Understanding]
New Political E(

A number of large-scale transformations have shaped the economy, polity and society of India over the past quarter century. This book provides a detailed account of three that are of particular importance: the advent of liberal economic reform, the ascendance of Hindu cultural nationalism and the empowerment of historically subordinate classes through popular democratic mobilizations.

Filling a gap in existing literature, the book goes beyond looking at the transformations in isolation, managing to:

- Explain the empirical linkages between these three phenomena
- Provide an account that integrates the insights of separate disciplinary perspectives
- Explain their distinct but possibly related causes and the likely consequences of these central transformations taken together

By seeking to explain the causal relationships between these central transformations through a coordinated conversation across different disciplines, the dynamics of India's new political economy are captured. Chapters focus on the political, economic and social aspects of India in their current and historical context. The contributors use new empirical research to discuss how India's multidimensional story of economic growth, social welfare and democratic deepening is likely to develop. This is an essential text for students and researchers of India's political economy and the growth economies of Asia.

Sanjay Ruparelia is an Assistant Professor of Politics at the New School for Social Research in the US. His current research examines the politics of the broader Indian left in contemporary Indian democracy in the wake of economic liberalization and Hindu nationalism.

Sanjay Reddy is an Associate Professor of Economics at the New School for Social Research in the US. His areas of work include development economics, international economics and economics and philosophy.

John Harriss is Professor of International Studies at Simon Fraser University, Canada. His current research concerns India's social policy in the context of liberalization.

Stuart Corbridge is Professor of Development Studies at the London School of Economics and Political Science in the UK. His previous publications include *Reinventing India: Liberalization, Hindu Nationalism and Popular Democracy* (2000, with John Harriss).

Understanding India's New Political Economy

A great transformation?

Edited by Sanjay Ruparelia,
Sanjay Reddy, John Harriss
and Stuart Corbridge

Routledge
Taylor & Francis Group

LONDON AND NEW YORK

First published 2011
by Routledge
2 Park Square, Milton Park, Abingdon, Oxon, OX14 4RN

Simultaneously published in the USA and Canada
by Routledge
711 Third Avenue, New York, NY 10017

Routledge is an imprint of the Taylor & Francis Group, an informa business

© 2011 Sanjay Ruparelia, Sanjay Reddy, John Harriss and Stuart Corbridge for selection and editorial matter, individual contributors; their contributions

The right of Sanjay Ruparelia, Sanjay Reddy, John Harriss and Stuart Corbridge to be identified as the authors of the editorial material, and of the contributors for their individual chapters, has been asserted in accordance with sections 77 and 78 of the Copyright, Designs and Patents Act 1988.

Typeset in Times by
Pindar NZ, Auckland, New Zealand
Printed and bound in Great Britain by
TJ International Ltd, Padstow, Cornwall

All rights reserved. No part of this book may be reprinted or reproduced or utilised in any form or by any electronic, mechanical, or other means, now known or hereafter invented, including photocopying and recording, or in any information storage or retrieval system, without permission in writing from the publishers.

British Library Cataloguing in Publication Data
A catalogue record for this book is available from the British Library

Library of Congress Cataloging-in-Publication Data
Understanding India's new political economy : a great transformation? / edited by Sanjay Ruparelia ... [et al].
 p. cm.
 Includes bibliographical references and index.
 1. India—Economic conditions—1991- 2. Social change—Economic aspects—India. 3. Economic development—Social aspects—India. I. Ruparelia, Sanjay.
 HC435.3U53 2011
 320.954—dc22   2010037065

ISBN13: 978-0-415-59810-1 (hbk)
ISBN13: 978-0-415-59811-8 (pbk)
ISBN13: 978-0-203-82960-8 (ebk)

Contents

List of figures and tables	vii
List of contributors	ix
Preface	xi
Abbreviations	xiii

1 Introduction: India's transforming political economy 1
   STUART CORBRIDGE, JOHN HARRISS, SANJAY RUPARELIA
   AND SANJAY REDDY

2 Democracy and economic transformation in India 17
   PARTHA CHATTERJEE

3 Economic liberalization, urban politics and the poor 35
   NANDINI GOOPTU

4 The politics of India's special economic zones 49
   ROB JENKINS

5 The contested geographies of federalism in post-reform India 66
   STUART CORBRIDGE

6 Patterns of wealth disparities in India: 1991–2002 81
   ARJUN JAYADEV, SRIPAD MOTIRAM AND VAMSI VAKULABHARANAM

7 Political economy of agrarian distress in India since the 1990s 101
   VAMSI VAKULABHARANAM AND SRIPAD MOTIRAM

8 How far have India's economic reforms been 'guided by compassion
   and justice'? Social policy in the neoliberal era 127
   JOHN HARRISS

9	The transformation of citizenship in India in the 1990s and beyond NIRAJA GOPAL JAYAL	141
10	Making citizens from below and above: the prospects and challenges of decentralization in India PATRICK HELLER	157
11	Hindutva's ebbing tide? RADHIKA DESAI	172
12	Expanding Indian democracy: the paradox of the third force SANJAY RUPARELIA	186
13	The Congress Party and the 'Great Transformation' JAMES MANOR	204
14	Indian foreign policy since the end of the Cold War: domestic determinants ACHIN VANAIK	221
	Glossary	237
	Consolidated Bibliography	238
	Index	260

Figures and tables

Figures

7.1	Agricultural investment as a percentage of GDP (1990–2006)	112
7.2	Input subsidies per hectare of Gross Cropped Area (GCA)	115

Tables

6.1	Major categories of total assets	84
6.2	Ownership rates by asset	85
6.3	Distributional measures	86
6.4	Gini by category	86
6.5	Share of assets and net worth by decile	87
6.6	Average per-capita wealth by expenditure decile	88
6.7	Increasing concentration of wealth at the upper end of the wealth distribution	89
6.8	Sociological breakdown of status variables	91
6.9	Sociological breakdown of white collar employment (from Sheth 1999)	92
6.10	Mean and median wealth breakdown by status category	92
6.11	Mean of assets by state income categorization	97
6.12	Mean of assets by regional categorization	98
7.1	Agricultural output growth in India	103
7.2	Area and land productivity growth in India	103
7.3	Average monthly per-capita expenditure for various classes (2005–6 values)	104
7.4	State-Wise Wage Rates of Agricultural Labor for Kharif Crops in India (Rs. per Man Day)	106
7.5	Average monthly per-capita expenditure for various castes (2005–6 values)	107
7.6	Rural poverty and poverty reduction rates in various regions	107
7.7	Inequality in rural and urban India	107

7.8	Comparison of mean monthly per-capita expenditure in rural and urban sectors	108
7.9	Fertilizer consumption in India	109
7.10	Irrigation trends in India ('000 hectares)	110
7.11	Agricultural investment in India	112
7.12	Summary of Liberalization Measures Introduced in the Agricultural Sector	114
7.13	Main sources of household credit and debt	116
7.14	Wholesale price index of food and non-food articles	116
7.15	Class composition of various castes (2003–4)	120
7.16	Caste Composition of Various Classes (2003–4)	121
13.1	'Backward caste' interests	211

Contributors

Partha Chatterjee is Professor of Political Science, Centre for Studies in Social Sciences, Calcutta, and Professor of Anthropology, Columbia University, New York. His most recent book is *The Politics of the Governed: Reflections on Popular Politics in Most of the World* (2004).

Stuart Corbridge is Professor of Development Studies, London School of Economics. His most recent monograph (with Glyn Williams, Manoj Srivastava and Rene Veron) is *Seeing the State: Governance and Governmentality in India* (2005).

Radhika Desai is Professor of Political Studies, University of Manitoba. Her books include *Slouching Towards Ayodhya: From Congress to Hindutva in Indian Politics* (2004) and *Developmental and Cultural Nationalisms* (2009). She is a co-editor of the *Future of Capitalism* book series, Pluto Press.

Nandini Gooptu is University Reader in South Asian Studies and Fellow of St Antony's College, Oxford. She is the author of *The Politics of the Urban Poor in Early Twentieth-Century India* (2001).

John Harriss is Professor of International Studies, Simon Fraser University, Vancouver. His most recent book is *Power Matters: Essays on Institutions, Politics and Society in India* (2006).

Patrick Heller is Professor of Sociology and International Studies, Brown University. He is the author of *The Labor of Development: Workers in the Transformation of Capitalism in Kerala, India* (1999) and co-author of *Social Democracy in the Global Periphery: Origins, Challenges, Prospects* (2006).

Arjun Jayadev is Assistant Professor of Economics, University of Massachusetts, Boston. He is interested in the linkage between finance and inequality. He has published widely, including in the *Journal of Development Economics*, *World Development* and *Economic and Political Weekly*.

Niraja Gopal Jayal is Professor at the Centre for the Study of Law and Governance, Jawaharlal Nehru University, New Delhi. Her recent publications include *Representing India: Ethnic Diversity and the Governance of Public Institutions* (2006) and *The Oxford Companion to Politics in India* (2010).

x Contributors

Rob Jenkins is Professor of Political Science, Hunter College and The Graduate Center, City University of New York, and Associate Director, Ralph Bunche Institute for International Studies. His most recent book (with Anne Marie Goetz) is *Reinventing Accountability* (2005).

James Manor is the Emeka Anyaoku Professor of Commonwealth Studies, School of Advanced Study, University of London. He has taught previously at Yale, Harvard, Leicester and Sussex Universities, and at the Institute for Social and Economic Change, Bangalore.

Sripad Motiram is Associate Professor, Indira Gandhi Institute of Development Research (IGIDR), Mumbai. Prior to IGIDR, he worked at the University of California, Berkeley, US and Dalhousie University, Halifax, Canada. His main areas of interest are development economics and microeconomics.

Sanjay Reddy is Associate Professor of Economics, New School for Social Research. His areas of work include development studies, political economy and philosophy and economics.

Sanjay Ruparelia is Assistant Professor of Political Science, New School for Social Research, New York. His research has been published in *Comparative Politics*, *Economic and Political Weekly* and other scholarly journals. He is completing a book, provisionally titled *Divided We Govern*, on India's federal coalition politics.

Vamsi Vakulabharanam is Assistant Professor of Economics, University of Hyderabad. His research examines agrarian change in India against the backdrop of policies towards globalization, and income distribution in India and China especially after market-oriented economic reforms were introduced in both countries.

Achin Vanaik is Professor of International Relations and Global Politics at the Department of Political Science, Delhi University. His writings and interests cover themes ranging from India's political economy and foreign policy, to communalism and secularism, to matters of nuclear disarmament.

Preface

This book is an attempt to map the transformations of modern India over the last three decades. From the 1930s until the 1960s, India galvanized attention throughout the world, given its centrality in the nationalist struggles that swept the world, in debates over planning, democracy and modernization in the post-colonial world and through the non-aligned movement during the Cold War. In contrast, it seemed to be a backwater in international affairs for much of the 1970s and 1980s, attracting less scholarly interest and media attention outside the country than many other regions. How different things are at the end of the first decade of the twenty-first century, when India is quite rightly seen as a major emerging power and one of the most important rising centres of the global economy. As India's enormous global significance has come to be recognized, interest in the country has grown. India could once, fairly safely, be ignored. This is no longer the case: there is now a massive demand for more information and better understanding. Of course, India is home to some of the finest social scientists and historians in the world, and their ideas and analyses of how their society has transformed itself over the last few decades deserve to be widely known and appreciated. And they increasingly are, as greater interaction occurs between them and scholars around the world.

This book emerged from one such encounter: an informal workshop organized by Sanjay Reddy and Sanjay Ruparelia at Columbia University in November 2003. A number of scholars from India, Europe and North America, crossing the disciplines, sought to understand India's many transformations, stimulated at least in part by the analysis presented by Stuart Corbridge and John Harriss in their jointly authored book, *Reinventing India*. Encouraged by the liveliness of these conversations the four of us organized a more formal workshop at Columbia in September 2007. The papers in this volume were originally written for that gathering. We believe that together they provide an original analysis, addressing the three most important large-scale transformations that have reshaped India since around 1980: the advent of liberal economic reform, the ascendance of Hindu cultural nationalism and the empowerment of historically subordinate classes through popular democratic mobilizations. Investigations of economic reform in India have illuminated its implications for economic growth, sectoral changes and social welfare; similarly, the rise of Hindu cultural nationalism has generated significant analysis of its implications for citizenship, welfare and India's relations with the world. Finally, many astute observers have examined the promise and limits of popular democratic politics. Given their scale and complexity, however, there are few analyses that attempt to explain the nexus between these three momentous transformations. *Understanding India's New Political Economy* aims to address this critical absence. Its underlying premise is that only an account that seeks to explain the causal relationships between these central transformations, through a coordinated interdisciplinary conversation, can adequately capture the dynamics of India's new political economy.

It is a pleasure for us to acknowledge, with gratitude, the friends and colleagues who have helped us from the inception of this project to its completion. We thank especially those who actively participated in the 2007 workshop – Ronald Herring, Jos Mooij, Arvind Rajagopal, Raka Ray and Rathin Roy – as well as those who contributed to it as discussants – Devesh Kapur, Sudipta Kaviraj, Atul Kohli, Dilip Mookherjee, Philip Oldenburg, Vyjayanthi Rao, Siddharth Varadarajan and Ashutosh Varshney. We also wish to express our appreciation to Vidya Dehejia, director of the Southern Asian Institute at Columbia, and her very able staff (especially Ann Levy, Zainab Mahmood and David Seidenberg) for graciously coordinating and hosting our two meetings and taking such good care of us during the proceedings. Our project would have been impossible to pursue without the generous support of the Southern Asian Institute, LSE-Columbia Alliance Collaborative Research Fund, Provost's Fund at Barnard College, Committee on Global Thought at Columbia University and the India China Institute at the New School. Last but far from least, we are grateful to our contributors for their patience, support and good humor in responding to our questions, comments and requests, and to Douglas Voigt and Vanessa Chan for helping us prepare the final typescript.

Sanjay Ruparelia, Sanjay Reddy,
John Harriss and Stuart Corbridge
New York, Vancouver and London,
April 2010

Abbreviations

AGP	Asom Gana Parishad
AIADMK	All India Anna Dravida Munnetra Kazagham
AIDIS	All-India Debt and Investment Survey
APL	Above Poverty Line
BIMARU	Bihar, Madhya Pradesh, Rajasthan, Uttar Pradesh
BJD	Biju Janata Dal
BJP	Bharatiya Janata Party
BJS	Bharatiya Jana Sangh
BKU	Bharatiya Kisan Union
BMD-TMD	Ballistic Missile Defense – Theater Missile Defense
BoA	Board of Approvals
BPL	Below Poverty Line
BSP	Bahujan Samaj Party
CEO	Chief Executive Officer
CM	Chief Minister
CMIE	Centre for Monitoring Indian Economy
CMP	Common Minimum Programme
CPI	Communist Party of India
CPI(M)/CPM	Communist Party of India (Marxist)
CR	citizenship regime
CRY	Child Rights and You
CTBT	Comprehensive Test Ban Treaty
DAE	Department of Atomic Energy
DFID	Department for International Development (UK)
DMK	Dravida Munnetra Kazagham
EGoM	Empowered Group of Ministers
EGS	Education Guarantee Scheme
EPW	*Economic and Political Weekly*
EPZ	Export Processing Zone
FB	All India Forward Bloc
FCI	Food Corporation India
FDI	Foreign Direct Investment
FENC	Far Eastern Naval Command

FII	Foreign Institutional Investors
GDP	Gross Domestic Product
GKS	Gujarat Khedut Samaj
GMO	Genetically Modified Organism
HYV	high yield variety
IAEA	International Atomic Energy Agency
ICDS	Integrated Child Development Scheme
ICRISAT	International Crops Research Institute for the Semi-Arid Tropics
IIM	Indian Institute of Management
IIT	Indian Institute of Technology
IMC	Indian middle class
INC	Indian National Congress
INC (T)	Indian National Congress (Tiwari)
IPCL	Indian Petrochemicals Corporation Limited
ISI	Import substitution industrialization
IT	Information Technology
ITeS	Information Technology-enhanced Services
JD	Janata Dal
JD (S)	Janata Dal (Secular)
JD (U)	Janata Dal (United)
JNNURM	Jawaharlal Nehru National Urban Renewal Mission
KMA	Kolkata Metropolitan Area
KRRS	Karnataka State Farmers' Association
KSSP	Kerala Sastra Sahitya Parishad
LAA	Land Acquisition Act
LF	Left Front
LJS	Lok Jan Shakti
LS	Lok Shakti
LTTE	Liberation Tigers of Tamil Eelam
MBC	Most Backward Class
MDG	Millennium Development Goal
MIDC	Maharashtra Industrial Development Corporation
MKKS	Mazdur Kisan Shakti Sangathan
MPVC	Madhya Pradesh Vikas Congress
NAM	Non-Aligned Movement
NCAER	National Council for Applied Economic Research
NCEUS	National Commission for Enterprises in the Unorganised Sector
NCO	National Classification of Occupations
NCP	Nationalist Congress Party
NDA	National Democratic Alliance
NEP	New Economic Policy
NF	National Front
NFHS	National Family Health Survey
NGO	Non-Governmental Organization
NPT	Non-Proliferation Treaty

NREGA	National Rural Employment Guarantee Act
NRI	Non-Resident Indian
NSS	National Sample Survey
OBC	Other Backward Class
OCI	Overseas Citizen of India
PAEG	People's Action for Employment Guarantee
PDP	People's Democratic Party
PIO	Person of Indian Origin
PPC	provincial propertied class
PSI	Proliferation Security Initiative
RJD	Rashtriya Janata Dal
RSP	Revolutionary Socialist Party
RSS	Rashtriya Swayamsevak Sangh
SAP	Samata Party
SC	Scheduled Caste
SEBI	Securities and Exchange Board of India
SEZ	Special Economic Zone
SHG	Self-Help Groups
SJP	Samajwadi Janata Party
SP	Samajwadi Party
Sh S	Shetkari Sanghatana
SS	Shiv Sena
ST	Scheduled Tribe
SVD	Samyukta Vidhayak Dal
TDP	Telegu Desam Party
TMC	Tamil Maanila Congress
TOT	Terms Of Trade
TRS	Telengana Rashtra Samiti
UF	United Front
UNICEF	United Nations International Children's Fund
UNPA	United National Progressive Alliance
UPA	United Progressive Alliance
VHP	Vishwa Hindu Parishad

1 Introduction

India's transforming political economy

*Stuart Corbridge, John Harriss,
Sanjay Ruparelia and Sanjay Reddy*

This book brings together essays first presented at a conference on India's political economy held at Columbia University in September 2007. The editors asked scholars from different intellectual backgrounds to consider whether and how India's political economy might have been fundamentally transformed in recent years. The volume seeks to describe, explain and assess the changes that have taken place in a rigorous, interdisciplinary and synoptic manner. In particular, it focuses on the three most important transformations in India's political economy since the 1980s: the influence of liberal economic reforms, the ascendance of Hindu cultural nationalism, and the empowerment of historically subordinate classes through popular democratic mobilizations.

Each of these large-scale transformations has received much scholarly attention in recent years. In contrast to previous decades, however, there have been very few attempts to provide a synoptic causal account of India's political economy. Ideally, a synoptic account would (a) explain the empirical linkages between these three phenomena; (b) provide an account that integrates the insights of separate disciplinary perspectives; and (c) explain their distinct but possibly related causes and the likely consequences of these central transformations taken together. Needless to say, constructing such an integrative perspective is extremely difficult for any individual. The lack of an encompassing view reflects the pace, scope and complexity of change set in motion by each of these transformations. Yet our capacity to grasp the contemporary dynamics of India's political economy, and to assess whether and how they are new, arguably requires such an analysis.

We seek to address this critical intellectual challenge. Our underlying premise is that only a synthetic account – one that seeks to explain the causal relationships between these central transformations through a coordinated intellectual conversation – can help to capture the dynamics of India's new political economy in their totality. Accordingly, this volume brings together work by both senior and younger scholars from a variety of disciplines. Each contribution examines how a particular actor, policy domain or spatial arena has shaped, and in turn been shaped by, India's transforming political economy since the 1980s. We hope that when read together, a larger view of the causes, nexus and consequences of economic liberalization, Hindu nationalism and popular democratic mobilization may emerge.

The challenge of writing such a synoptic causal account of India's new political economy raises a critical question signalled by our title: do these three major transformations, taken together, constitute a "great transformation"? Our motivation for using this term is twofold. The first meaning of "a great transformation," in simple language, is wide: to what extent have liberal economic reform, popular democratic mobilization and ascendant cultural nationalism fundamentally reordered relations of power, wealth and status in India? Or are the changes set in motion by these phenomena ephemeral and susceptible to reversal? The second meaning is more specific. To what extent can one understand the changes that have taken place in the Indian political economy through the idea of a "double movement," to use Karl Polanyi's well-known phrase developed in reference to the historical European case, in which the attempt to create a market-oriented society from above compels a movement from below to moderate its severely dislocating effects? The question mark in the title of the book registers our openness towards such questions while intimating differences of interpretation amongst the different authors. Our aim was to foster a critical debate, informed by rich empirical detail and sharp theoretical analysis, but unified by common questions.

The "economic reforms" that have taken shape in India over the past 30 years, reaching back at least to certain pro-business initiatives enacted by Prime Ministers Indira and Rajiv Gandhi in the 1980s, and carried further by the economic policy changes that began to be implemented by a recently elected Congress government in 1991, represent a shift – albeit a moderate one – towards neoliberalism. It is for this reason that Polanyi's work, about earlier attempts to make a reality of the "self-regulating market" – which is what he meant by "the Great Transformation" – provides one key point of reference in thinking about the political economy of India today. Most contributors to this book, however, pay close attention as well to transformations that are more plural and perhaps even lower case. They are at least fivefold, and they are strongly interlinked. First, there is the economic transformation of India since about 1980. We inquire collectively into its chronology, mainsprings and consequences. Second, we note that economic liberalization has coincided with a period that saw the re-emergence of Hindu nationalism. We take seriously the proposition that these first two transformations are linked in important ways, not least in regard to the formation of identities and political projects among India's urban middle classes. Likewise, we contend that the rise of Hindu nationalism and the pace of economic reform must be understood in relation to a third transformation: the slow-burning but significant deepening of India's democracy. We ask how far and in what ways Indians from among the Backward Classes have been brought into the country's main circuits of political and economic power, and on what terms. Are India's subaltern communities beginning to enjoy forms of political citizenship and market access in anything like the same terms as the country's middle classes, and if so, where: in which parts of India? How too are they engaged in forms of political struggle, including Naxalism and anti-dam movements, which cut against the grain of the production of India as a visibly "new" centre of economic production and exchange?

Finally, we begin to describe and think through what will possibly be India's greatest transformations in the 20 years ahead: the expected movement of perhaps 200–300 million more men and women from the countryside to its towns and cities, and changes in India's geopolitical position. How will political and economic power be redistributed in the wake of such a rural–urban transformation? How, indeed, should we think about the unity of India in the wake of these enormous shifts in labour power, and in the train of growing social inequalities between sectors and regions at the heart of India's economic reform agendas and those that are locked out of them? And what changes can we expect in India's foreign policy? Will India continue to move closer to the United States and other Western powers, or will it establish a more independent path?

There are many ways of thinking about these questions. As editors, we asked authors to deal with one or more aspect of India's "Great Transformation" in relation to the extraordinary shifts in power, identity and wealth that symbolically were prefigured by the controversies around the so-called Mandal report (on reservations), the mandir/mosque dispute that erupted in Ayodhya in 1992 and the pro-market tilt of Manmohan Singh's July 1991 budget. We certainly didn't expect all authors to deal with all the lines of enquiry set out above.

We begin with a reflective paper by Partha Chatterjee. Chatterjee's account of "Democracy and economic transformation in India" was produced for and played a prominent role in the 2007 New York conference. More recently it was published in *Economic and Political Weekly*, India's leading journal of political economy and public record. Since its publication in April 2008, Chatterjee's analysis has been challenged by several commentators, including Mary John and Satish Deshpande (2008), Amita Baviskar and Nandini Sundar (2008) and Mihir Shah (2008). These commentaries inform some of the papers that follow: papers that were prepared first for September 2007, but which in all cases have been re-written in light of further reading and recent events, and exchanges with other workshop participants.

Chatterjee begins his essay by declaring that the Indian economy has been undergoing a series of profound changes that have "since the 1990s ... transformed [an earlier] framework of class dominance." Nehru and Mahalanobis sought the development of India's economy along the classic lines of capital goods-based import-substituting industrialization. India's push for growth was, however, turned back by the country's dominant proprietary elites. These have been described by Pranab Bardhan (1984) as its monopoly industrial bourgeoisie, its richer farmers, and its better-placed bureaucrats. The first of these groups blocked industrial competition and innovation. The richer farmers in turn blocked agrarian reform, pushing the country instead to a Green Revolution that gathered pace in the 1970s, while many bureaucrats worked the planning and license Raj to their personal advantage and to the advantage of many of the politicians they served. Planning was suspended in India from 1966 to 1969 and the country's first experiments with state-directed development stalled sharply. What Chatterjee now describes as the first stage in India's "passive revolution" delivered improvements in average per capita incomes of little more than 1 percent per annum.[1] By the time that Indira Gandhi returned to power in 1980 it was clear that the economy would need to be kick-started in other ways. Deficit financing was one option that was pursued vigorously in the 1980s, not least in the form of subsidies into and out of the agricultural economy, but this led to a burgeoning debt crisis by the end of the decade. Atul Kohli (2006) has also documented a tilt in favour of pro-business policies in the 1980s under Indira Gandhi and her elder son, Rajiv.

Per capita income growth rose to close to 4 percent per annum between c.1980 and 2003, before shifting closer to 6 percent after 2003 (at least until 2008). Chatterjee attributes this "major spurt" to "much greater confidence among Indian capitalists to make use of the opportunities opened up by global flows of capital, goods and services." The earlier dominance of India's economy by a "few 'monopoly' houses drawn from traditional merchant backgrounds and protected by the license and import substitution regime" has ended. Chatterjee instead sees the emergence of a vibrant and increasingly urbanized economy which is pulling younger people in their millions from a countryside mired in torpor, hardship and uncertainty.

Chatterjee's broader argument is that capital's pursuit of accumulation by dispossession is tempered by various path dependencies in India's democratic polity. Governmental commitments to welfare still bring education, health and subsidies to India's villages, and sanitation and water-pumps to its urban slum-dwellers. The picture that Chatterjee paints is of a double movement. Even as the larger economic pendulum swings in favour of "reform" and liberalization, the fully fledged sway of capital is reined in both by local resistance and by the commitment of government in India to "revers[e] the effects of primitive accumulation" by other forms of market intervention. The state in India remains committed to providing for "a culturally determined sense of what is minimally necessary for a decent life." India's poor might not have gained much directly from the country's pro-market reforms – elasticities of poverty reduction remain disgracefully low by East Asian standards – but the voting power of named communities of the poor (SCs, STs, BPLs, slum dwellers, etc.) still translates into claims on the Indian fisc through what Chatterjee calls political society.[2]

Here is the nub of Chatterjee's argument, which is developed at greater length in *The Politics of the Governed* (2004). Chatterjee suggests that what we are seeing in India is the rise to political power of a corporate capitalist class. This class has established an increasing role in a number of India's states – in Gujarat most notably, but also in Mahrashtra, Tamil Nadu and elsewhere – and is minded more and more to view government as corrupt and inefficient. Calls are growing for the reform of government along "Western" lines, or at least along the lines that Western government is imagined by CEOs, senior managers and a new wave of maverick politicians trained in US universities and management consultancies. Bangalore, not Delhi, is the new model, with some among this camp of competitive capitalists looking to new emerging leaders (such, perhaps, as Rahul Gandhi) to modernize India's polity as comprehensively as entrepreneurs like Nandan Nilekani and Mukesh Ambani are modernizing the economy.

But while this push for rule by experts is growing, Chatterjee suggests that it is restricted as yet to English-speaking elites in urban India. The urban middle class *is* now coming under "the moral-political sway of the bourgeoisie." Its members also enjoy the protections of the rule of law and the privileges that accrue to those living in properly civil societies. Where India continues to depart from Western capitalist democracies, however, Chatterjee suggests, is in regard to the dominance of political society in the lives of its social majorities. Ordinary people don't make claims on government in the form of rights or with regard to abstract laws and constitutions. They instead negotiate ad hoc, unstable and often illegal forms of access to basic public services through their political bosses or agents of the state, who acquiesce through acts of omission or commission. In West Bengal, until recently, this patronage democracy was brokered almost exclusively by the CPM; in Mumbai, the Shiv Sena has performed a similar function, offering services in return for votes and occasional acts of thuggery. Meanwhile, in both states, Chatterjee concludes, ruling elites have moved to embrace liberalization. "[A]s far as the party system is concerned, it does not matter which particular combination of parties comes to power in the centre or even in most of the states; state support for rapid economic growth is guaranteed to continue. This is evidence of the current success of the passive revolution."

Chatterjee's depiction of an India increasingly divided between elites and masses, between city and countryside, and between the life-worlds of civil and political societies, will find many takers. There is no doubt that social and spatial inequalities in income and consumption have increased. Trickle-down is generally notable by its absence in the poorest regions of India, and matters are not helped by demographic pressures that are delivering more and more young people into labour markets. During the next two decades India should reap a demographic dividend as the ratio of workers to dependents becomes more favourable. But this can go badly wrong if rates of human capital formation remain low or if educated youths fail to get decent jobs.

What is less clear from Chatterjee's analysis is whether we should expect the urban and the civil to gain hegemony over the rural and the political – whether, to be blunt, we should expect a tenuous equilibrium to be maintained (for fear perhaps of the continuing power of the rural vote), or whether "the inevitable story of primitive accumulation" will progressively break free from governmental duties to provide welfare for the poor and create a volatile disequilibrium in the new India.[3]

Chatterjee argues that it all depends on politics, which of course it does. Still, his critics want to know more about his understanding of the dynamics and aims of "political struggle." Some of them are uncomfortable with Chatterjee's neat mappings of corporate capital on to civil society and of non-corporate capital on to political society. Isn't it the case, ask Amita Baviskar and Nandini Sundar, that many of India's most civil and progressive welfare measures have been pushed for at "the insistence of ... 'political society' or even non-society marginal groups"? (2008: 87): they have in mind the National Rural Employment Guarantee Act, the Forest Rights Act and the Right to Information Act. And isn't it also the case that corporate India has been anything but civil or law-abiding in its militaristic adventures in Kashmir, Singur or in Naxalite India? In their view, "Chatterjee inverts what is actually the case: generally, it is members of the so-called civil society who break laws with impunity and who demand that the rules be waived for them, whereas members of political society strive to become legal, to gain recognition and entitlements from the state" (ibid.: 88).

Of course, we don't have to reverse Chatterjee's arguments to engage them. In the essays that follow we find a nuanced range of positions being explored by authors keen to grapple seriously with Chatterjee's broad theses. Nandini Gooptu focuses directly on one of Chatterjee's main themes when she examines the links between economic liberalization, cities and the poor. She points out that efforts to tidy the poor out of India's cities are hardly new. India's urban elites have been keen for decades to punish those who can be coded as dirty, ill-kempt or "un-modern." Evictions, demolition and imprisonment have long and troubling histories in urban India. Gooptu accepts even so that India's obsession with neoliberal urban policies is changing the terms under which "new" urban governance systems are being imagined and put into practice. India's ruling elites are increasingly buying into the view that cities are or should be sites of innovation and entrepreneurship. This is very much the view of the "New Economic Geography."[4] Far from being landscapes of predation – the "old" politics of urban bias, or of "Bharat versus India" – the city is now configured as fully authentic (*contra* Gandhi) and necessarily dynamic: so long, that is, that urban space can be liberated from chaos and cows, and remade as sleek, linear and above-all "professional."

Gooptu explores the differential emergence of the new urbanism in India and the booming property markets and gentrification that come in its wake. She shows how gentrification can lead to revanchism, or the politics of revenge against the poor. More significantly, she explores how a desire to push the poor out of desirable urban space is being mirrored in cities like Delhi and Mumbai by increased middle-class distaste for democracy. The sheer numbers of urban poor, Gooptu reminds us, and the continued existence of vote-bank politics, threaten the bourgeois project of city upgrading. Democracy gets in the way of development. Worse, it points to Patna, not Mumbai. It is no coincidence, Gooptu suggests, that Mumbai is then such a heartland of rabid Hindu nationalism. Urban elites mobilize Hindutva politics as a way of resisting mass mobilizations from below, which they find threatening. Key here are the mobilizations of poor voters and of poor migrants.

In practice, the poor simply can't be expelled from India's largest cities, as opposed to being removed from their glossiest colonies. Gooptu ends her paper by showing how India's ruling elites are proposing an ideology of urban regeneration that aims to turn slum dwellers into stakeholder entrepreneurs. (Inevitably, this is on the small scale that most appeals to NGOs, foreign funders and microfinance institutions). India's urban poor are certainly not marginal to the country's changing economy. Gooptu concludes nonetheless that they are increasingly being stripped of just those forms of group identification and solidarity that have provided them with the protections of political society. One danger facing India's urban poor is that they become so "individualized" (as proto-entrepreneurs) that their increasing vulnerability in labor markets is matched by greater vulnerability in the political arena.

It is to be hoped this will not happen. Much will depend on the rate of growth of the economy as a whole, and more so on the terms under which non-elite groups negotiate access to jobs, savings, education and healthcare. Rob Jenkins, in the next paper, explores the role that Special Economic Zones are coming to play in the New India, or at any rate in imaginaries of the New India. SEZs are winning a special place of affection in the hearts of India's reformers. Not only do they call to mind successes further east in Asia, they also promise to deliver capital from the state and politics. SEZs offer the prospect of growth unbound, and of cascading benefits to local workers and households. They announce yet another site of unbridled entrepreneurship.

As Jenkins reports, however, the reality of SEZs is very different. Export-processing zones in India date back to the 1960s, although the real push came after Murasoli Maran, then Union Commerce Minister, made a visit to China in 2000. In 2005, India passed the Special Economic Zone Act, and within four years about 600 SEZs had been approved. Many are in construction and a few are now operational. SEZs provide investors with tax breaks and an end to red tape. As Jenkins adroitly notes, they offer capital a chance to "secede from the rest of India," a theme picked up also by Gooptu. But therein lies a problem. Jenkins reports that the visibility of SEZs has ensured that they have become a lightning rod for protest by groups outside "the project" (or inside the rest of India). Paradoxically, the multiplication of SEZs illustrates the limits of economic reform in India.

Jenkins has often argued that India's economic reform agenda has been negotiated by stealth and side-payments, and by exploiting a multiplicity of governance jurisdictions. States have been played against States, metros against metros. Now, though, just at a time when the introduction of SEZs on a large scale seems to consolidate the power of capital to produce space in its own image, a powerful coalition has emerged to contest the main instrument that makes them possible. Jenkins focuses in the middle part of his paper on the Land Acquisition Act. Promulgated in 1894 for the purpose of acquiring land for a public purpose, the LAA is now widely seen as a vehicle for private land grabs and real estate manipulation. Some industrialists have joined with grass roots organizations to oppose land acquisitions that too often benefit limited coalitions of state-level politicians and private developers. As Jenkins very fairly points out, public outrage at land acquisitions in West Bengal (notably at Nandigram), Orissa, Punjab and Maharashtra has dramatically exposed not only caste and class cleavages around the accumulation process, but also the limits of Jenkins' own thesis about reform by stealth (Jenkins 1999). Growing opposition to India's SEZs highlights not so much political competence in the States as political incompetence. "A compromised Indian state ... undermines the confidence required of people with which the state would like to enter into compacts, without which a political consensus to deepen economic reform will be difficult to engender."

Nowhere is this consensus less evident than in eastern India. Both Jenkins and Chatterjee refer to Nandigram. Stuart Corbridge, in the next chapter, builds on their observations to present a broad account of geography-making in contemporary India. Federalism in India has been reconfigured in the wake both of economic reform and the rise of largely state-based political parties. Increasingly, India's federalism is without a centre, as Lawrence Saez (2002) puts it. Corbridge goes further, and documents the drive for the production of abstract space that is embodied in

India's most competitive States not only by SEZs, but also by four-lane highways, new subway systems, giant shopping malls and urban spaces like Gurgaon and Bandra Kurla (in Mumbai). Here is the dull, homogenized, rational space that capital needs for the efficient production and circulation of its outputs. As Henri Lefebvre once put it, capitalism survives "by occupying space, by producing space" (quoted in Harvey 2001: 376).

Corbridge also explores the limits of the competition states hypothesis. Why haven't the pressures of inter-provincial competition weighed as heavily in Bihar, Orissa, Jharkhand and Chhattisgarh, even in West Bengal and large parts of Madhya Pradesh and Uttar Pradesh, as they have done in Delhi, Haryana, Gujarat, Punjab and Maharashtra? The answers he proposes are fourfold. First, much of eastern India is paying the price of years of relative under-investment or ineffectiveness of investment in its public infrastructure. Some natural resource-rich areas have also suffered from the operation of Freight Equalization Acts, which have removed their pre-existing advantages as sites of industrial production. Second, the cost of building a functioning infrastructure in eastern India is running up against a hard budget constraint. This constraint eased substantially from c.2003–2008 but is building again. Annual GDP growth in India slowed to less than 6 percent in 2009, by which time the combined fiscal deficit of the Centre and the States was back above 8 percent of GDP (Govinda Rao 2009). Third, political forces like the (Rashtriya) Janata Dal in Bihar and the Bahujan Samaj Party in UP were able to remain in power for years without feeling the need to respond to the forces of inter-provincial competition. Lalu Prasad Yadav offered honour and empowerment to his Yadav and Kurmi supporters, and protection to Bihar's Muslims. Economic development was taken off the agenda, along with serious attempts at building an adequately functioning polity. Finally, the degradation of public services in eastern India over many years, and the hollowing out of government, has paved the way for other political actors: notably the Communist Party of India (Maoist), as the newly consolidated Naxalite movement is now called. Like many authors in this collection, Corbridge concludes on a cautionary note. His argument is not that eastern India cannot be delivered to the reform project or to a growing middle class. He simply notes that political opposition to this project is now entrenched in Naxalite India, and that the costs of reclamation will be high.

The nature of emerging inequalities in India is explored further in the next two papers, those by Arjan Jayadev, Sripad Motiram and Vamsi Vakulabharanam and by Vakulababharanam and Motiram. Jayadev et al. break new ground by exploring changes in wealth disparities in India between 1991 and 2002. The more usual focus has been on consumption or income inequalities. Like Chatterjee and Gooptu, Jayadev et al. are able to document the rise and consolidation of an urban elite that they say corresponds "roughly to the notion of the Indian middle class/white collar workers/new middle class." This group is comfortably maintaining its share of wealth in India, a country where the top 10 percent of households continue to own just over 50 percent of total assets.

Jayadev et al. also document the continuing power and wealth of a dynamic rural elite. Here they depart from Chatterjee, and from Dipankar Gupta (2005), whom

Chatterjee presents as a herald of India's vanishing villages. This elite has its roots in land but increasingly is involved in non-agricultural activities. It also bridges to India's small towns and cities. There is undoubtedly a crisis in much of Indian agriculture, and horrible signs of distress in parts of the countryside. Famine conditions in Kalahandi and farmer suicides in several states are rightly cited with some regularity. This is painstakingly documented in the paper by Vakulababharanam and Motiram, which also notes (*pace* Chatterjee) that the state is manifestly failing to discharge a governmental duty of welfare to many poor rural households. Yet they also report on India's growing foodgrain stocks, and point towards remarkable sites of agricultural prosperity. These would include fast-growing agricultural economies like Hadar District in Madhya Pradesh, for example, where rich farmers are growing much richer still on the back of local wheat and soybean booms.[5] Rising global prices for grains and horticultural products have ensured that India's countryside is very far from being uniformly in distress or devoid of young men and women. Vakulabharanam and Motiram argue instead that we are witnessing the consolidation of "hunger amidst plenty," in savage mimicry of broader social and spatial trends in India's political economy.

This suggests that India's urban economy is not yet capable of creating enough urban jobs to accommodate the aspirations of potential migrants out of rural India. There is no Lewisian transformation on the cards that might turn India into the next China, at least not yet, and not in these comforting terms. Migrants to the city are likely to end up in slums and without decent jobs. A new future beckons that is bound up with the urbanization of poverty. And this in turn will begin to change the terms of politics in India. Can the urban poor (or the rural poor for that matter) begin to make headway into the circuits of civil society that Chatterjee believes are closed to them? What forms of politics and what forms of citizenship claims are now open to different groups of the poor in post-reform India? The next three papers, by John Harriss, Niraja Gopal Jayal and Patrick Heller, address these questions, among others.

Harriss takes as his starting point a phrase from Yaswant Sinha's Budget speech in 2000. India's reforms, said Sinha, were being "guided by compassion and justice." Harriss begins by addressing the issue of compassion, broadly conceived. While he accepts that claims about "jobless growth" are exaggerated, Harriss notes that average real daily wages of regular workers have stagnated in recent years (particularly for females). Jobs have come to post-reform India, but they have too often been of poor quality and/or linked to an increase in part-time work or home-working.

As Harriss points out, this helps us to understand why reasonably high and sustained rates of GDP growth have led to lower rates of poverty reduction than might have been expected. So-called "absolute" (income/consumption) poverty has been reduced significantly since the late 1970s, when over 50 percent of Indians were struggling with malnutrition. According to the 61st round of the National Sample Survey, 27.5 percent of Indians were below the poverty line in 2004–5.[6] This achievement, however, while considerable, has been far less notable than in China, where one percent increases in GDP growth translated over the same period into 1 percent poverty reductions (compared to around –0.65 percent in India).[7]

Poorer people are still not accessing the benefits of generalized growth in effective fashion outside Kerala and one or two other states (where they have been helped by high literacy rates and greater equality in the distribution of assets, notably land). Harriss also notes that declines in income poverty have not been matched by declines in most non-income measures of poverty – for example, malnutrition in children. It is hard to maintain that India is shining when 42 percent of children were recorded by UNICEF in 2007 as being underweight, as against 20 percent in sub-Saharan Africa.

Harriss accepts that the prevalence of ill-being in India can hardly be laid at the door of neoliberalism. It has long and deep roots. But he does insist that India's social welfare regime has been reworked in the reform period in a manner that is inconsistent with government commitments to poverty reduction, or compassion. Public spending on health and education gives the lie to this part of Sinha's homily, as indeed does the poor performance of a supposedly better "targeted" Public Distribution System. Harriss points out that barely more than 150 households in Dharavi, Mumbai, had been issued with BPL cards at the end of the 1990s, despite this being Asia's largest "slum."

Rhetoric continues to loom larger than resources when it comes to India's social policies. The situation might be slightly better, Harriss suggests, when it comes to various recent developments that can be placed under the heading of "justice" – notably, the success of rights-based campaigns for access to education, information, food and employment. Harriss notes that most of these campaigns have been driven by middle-class intellectuals, and certainly they are focused in large degree on individual rights, as per the broader agendas of liberalism. As Niraja Gopal Jayal reminds us, however, in the next essay, citizenship regimes in post-Independence India were written from the start around the figure of the sovereign individual, equal before the law and bearing the right to vote in an ostensibly secular Republic. The main exceptions to this regime were meant to hasten disadvantaged groups into this form of citizenship. This was the ambition both of compensatory discrimination for India's Scheduled Communities and separate personal laws for named religious groups.

By 2000 this citizenship regime seemed to be in the process of transformation. To begin with, the rise of the "BJP and its affiliates in the Sangh Parivar invented new forms of exclusion which were backed with grotesque violence." And second, "the caste-based political parties of north India invented new forms of inclusion, expressed in higher levels of representation for members of the backward castes in legislative bodies and a presence in the institutions of governance." This has variously been described as the "second great democratic upsurge" in India (Yadav 2000), or less positively, as the collapse of universal forms of citizenship in favour of the rise of patronage politics controlled by the Backward Classes (Chandra 2004).

Jayal notes, however, that while this transformation is real enough, the contours of change are more nuanced than a Great Transformation narrative might suggest. Most of the gains made by the Backward Classes have accrued to its "creamy layers," some of whose members are now engaged in oppression of more subaltern communities. Set against this, there is some evidence that women are beginning to make headway in India's newly vibrant Panchayati Raj institutions, including as *sarpanches*. This is poor compensation, however, for various developments that are impacting India's women in the field of biological citizenship. In some of India's most affluent and reform-affected Districts – including in Punjab, Haryana and Gujarat – there is evidence that sex-ratios are worsening, so much so that ratios of less than 850 females for every 1000 men are not uncommon. Maternal mortality in India meanwhile remains appallingly high at around 330 per 100,000 live births. As Jayal reports, "if a woman gets pregnant three times in her life, the chance of her dying is 1 in 101." Jayal suggests that developments in citizenship regimes that have an impact on the substantive social and economic claims of members of the society, gender relations, the status of non-citizens (including refugees from Pakistan) might be of great significance in the long run.

Much will depend in the years ahead on how well women and other disadvantaged groups can mobilize for citizenship rights and welfare entitlements in the political arena, whether through new forms of decentralized governance and/or with the help of organized political forces.

Patrick Heller begins his discussion of these issues with an account of democratic deepening that takes a more positive line than either Harriss or Jayal. Heller notes that "the democratic deficit in India is both associational and institutional. Despite formal democratic rights, ordinary citizens find it difficult to engage the state meaningfully [while] pervasive and durable inequalities severely constrain the associational capacities of many social categories." The gist of his argument, nonetheless, is that both vertical and horizontal deepening in India's democracy is now apparent. And this is not just in Kerala – what might be called the "usual suspect" in upbeat accounts of the possibility of progressive social mobilizations in civil society. Heller also directs attention to Madhya Pradesh.

Heller, like John Harriss for the most part, thinks of civil society as a zone of free association and mobilization between the state and the household. He does not equate civil society with civility and the rule of law, as Partha Chatterjee is inclined to do. Heller provides strong reasons for believing that citizens are participating more meaningfully and effectively in political life than was the case 20 years ago. Local democracy has made a difference, and so too have repeat plays in other "democratic games," such as participation in village education committees or forest management institutions. Men and women are learning by doing, however slowly and fitfully. Above all, Heller suggests, the "significance of Panchayati Raj is that it represents a potentially very significant expansion of the political opportunity structure." When combined with a deep churning among India's subordinate groups, we might be witnessing, Heller concludes, not only a second or third democratic upsurge in India, but something close to a "silent revolution" (see Jaffrelot 2003) in the ways in which political business can be transacted and how poor people see and engage the state.

Heller's qualified optimism finds supporting documentation in randomized experiments carried out by some economists. Chattopadhyay and Duflo (2004) find that elected women politicians in rural West Bengal are more likely than men to prioritize issues of importance to women, including water provision and collection.

Besley, Pande and Rao (2006) argue that more educated village representatives are less likely to be 'corrupt' or sectional than their less-educated counterparts. Others, however, are less persuaded. John Harriss (2007) and Karen Coelho (2005) largely concur with Partha Chatterjee about the difficulties that poor urban Indians face in dealing with government, where they are generally treated with disdain or as troublesome members of "crowds." As ever, more work is required and we need to be wary of all-India generalizations.

Similar caution is warranted when it comes to formal politics at state and national levels. Three common propositions that were advanced in the 1990s were that national parties were on the wane in India, save perhaps for the BJP; that the unity of India would be enormously weakened by the rise of political parties that pandered to caste, religion or region; and that governmental capacity in India would be eroded by the post-1989 arrival of national coalition governments.

The rise of Hindu nationalist forces is dealt with most directly in this collection by Radhika Desai in her essay on "the great Hindutva transformation." Desai argues forcefully that economic liberalization since the late 1960s has been decisive in advancing Hindu nationalism, as well as the fortunes of India's provincial propertied classes (PPCs). In turn, the BJP and the Sangh Parivar have stood squarely behind the bourgeois agenda of economic reform, notwithstanding their internal debates over the desirability of *swadeshi* in a post-liberalization era. What is distinctive in this argument is not that links are drawn between Hindutva politics and liberalization, but rather its chronology. Desai contends that economic liberalization in India began in 1969 with the Green Revolution. It was at this point that "developmentalism" was laid to rest, and it was from this time that a slow sea change occurred in India's political and economic landscapes. Desai argues that a focus on 1990–2 fails to register the turn to "plutocratic politics" that has accompanied the rise of India's post-Green Revolution regional bourgeoisies. In her view, non-liberal forms of government in India were ended in the near-famine conditions that gripped parts of India in 1966 and 1967. To some degree, too, they were anticipated by the rise to power in western Uttar Pradesh of Charan Singh. Desai accepts that the rise of caste-based parties like the Bahujan Samaj Party (BSP) is indicative of democratic deepening in post-1990 India. Her broader argument, however, is that this moment of deepening has been offset by the rise of various PPCs – political groupings that turned their backs on the Green Revolution that Congress (finally) had given them in favour of a Hindutva politics that allowed them to contest the (prospective) rise to power of the Backward Classes.

Desai suggests that the BJP achieved power in New Delhi by forging a political coalition of the propertied classes that stretched across India's rural–urban divide. This was also the achievement of the BJP in Gujarat, Haryana, Himachal Pradesh and Rajasthan. Desai recognizes, however, that Hindutva forces have been less successful outside their heartlands in central and north-west India, and that Congress has slowly regrouped following its defeat in the 1999 general election. When in power, too, the BJP has had to moderate its agendas to conform with the centrist nature of Indian politics. It has also had to form coalition governments in alliance with other political parties – just like the Congress Party since 1989 – and in the teeth of opposition, at least in the late 1980s and 1990s, from a Third Force of political parties that have been demanding "greater cultural recognition and political devolution" (as Sanjay Ruparelia puts it in his paper here). The Third Force came to power in India for the first time in 1989 in the form of a seven-party coalition named the National Front (NF). Ruparelia contends that despite "its short-lived tenure ... the election of the National Front constituted a watershed in modern Indian democracy ... [I]t ushered in a 'post-Congress' polity in which state-level dynamics would determine the face of government in New Delhi."

Ruparelia focuses on the reasons for and significance of the rise to power in New Delhi both of the National Front governments of 1989–91 (led by V. P. Singh and Chandra Shekhar) and the United Front governments of Prime Ministers H. D. Deve Gowda and I. K. Gujral in 1996–8. He notes that it is tempting to read the failure to create a durable national alternative to the Congress or BJP after 1989 "as the chronicle of a death foretold." Most observers thought the NF and UF governments were doomed from the start, the inevitable victims of vicious in-fighting, diverse class, caste and regional interests and an apparent lack of coherent ideologies. Ruparelia, however, shows that this perspective is marked more by pessimism and teleology than by empirical insight. What is most remarkable about both governments is that they achieved so much. This was true both in foreign policy – Ruparelia directs attention to the NF government's commitment to better relations with Pakistan – and at home. It was V. P. Singh's government, after all, which acted on many of the recommendations of the Report of the Second Backward Classes Commission (the so-called Mandal Report), which led to increased reservation of jobs for India's Other Backward Classes, just as India's one true neoliberal (as James Manor describes him in the next chapter), P. Chidambaram, cut his teeth as Finance Minister in Deve Gowda's UF government. As Ruparelia notes, "[t]he capacity of the United Front to advance the agenda of liberalization disproved the view that a heterogeneous centre-left coalition would stymie the reform process."

In the end the Third Force was not able to hold together as a coherent opposition to the BJP (whose progress it still helped to slow), or the Congress, even though its elements continue to shape the politics of the latter two parties. On the one hand, the dictates of economic liberalization deepened the regionalization of politics that gave rise to the parties of the third force, which paradoxically made it harder to cohere as a national political front over time. On the other, these conditions simultaneously increased the importance and difficulty of its leaders' exercising good political judgment. They failed to live up to the task. The Congress has learned to adapt to the new rules of federal power-sharing that have shaped politics in India since 1989, most especially so in the 2004 Lok Sabha elections, and in lesser degree in 2009, when the Congress Party of Prime Minister Manmohan Singh translated a 28.6 percent vote share into 206 seats.

What might be called the rise and fall and rise again of the Congress Party is the subject of the penultimate essay in this volume, by James Manor. Manor begins his essay with an interesting portrait of Narasimha Rao, the Congress Prime Minister of India during the first phase of economic reforms (1991–6). Manor depicts Rao as a political manager who backed off confrontation and who was anything but a neoliberal. Nor, says Manor, is Manmohan Singh, Rao's Finance Minister and now the Prime Minister, a neoliberal. Rao was sceptical of the possibility of trickle-down economics and both men embraced social democracy. The reform agenda in India was driven more by events than by ideas, and Rao deserves to be remembered, Manor concludes, more for what he held back (cuts to "huge government subsidies on many goods") than for what he authorized by way of economic liberalization. The pace of reform had much to do with Rao's temperament, and it was generally a slow pace that ensued.

Manor also considers the threats posed to the Congress Party by the rise of the BJP and by the "Backward Castes issue." He finds in both cases that mainstream perspectives have exaggerated the challenge to Congress, except in regard to Hindutva forces in Gujarat. The Congress has faced a far greater threat from regional forces, and has largely been driven from power in States like Bihar, West Bengal and Tamil Nadu by "regional parties" of very different hues – ethnic, casteist, communist. Manor, though, more so than many observers, notes that the Congress Party has been reforming itself since the dark days of "Indira is India, India is Indira." Again, Narasimha Rao played a key role in reviving Congress fortunes, before handing on in due course to Sonia Gandhi and Manmohan Singh (who may now, perhaps, pass the baton to Rahul Gandhi). Neither the Congress Party nor the Nehru-Gandhi dynasty is dead, a point proved with great vigour in the 15th Lok Sabha elections. The Congress Party still retains the services of many senior politicians who are skilled in exploiting protests against Hindutva and Third Force agendas. It is also beginning to appeal again to a younger, more middle-class India, confidently promoting Rahul Gandhi as the future face of a more upbeat, managerial and still all-India political party.

This new confidence extends to the Congress Party's dealings with the wider world. India now forcefully articulates a claim to permanent membership of the UN's Security Council, something that its large and growing economy, not to mention its status as a nuclear weapons state, would seem to mandate. It is already a regional power, doing its best over the past decade to extend its presence in Central Asia and in Afghanistan through increased developmental aid and foreign investment, in the process creating a sense of encirclement in Pakistan. India has also moved closer to the US and, less publicly, to Israel, stoking fears about its commitments to foreign policy independence and to secular politics. These worries increased sharply when the BJP was in power in New Delhi from 1998 to 2004, and especially so at the time of the nuclear tests that Prime Minister Vajpayee authorized in Pokhran in May 1998.

Achin Vanaik, in the book's concluding essay, explores some of these developments. He deploys a vigorously realist sensibility that guards him against the view that only the BJP has supported a Hindutva agenda. According to Vanaik, "The great irony of our times is that although socially-electorally the Congress today is, proportionately speaking, more than ever before in its post-independence history, a party of the lower castes and lower classes. Yet in its policy orientation and behaviour it has never been so right-wing!" The focus on existing politics also leads him to expose the myths of national interest and complete State autonomy that proponents of Realism in the discipline of international relations in India are determined to promote.

Vanaik ends by coming close to Chatterjee. He argues that a decline in the power of India's agrarian bourgeoisie has opened the way to the ascendancy of "Big capital, Indian and foreign, [which] is increasingly powerful." As these capitals have become more mobile and transnationalized, India and its ruling elites have been brought closer to the US. India's elites have recognized that even mobile capitals have to be regulated within nation-states. India might also need the protection – in extremis: as in 2008–9, as in a war with China – of a hegemon that helps to provide order in a world that tends otherwise to anarchy. This is the real reason, Vanaik concludes, why India is edging closer to the US and to its militaristic commitments to making the world safe for capital (a project usually glossed as "globalization").

For Vanaik this is a tragedy. It is confirmation that the vision of a Third Way, or a New India, proposed by Nehru, and fought for by the Freedom Movement, has been sold out in favour of emulation of a capitalist country that Nehru and Gandhi would have abjured. For others, it is simply confirmation that the pendulum has swung a long way since the deaths of Gandhi in 1948 and Nehru in 1964. The great transformations in India's political economy that are debated here are now being paralleled by significant changes in India's geopolitical and geoeconomic relationships. Achin Vanaik offers a first glimpse into these complex re-inscribings of space and politics.

All countries are in continuous process of transformation. It is probably also true to say that the transformations that have been seen in India over the last two decades have not been as great as those that have occurred in China since the death of Mao, or in Russia since the collapse of state socialism. The spread of capitalist market relations in South Asia is taking place in countries that have not been blighted by concerted attempts to suppress the profit motive.

In other respects, however, the transformations now being negotiated in India, and more broadly across South Asia, are every bit as great and contested. At stake, crucially, are the citizenship, welfare and foreign policy regimes that either connect the region's social majorities to the accumulation projects of ruling elites, or which leave them excluded, dispossessed and angry. The future of India looked dark in the years either side of 1990. It looks far better in 2010, thanks to the efforts of some of its leading politicians, both mainstream and oppositional. But India's continuous and smooth ascent to global power status is far from assured. Much will depend on how the pendulum shifts over the next 20 years, and on whether India can shift its accumulation strategy in a more inclusive direction, better encompassing in both the economic and the political process of the poorer and those who have been socially excluded on the basis of caste, gender or religion. Over the past 20 years, India's elites have been in revolt against earlier models of economic accumulation and social regulation. Whether and how they will make space for forms of governance that are more expansive – if not quite "pro-poor" – remains the key issue facing India in the years ahead.

Notes

1 Chatterjee takes the phrase "passive revolution" from Gramsci. It refers to an expensive and technocratic approach to capitalist development from on high that takes the place of (and substitutes for) social transformations from below. India's poor economic performance in the 1970s is often described with reference to the so-called "Hindu rate of growth."
2 The conventional definition of "political society," as used by political scientists, depicts the formal realm of electoral contestation between political parties, legislative assemblies and the institutions that govern the ballot. By expanding its coverage to subaltern classes in the informal sector, Chatterjee offers an alternative meaning.
3 We owe this formulation to Atul Kohli.
4 Paul Krugman and Anthony Venables have been key figures in this enterprise. For a detailed exposition, see World Bank (2009).
5 See Krishnamurthy (2009).
6 Using the Uniform Reporting System that allows for comparability in poverty rates and trends over time. For discussion, see Himanshu (2007).
7 See Besley et al. (2005).

2 Democracy and economic transformation in India[1]

Partha Chatterjee

Peasant society today

The first volume of *Subaltern Studies* was published in 1982. I was part of the editorial group that launched, under the leadership of Ranajit Guha, this critical engagement with Indian modernity from the standpoint of the subaltern classes, especially the peasantry. In the quarter of a century that has passed since then, there has been, I believe, a fundamental change in the situation prevailing in postcolonial India. The new conditions under which global flows of capital, commodities, information and people are now regulated – a complex set of phenomena generally grouped under the category of globalization – have created both new opportunities and new obstacles for the Indian ruling classes. The old idea of a Third World, sharing a common history of colonial oppression and backwardness, is no longer as persuasive as it was in the 1960s. The trajectory of economic growth taken by the countries of Asia has diverged radically from that of most African countries. The phenomenal growth of China and India in recent years, involving two of the most populous agrarian countries of the world, has set in motion a process of social change that is, in its scale and speed, unprecedented in human history.

In this context, I believe it has become important to revisit the question of the basic structures of power in Indian society, especially the position of the peasantry, under conditions of postcolonial democracy. This is not because I think that the advance of capitalist industrial growth is inevitably breaking down peasant communities and turning peasants into proletarian workers, as has been predicted innumerable times in the last century and a half. On the contrary, I will argue that the forms of capitalist industrial growth now under way in India will make room for the preservation of the peasantry, but under completely altered conditions. The analysis of these emergent forms of postcolonial capitalism in India under conditions of electoral democracy requires new conceptual work.

Let me begin by referring to the recent incidents of violent agitation in different regions of India, especially in West Bengal and Orissa, against the acquisition of agricultural land for industry. There have also been agitations in several states against the entry of corporate capital into the retail market for food and vegetables. The most talked about incidents occurred in Nandigram in West Bengal in 2007–8, on which much has been written. If these incidents had taken place 25 years ago, we would have seen in them the classic signs of peasant insurgency. Here were the long familiar features of a peasantry, tied to the land and small-scale agriculture, united by the cultural and moral bonds of a local rural community, resisting the agents of an external state and of city-based commercial institutions by using both peaceful and violent means. Our analysis then could have drawn on a long tradition of anthropological studies of peasant societies, focusing on the characteristic forms of dependence of peasant economies on external institutions such as the state and dominant classes such as landlords, moneylenders and traders, but also on the forms of autonomy of peasant cultures based on the solidarity of a local moral community. We could have also linked our discussion to a long tradition of political debates over the historical role of the peasantry under conditions of capitalist growth, beginning with the Marxist analysis in Western Europe of the inevitable dissolution of the peasantry as a result of the process of primitive accumulation of capital, Lenin's debates in Russia with the Narodniks, Mao Zedong's analysis of the role of the peasantry in the Chinese Revolution, and the continuing debates over Gandhi's vision of a free India where a mobilized peasantry in the villages would successfully resist the spread of industrial capitalism and the violence of the modern state. Moreover, using the insights drawn from Antonio Gramsci's writings, we could have talked about the contradictory consciousness of the peasantry in which it was both dominated by the forms of the elite culture of the ruling classes and, at the same time, resistant to them. Twenty-five years ago, we would have seen these rural agitations in terms of the analysis provided by Ranajit Guha in his classic work *Elementary Aspects of Peasant Insurgency in Colonial India* (1983).

I believe that analysis would be inappropriate today. I say this for the following reasons. First, the spread of governmental technologies in India in the last three decades, as a result of the deepening reach of the developmental state under conditions of electoral democracy, has meant that the state is no longer an external entity to the peasant community. Governmental agencies distributing education, health services, food, roadways, water, electricity, agricultural technology, emergency relief and dozens of other welfare services have penetrated deep into the interior of everyday peasant life. Not only are peasants dependent on state agencies for these services, they have also acquired considerable skill, albeit to a different degree in different regions, in manipulating and pressurizing these agencies to deliver these benefits. Institutions of the state, or at least governmental agencies (whether state or non-state), have become internal aspects of the peasant community. Second, the reforms since the 1950s to the structure of agrarian property, even though gradual and piecemeal, have meant that except in isolated areas, for the first time in centuries, small peasants possessing land no longer directly confront an exploiting class within the village, as under feudal or semi-feudal conditions. This has had consequences that are completely new for the range of strategies of peasant politics. Third, since the tax on land or agricultural produce is no longer a significant source of revenue for the government, as in colonial or pre-colonial times, the relation of the state to the peasantry is no longer directly extractive, as it often was in the past. Fourth, with the rapid growth of cities and industrial regions, the possibility of peasants making a shift to urban and non-agricultural occupations is no longer a function of their pauperization and forcible separation from the land, but is often a voluntary choice, shaped by the perception of new opportunities and new desires. Fifth, with the spread of school education and widespread exposure to modern communications media such as the cinema, television and advertising, there is a strong and widespread desire among younger members, both male and female, of peasant families not to live the life of a peasant in the village and instead to move to the town or the city, with all its hardships and uncertainties, because of its lure of anonymity and upward mobility. This is particularly significant for India, where the life of poor peasants in rural society is marked not only by the disadvantage of class but also by the discriminations of caste, compared to which the sheer anonymity of life in the city is often seen as liberating. For agricultural labourers, of whom vast numbers are from the *Dalit* communities, the desired future is to move out of the traditional servitude of rural labour into urban non-agricultural occupations.

A new conceptual framework

I may have emphasized the novelty of the present situation too sharply; in actual fact, the changes have undoubtedly come more gradually over time. But I do believe that the novelty needs to be stressed at this time in order to ask: how do these new features of peasant life affect our received theories of the place of the peasantry in postcolonial India? Kalyan Sanyal has attempted a fundamental revision of these theories in his recent book *Rethinking Capitalist Development* (2007). In the following discussion, I will use some of his formulations in order to present my own arguments on this subject.

The key concept in Sanyal's analysis is the *primitive accumulation of capital* – sometimes called primary or original accumulation of capital. Like Sanyal, I too prefer to use this term in Marx's sense to mean the dissociation of the labourer from the means of labour. There is no doubt that this is the key historical process that brings peasant societies into crisis with the rise of capitalist production. Marx's analysis in the last chapters of volume one of *Capital* shows that the emergence of modern capitalist industrial production is invariably associated with the parallel process of the loss of the means of production on the part of primary producers such as peasants and artisans.[2] The unity of labour with the means of labour, which is the basis of most pre-capitalist modes of production, is destroyed and a mass of labourers emerge who do not any more possess the means of production. Needless to say, the unity of labour with the means of labour is the conceptual counterpart in the political economy of the organic unity of most pre-capitalist rural societies by virtue of which peasants and rural artisans are said to live in close bonds of solidarity in a local rural community. This is the familiar anthropological description of peasant societies as well as the source of inspiration for many romantic writers and artists portraying rural life. This is also the unity that is destroyed in the process of primitive accumulation of capital, throwing peasant societies into crisis.

The analysis of this crisis has produced, as I have already indicated, a variety of historical narratives ranging from the inevitable dissolution of peasant societies to slogans of worker-peasant unity in the building of a future socialist society.

Despite their differences, the common feature in all these narratives is the idea of transition. Peasants and peasant societies under conditions of capitalist development are always in a state of transition – whether from feudalism to capitalism or from pre-capitalist backwardness to socialist modernity.

A central argument made by Sanyal in his book is that under present conditions of postcolonial development within a globalized economy, *the narrative of transition is no longer valid*. That is to say, although capitalist growth in a postcolonial society such as India is inevitably accompanied by the primitive accumulation of capital, the social changes that are brought about cannot be understood as a transition. How is that possible?

The explanation has to do with the transformations in the last two decades in the globally dispersed understanding about the minimum functions as well as the available technologies of government. There is a growing sense now that certain basic conditions of life must be provided to people everywhere and that if the national or local governments do not provide them, someone else must, whether it is other states or international agencies, or non-governmental organizations. Thus, while there is a dominant discourse about the importance of growth, which in recent times has come to mean almost exclusively capitalist growth, it is, at the same time, considered unacceptable that those who are dispossessed of their means of labour because of the primitive accumulation of capital should have no means of subsistence. This produces, says Sanyal, a curious process in which, on the one side, primary producers such as peasants, craftspeople and petty manufacturers lose their land and other means of production, but, on the other, are also provided by governmental agencies with the conditions for meeting their basic needs of livelihood. There is, says Sanyal, primitive accumulation as well as a parallel process of the *reversal of the effects of primitive accumulation*.

It would be useful to illustrate this process with some examples. Historically, the process of industrialization in all agrarian countries has meant the eviction of peasants from the land, either because the land was taken over for urban or industrial development or because the peasant no longer had the means to cultivate the land. Market forces were usually strong enough to force peasants to give up the land, but often direct coercion was used by means of the legal and fiscal powers of the state. From colonial times, government authorities in India have used the right of eminent domain to acquire lands to be used for 'public purposes', offering only a token compensation, if any. The idea that peasants losing land must be resettled somewhere else and rehabilitated into a new livelihood was rarely acknowledged. Historically, it has been said that the opportunities of migration of the surplus population from Europe to the settler colonies in the Americas and elsewhere made it possible to politically manage the consequences of primitive accumulation in Europe in the eighteenth and nineteenth centuries. No such opportunities exist today for India. More importantly, the technological conditions of early industrialization that created the demand for a substantial mass of industrial labour have long passed. Capitalist growth today is far more capital-intensive and technology-dependent than it was even some decades ago. Large sections of peasants who are today the victims of the primitive accumulation of capital are completely unlikely to be absorbed into the new capitalist sectors of growth. Therefore, without a specific government policy of resettlement, the peasants losing their land face the possibility of the complete loss of their means of livelihood. Under present globally prevailing normative ideas, this is considered unacceptable. Hence, the old-fashioned methods of putting down peasant resistance by armed repression have little chance of gaining legitimacy. The result is the widespread demand today for the rehabilitation of displaced people who lose their means of subsistence because of industrial and urban development. It is not, says Sanyal, as though primitive accumulation is halted or even slowed down, for primitive accumulation is the inevitable companion to capitalist growth. Rather, governmental agencies have to find the resources to, as it were, reverse the consequences of primitive accumulation by providing alternative means of livelihood to those who have lost them.

Several governmental technologies became widespread in the second half of the twentieth century to soften the blows dealt by primitive accumulation. They have become part of the political-economic technologies of democracy in India. Thus, it is not uncommon for developmental states to protect certain sectors of production that are currently the domain of peasants, artisans and small manufacturers against competition from large corporate firms. But this may be interpreted as an attempt to forestall primitive accumulation itself by preventing corporate capital from entering into areas such as food crop or vegetable production or handicraft manufacture. However, there are many examples in many countries, including India, of governments and non-government agencies offering easy loans to enable those without the means of sustenance to find some gainful employment. Such loans are often advanced without serious concern for profitability or the prospect of the loan being repaid, since the money advanced here is not driven by the motive of further accumulation of capital but rather by that of providing the livelihood needs of the borrowers – that is to say, by the motive of reversal of the effects of primitive accumulation. In recent years, these efforts have acquired the status of a globally circulating technology of poverty management: a notable instance is the micro-credit movement initiated by the Grameen Bank in Bangladesh and its founder, the Nobel Prize winner Mohammed Yunus. Most of us are familiar now with stories of peasant women in rural Bangladesh forming groups to take loans from Grameen Bank to undertake small activities to supplement their livelihood and putting pressure on one another to repay the loan so that they can qualify for another round of credit. Similar activities have been introduced quite extensively in India in recent years.

Finally, as in other countries, government agencies in India provide some direct benefits to people who, because of poverty or other reasons, are unable to meet their basic consumption needs. This could be in the form of special poverty-removal programmes, or schemes of guaranteed employment in public works, or even direct delivery of subsidized or free food. Thus, there are programmes of supplying subsidized food grains to those designated as 'below the poverty line', guaranteed employment for up to 100 days in the year for those who need it, and free meals for children in primary school. All of these may be regarded, in terms of our analysis, as direct interventions to reverse the effects of primitive accumulation.

It is important to point out that except for the last example of direct provision of consumption needs, most of the other mechanisms of reversing the effects of primitive accumulation involve the intervention of the market. This is the other significant difference in the present conditions of peasant life from the traditional models we have known. Except in certain marginal pockets, peasant and craft production in India today is fully integrated into a market economy. Unlike a few decades ago, there is almost no sector of household production that can be described as intended wholly for self-consumption or non-monetized exchange within a local community. Virtually all peasant and artisan production is for sale in the market and all consumption needs are purchased from the market. This, as we shall see, has an important bearing on recent changes in the conditions of peasant politics.

It is also necessary to point out that 'livelihood needs' do not indicate a fixed quantum of goods determined by biological or other ahistorical criteria. It is a contextually determined, socially produced sense of what is necessary to lead a decent life of some worth and self-respect. The composition of the set of elements that constitute 'livelihood needs' will, therefore, vary with social location, cultural context and time. Thus, the expected minimum standards of health care for the family or minimum levels of education for one's children will vary, as will the specific composition of the commodities of consumption such as food, clothes or domestic appliances. What is important here is a culturally determined sense of what is minimally necessary for a decent life, one that is neither unacceptably impoverished nor excessive and luxurious.

Transformed structures of political power

To place these changes within a structural frame that describes how political power is held and exercised in postcolonial India, I also need to provide an outline of the transformation that, I believe, has taken place in that structure in recent years. Twenty-five years ago, the structure of state power in India was usually described in terms of a coalition of dominant class interests. Pranab Bardhan identified the capitalists, the rich farmers and the bureaucracy as the three dominant classes, competing and aligning with one another within a political space supervised by a relatively autonomous state (Bardhan 1984). Achin Vanaik also endorsed the dominant coalition model, emphasizing in particular the relative political strength of the agrarian bourgeoisie, which, he stressed, was far greater than its economic importance. He also insisted that even though India had never had a classical bourgeois revolution, its political system was nevertheless a bourgeois democracy that enjoyed a considerable degree of legitimacy not only with the dominant classes but also with the mass of the people (Vanaik 1990). Several scholars writing in the 1980s, such as for instance Ashutosh Varshney (1995) and Lloyd and Susanne Rudolph (1987), emphasized the growing political clout of the rich farmers or agrarian capitalists within the dominant coalition.

The dominant class coalition model was given a robust theoretical shape in a classic essay by Sudipta Kaviraj in which, by using Antonio Gramsci's idea of the 'passive revolution' as a blocked dialectic, he was able to ascribe to the process of class domination in postcolonial India its own dynamic (Kaviraj 1988). Power had to be shared between the dominant classes because no one class had the ability to exercise hegemony on its own. But 'sharing' was a process of ceaseless push and pull, with one class gaining a relative ascendancy at one point, only to lose it at another. Kaviraj provided us with a synoptic political history of the relative dominance and decline of the industrial capitalists, the rural elites and the bureaucratic-managerial elite within the framework of the passive revolution of capital. In my early work, I too adopted the idea of the passive revolution of capital in my account of the emergence of the postcolonial state in India (Chatterjee and Mallik 1975; Chatterjee 1986; Chatterjee 1998).

The characteristic features of the passive revolution in India were the relative autonomy of the state as a whole from the bourgeoisie and the landed elites; the supervision of the state by an elected political leadership, a permanent bureaucracy and an independent judiciary; the negotiation of class interests through a multi-party electoral system; a protectionist regime discouraging the entry of foreign capital and promoting import substitution; the leading role of the state sector in heavy industry, infrastructure, transport, telecommunications; mining, banking and insurance; state control over the private manufacturing sector through a regime of licensing; and the relatively greater influence of industrial capitalists over the central government and that of the landed elites on the state governments. Passive revolution was a form that was marked by its difference from classical bourgeois democracy. But to the extent that capitalist democracy as established in Western Europe or North America served as the normative standard of bourgeois revolution, discussions of passive revolution in India carried with them the sense of a transitional system – from pre-colonial and colonial regimes to some yet-to-be-defined authentic modernity.

The changes introduced since the 1990s have, I believe, transformed this framework of class dominance. The crucial difference now is the dismantling of the licence regime, greater entry of foreign capital and foreign consumer goods; and the opening up of sectors such as telecommunications, transport, infrastructure, mining, banking, insurance, etc. to private capital. This has led to a change in the very composition of the capitalist class. Instead of the earlier dominance of a few 'monopoly' houses drawn from traditional merchant backgrounds and protected by the licence and import substitution regime, there are now many more entrants into the capitalist class at all levels and much greater mobility within its formation (see Damodaran 2008). Unlike the earlier fear of foreign competition, there appears to be much greater confidence among Indian capitalists to make use of the opportunities opened up by global flows of capital, goods and services, including, in recent times, significant exports of capital. The most dramatic event has been the rise of the Indian information technologies industry. But domestic manufacturing and services have also received a major spurt, leading to annual growth rates of 8 or 9 per cent for the economy as a whole in the last few years until the slump of 2008–9.

There have been several political changes as a result. Let me list a few that are relevant for our present discussion. First, there is a distinct ascendancy in the relative power of the corporate capitalist class as compared to the landed elites. The political means by which this recent dominance has been achieved needs to be investigated more carefully, because it was not achieved through the mechanism of electoral mobilization (which used to be the source of the political power of the landed elites).[3] Second, the dismantling of the licence regime has opened up a new field of competition between state governments to woo capitalist investment, both domestic and foreign. This has resulted in the involvement of state-level political parties and leaders with the interests of national and international corporate capital in unprecedented ways. Third, although the state continues to be the most important mediating apparatus in negotiating between conflicting class interests, the autonomy of the state in relation to the dominant classes appears to have been redefined. Crucially, the earlier role of the bureaucratic-managerial class, or more generally of the urban middle classes, in leading and operating, both socially and ideologically, the autonomous interventionist activities of the developmental state has significantly weakened. There is a strong ideological tendency among the urban middle classes today to view the state apparatus as ridden with corruption, inefficiency and populist political venality and a much greater social acceptance of the professionalism and commitment to growth and efficiency of the corporate capitalist sector. The urban middle class, which once played such a crucial role in producing and running the autonomous developmental state of the passive revolution, appears now to have largely come under the moral-political sway of the bourgeoisie.

It would be a mistake, however, to think that the result is a convergence of the Indian political system with the classical models of capitalist democracy. The critical difference, as I have pointed out earlier, has been produced by a split in the field of the political between a domain of properly constituted *civil society* and a more ill-defined and contingently activated domain of *political society* (Chatterjee 2004b). Civil society in India today, peopled largely by the urban middle classes, is the sphere that seeks to be congruent with the normative models of bourgeois civil society and represents the domain of capitalist hegemony. If this were the only relevant political domain, then India today would probably be indistinguishable from other Western capitalist democracies. But there is the other domain, of what I have called political society, which includes large sections of the rural population and the urban poor. These people do, of course, have the formal status of citizens and can exercise their franchise as an instrument of political bargaining. But they do not relate to the organs of the state in the same way that the middle classes do, nor do governmental agencies treat them as proper citizens belonging to civil society. Those in political society make their claims on government, and in turn are governed, not within the framework of stable constitutionally defined rights and laws, but rather through temporary, contextual and unstable arrangements arrived at through direct political negotiations. The latter domain, which represents the vast bulk of democratic politics in India, is not under the moral-political leadership of the capitalist class.

Hence, my argument is that the framework of passive revolution is still valid for India. But its structure and dynamic have undergone a change. The capitalist class has come to acquire a position of moral-political hegemony over civil society, consisting principally of the urban middle classes. It exercises its considerable influence over both the central and the state governments not through electoral mobilization of political parties and movements but largely through the bureaucratic-managerial class, the increasingly influential print and visual media, and the judiciary and other independent regulatory bodies. The dominance of the capitalist class within the state structure as a whole can be inferred from the virtual consensus among all major political parties about the priorities of rapid economic growth led by private investment, both domestic and foreign. It is striking that even the CPI(M) in West Bengal, and slightly more ambiguously in Kerala, have, in practice if not in theory, joined this consensus. This means that as far as the party system is concerned, it does not matter which particular combination of parties comes to power at the Centre or even in most of the states; state support for rapid economic growth is guaranteed to continue. This is evidence of the current success of the passive revolution.

However, the practices of the state also include the large range of governmental activities in political society. Here there are locally dominant interests, such as those of landed elites, small producers and local traders, who are able to exercise political influence through their powers of electoral mobilization. In the old understanding of the passive revolution, these interests would have been seen as potentially opposed to those of the industrial bourgeoisie; the conflicts would have been temporarily resolved through a compromise worked out within the party system and the autonomous apparatus of the state. Now, I believe, there is a new dynamic logic that ties the operations of political society with the hegemonic role of the bourgeoisie in civil society and its dominance over the state structure as a whole. This logic is supplied by the requirement, explained earlier, of reversing the effects of primitive accumulation of capital. To describe how this logic serves to integrate civil and political society into a new structure of the passive revolution, let me return to the subject of the peasantry.

Political society and the management of non-corporate capital

The integration with the market has meant that large sections of what used to be called the subsistence economy, which was once the classic description of small peasant agriculture, have now come fully under the sway of capital. This is a key development that must crucially affect our understanding of peasant society in India today. There is now a degree of connectedness between peasant cultivation, trade and credit networks in agricultural commodities, transport networks, petty manufacturing and services in rural markets and small towns, etc. that makes it necessary for us to categorize all of them as part of a single, but stratified, complex. A common description of this is the unorganized or informal sector, recently given official recognition by the National Commission for Enterprises in the Unorganized Sector (NCEUS) which has treated agricultural and non-agricultural activities in the unorganized sector in both rural and urban areas, including farming and household work, as differentiated parts of the same economic category (NCEUS 2007).

Usually, a unit belonging to the informal sector is identified in terms of the small size of the enterprise, the small number of labourers employed, or the relatively unregulated nature of the business. In terms of the analytical framework I have presented here, I will propose a distinction between the formal and the informal sectors of today's economy in terms of a difference between corporate and non-corporate forms of capital. Interestingly, the NCEUS too has settled for a similar definition: 'The unorganized sector consists of all unincorporated private enterprises … with less than ten total workers' (NCEUS 2007: 3). The classification by size, necessary for purposes of counting, is of course arbitrary; the identification of the unorganized with the unincorporated sector, however, is conceptual.

My argument is that the characteristics I have described of peasant societies today are best understood as the marks of *non-corporate capital*. To the extent that peasant production is deeply embedded within market structures, investments and returns are conditioned by forces emanating from the operations of capital. In this sense, peasant production shares many connections with informal units in manufacturing, trade and services operating in rural markets, small towns and even in large cities. We can draw many refined distinctions between corporate and non-corporate forms of capital. But the key distinction I wish to emphasize is the following. The fundamental logic that underlies the operations of corporate capital is further accumulation of capital, usually signified by the maximization of profit. For non-corporate organizations of capital, while profit is not irrelevant, it is dominated by another logic – that of providing the livelihood needs of those working in the units. This difference is crucial for the understanding of the so-called informal economy and, by extension, as I will argue, of peasant society.

Let me illustrate with a couple of familiar examples from the non-agricultural informal sector and then return to the subject of peasants. Most of us are familiar with the phenomenon of street vendors in Indian cities. They occupy street space, usually violating municipal laws; they often erect permanent stalls, use municipal services such as water and electricity, and do not pay taxes. To carry on their trade under these conditions, they usually organize themselves into associations to deal with the municipal authorities, the police, credit agencies such as banks and corporate firms that manufacture and distribute the commodities they sell on the streets. These associations are often large and the volume of business they encompass can be quite considerable. Obviously, operating within a public and anonymous market situation, the vendors are subject to the standard conditions of profitability of their businesses. But to ensure that everyone is able to meet their livelihood needs, the association will usually try to limit the number of vendors who can operate in a given area and prevent the entry of newcomers. On the other hand, there are many examples where, if the businesses are doing particularly well, the vendors do not, like corporate capitalists, continue to accumulate on an expanded scale, but rather agree to extend their membership and allow new entrants. To cite another example, in most cities and towns of India, the transport system depends heavily on private operators who run buses and auto-rickshaws. Here too there is frequent violation of regulations such as licences, safety standards and pollution norms – violations that allow these units to survive economically. Although most operators own only one or two vehicles each, they form associations to negotiate with transport authorities and the police over fares and routes, and control the frequency of services and entry of new operators to ensure that a minimum income, and not much more than a minimum income, is guaranteed to all.

In my book *The Politics of the Governed* (2004), I have described the form of governmental regulation of population groups such as street vendors, illegal squatters and others, whose habitation or livelihood verge on the margins of legality, as *political society*. In political society, I have argued, people are not regarded by the state as proper citizens possessing rights and belonging to the properly constituted civil society. Rather, they are seen to belong to particular population groups, with specific empirically established and statistically described characteristics, which are targets of particular governmental policies. Since dealing with many of these groups implies the tacit acknowledgement of various illegal practices, governmental agencies will often treat such cases as exceptions, justified by very specific and special circumstances, so that the structure of general rules and principles is not compromised. Thus, illegal squatters may be given water supply or electricity connections but on exceptional grounds so as not to group them with regular customers having secure legal title to their property, or street vendors may be allowed to trade under specific conditions that distinguish them from regular shops and businesses that comply with the laws and pay taxes. All of this makes the claims of people in political society a matter of constant political negotiation and the results are never secure or permanent. Their entitlements, even when recognized, never quite become rights. These features of the everyday practices of government are now receiving increased scholarly attention (Gupta 1998; Fuller and Bénéï, eds, 2001; Tarlo 2003).

To connect the question of political society with my earlier discussion on the process of primitive accumulation of capital, I now wish to advance the following proposition. *Civil society is where corporate capital is hegemonic, whereas political society is the space of management of non-corporate capital.* I have argued above that since the 1990s, corporate capital, and along with it the class of corporate capitalists, have achieved a hegemonic position over civil society in India. This means that the logic of accumulation, expressed at this time in the demand that national economic growth be maintained at a very high rate and that the requirements of corporate capital be given priority, holds sway over civil society – that is to say, over the urban middle classes. It also means that the educational, professional and social aspirations of the middle classes have become tied up with the fortunes of corporate capital. There is now a powerful tendency to insist on the legal rights of proper citizens, to impose civic order in public places and institutions and to treat the messy world of the informal sector and political society with a degree of intolerance. A vague but powerful feeling seems to prevail among the urban middle classes that rapid growth will solve all problems of poverty and unequal opportunities.

The informal sector, which does not have a corporate structure and does not function principally according to the logic of accumulation, does not, however, lack organization. As I have indicated in my examples, those who function in the informal sector often have large, and in many cases quite powerful and effective, organizations. They need to organize precisely to function in the modern market and governmental spaces. Traditional organizations of peasant and artisan societies are not adequate for the task. I believe this organization is as much of a *political* activity as it is an economic one. Given the logic of non-corporate capital that I have described above, the function of these organizations is precisely to successfully operate within the rules of the market and of governmental regulations in order to ensure the livelihood needs of its members. One of the striking findings of the NCEUS was the huge predominance among unorganized enterprises, not merely in the rural but also in urban areas, of self-employed owners operating with family labour and virtually no hired employees. Resorting to self-exploitation by stretching out the working hours, their overwhelming goal is merely to sustain their livelihoods (NCEUS 2007: 49–57). Most of those who provide leadership in organizing people, both owners and workers, operating in the informal sector are actual or potential political leaders. Many such leaders are prominent local politicians and many such organizations are directly or indirectly affiliated to political parties. Thus, it is correct to say that the management of non-corporate capital under such conditions is a political function that is carried out by political leaders. The existence and survival of the vast assemblage of so-called informal units of production in India today, including peasant production, is directly dependent on the successful operation of certain *political* functions. That is what is facilitated by the process of democracy.

The organizations that can carry out these political functions have to be innovative – necessarily so, because neither the history of the cooperative movement nor that of socialist collective organization provides any model that can be copied by these non-corporate organizations of capital in India. What is noticeable here is a strong sense of attachment to small-scale private property and, at the same time, a willingness to organize and cooperate in order to protect the fragile basis of livelihood that is constantly under threat from the advancing forces of corporate capital. These organizations of political society often borrow their forms from those of associations in civil society, but other modalities such as kinship, patron–client relations, even protection rackets and mafia-like networks are not entirely uncommon. The informal economy, regulated by political society rather than by the legal organs of the state, also creates its own domain of revenue generation and expenditure in the collective interest of the organized group. Thus, a particular group of employers or workers in the informal sector may form an association that requires each member to pay regular contributions, managed by the leadership, to meet expenses that may include benefits such as medical costs as well as payments of bribes, fines, etc. The circulation of such revenues and expenditures constitutes an economic domain parallel to that of the legal domain of the organized economy and is one more indicator of its 'negative' status from the standpoint of the formal domain of the state and civil society.

However, it appears that these organizations of non-corporate capital are stronger, at least at this time, in the non-agricultural informal sectors in cities and towns and less so among the rural peasantry. This means that while the organization of non-corporate capital in urban areas has developed relatively stable and effective forms and is able, by mobilizing governmental support through the activities of political society, to sustain the livelihood needs of the urban poor in the informal sector, the rural poor, consisting of small peasants and rural labourers, are still dependent on direct governmental support for their basic needs and are less able to make effective organized use of the market in agricultural commodities. This challenge lies at the heart of the recent controversies over farmer suicides as well as the ongoing debates over acquisition of agricultural land for industry. It is clear that in the face of rapid changes in agricultural production in the near future, Indian democracy will soon have to invent new forms of organization to ensure the survival of a vast rural population increasingly dependent on the operations of non-corporate forms of capital.

What I have said here about the characteristics of non-corporate capital are, of course, true only in the gross or average sense. It is admittedly an umbrella category, hiding many important variations within it. Informal or non-corporate units, even when they involve significant amounts of fixed capital and employ several hired workers, are, by my description, primarily intended to meet the livelihood needs of those involved in the business. Frequently, the owner is himself or herself also a worker. But this does not mean that there do not exist any informal units in which the owner strives to turn the business toward the route of accumulation, seeking to leave the grey zones of informality and enter the hallowed portals of corporate capitalism. This too might be a tendency that would indicate upward mobility as well as change in the overall social structure of capital.

Peasant culture and politics

In a recent lecture, the sociologist Dipankar Gupta has taken note of many of these features of changing peasant life to argue that we need a new theoretical framework for understanding contemporary rural society (Gupta 2005). One of the features he has emphasized is the sharp rise in non-agricultural employment among those who live in villages. Between 1983 and 2004–5, employment in agriculture fell in India from 68.6 to 56.6 per cent.[4] In almost half of the states of India, more than 40 per cent of the rural population is engaged in non-agricultural occupations today and the number is rising rapidly. A significant part of this population consists of rural labourers who do not own land but do not find enough opportunity for agricultural work. But more significantly, even peasant families that own land will often have some members engaged in non-agricultural employment. In part, this reflects precisely the pressure of market forces that makes small peasant cultivation unviable over time because it is unable to increase productivity. As the small peasant property is handed down from one generation to the next, the holdings get subdivided even further. I have seen in the course of my own fieldwork in West Bengal in the last three years that there is a distinct reluctance among younger members of rural landowning peasant families – both men and women – to continue with the life of a peasant. There is, they say, no future in small peasant agriculture and they would prefer to try their luck in town, even if it means a period of hardship. Needless to say, this feeling is particularly strong among those who have had some school education. It reflects not just a response to the effects of primitive accumulation, because many of these young men and women come from landowning families that are able to provide for their basic livelihood needs. Rather, it reflects the sense of a looming threat, the ever-present danger that small peasant agriculture will, sooner or later, have to succumb to the larger forces of capital. If this feeling becomes a general feature among the next generation of rural families, it would call for a radical transformation in our understanding of peasant culture. The very idea of a peasant society whose fundamental dynamic is to reproduce itself, accommodating only small and slow changes, would have to be given up altogether. Here we find a generation of peasants whose principal motivation seems to be to stop being peasants.

Based on findings of this type, which are now accumulating rapidly, Dipankar Gupta has spoken of the 'vanishing village': 'Agriculture is an economic residue that generously accommodates non-achievers resigned to a life of sad satisfaction. The villager is as bloodless as the rural economy is lifeless. From rich to poor, the trend is to leave the village ...' (Gupta 2005: 757). I think Gupta is too hasty in this conclusion. He has noticed only one side of the process, which is the inevitable story of primitive accumulation. He has not considered the other side, which is the field of governmental policies aimed at reversing the effects of primitive accumulation. It is in that field that the relation between peasants and the state has been, and is still being, redefined.

I have mentioned before that state agencies, or governmental agencies generally, including NGOs that carry out governmental functions, are no longer an external entity in relation to peasant society. This has had several implications. First, because various welfare and developmental functions are now widely recognized to be necessary tasks for government in relation to the poor, which includes large sections of peasants, these functions in the fields of health, education, basic inputs for agricultural production and the provision of basic necessities of life are now demanded from governmental agencies as a matter of legitimate claims by peasants. This means that government officials and political representatives in rural areas are constantly besieged by demands for various welfare and developmental benefits. It also means that peasants learn to operate the levers of the governmental system, to apply pressure at the right places or negotiate for better terms. This is where the everyday operations of democratic politics, organization and leadership come into play (see e.g. Drèze and Sen 1995). Second, the response of governmental agencies to such demands is usually flexible, based on calculations of costs and returns. In most cases, the strategy is to break up the benefit-seekers into smaller groups, defined by specific demographic or social characteristics, so that there can be a flexible policy that does not regard the entire rural population as a single homogeneous mass but rather breaks it up into smaller target populations. The intention is precisely to fragment the benefit-seekers and hence divide the potential opposition to the state (see Corbridge et al. 2005). Third, this field of negotiations opened up by flexible policies of seeking and delivering benefits creates a new competitive spirit among benefit-seekers. Since peasants now confront, not landlords or traders as direct exploiters, but rather governmental agencies from whom they expect benefits, the state is blamed for perceived inequalities in the distribution of benefits. Thus, peasants will accuse officials and political representatives of favouring cities at the cost of the countryside, or particular sections of peasants will complain of having been deprived while other sections belonging to other regions or ethnic groups or castes or political loyalties have been allegedly favoured. The charge against state agencies is not one of exploitation but discrimination. This has given a completely new quality to peasant politics, one that was missing in the classical understandings of peasant society. This is where the everyday operations of democratic politics, organization and leadership come into play. Fourth, unlike the old forms of peasant insurgency that characterized much of the history of peasant society for centuries, there is, I believe, a quite different quality in the role of violence in contemporary peasant politics. While subaltern peasant revolts of the old kind had their own notions of strategy and tactics, they were characterized, as Ranajit Guha showed in his classic work, by strong community solidarity on the one side and negative opposition to the perceived exploiters on the other. Today, the use of violence in peasant agitations seems to have a far more calculative, almost utilitarian logic, designed to draw attention to specific grievances with a view to seeking appropriate governmental benefits. A range of deliberate tactics are followed to elicit the right responses from officials, political leaders and especially the media. In other words, violence of this sort has become part of the performative strategies for building chains of equivalence that might bring about a populist consolidation against the ruling authorities. This is probably the most significant change in the nature of peasant politics in the last two or three decades.

As far as peasant agriculture is concerned, however, things are much less clearly developed. Small peasant agriculture, even though it is thoroughly enmeshed in market connections, also feels threatened by the market. There is, in particular, an unfamiliarity with, and deep suspicion of, corporate organizations. Peasants appear to be far less able to deal with the uncertainties of the market than they are able to secure governmental benefits. In the last few years, there have been hundreds of reported suicides of peasants who suddenly fell into huge debt because they were unable to realize the expected price from their agricultural products, such as tobacco and cotton. Peasants feel that the markets for these commercial crops are manipulated by large mysterious forces that are entirely beyond their control. Unlike many organizations in the informal non-agricultural sector in urban areas that can effectively deal with corporate firms for the supply of inputs or the sale of their products, peasants have been unable thus far to build similar organizations. This is the large area of the management of peasant agriculture, not as subsistence production for self-consumption, but as the field of non-corporate capital, that remains a challenge. It is the political response to this challenge that will determine whether the rural poor will remain vulnerable to the manipulative strategies of capital and the state or whether they might use the terrain of governmental activities to assert their own claims to a life of worth and dignity.

It is important to emphasize that contrary to what is suggested by the depoliticized idea of governmentality, the quality of politics in the domain of political society is by no means a mechanical transaction of benefits and services. Even as state agencies try, by constantly adjusting their flexible policies, to break up large combinations of claimants, the organization of demands in political society can adopt highly emotive resources of solidarity and militant action. Democratic politics in India is daily marked by passionate and often violent agitations to protest discrimination and to secure claims. The fact that the objectives of such agitations are framed by the conditions of governmentality is no reason to think that they cannot arouse considerable passion and affective energy. Collective actions in political society cannot be depoliticized by framing them within the grid of governmentality because the activities of governmentality affect the very conditions of livelihood and social existence of the groups they target. At least that part of Indian democracy that falls within the domain of political society is definitely not anaemic and lifeless.

Interestingly, even though the claims made by different groups in political society are for governmental benefits, these cannot often be met by the standard application of rules and frequently require the declaration of an exception. Thus, when a group of people living or cultivating on illegally occupied land or selling goods on the street claim the right to continue with their activities, or demand compensation for moving somewhere else, they are in fact inviting the state to declare their case as an exception to the universally applicable rule. They do not demand that the right to private property in land be abolished or that the regulations on trade licences and sales taxes be set aside. Rather, they demand that their cases be treated as exceptions. When the state acknowledges these demands, it too must do so not by the simple application of administrative rules but rather by a political decision to declare an exception. The governmental response to demands in political society is also, therefore, irreducibly political rather than merely administrative.

I must point out one other significant characteristic of the modalities of democratic practice in political society. This has to do with the relevance of numbers. Ever since Tocqueville in the early nineteenth century, it is a common argument that electoral democracies foster the tyranny of the majority. However, mobilizations in political society are often premised on the strategic manipulation of relative electoral strengths rather than on the expectation of commanding a majority. Indeed, the frequently spectacular quality of actions in political society, including the resort to violence, is a sign of the ability of relatively small groups of people to make their voices heard and to register their claims with governmental agencies. As a matter of fact, it could even be said that the activities of political society represent a continuing critique of the paradoxical reality in all capitalist democracies of equal citizenship and majority rule, on the one hand, and the dominance of property and privilege, on the other.

But the underside of political society is the utter marginalization of those groups that do not even have the strategic leverage of electoral mobilization. In every region of India there exist marginal groups of people who are unable to gain access to the mechanisms of political society. They are often marked by their exclusion from peasant society, such as low-caste groups who do not participate in agriculture or tribal peoples who depend more on forest products or pastoral occupations than on agriculture. Political society and electoral democracy have not given these groups the means to make effective claims on governmentality. In this sense, these marginalized groups represent an outside beyond the boundaries of political society.

The important difference represented by activities in political society, when compared to the movements of democratic mobilization familiar to us from twentieth-century Indian history, is its lack of a perspective of transition. While there is much passion aroused over ending the discriminations of caste or ethnicity or asserting the rightful claims of marginal groups, there is little conscious effort to view these agitations as directed towards a fundamental transformation of the structures of political power, as they were in the days of nationalist and socialist mobilizations. On the contrary, if anything, it is the bourgeoisie, hegemonic in civil society and dominant within the state structure as a whole, which appears to have a narrative of transition – from stagnation to rapid growth, from backwardness and poverty to modernity and prosperity, from third-world insignificance to major world-power status. Perhaps this is not surprising if one remembers the class formation of the passive revolution: with the landed elites pushed to a subordinate position and the bureaucratic-managerial class won over by the bourgeoisie, it is the capitalist class that has now acquired a position to set the terms to which other political formations can only respond.

The unity of the state system as a whole is now maintained by relating civil society to political society through the logic of reversal of the effects of primitive accumulation. Once this logic is recognized by the bourgeoisie as a *necessary political condition* for the continued rapid growth of corporate capital, the state, with its mechanisms of electoral democracy, becomes the field for the political negotiation of demands for the transfer of resources, through fiscal and other means, from the accumulation economy to governmental programmes aimed at providing the livelihood needs of the poor and the marginalized. The autonomy of the state, and that of the bureaucracy, now lies in their power to adjudicate the quantum and form of transfer of resources to the so-called 'social sector of expenditure'. Ideological differences, such as those between the Right and the Left, for instance, are largely about the amount and modalities of social sector expenditure, such as poverty removal programmes. These differences do not question the dynamic logic that binds civil society to political society under the dominance of capital. Once again, it is significant, but not surprising, that despite the freedom acquired by the Congress Party in the 2009 elections in running the national government without any contrary pull exerted by the Left parties, there continues to be the same attention paid to social sector expenditure as a complement to the emphasis on economic reforms to promote growth.

Let me summarize my main argument. With the continuing rapid growth of the Indian economy, the hegemonic hold of corporate capital over the domain of civil society is likely to continue. This will inevitably mean continued primitive accumulation. That is to say, there will be more and more primary producers, i.e. peasants, artisans and petty manufacturers, who will lose their means of production. But most of these victims of primitive accumulation are unlikely to be absorbed in the new growth sectors of the economy. They will be marginalized and rendered useless as far as the sectors dominated by corporate capital are concerned. But the passive revolution under conditions of electoral democracy makes it unacceptable and illegitimate for the government to leave these marginalized populations without the means of labour to fend for themselves. That carries the risk of turning them into the 'dangerous classes'. Hence, a whole series of governmental policies are being, and will be, devised to reverse the effects of primitive accumulation. This is the field in which peasant societies are having to redefine their relations with both the state and with capital. Thus far, it appears that whereas many new practices have been developed by peasants, using the mechanisms of democratic politics, to claim and negotiate benefits from the state, their ability to deal with the world of capital is still unsure and inadequate. This is where the further development of peasant activities as non-corporate capital, seeking to ensure the livelihood needs of peasants while operating within the circuits of capital, will define the future of peasant society in India. As far as I can see, peasant society will certainly survive in India in the twenty-first century, but only by accommodating a substantial non-agricultural component within the village. Further, I think there will be major overlaps and continuities in emerging cultural practices between rural villages and small towns and urban areas, with the urban elements gaining predominance.

I have also suggested that the distinction between corporate and non-corporate capital appears to be coinciding with the divide between civil society and political society. This could have some ominous consequences. We have seen in several Asian countries what may be called a revolt of 'proper citizens' against the unruliness and corruption of systems of popular political representation. In Thailand, there have been two army-led coups, in 2006 and 2009, which ousted popularly elected governments. These actions seemed to draw support from the urban middle classes, which expressed their disapproval of what they considered wasteful and corrupt populist expenditure aimed at gaining the support of the rural population. In 2007, there was a similar army-backed coup in Bangladesh, initially welcomed by the urban middle classes. In India, a significant feature in recent years has been the withdrawal of the urban middle classes from political activities altogether. There is widespread resentment in the cities of the populism and corruption of all political parties which, it is said, are driven principally by the motive of gaining votes at the cost of ensuring the conditions of rapid economic growth. There is no doubt that this reflects the hegemony of the logic of corporate capital among the urban middle classes. The fact, however, is that the bulk of the population in India lives outside the orderly zones of proper civil society. It is in political society that they have to be fed and clothed and given work, if only to ensure the long-term and relatively peaceful well-being of civil society. That is the difficult and innovative process of politics on which the future of the passive revolution under conditions of democracy depends.

Notes

1 This essay has been previously published in *Economic and Political Weekly*, 19 April, 2008: 53–62.
2 Karl Marx, *Capital*, vol. 1, tr. Samuel Moore and Edward Aveling (1887; Moscow: Progress Publishers, 1968), chs. Xxvi–xxxiii.
3 For an account of the 'stealthy' introduction of economic reforms in the 1990s, see Rob Jenkins, *Democratic Politics and Economic Reform in India* (Cambridge: Cambridge University Press, 1999).
4 National Sample Survey, 61st Round, Employment Tables.

3 Economic liberalization, urban politics and the poor

Nandini Gooptu

An emerging literature on contemporary urban India has highlighted developments that cater to the middle classes (Fernandes 2006; Chatterjee, P. 2004b: chapter 7), marginalize the poor and cause the 'polarization of [post-Fordist] city space' (Banerjee-Guha 2007: 277). Scholars have identified increasing urban 'informality' as 'a regime of exploitation and exclusion' of the poor (Breman 2003: 220), who lack the relevant skills or resources to enter the new service and entrepreneurial economy, except at its lowest rungs. Emphasis has been placed on the growing tendency to discipline the poor, and on increasing middle-class and élite intolerance, verging on Social Darwinism, towards those who are seen to fail to contribute to, or hinder, the development of India's new liberalized economy (Fernandes 2006: 182–6; Breman 2003: 12). The demolition of slums and the eviction of the poor from their habitat, as well as the removal of pavement dwellers, hawkers and 'unwanted economic activities' in cities have also received much scholarly attention (Mahadevia, 2006). These are apposite and illuminating observations on the adverse impact of contemporary urban change on the poor. However, from an historical perspective, it is evident that slum demolitions, sanitizing or disciplining of the poor, and their concentration in the lower reaches of the urban economy are by no means novel features of India under economic liberalization. Similarly, urban class relations have, for a long time, been defined through the politics of space and differentiated consumption practices and economic experiences. Moreover, spatial restructuring has been an important feature of urban change in the past three decades or so in many parts of the globe. What, if anything, then is new or distinctive about the present and about the Indian case? This question is taken as the point of departure in this paper to explore the interplay of economic liberalization and urban class relations. The first part of this paper attempts to answer this question with reference to the emergence of the 'entrepreneurial city' in India and the process of urban gentrification as a form of 'elite revolt'.

In the international literature on neoliberal urban transformation, it is now widely recognized that cities are 'central to the reproduction, mutation and continual reconstitution of neoliberalism', and they have witnessed 'an increasingly broad range of neoliberal policy experiments, institutional innovations and politico-ideological projects' (Brenner and Theodore 2002: 28). Neoliberalism is taken to imply an ideological emphasis on market ethic, competition and commodification, but 'actually existing neoliberalism' (Brenner and Theodore 2002) had various manifestations and pathways in different national contexts (Ong 2006), and there is no ideal type in practice. Broadly speaking, the early and more aggressive neoliberal doctrines, usually associated with Thatcher and Reagan (Harvey 2005), were not espoused everywhere, and even the US and the UK gradually adopted modified versions in the Clinton era and under Blair's 'Third Way'. These transitions were reflected in a gradual shift in emphasis in urban development policy in the West, first, with social policies to temper and manage the ill-effects of neoliberal economic change of the previous period, and, second, with penal regimes, targeting those adversely affected by neoliberal policies for social control and policing. Thus emerged an urban policy combination of 'socializing individualized [neoliberal] subjects' and 'disciplining the non-compliant' (Peck and Tickell 2002: 42). The neoliberal policy repertoire was stretched to include community regeneration and voluntary associations, based on notions of social responsibility, social capital and partnership (Peck and Tickell 2002: 43). Theorizing the changing trajectory of neoliberal urban policy along these lines, Bob Jessop draws attention to the increasingly 'perceived need to re-embed neoliberalism in society, to make it more acceptable socially and politically …'. 'Here Polanyi lives!', he concludes (Jessop 2002: 120). This is not to suggest that a process of social regulation, re-embedding and decommodification a` la Polanyi is afoot either in the West or anywhere else. Rather, as Ronaldo Munck argues, Polanyi's concept of the double movement serves as a metaphor to open enquiries into counter-hegemonic forces and into the processes through which the effects of neoliberalism are sought to be negotiated or contested (Munck 2002: 18).

There are, of course, parallels of this revisionist neoliberalism in the world of development practice and theory (Hart 2002), with the Washington Consensus giving way to the Post-Washington Consensus precepts of governance reforms, participation, subsidiarity, partnership, empowerment, safety nets, poverty alleviation, and the Millennium Development Goals. In the case of urban centres in developing countries, the idea of the 'inclusive city' has for some time now held sway in official and development circles, with a recent reiteration in the form of the UN-Habitat initiative to promote 'harmonious cities', based on the twin pillars of equity and sustainability. Writing about Latin American cities in the neoliberal era, Bryan Roberts noted that the delegation of functions by central government to lower-order authorities and local-level implementation of targeted national programmes as well as increasing NGO activism led to 'widespread external intervention in the lives of the poor'. Roberts commented pithily: 'No one leaves the poor alone anymore' (Roberts 2004). Recent literature on India similarly suggests that the detrimental consequences of primitive accumulation under neoliberalism are sought to be mitigated or contained, first, through targeted social policy and anti-poverty measures, and second, through the democratic accommodation of a vibrant 'political society', which allows space for manoeuvre to those in the 'informal sector' and the subaltern classes (Chatterjee 2008). In light of the above, the second part of this paper seeks to go beyond the theme of marginalization of the urban poor, to probe the nature of the integration of the poor in the neoliberal city and the terms of their inclusion. What attempts have been made for the 'construction of consent' (Harvey 2005) to create neoliberal subjectivities and to elicit the acquiescence or compliance of the poor, and with what implications?

The neoliberal entrepreneurial city

Launching the Jawaharlal Nehru National Urban Renewal Mission (JNNURM) in December 2005, covering 60 cities, Manmohan Singh, the Prime Minister of India, described it as 'the single largest initiative of the Government of India for a planned development of our cities'. Proclaiming the momentous significance of the Mission, he explained: 'Our urban economy has become an important driver of economic growth. It is also the bridge between the domestic economy and the global economy. It is a bridge we must strengthen' (Singh, M. 2005). Elsewhere, he celebrated 'the emergence of a new generation of Indian enterprise' and entrepreneurs in recent years as an unparalleled phenomenon in the developing world and as 'one of the great success stories of our time', which has contributed to the development of scores of Indian towns and cities (Singh, M. 2007). Alongside enterprise development, in official and policy circles, it is now commonplace to emphasize the need for efficient city management and urban infrastructure improvement for 'accelerating the momentum of economic growth' and for 'productivity enhancement' (Mohan 2005). These perspectives on urbanization are not, of course, confined within the walls of government buildings. Nandan Nilekani, an iconic figure in India's private corporate sector and in the public media as the Chairman of India's flagship IT firm, Infosys, and as a key government adviser and a member of several official and non-official public bodies, including the National Knowledge Commission and the Review Committee of JNNURM, has recently argued in his bestselling book that one of the most powerful 'ideas for the new century' that has dynamized India is the unprecedented focus on cities as the cradle of enterprise, innovation and growth, decisively displacing the countryside from the public imagination as the quintessence of India. Nilekani also advocates the establishment of autonomous city governance institutions, with the active involvement of the private corporate sector for managerial input (Nilekani 2008).

The selective, but representative and influential, sample of views on cities cited here demonstrates a remarkable convergence of public and private sector attitudes to Indian cities in the post-economic reforms era. Cities are now seen as 'generators of economic momentum' and are expected to act as growth engines for the economy as a whole, eventually accounting for 65 per cent of total GDP by 2011 (Government of India 2005). However, Indian cities experienced a deceleration in their rates of growth in the 1980s and 1990s (Sivaramakrishnan, Kundu and Singh 2005: chapter 3; Mohan 1996). The regeneration of cities and the revival of urban economies thereafter assumed utmost urgency, in the context of economic policies that prioritized growth above all else from the 1990s. This led to concerted attempts on the part of several regional state governments to adopt policies to attract investment and stimulate private enterprise, with the hope of unleashing high growth rates. Thus was born, in the late 1990s and early 2000s, the policy of growth-oriented urban developmentalism and 'entrepreneurial cities', in a large number of big and small urban areas. Upgradation and expansion of city infrastructure, particularly transport arteries and hubs, came to be considered one of the main pre-conditions of growth, and often received international donor funding or loans. 'Entrepreneurial cities' are characterized by three main elements: (1) politics and policies designed to boost entrepreneurial activity, and cities being reconceived as sites primarily of an emerging entrepreneurial culture; (2) governments becoming more entrepreneurial in promoting urban capital accumulation, investment and growth, particularly through private-public partnerships; and (3) cities and municipal governments being run in a more business-like and cost-efficient fashion, along the lines of profit-making private firms. With such extensive city development efforts, it is not surprising that according to one estimate, out of India's top 35 cities with populations of between one and 16 million, 24 are in the world's 100 fastest growing cities (City Mayors n.d.)

The overwhelming importance attached to urban growth prompted government ministries at the top of the state administration and parastatals to seize the initiative of urban 'boosterism', in cooperation with commercial investors and private corporate groups, who have been offered a range of incentives, concessions and relaxation of rules and regulations, particularly relating to land use. A significant role has been played in many cities by business, IT and real estate lobbies or by international consultancy firms giving expert planning advice. The strategy of boosting entrepreneurial cities by state governments has required the control of local-level dissent and contestation that might jeopardize city growth. Often, the trend has been to bypass local representative political processes and to subordinate urban local councils, by adopting a largely centralized planning process in the states. Government ministers and those at the top of the party political hierarchy have pushed forward growth policies, often securing compliance of local political representatives or overcoming opposition through mechanisms of internal party control (Benjamin 2000; Benjamin and Bhuvaneswari 2006). Municipal councils have been reduced to the role of implementing urban development schemes of central and state governments. This erosion of municipal autonomy and the constraints placed on the capacity of elected local representatives to influence policy have been shown to have had particularly adverse consequences for the poor. As several scholars have noted, the poor depend on politicians in the locality and lower down in party hierarchies to represent their needs (Benjamin 2000; Harriss 2007; Jha, Rao and Woolcock 2007). The local political field, in which the poor operate, has thus been rendered dependent on higher levels of the state administration and party, to which the poor have no access.

Urban gentrification, revanchism and elite revolt

A significant, and often the primary, driver of growth in most towns, large and small, has been real estate and property development. *The Financial Express*, for instance, reported on 28 December 2006, that the Indian real estate sector, worth approximately US$12–16 billion, had witnessed a 'gold rush', with 'some of the country's biggest land deals', and was growing at 30 per cent per annum. This real estate boom, although now somewhat abated in the context of the global economic downturn from late 2008, is underpinned partly by the urge to create 'world class' cities as centres of financial and knowledge-based services, but more importantly by the demand, in a large number of cities of varying sizes, for middle-class residential, office and commercial spaces, including new format, organized retail space in shopping malls. This kind of urban spatial gentrification, or a process of urban neighbourhood change in favour of middle classes, has marked the neoliberal transformation of cities all over the world (Atkinson and Bridge 2005). In India, as elsewhere, gentrification has emerged as an important feature of urban development through the operations of the land and property markets and the creation of profits through rents (Smith 2002; Whitehead and More 2007). Restructuring of space and real estate development have become important factors in urban development because capital investment has increasingly focused on the built environment. Urban land development for middle-class housing has been an important thrust of local policy for many decades, but hitherto land and space had not been targeted by state agencies or through private–public partnerships on such an extensive scale for investment. The use of space as the 'privileged instrument' of neoliberal urban strategy (Brenner and Theodore 2002: Preface) and the shift of capital from primary circuits of production in the manufacturing sector to the secondary circuit of the built environment (Harvey 1985) noticed in other geographical regions of the world, are thus evident in India too (Banerjee-Guha 2007, 2009). However, there are important contextual specificities in India.

Gentrification here is anchored in the rise and expansion of India's middle classes and the consumer revolution that occurred in the course of gradual economic liberalization from the late 1980s. Gentrification has been fuelled by a move of upwardly mobile middle classes to ownership properties in housing complexes and high-rise developments in newly created enclaves, both within the city and in suburban areas or newly developed townships in urban outskirts. This has been the major impetus behind urban development and spatial restructuring in a large number of smaller towns in particular, where IT and similar industries have not been prominent. Residential developments have been accompanied by the growth of retail units, and private health and educational facilities and leisure, entertainment and hospitality provision, as lucrative avenues of investment for a diverse range of entrepreneurs. In larger cities, urban morphology has also been reshaped by prioritizing the use of land for new middle-class occupations in the IT and IT-enabled services, and in financial and management services and corporate offices. Cities, though, continue to support and expand informal and unorganized sector trade and manufacture, with exploitative labour and credit arrangements, and working conditions. Urban areas are thus increasingly characterized by spatial dualism and power asymmetry between the 'corporate' economy of financial and information services and the 'local' economy, which provides work and livelihood to the poor (Benjamin 2000).

Urban residential and occupational gentrification is, however, not an automatic or inevitable outcome of India's middle-class consumer revolution and upward lifestyle mobility, but its major agents are private property developers, with state support (Fernandes 2006). Middle-class preferences and aspirations are not always symmetrically aligned with the interests of private investors. Investors have, therefore, actively created a market demand for housing and consumption practices through a vigorous advertising campaign, aimed at diverse sections of the middle class, defining new aspirations, lifestyle practices and status markers. Reconfiguration of space for new types of middle-class workplaces, leisure activities, consumption, housing, education and health are also being ideologically and politically promoted as the hallmark of new urbanism. Change in land use and its commodification are projected as the route to economic growth, urban regeneration, modernization and upward social and status mobility.

In tandem with the above, middle-class civic activism and a proactive media have also advanced environmental and public order arguments about changing land use, sanitizing space and creating safe, secure and clean cities (Baviskar 2006). These arguments are reinforced by notions of obsolescence of certain sectors of the economy and of urban residents associated with them. This is particularly true of formerly industrial cities like Mumbai, Kolkata or Ahmedabad, where the motto of 'mills to malls' governs urban development. As widely noted, urban spatial change has caused the displacement and dispossession of many sections of the poor, especially slum and pavement dwellers and residents of squatter settlements. Not only have local policy and property developers been implicated in this process, but an important role has been played by the judicial system, with several controversial court judgements that have upheld the rights of middle-class urban residents to clean and salubrious habitat, while denying the poor their entitlement to urban housing and workspace (Ghertner 2008). Unprecedented claims have been placed on urban public space by the middle class, and such demands have then been met by the state, through the adaptation of public land for middle-class use (Fernandes 2006). Open land, municipal markets and bazaars, that hitherto had free access, are being modernized and privately redeveloped into 'beautified' parks and shopping malls for dedicated middle-class use. Their demarcation and redesignation as exclusive spaces is established through the presence of private security guards, who ensure restricted entry. There are strident, and frequently met, demands for clearance of street vendors and hawkers, and for road improvement and flyover construction to alleviate the problems of vehicular traffic flow. In sum, a new image of sanitized spaces in a 'happening city', mutating from 'dusty to glitzy', dominate the new politics of entrepreneurial cities.

Thus far, the story of India's neoliberal cities has proceeded along predictable lines, consistent with developments elsewhere, albeit with the contextual factor of the middle-class consumer revolution in India. In addition, the processes of gentrification and an increasing middle-class and elite orientation to land use arguably has an element of revanchism, as conceptualized by Neil Smith (1996) as middle-class revenge in New York against the assertive lower orders and the socially marginalized, and a strategy to contain, control and discipline them (Whitehead and More 2007). The Indian case, however, has its own dynamics related to specific political processes, practices and struggles. Here urban development and control over urban space have emerged as increasingly important articulations of elite and middle class politics in the context of democratization of Indian politics (Yadav 1999a).

Much has been written about India's recent democratic participatory upsurge, with significantly expanded participation of the lower classes and castes in electoral politics, their entry into formal political institutions (Yadav 1999a). Scholars have also noted the consequent 'elite revolt' (Corbridge and Harriss 2000), in the form of withdrawal of elites, middle classes and upper castes from electoral politics and their condemnation and denial of the legitimacy of democratic politics as being increasingly corrupt and driven by the imperatives of electoral mobilization. In this context, 'elite revolts' (Corbridge and Harriss 2000) and revanchism are relevant to our understanding of Indian city development in three ways, as follows.

First, revanchism, coupled with a sense of moral panic, manifests itself as righteous civic opposition to the supposed lawlessness of the poor, represented above all by their seeming propensity to stake an unfounded claim on urban land; to cling tenaciously and illegally to land as squatters, pavement dwellers and hawkers. Moreover, if the poor break the law in one respect, they are assumed to be essentially lawless in every respect, and by extension, also considered pathologically prone to crime, criminality and immorality. Thus, for example, 'Common Cause', a citizens' organization that filed a court case in 1993 against the legalization or regularization of squatter colonies in Delhi, stated in its petition:

> [I]n the process of sponsoring, motivating and encouraging the setting up of these unauthorized, and subsequently, regularized colonies, the interests of the underprivileged persons do not really get served; they are encouraged to act illegally and to gain from such illegal acts; their moral fabric gets undermined ... these measures inevitably generate an atmosphere of crime ... and a general lowering of the standards of morals.
>
> (cited in Sethi 2008)

Not surprisingly, slum and pavement clearance with force and coercion enjoy the support of urban elites and middle classes as campaigns against lawlessness and criminality of the poor.

Second, revanchism and 'elite revolt', in the urban context, are directed against the supposed ability of the poor to use the ballot to hold politicians to ransom and to extract various inappropriate policies and undeserved rights and entitlements, all on the back of electoral politics as mobilized voters. Such 'vote-bank' politics is seen to threaten mob rule and ride roughshod over the rule of law and political reason as well as undermine democracy and jeopardize development. Slums and squatter colonies, in particular, are seen as the outcome of politicians pandering to their mass electorate. Slum and pavement clearance thus plays a central symbolic role in concretizing the sentiment of revenge against the political assertion of the poor. This was aptly expressed by a journalist when a controversy raged in Mumbai in 2005 about slum demolitions:

> The one difference between development the way it is happening in China and India is the *encumbrance of politics* ... the problem being the *exigencies of power and vote-bank politics* ... Pollution, encroachment, traffic congestion

and unplanned urbanization have taken their toll on India's commercial capital, but *the worst has been the sea of slum dwellers* who have taken root in Mumbai and who are *encouraged and protected by political parties of every hue as they provide a huge catchment area of votes.*

(Srivastava 2005, emphasis added)

In keeping with these sentiments, eleven prominent citizens moved the Bombay High Court in 2004 to bar slum dwellers from voting, and in the following year, the Municipal Corporation asked the Chief Electoral Officer to drop residents of demolished slums from the voters' lists (Sainath 2005).

Finally, revanchism is also directed at the political mobilization of working classes and at what is seen as destructive political militancy that is inimical to economic efficiency and productivity and that had hitherto stifled urban growth and development (Fernandes 2006). The image of erstwhile industrial cities like Mumbai, Kolkata and Ahmedabad is being re-engineered with apparently negative images of not only poverty and industrial squalor, but also political unrest and public protest being obscured. In several Indian cities now, political demonstrations are not permitted to take place in the vicinity of the administrative areas or in specialized business and commercial zones, reminiscent of colonial prohibitions against nationalist demonstrations in central areas and government districts (Nair 2005: 213–14). Date (2006) reports that the role model for some of the young politicians of Mumbai is New York's erstwhile Mayor Rudy Giuliani, 'known for his distaste for civil liberties and demonstrations' and for his success in forcibly cleaning up New York's central areas.

Inclusive growth and the incorporation of the poor in the neoliberal city

The developments described thus far tell the story of divided cities, marked by the political and spatial marginalization of the poor. As mentioned at the beginning, the perspective of marginality, however, provides only a limited understanding of the complexity of urban change today. The realization that polarized economic development and exacerbation of the vulnerability of the poor might jeopardize economic growth through political instability, violence or urban environmental and health crises, has gradually led to a declared commitment to 'inclusive growth'. The poor in towns are not just victims of clearance and improvement drives or helpless in the face of onslaught of property developers, but they are also the beneficiaries of a range of targeted policy initiatives. One obvious development, for instance, has been an increase in centrally devised schemes and intervention for 'Below Poverty Line' (BPL) and slum populations for the delivery of basic services and for income generation, often funded by foreign donors and lenders or through public-private partnerships, including extensive NGO involvement. Clearly, the poor are sought to be included in the project of neoliberal urban transformation, and it is worth asking whether this has helped to mute protest or opposition to processes of dramatic change, a great deal of which is anti-poor in orientation and outcome. Two key forms of inclusion of the poor are discussed here: (1) the poor as entrepreneurs; and (2) the poor as stakeholder citizens.

Entrepreneurship is now construed as a nation-building activity, with two different, but related, conceptions of enterprise being publicly projected: one that refers to business as an economic activity, and another that refers to character attributes and personal qualities, such as risk-taking, courage, innovation, initiative and work ethic – all to be pressed into action for both individual upwardly mobility and the collective good. In this context, the urban poor have been increasingly construed as latent entrepreneurs, who can contribute to the economy of the entrepreneurial city, if given suitable incentives. Enterprise solutions to the problems of urban poverty are more and more systematically propounded, through a plethora of government- and international donor-funded and NGO schemes for income generation through micro-enterprises, and through Self-Help Groups (SHGs) for micro-credit and self-employment. Indeed, in contrast to the official employment guarantee scheme in rural areas, enterprise promotion and self-employment are the centrepiece of urban poverty alleviation policy. Enterprise promotion initiatives are expected to chart a route out of poverty based on individual mobility, rather than structural or societal ones, and they rely on an ideology of self-reliance and individual initiative (Joseph 2007: 3216). Not only state agencies, but private sector micro-finance institutions are beginning to catch up with the provision of urban micro-credit, as the livelihood needs of the poor are increasingly seen to be 'bankable' and a source of profits. Enterprise and inclusiveness have even been invoked to justify slum demolition in Mumbai. Mukesh Mehta, the property developer responsible for the highly controversial redevelopment of Asia's largest slum in Dharavi, is reported to have said: 'The slum dwellers ... need to be integrated into mainstream society ... They are *enterprising people* who have come here to make a better life for themselves and their families ... redeveloping Dharavi will become an engine for economic development' (BBC 2006).

How far the poor have bought into this enterprise culture and turned entrepreneurial is a question that was addressed in recent research among slum dwellers, families of former industrial workers and urban informal sector workers in some municipalities within the Kolkata Metropolitan Area (KMA), and among workers in shopping malls in the city.[1] One of the municipal councils covered in this research has been particularly active and successful in promoting a large number of SHGs and providing training for self-employment and micro-enterprise to numerous groups of women, and some young men too. In some municipal wards, inhabited by families of former mill workers, rickshaw pullers, tailors, construction workers, hawkers, rag-pickers, etc. almost every household had a member in a SHG. At the same time, extensive slum improvement has taken place with international donor-funding, with paved roads, provision of domestic latrines and water supply, improvement of drainage and sewerage, and street lighting. Local women eagerly state that they now live in much better and more salubrious neighbourhood conditions and that this is also reflected in the general condition of their own houses, their clothing, their attitude to health and hygiene, and their sense of self-esteem. The streets, they say, are well-lit and safer. There are more new shops and a range of goods are available in close proximity. Women are also well clued into projects and schemes launched through the municipality, many of which are gender-based. Their local councillors and party political activists provide them regular information about various schemes for poverty alleviation and for BPL families. They themselves go to regular party and municipal meetings, where there is always an opportunity to learn about what is going on and the benefits to which one might be entitled. Compared to a few years ago, they are now much better off, these women said emphatically. Anger and frustration, overwhelmingly noticeable a few years ago in these areas of closed mills (Gooptu 2007), are now somewhat muted. This is not because the crisis of employment in these declining industrial areas has blown over or because the terms and conditions of work have improved. Instead, they explained, this is because, 'no one sits around any more these days'. Instead of sitting idly and lamenting their predicament, everyone, including women, now does something and seizes every available opportunity. As they explained: 'We all want to live and eat well, so we work harder'.

Men find it difficult to get regular work, but nonetheless try to keep themselves occupied with whatever they can get, and move from job to job, alternating between wage work and petty trade. The more dynamic and literate have taken up new kinds of initiatives suitable for today's needs: catering, mobile phone and TV repairing, and the like. Some have started workshops of gold and silver embroidery on *sarees*, supplied to wholesalers for export; while others have sought work in the emerging new sectors of the economy in retail, entertainment and hospitality. Women seldom sit idle, and always manage to find some home-based work, such as sewing, embroidery, *bindi*-making and paper bag making, even if paid a pittance. With everyone working intensively, they say, they no longer worry about the family not having at least one square meal a day. '*Dhanda*', which means seizing or seeking out a lucrative opportunity as well as own-account business venture, is much coveted, and is indeed the preferred career choice of most, including many local school children. However, it is also noted that in these self-employed activities, it is difficult for them to expand and scale-up beyond a certain point, for lack of capital. Faced with these problems, they have pragmatically reoriented their family income strategy to develop the widest possible portfolio of economic activities, involving all members of the family, except children, if possible, whom they try to send to school, as their only ticket to future upward mobility. These modes of addressing economic problems based on individual initiative in pursuit of economic activities, also tend to foster individualism – 'everybody now goes about on their own "*dhanda*" or business', as it is frequently said. In turn, this individualism militates against collective action on issues of livelihood and work.

This individualistic tendency was particularly explicit among young men and women from poorer families who have joined the newly emerging retail economy as lower-level workers and shop assistants in the increasing number of urban shopping malls (Gooptu 2009), either through their own initiative or through training and placement organized by municipal councils as a poverty alleviation initiative. Mall workers are willing to work very hard to show results in meeting sales and other targets and thus attain a higher pay packet. Rapid work mobility and taking risks to abandon a job and to seek better opportunities elsewhere constitute an important feature of their career strategy. Many of these workers associate their work with personal autonomy and independence, and with a range of choices and opportunities available to them, through exposure to a variety of experiences. The retail world is not, however, an ideal workplace. Workers tell of long hours and monotony, physical exhaustion, intense competition among workers, surveillance and discipline by management, arbitrary dismissals, tyranny of sales targets and a lack of career structure or future prospects and promotions. No one, however, countenanced the possibility of expressing these grievances to their employers, let alone contemplating collective action to address these issues. Indeed, collective action and more generally 'politics' is almost unanimously considered either detrimental or futile in improving their economic well-being and life chances. Instead, they emphasized hard work, achievement, ambition, drive, initiative, enhancing ones skills and competences, unambiguous self-advancement to realize one's own aspirations, and individualistic career development in pursuit of a better life for oneself and one's family.

Are we to conclude from the above then that these poor people have managed to imbibe the spirit of enterprise and have become a part of the entrepreneurial economy? Certainly, they demonstrate some entrepreneurial characteristics – work ethic, risk-taking, flexibility, pursuit of profit, creative diversification of activities, following multiple strategies, seizing any opportunity that presents itself. This entrepreneurial turn may be in part a product of rising expectations. However, in the main, it seems to be distress-induced, rather more than being incentivized by a favourable new urban economic milieu that presents lucrative new economic opportunities, of the kind enjoyed by more substantial entrepreneurs or middle classes. Moreover, this mode of entrepreneurial incorporation enhances their vulnerability and reinforces their subordination within the urban economy, and thus gives rise to the 'paradox of inclusion', to borrow a term from Joel Handler's analysis of workfare policies in the West (Handler 2004), by forcing them to struggle at the lowest and most insecure and unstable rungs of the urban economy.

Not surprisingly then, while these slum-dwellers and young workers express a degree of satisfaction that they are better off as a result of harder work in the present, they do point to persistent inequality, insecurity and disparity, and particularly the paucity of present opportunities and the lack of future prospects for themselves, in contrast to the plethora of obvious channels of middle-class upward mobility in India's liberalized economy. They worry about the future, for there is little scope for savings, let alone planning for contingencies or for a stage when they may not be able to work. The poor then appear to be becoming reluctant entrepreneurs. This is consistent with the findings of Portes and Hoffman (2003) about the Latin American urban poor, that increased inequality and the stagnation of employment led to a range of adaptive solutions, most important of which was informal self-employment and petty enterprise. This is also in tune with Breman's description of Ahmedabad and the increasing self-exploitation of the poor in a milieu of highly fluid and insecure work (Breman 2004: chapter 9). What is different, and apparently new, here is that at least some among the poor have come to develop coping mechanisms that seem to be bringing about a degree of relief to their income poverty in the present, even if not reversing their precarious predicament or vulnerability.

This has helped to generate a perceived sense of present well-being, notwithstanding an awareness of exploitation and insecurity. Moreover, some young people appear to have embraced the notions of freedom and choice, personal drive and initiative, as well as individualistic norms and values that are associated with neoliberal subjectivity and enterprise culture (Harvey 2005; Heelas and Morris 1992). All this arguably contributes to their acquiescence of the entrepreneurial culture and economy of the city, and may well account for their political quietism.

Trends of incorporation of the poor are also discernible in urban local politics, particularly under the rubric of decentralization and participation. Linked to the creation of entrepreneurial cities is the development of entrepreneurial and managerial modes of city governance, the main thrust of which is to make urban local bodies commercially viable and financially sustainable, by adopting business norms and practices, often in response to international donor and lender conditionalities or advice. Service delivery is sought to be isolated from messy local politics, its pressures, lobbies and 'vote banks', in order to ensure cost-effective professionalism. Transparency, accountability, efficiency, target delivery, and evaluation through performance indicators are the key concepts to help achieve economy, alongside electronic assessment and collection of taxes, better accounting systems and commodification of some services through the introduction of user charges and privatization, as undertaken throughout the KMA. In this reconfiguration of the nature and functions of local government, citizens are conceived as consumers of services and stakeholders in local affairs. The most powerful tool of citizens in local democracy of this nature is not the law, constitution or the ballot but citizens' charters that guarantee a minimum level of service, consumer satisfaction surveys and citizens report cards, of the kind that has now been implemented in almost every municipality in the KMA. Cost-efficiency also requires the engagement of active, informed citizen-consumers to hold local bodies accountable. Their participation and consent are also solicited for bearing some of the costs of local services through user charges, and for shouldering the responsibility of maintaining and operating local infrastructure and services, such as water taps, public latrines, solid waste management systems and so on, in order to minimize the cost to local bodies. A growing concern with urban environmental sustainability has also focused attention on the monitoring and maintenance role of active citizens in the locality. In this context, the poor are increasingly courted by local authorities. Moreover, the involvement of international donors, such as DFID, and the requirements of the 74th Constitutional Amendment, have led to an emphasis on community participation in decentralized local government, prompting municipalities to mobilize local communities from above, including women, whose involvement is specifically required in local institutions and in development projects.

The recasting of the poor as stakeholder citizens in this way has led to a reorientation in the everyday terms of interaction between the poor and representative institutions in the locality. For instance, Ward Committees have been constituted in all local bodies, through nomination of local residents by the ward councillor and municipal chairman (Ghosh and Mitra 2004). Bustee [Slum] Works Maintenance Committees have also been formed to implement environmental upgradation and slum improvement programmes. Community Development Societies have been formed in the municipality with female members of Self Help Groups. All these have, in theory, provided new institutional fora for neighbourhood residents to represent their interests in local affairs, although, in practice, their role is confined to monitoring, supervision and maintenance. Planning activity, if at all possible, is circumscribed by the priorities preset by state policy. Local politicians, on their part, have, however, found these new institutional arenas of service-oriented relationship particularly useful for mobilizing the poor for electoral politics. This has further strengthened already well-entrenched local patronage-based politics, especially in a context where the Left Front government, led by the Communist Party of India (Marxist), which has held power in the state of West Bengal since the late 1970s, has gradually turned away from agitational and radical politics and relied increasingly on clientelistic relations as the instrument of electoral mobilization. Local people, particularly women, now engage far more vigorously with municipal issues. Their consequent sense of participation has enhanced their perception of well-being, mentioned earlier. This appears to have diffused or at least muted discontent against the more exclusionary aspects of current economic and social transitions. At the same time, participatory development initiatives in the locality, because of their very limited service orientation, have come to be interpreted by the poor as individual or group opportunities to cultivate patronage networks and to extract benefits to address specific material or practical problems.

In this process, poor people's largely pragmatic and cynical view of party and electoral politics has been consolidated further. They see party politics as a resource in everyday problem-solving in the locality and a bargaining counter to secure their individual or collective interests in return for electoral support. This is not new, but is becoming more pervasive and striking deeper, institutionalized roots. Paradoxically then, institutional decentralization, along with the elevation of the poor to the status of stakeholder or consumer citizens, have increased the involvement of the poor in local affairs on the one hand, but on the other hand, proliferated existing forms of transactional political relations with their local representatives and politicians in multiple fragmented and localized arenas. This has increased the dependence of the poor on local politicians and leaders. Similar processes have been noted for Latin American cities in the neoliberal era, where decentralization has meant that the political activities of the poor have become fragmented and territory-based, instead of class-based, 'dealing with the consequences, not the root cause of misdistribution and poverty' (Roberts and Portes 2006). Moreover, as Chatterjee emphasizes, the 'governed' population of the poor in 'political society' can make claims on the government, and can interact with the formal domain of institutional politics and civil society, only through protean, contingent and unstable arrangements (Chatterjee 2004, 2008). The poor are then compromised democrats and circumscribed citizens in the neoliberal urban order, as they are reluctant entrepreneurs. Indian cities now appear to lack overt political mobilization among the poor in the process of economic transformation, other than sporadic engagement in specific issue-based activism under NGO leadership or involvement in identity politics. The inclusion of the poor in local political and development institutions, albeit in circumscribed and constrained ways, appears to have contained overt political dissent.

Conclusion

Although the present process of the marginalization of the urban poor is not novel or unique, it is certainly distinctive, and powerful structural forces do serve to marginalize the poor in the neoliberal entrepreneurial city far more than in the past, for two reasons. First, it is a structural feature of the process of creation of entrepreneurial cities as growth engines and it is central to urban spatial reorganization as a mode of capital accumulation and investment. The urban built environment has never before, in this way, been the prime target of investment, nor seen as a major lever of growth. Second, the emergence of the polarized city has a causal link, not only with middle-class revolution in India, but also with elite revolt and middle-class revanchism against the politicization and democratic mobilization of the poor, with the middle classes now asserting their hegemony over urban economy and politics. However, the concept of marginality is of limited analytical efficacy in understanding the dynamics of urban class relations. For the poor are not marginal in the sense of being left behind or driven beyond the pale. Instead, they are sought to be integrated in the urban economy and city governance, albeit in ways that are not always in their interest. The concept of social exclusion provides a better analytical tool, for it refers to differentiated, subordinated or exploitative inclusion in a social system (Roberts 2004: 197). Yet this limited or even exploitative inclusion can paradoxically have a palliative or ameliorative effect, and can help to elicit the complicity or compliance of the poor to the neoliberal order, and head off any resistance or protest, except perhaps of those who are forcibly and violently dispossessed. 'New urban poverty' in India, as in Latin America (Roberts 2004), is characterized by increasing inequality, insecurity and vulnerability on the one hand, and on the other it is embedded in a framework of electoral democracy, decentralized participation and targeted interventions, which helps to make the bitter pill more swallowable, and thus to foster political quietism.

Note

1 Interviews and discussions were conducted in two municipalities of the Kolkata Metropolitan Area with (1) municipal officers, staff and development workers; (2) poor women involved in SHGs, enterprise and skills training sessions, neighbourhood committees; (3) men and women in slums; (4) young people in neighbourhood clubs in slum areas. Interviews and discussions were conducted with nearly 50 shopping mall workers in Kolkata between 2006 and 2008; 200 questionnaires were also administered, of which about 50 per cent fully or partially completed forms were returned.

4 The politics of India's special economic zones

Rob Jenkins

Introduction

India's Special Economic Zone Act 2005 and the regulations to govern its implementation came into force in February 2006. Policy regimes have been formulated in various states pursuant to the central SEZ Act. These, as well as the Government of India's own SEZ guidelines, have been revised on many occasions. 'Implementation', in the form of approvals for the creation of SEZs, has moved forward rapidly. Close to 600 have been approved at the time of writing. Many of these are under construction and many are now operational.

This paper assesses the political dynamics that have arisen in the wake of the Act's passage. There are inherent dangers in using a single policy domain to derive generalizations about processes of much broader scope. But if ever a single policy initiative were capable of serving as a microcosm for the politics of reform it would be India's SEZ Act, which draws within its ambit such diverse issues as foreign investment, trade, taxation, industrial relations, land, and environmental sustainability. There are implications for federal relations and the functioning of India's system of local government as well.

Such a multifaceted process makes generalizations elusive. Nevertheless, the story of India's SEZ policy to date holds three important lessons. First, in implementing the SEZ policy, India's policymaking establishment seems to have run up against the limits of what can be achieved by practicing 'reform by stealth', or by insulating policymaking from the effects of 'mass politics'.

Second, the political dilemmas accompanying the implementation of the SEZ policy highlight a structural weakness of India's political system in the process of its economic transformation: the increasing inability of the state to broker political accommodations that advance policy objectives. This is largely a result of pervasive corruption and a recent history littered with broken promises – both of which were integral to the process of reforming by stealth.

Third, SEZs represent a desire by both political elites and those who aspire to middle-class status to, in a sense, secede from the rest of India – that is, to escape the consequences of India's recent 'democratic upsurge'. To many people, the political ascendancy of historically oppressed groups threatens to sabotage the dream of a more prosperous, efficient, and powerful India. SEZs offer a means for the inhabitants of this upwardly mobile India to pursue this dream.

The chapter is organized as follows: Section I overviews the SEZ concept and some of the policy decisions through which it has taken root in India; Section II outlines the political logic underlying SEZ reform, particularly with respect to theories of how India's reformers have contended with the constraints imposed by democracy; Section III examines the forms of opposition to which the SEZ policy has given rise; Section IV summarizes the government's response; Section V concludes by elaborating on the three propositions advanced in this introduction.

I. India's SEZ policy

An SEZ is a geographic region within a nation-state in which a distinct legal framework provides for more liberal economic policies and governance arrangements than prevail in the country at large. The ostensible purpose of SEZs is to attract large volumes of investment by providing world-class infrastructural facilities, a favourable taxation regime, and incentives for sectoral clustering. The benefits for the wider economy are, in theory, more exports, particularly in high-value-added sectors, increased employment, and ultimately faster economic growth.

India's SEZ policy can be thought of as ushering in a third generation of economic reforms: while the first two phases were dominated, respectively, by efforts to liberalize the macro policy environment, and by the creation of institutions for regulating a market economy, phase three emphasizes the facilitation of a global presence for India's largest private-sector firms and a rapid enhancement of the physical infrastructure within which such firms operate.[1]

Though India did not pass an SEZ Act until 2005, it has been experimenting with the concept since the 1960s. The Kandla Export Processing Zone (EPZ) in Gujarat is said to have been the world's first. A private-sector EPZ in Surat was the first to emerge under a new 1994 EPZ policy (Ranjan 2006). But India's push toward a more comprehensive SEZ policy began in earnest following a visit by then Commerce Minister Murasoli Maran to China in 2000. Impressed by China's SEZs, Maran acted quickly to initiate a change in India's policy regime. This took the form of new SEZ rules notified in the Commerce Ministry's Export-Import Policy, which allowed conversion of existing EPZs into SEZs. Whereas EPZs were akin to industrial estates, SEZs often contain the full array of social facilities – housing, hospitals, schools, retail developments – that make up a small city. Moreover, SEZs are designed to operate on the principle of 'self-certification' on tax-exempt transactions, whereas EPZs usually require official attestation.

For a major piece of economic legislation with such far-reaching implications, the SEZ Act 2005 was passed relatively quickly – just a year after the UPA government's arrival in power. Debate in parliament was minimal, in contrast to the prolonged discussions that accompanied passage of the National Rural Employment Guarantee Act (NREGA) during the same session. The SEZ Act's drafters built upon earlier policy development work conducted under the previous (BJP-led) government, notably the *Report of the Steering Group on Foreign Direct Investment*, prepared by the Planning Commission in 2002 (Government of India 2002). This report quoted liberally from studies conducted by international management consulting firms about problems faced by foreign investors in India.

The Act sought to attract investors with, among other things, a package of tax and non-tax incentives, including exemption from export and import duties, excise duties, and central and state sales tax. Businesses were to receive tax deductions on 100 per cent of profits from exports for the first five years of operation within an SEZ; 50 per cent of profits from exports for the next five years; and up to 50 per cent of profits for a further five years.[2] In addition, firms operating within SEZs need not acquire licenses for, or pay taxes for, importing capital goods or raw materials and can start joint ventures with up to 100 per cent FDI without seeking approval (except in a small number of industries).

SEZs can be developed by state governments, private promoters, or a mixture of the two. Applications for the establishment of an SEZ require various certifications and evidence of 'proof of intent' and competency. But the approval process takes place via a 'single window', the Board of Approvals (BoA), led by the Ministry of Commerce and Industry. Though in theory it is possible to submit an application directly to the BoA, in practice firms seeking to establish an SEZ choose the option of routing their applications through the relevant state government, without whose support it stands little chance of succeeding. The BoA operates under guidelines that have been subject to much revision since they were originally issued in early 2006. Application documents and guidelines are available on the government's SEZ website, though success depends on the applicant's mastery of unwritten rules and political influence. As of July 2009, the BoA had given approval (some 'in principle', others formally) to nearly 600 SEZs. Hundreds of others were 'pending'.

In addition to the BoA, the SEZ rules stipulate the creation, for each SEZ, of a 'Unit Approval Committee' (UAC), headed by a government-appointed civil servant, the Development Commissioner. The UAC, consisting of a mixture of private-sector and government officials, approves the entry of new businesses into a particular SEZ and decides on the application of other rules (regarding the location of social facilities, the measurements to be used in determining 'processing area', etc.).

Even a preliminary assessment of India's SEZ policy – examining the policy approach in general terms rather than its impact – encounters the difficulty of determining which metrics are most relevant. In many countries, SEZs have been regarded as part of a 'regional development' paradigm emphasizing the benefits of geographic clustering among firms within and across economic sectors. SEZs can, in theory, facilitate more efficient linkages among end-product manufacturers and their suppliers and kickstart entrepreneurial activity within related industries. SEZs can also serve as an element of a 'regional growth pole', from which an expanding area of economic dynamism can emerge.

A major objective of SEZ policies in most countries is to create the world-class infrastructure that firms need to make their operations globally competitive. Governments unable to provide high-quality road and rail systems, communication networks, water-supply systems, or electricity grids on a countrywide basis have sought to concentrate investment in locations of intensive economic activity. The ability of centres of innovation to catalyze a wider growth dynamic, from which areas beyond the SEZs themselves would benefit, has been the standard justification for concentrating infrastructure investment rather than ensuring a more even geographic spread.

To yield the desired economic payoffs, however, each SEZ was expected to operate on a large scale. Infrastructural investments would be worthwhile only if they covered a wide enough area. A critical mass of firms was required for the benefits of clustering to emerge. A very large increase in entrepreneurial dynamism was necessary before localized growth would spread to surrounding areas.

India's approach to SEZs has deviated from this logic in three key respects. First, whereas in China the public sector was responsible for developing SEZs, in India the private sector has been in the forefront, though in many cases private SEZ promoters have partnered with government entities. Second, India's model does not use SEZs as a way of promoting under-industrialized areas. India's SEZs are – unlike Chinese SEZs and because of the incentives created by the policy design – overwhelmingly located in areas that are already highly developed.[3] The third difference concerns scale. India's SEZ Act specifies extremely low minimum size requirements to establish an SEZ: 1,000 hectares for 'multi-product' SEZs and 100 hectares for sector-specific SEZs, except for Information Technology and IT-enhanced Services (IT/ITeS) SEZs, which can be as small as 10 hectares (Government of India 2006c). Small SEZs account for a disproportionate amount of the total approved.

II. Political constraints and the hedging of political risk

India's gradual shift toward a more internationally integrated market economy over the past quarter-century has generated considerable – if fluctuating – political resistance. How opposition has been successfully managed is a matter of some disagreement. In the 1990s, Varshney pointed to reformers' tendency to evade policy decisions that impinge on the lives of ordinary Indians, in effect leaving the domain of 'mass politics' relatively untouched by liberalization. Identity-based mobilization helped to insulate policymaking from the vagaries of democratic politics (Varshney 1999). Jenkins, granting the less-than-aggressive nature of India's reform efforts, stressed the capacity of democratic institutions, and the politicians and parties that operate within them, to undercut key sources of resistance – by fragmenting opposition to reforms, by shifting blame and political burdens away from decision-makers, by sequencing policy measures in ways that forestall political confrontations until more propitious circumstances prevail, by brokering agreements between contending interests, and by efficiently steering compensation to the most potentially disruptive groups among 'losers' of reform (Jenkins 1999). Even if reform was not as comprehensive as often suggested, and even if the salience of non-economic cleavages prevented anti-reform groups from coalescing into an effective electoral bloc, India's liberalizers still faced an uphill task and have proved themselves surprisingly agile.

How can we interpret the SEZ policy in light of the political dynamics that have attended India's reform trajectory since 1991 – or whichever watershed date one uses to mark the onset of liberalization?[4] Does the pursuit of a far-reaching SEZ policy – in which catering to the global market and welcoming foreign investors are visible features – signal a retreat from the political caution that characterized India's earlier reform process? Has India's accelerated growth rate of recent years – or the disarray in which opponents of liberalization have found themselves after a decade and a half of creeping marketization – emboldened reformers to take greater political risks? Because the SEZ Act impinges on so many aspects of economic policy; because its implementation involves so many government departments and levels of the political system; because it touches on sensitive political issues – for these and other reasons one might have expected a state with a reputation for political timidity to be highly wary of championing SEZs.

And, yet, the nature of the SEZ policy also raises the opposite question: is not the defining characteristic of the SEZ policy – the limit of its geographic extent – an indication of the continued risk-aversion of India's liberalizers? If governing elites were so confident of their ability to pursue a bold reform agenda, why haven't the floodgates been opened to foreign investment in the country at large, rather than in confined enclaves? Why not introduce the governance reforms contained within the SEZ Act to the entire country? If firms and people residing in SEZs are so certain to benefit from streamlined regulatory procedures, is not the government's unwillingness to cut red tape with similar zeal in the rest of India an admission that realities of democratic politics prevent it from doing so?

Paradoxically, the answer to these two seemingly contradictory sets of questions is 'yes'. The SEZ policy reflects both the full-throttle ambition of liberalizers as well as the stubbornly persistent constraints that a liberal political system imposes. Even if SEZs have brought reform directly into the arena of mass politics – notably through the land-acquisition process – time-tested techniques of political management have been clearly in evidence. Indeed, the SEZ policy's initial mode of entry, through the backdoor of the Exim Policy, was consistent with the stealthy tactics through which earlier reforms were introduced.

SEZs represent an attractive way, politically speaking, of introducing reforms from which liberalizers have otherwise shied away. The SEZ policy is a convenient means of overcoming the huge obstacles (bureaucratic and legal, but ultimately political) to urban redevelopment. Barriers range from the diversity of agencies and authorities with overlapping jurisdictions (each with its own set of entrenched political defenders), to outmoded legislation such as the Urban Land Ceiling Act and the Rent Control Act, which have proven difficult to revise (*The Economist*, 2007).[5] The SEZ policy may also be seen as a response to the failure (for political reasons) of the Electricity Act 2003 to generate the anticipated flood of new investment in this crucial infrastructure sector (*Economic and Political Weekly*, 2006c).

Politicians and party strategists who, having weighed the risks, decided to make SEZs a priority on the UPA government's legislative agenda anticipated that implementing the SEZ policy would encounter political opposition. Pursuing the SEZ policy was considered politically *feasible* – which is distinct from why it was considered politically *desirable* – by the managers of economic reform for several reasons.

First, the SEZ policy would reside mainly in the domain of 'elite politics', the other half of Varshney's dichotomy. It would interest policy analysts, business associations, and the financial press. Policy discussions concerning SEZs, it was believed, would over time grow highly technical. It was reasonable for the UPA's political strategists to predict that even politically engaged people – to say nothing of ordinary citizens – would grow weary of these debates as more visible events and controversies came to the forefront. This is more or less what happened: during the two years following the Act's passage, newspaper headlines, parliamentary maneuvering, and political agitations focused on such hot-button issues as OBC reservations in educational institutions, the remnants of the Bofors case, and the Indo–US nuclear deal.

Second, reformers expected resistance to the SEZ policy to be fragmented in two senses: *geographically* dispersed, and divided on the *basis* of the opposition. As SEZs are implemented, by definition, in precisely demarcated areas, the most immediately affected constituencies – the main sources of potential resistance – would be localized in nature. Those opposed to a given SEZ would be isolated within a contained area, where the political fallout could be minimized. Protestors from different SEZ sites within a state would face distinct local circumstances, while those from different states would encounter barriers of distance, language and political priorities.

Moreover, the *basis* for opposition to the SEZ policy would vary from place to place, from group to group, and even between individuals. When the draft legislation was being discussed in 2005, it was apparent that some critics were concerned mainly with particular aspects of the policy (excessively generous or sectorally untargeted tax breaks), while others were opposed on broad ideological grounds, seeing in SEZs a Trojan Horse for a new wave of liberalization.

The architects of the SEZ policy foresaw the possibility of addressing the complaints of each group individually and serially, picking off discontented constituencies one at a time. Ideological opponents who considered SEZs further evidence of the government's embrace of 'market fundamentalism' would be neutralized by the UPA's concurrent efforts to tackle the iniquities of liberalization by passing the NREGA. Those who complained that SEZs would erode labour rights and environmental protections could be countered with evidence of the UPA's commitment to transparent governance, manifested in the passage of the Right to Information Act of 2005.

Third, political strategists in Delhi expected political resistance to be managed, in part, by state governments. Most state governments, they reasoned, would want to attract SEZ promoters – because they wanted to create jobs and build their economies, and for less public-spirited reasons as well. Political managers in Delhi were confident of the ability of state-level politicians to arrange accommodations between contending groups and to compensate policy 'losers' to the extent that political expediency required (Sinha 2007). This is consistent with the assumption of neoliberal policy advocates, who are aware of the dislocations policy shifts can cause, but argue that adversely affected interests can be won over with compensatory adjustments (Jain and Mukand 2003).

That the political risk of pursuing fairly radical policies within defined geographic zones was considered by India's governing elites to reside within manageable bounds points to a belief that the SEZ Act represented a logical extension of the cautious approach to political risk-taking, and stealthy tactics, pursued since 1991. The SEZ policy reflected an appreciation of the political constraints, but also the state's capacity to extend the boundaries of the possible.

III. SEZs as political lightning rods

The passage of the SEZ Act by India's parliament in 2005 was not without controversy. There was the usual ideological opposition to what was seen as further entrenchment of an excessively pro-business economic framework. This emerged mainly from the left, but also from *swadeshi* voices in the Sangh Parivar. Another line of critique asked why, if export zones were to be created, they could not be developed by the public sector. Another called into question the UPA government's purported concern with regional imbalances, asking why the policy's incentives were not designed to steer investment toward under-industrialized regions.

Finance Ministry concerns about revenue implications of SEZs were evident from the outset and seized upon by people of almost all political stripes, including highly respected economists such as former IMF official Raghuram Rajan, who called the tax incentives a 'give away' (Mukherjee 2006). Critics argued that the 'additional' economic activities produced by SEZs were not additional at all: they would have taken place anyway, and so would have generated tax receipts that now must indeed be foregone. Critics also pointed to revenue that would be lost due to the inevitable abuses – for instance, the smuggling of duty-free goods from SEZs to the Domestic Tariff Area (DTA) (Rao 2007). A related charge was that already-thriving sectors would be among the main beneficiaries of tax concessions. As one analyst put it, IT companies were merely shifting into 'mini-SEZs' as a way of extending tax holidays due to expire in 2009 (Aiyar 2007).

Activists have also voiced deep apprehension about the seemingly undemocratic mode of governance envisioned for SEZs. SEZ promoters were dubbed the 'new landlord class', while SEZs heralded the emergence of 'corporate colonial rule'.[6] People residing or working within SEZs might find themselves in a legal grey area, where neither the voice of the majority nor the rights of the minority would be respected. One author highlighted the unclear 'legal regime affecting the functioning of an enterprise working within the SEZ', to say nothing of the people living there (Burman 2007).

The creation of distinct zones of governance in India is not entirely new: government forms differ between urban and rural areas, between notified tribal areas and other locations, and between industrial townships, such as Jamshedpur, a century-old company town, and other municipalities. Governance problems afflict even smaller-scale industrial sites (Singh 2006). But never have distinct regulatory spaces proliferated so widely, so rapidly, and with the expenditure of such vast resources. As Burman put it, India's SEZ Act provides enormous 'latitude to the concerned governments to regulate, or more importantly, not regulate the operation of companies within an SEZ' (Burman 2007). Burman examines this from the perspective of corporate governance – a relevant issue since firms will assume substantial responsibility for governing territories where millions of people will conduct their social lives (educating their children, engaging in religious worship, pursuing leisure activities).

The role of the Development Commissioner, discussed in Section 11 of the Act, is a point of particular suspicion. The Commissioner must consult with state-government officials on certain issues (e.g. compliance with environmental standards), but for many matters would seem to exercise a combination of legislative, executive, and judicial powers as the pre-eminent member of a governing body over which corporate developers would have significant influence. State governments may delegate to Commissioners any powers they deem necessary.

Press reports and activist manifestos have stoked fears that state governments seek to establish permissive legal regimes for SEZs.[7] Section 49 of the Act is a particular source of worry because it specifies that the central government can declare any of its acts inapplicable within SEZs. The uses to which this provision could, in practice, be put are less alarming than they might appear in the fervid imaginings of some activists. But it is a legitimate worry, not least because businesses (some of which have already circumvented the law while *establishing* SEZs) clearly seek to water down already weakly enforced laws.

Section 23 of the Act is another commonly criticized provision. It empowers state governments to establish special courts to adjudicate civil cases. Though Section 24 of the Act specifies the right of appeal to a state's High Court, there are reasonable grounds for concern that this provision will furnish firms operating within SEZs a convenient forum for harassment litigation against unions, activist groups, or individuals seen to be instigating trouble.

Potentially more problematic from the perspective of democratic accountability is the seeming exemption of SEZs from the provisions of the 74th Amendment, which provides for local participation in municipal governance. How and where municipal authorities can or will be established in newly urbanized areas created by SEZs is not clear.

While most of the concerns discussed thus far are speculative in nature, involving problems that *could* arise once SEZs are up and running, land issues have been of immediate relevance to the *establishment* of SEZs. Land acquisition has been instrumental in fusing diverse strands of discontent into a powerful political force. Land issues have helped to forge a broad-based anti-SEZ movement in part because they focus attention on liberalization's neglect of agriculture. As Sainath (2007) put it, 'In 60 years we haven't managed – except in three States – to push through any serious land reforms or tenancy reforms. But we can clear a Special Economic Zone … in six months.'

At the heart of the protests are perceived abuses of the Land Acquisition Act, especially the doctrine of 'eminent domain', originally intended to advance 'public purpose', not private profit. It is notable that many members of the growing chorus of critics on this issue are not the usual suspects. One is industrialist Rahul Bajaj, now a member of the Rajya Sabha, who claimed that real estate developers were using SEZs to perpetrate, with government connivance, a massive 'land scam'.[8]

State governments have shown themselves less politically astute than the political strategists in Delhi had hoped. Many states clearly expected protests to die down, or for them to have little electoral effect. In some states, such as Punjab and Uttar Pradesh (UP) in late 2006 and early 2007, ruling parties clearly considered their days in office numbered, which made it rational for them to milk the SEZ land-acquisition process before leaving power.

A more sophisticated calculation prevailed in other states, where kickbacks from the transfer of forcibly acquired land to private developers were said to have constituted a major source of ruling-party election finance. In Andhra Pradesh, early SEZ sites were reportedly chosen with caste calculations in mind. Groups that traditionally voted for the ruling party (or might be courted in the campaign) were allegedly spared the pain of compulsory land acquisition.

Over time, the UPA government found it increasingly difficult to distance itself from abuses committed by state governments, particularly in Congress-ruled states. The original intention was to shift blame onto the state governments, which had considerable latitude in operationalizing the SEZ policy. Political discontent was, however, increasingly directed at the centre – because it initiated the SEZ policy; because the BoA in Delhi approves projects; and because it is expected to frame regulations and exercise oversight.

Grass-roots opposition to land acquisition became most visible in the case of an SEZ approved for Nandigram, in West Bengal's East Midnapore district. In March 2007 violence erupted between the police and protestors. Fourteen people were killed. Another spasm of violence occurred in late 2007. Nandigram become a *cause célèbre* for anti-SEZ activists across India. Considerable controversy surrounds what took place there, the apportioning of blame following largely party lines. The ruling CPI(M)'s account of events was elaborated in an op-ed piece by MP and Politburo member Brinda Karat. Karat acknowledged that mistakes had been made, but accused protestors of being largely from outside the area, motivated by partisan agendas, and supplemented by paid muscle (Karat 2007). Karat's version of events was widely criticized.

But Nandigram is just the tip of the iceberg. Land acquisition for SEZs sparked protests in cases where charges of interference by outside agitators were even more difficult to sustain. Activist complaints have taken a wide range of forms. Documents presented by Orissa's state government at a BoA meeting in September 2006 stated that only 'waste' or 'barren' land, or that which supported only a single annual crop, would be forcibly acquired for SEZs (Government of Orissa, Department of Revenue 2006). Activists from Orissa, however, claimed that much of the land acquired was highly fertile, supporting multiple crops. The resulting controversy was sufficient to convince the promoters of a 1,800-hectare SEZ to reduce its size by more than 10 per cent.

Protests have erupted whether SEZ developers have acquired land directly from landowners or through state governments employing the Land Acquisition Act. Many SEZs have combined the two procedures. One firm, seeking to establish a

SEZ near Gurgaon, was alleged to have obtained the collaboration of the Haryana government in pressuring landowners to sell. Though the government had announced that it would not employ the Land Acquisition Act, officials reportedly threatened landowners with withdrawal of infrastructure and informed landowners that their property values would decline once the SEZ was established due to industrial pollution and reduced water availability, both of which would occur 'naturally', but could also be engineered by government agencies.[9]

Outrage at the use of underhand tactics led to protests against several projects in Maharashtra, a major destination for SEZ investment. The proposed 1,900-hectare Videocon SEZ on the eastern outskirts of Pune generated repeated protests, backed by several opposition party leaders. Their complaint, submitted to the Pune District Collector's office in May 2007, was a familiar one: that members of a prominent political family were using the official land acquisition process – and informal strong-arm tactics – to 'grab land' (*India Realty News* 2007).

The tendency for protests against land-acquisition practices to seep from social activism into party politics has strengthened SEZ resistance. The 2007 assembly elections in Punjab in 2007 showed how SEZs could serve as both a symbolic issue and one of material relevance to affected groups. During the campaign, opposition leaders criticized Amarinder Singh's Congress government for 'squeezing' farmers when acquiring land for SEZs. The Congress's electoral loss in Punjab cannot be blamed on its approach to SEZ implementation, but the issue provided a continuing focal point for opponents of the policy. In neighbouring Haryana, land-acquisition protests took on an intra-party dimension when opposition to a large SEZ planned for Jhajjar provided an excuse for Congress dissidents to criticize the party's leadership. In July 2007 a prominent Congress MP from the state, Kuldeep Bishnoi, complained about corruption related to this SEZ, accusing Congress president Sonia Gandhi of being a 'party to the deal'. Bishnoi stated that Haryana's chief minister, along with Gandhi and other senior Congress leaders, had all 'received money' from a deal with the SEZ's developer (*UNI* 2007a). These charges, regardless of their veracity, have been quoted by all manner of SEZ critics.

The lack of sustained, national party-based opposition to the SEZ policy reflects the dispersal of power throughout India's federal system. Because they have supported SEZ projects in states where they govern, non-UPA parties that might have railed against the SEZ policy have found themselves hamstrung by minimal requirements of consistency. This has not constrained them from complaining about implementation of the SEZ policy in states where they are not in power. In October 2006, BJP leaders stated that the party opposed *not* the SEZ policy itself, but only its implementation by the governments of states such as Andhra Pradesh, where the BJP sat in opposition. In Orissa, members of the oppositional CPI(M) levelled the same criticisms against the Orissa government that were made against the CPI(M)-led government in West Bengal (*Frontline* 2007). This dynamic worked the other way around in states where Congress was out of power. The Congress leadership in Karnataka repeatedly attacked the BJP-led state government on land acquisition for several SEZs. Karnataka's Congress president clarified that he was not opposed to the *idea* of SEZs, but that compulsory acquisition by the state at unfairly low prices was intolerable (*UNI* 2007b). Karnataka's ruling coalition was not about to permit state Congress leaders, whose party sponsored the SEZ Act itself, to play both sides of the fence, and soon began protesting against the UPA government's alleged failure to provide coherent guidelines for implementing the Act.

Not all states have responded with equal callousness and political ineptitude on the question of land acquisition for SEZs.[10] Different states pursue different policies on a number of policy parameters. Karnataka, for instance, has its own standard for deciding what kind of land can be acquired. The Karnataka Industrial Areas Development Board permits up to 10 per cent of a SEZ's area to come from fertile agricultural land. The compensation offered to landowners varies considerably across states as well, as does the credibility of governments that offer it. West Bengal, for instance, pays 30 per cent above the market rate for compulsorily acquired lands, and a much higher payout to sharecroppers than is recommended in national guidelines. It also has extracted more generous, legally enforceable, promises from SEZ developers for retraining and other facilities. None of this prevented India's most vociferous anti-SEZ movement from taking root in West Bengal, however.

IV. Government revision of the SEZ policy

As complaints mounted, the central government reversed its initial insistence that the SEZ rules would not be revised for two years. The rationale for non-revision had been that stable expectations were needed for investors to feel confident enough to commit the financial resources necessary to establish an initial wave of SEZs. Politics soon overtook this stance.

Following the initial set of SEZ rules, first framed in February 2006, successive waves of revisions have come roughly every six months. Key policy changes have come primarily from the so-called Empowered Group of Ministers (EGoM), established in mid 2006. The initial impetus was the 'success' of the policy, measured in terms of the rate at which SEZs were being approved. More significant, however, were complaints from the Finance Ministry that their two representatives on the BoA were being consistently overruled when they voiced objections about the adverse revenue implications of proposed SEZs.

Other issues that over time required clarification included the ability of existing businesses (operating in the DTA) to shift operations into an SEZ using existing equipment; the creation of a regulator to determine how much newly created SEZ infrastructure could be offset for tax purposes; and the area allowed for 'non-processing' activities (e.g. housing, commercial developments, schools). The EGoM reached compromise decisions on a number of matters, and developed procedural reforms to deal with others (*Business World* 2006b). Many decisions required refereeing by the Prime Minister's Office (PMO).

Another set of amendments was issued in March 2007. The government had begun to have serious doubts about the capacity of states to implement the land-acquisition portion of the SEZ policy without generating a backlash that would tarnish the entire effort. It therefore temporarily halted the process of approving new SEZs while the EGoM examined a range of issues. Within weeks of putting the approval process on hold, however, the BoA had resumed considering and clearing SEZ applications. Many observers considered the government to be acting in undue haste. The *Economic and Political Weekly* called the changes to the SEZ guidelines 'piecemeal tinkering' (*Economic and Political Weekly* 2007). The *EPW* also pointed out that the government had still not instituted 'a legally enforceable re-settlement and rehabilitation' policy that would hold SEZ promoters (or the state) accountable.[11]

Two substantial changes were announced during this period. First, one provision in the government order issued on 16 March 2007 appeared to accord the BoA wide latitude in changing the classification of land in an SEZ. Second, in early April 2007 the EGoM decided to prohibit the involvement of state governments in the acquisition of land for SEZ projects. An *EPW* editorial portrayed this as 'leaving peasants and landowners at the mercy of market forces', though many farmers no doubt preferred a (voluntary) market transaction to a compulsory sale engineered by corrupt officials acting at the behest of corrupt politicians. The *EPW* was on firmer ground when it claimed that the government was continuing 'to pander to the whims of SEZ promoters/developers'.

The government, eager to be seen as addressing the rising political discontent, made other largely cosmetic changes in 2007. It reduced the proportion of land within an SEZ that could be used for non-processing activities – from 65 to 50 per cent. The other high-profile policy change, transparently devised to provide the appearance of getting tough on developers, was to set a ceiling of 5,000 hectares on 'multi-product' SEZs. A subsequent ruling that allowed certain exemptions led critics to claim that the new ceiling was a political gimmick.

A new round of policy changes was under consideration by the EGoM at the end of August 2007 (*Economic Times* 2007), including a provision allowing states to acquire up to 30 per cent of an SEZ's land compulsorily, if the private developers could acquire 70 per cent of the land themselves.

State governments have also occasionally revised their own SEZ policies. Soon after coming to power in 2007, the new UP Chief Minister announced that the state government was indefinitely suspending the Anil Ambani Reliance group's planned SEZ in Noida. The Chief Minister claimed it was merely following the recommendation of a committee established by the previous government (*The Tribune* 2007). No one was in any doubt, however, that the decision on the Noida SEZ was driven largely by Ambani's political proximity to the Samajwadi Party, the chief minister's main rival.

Other state governments took steps to revise their policy frameworks – for instance, regarding the permitted size of SEZs, the nature of tax concessions, the sectors that would receive priority for SEZ development, the types of land available for acquisition, the procedures for acquiring land, and the compensation payable to landowners. Notable among these were Haryana, Maharashtra, Orissa, and West Bengal – states, not coincidentally, where some of the most visible and sustained protests took place.

Finally, to place the policy-revision process in political perspective, it is worth noting that frequent iteration of the SEZ policy framework (at state or central level) can spur rent-seeking. It provides incentives for private actors to influence successive rounds of revision, or to purchase inside information before key decisions are announced. Frequent policy changes also create ambiguities that provide bureaucrats greater scope to exercise discretion. For astute and well-networked officials, 'permanent reform' helps to generate illicit income.

V. Implications: taking stock of the politics of SEZs

Reviewing patterns that have emerged in the formulation of the SEZ policy, calculations concerning its political feasibility, resistance arising in the course of implementation, and subsequent attempts at policy revision, three arguments can be advanced.

First, India's reform process may have reached the limits of what can be achieved through shrewd and stealthy political management. Partisan blame-shifting, institutional burden-spreading, reverse forum-shopping, the purposeful division of adversely affected constituencies, tactical policy sequencing – these and other techniques for reducing political resistance (including some that rely on systematic illegality) have been important contributors to India's ability to gradually transform its economic framework in the last two decades. But a strategy based on manipulating incentives and disrupting the tactical calculus of key interest groups and elites is increasingly unviable.

The chief irony of more than three years of SEZ policy formulation, implementation, and revision is that an approach designed to effect an end run around formidable legal and political obstacles has generated not only a serious backlash against the SEZ policy, but a sense of disenchantment about the state's approach to liberalization more generally – in particular its lack of attention to the agricultural sector and its disregard of the rural poor.

India's SEZ policy has created a potent symbol around which opponents of liberalization – from grass-roots activists to national political leaders – have rallied. Indeed, one would be hard-pressed to imagine a single action more likely to unite the various anti-reform groups that for the past two decades have been fighting dispersed battles on a variety of lonely fronts. SEZs have brought economic reform firmly into the domain of mass politics.

SEZs have also fuelled serious political discontent. Protests that initially appeared sporadic and dispersed among far-flung sites (manageable by local officials and state governments) have coalesced. Over time, complaints about SEZ implementation became so widespread that the central government's excuse – that state governments were to blame – began to ring hollow. The conceptual firewall between policy and implementation was revealed as spurious: if implementation could be so consistently abusive, then there must be something wrong with the policy.

The second argument is closely related to the first. The political troubles that the SEZ policy has encountered underscore one of the costs of corruption that has largely been overlooked. The costs of corruption are typically measured in terms of either efficiency or equity. Efficiency-related costs stem from incentives for rent-seeking (Mauro 1996). Equity-related costs, which have received increasing attention in recent years, become more apparent when one examines the forms of corruption that particularly afflict the poor (Jenkins and Goetz 2003).

The systemic abuses that have attended SEZ implementation highlight the interdependence of efficiency- and equity-depleting forms of corruption. Attempts by governments to mitigate the effects of corruption on segments of the population that have not benefited from liberalization – the rural poor in particular – have often been foiled by middlemen and corrupt officials' siphoning of funds. This also damages the state's ability to build political consensus behind reforms designed to reduce structural inefficiencies in the economy. In other words, corruption that afflicts the poor not only undermines equity, it can also, indirectly, harm efficiency, by denting the political prospects for the creation of a more efficient economy (Jenkins 2006).

This syndrome is directly relevant to the fate of India's SEZ policy. The lack of faith among ordinary people in the state's ability to design and administer a program in which benefits will reach the intended beneficiaries would be a huge obstacle for any new, more comprehensive, approach to compensating losers from the SEZ process. The large SEZ projects being planned in and around Mumbai are a case in point. Reputable NGOs working in the city report that promises of employment for those whose land is acquired were particularly suspect in the eyes of residents.[12] Pledges from SEZ promoters as well as the state government come in the wake of a series of broken promises regarding land acquisition.

The Maharashtra Industrial Development Corporation (MIDC), like similar agencies in other states, has sought to assure landowners that they will be assigned plots in the SEZs in which the MIDC is an equity partner. The MIDC has also promised assistance in setting up business units in adjacent areas likely to undergo rapid development. But farmers have been unreceptive, referring to earlier episodes where landowners were treated unfairly. The land acquisition process for the Ispat Denro plant in Raigad and the IPCL plan at Nagothane loomed large in these accounts, according to spokespeople from activist groups such as Ekvira Jameen Bachao Andolan (*Frontline* 2007). Given the dismal record of the Maharashtra government in living up to its commitments, is it any wonder that landowners are not convinced by the assurances offered by the MIDC? It is not that farmers are clinging to land out of some atavistic attachment to real property; they have a rational belief, based on experience, that promises will not be kept.

The credibility of the Indian state as a broker of compromises on a large scale is so damaged by its repeated failures to stem corruption among the frontline bureaucracies charged with delivering compensation packages that compensation-based schemes find few takers and become unviable as deadlock-breaking solutions. This is a pathological condition for a democratic political system that must rely on such accommodations to effect policy change.

It is sometimes suggested that private-sector firms are better at developing compensation packages that landowners find attractive. The kinds of compensation offered are seen as more direct and backed by specific contracts for individuals rather than revocable policy commitments for classes of landowners, it is argued. The problem with contracts between firms and landowners is that these too rely on the enforcement machinery of the state, including a grotesquely corrupt legal system. A compromised Indian state, in short, undermines the confidence required of people with which the state would like to enter into contracts, without which a political consensus to deepen economic reform will be difficult to engender.

Recent government efforts to arrive at policy compromises on SEZ-related land issues may well generate even further suspicion. The proposed 70:30 policy on land acquisition – allowing state governments to acquire 30 per cent of SEZ land compulsorily if developers can acquire the other 70 per cent privately – enhances the negotiating leverage of SEZ promoters by considerably more than 30 per cent. Developers will attempt to convey the impression to *all* potential sellers that the firm is approaching the 70 per cent threshold, increasing pressure on landowners to sell – at what the developer will claim is a good price. The mere threat of being subjected to compulsory purchase – through a state land-acquisition process known to be corrupt and unreliable – will exert downward pressure on the market prices available to landowners. Industry analysts have welcomed such a policy because it ensures that 'projects will not be held to ransom' by recalcitrant landowners.[13]

Farmers have cause to be suspicious of a state that has done little to improve the conditions facing agriculture – a state that has in effect created the push factors that cause many to consider selling their land their only option. Pani has argued that encouraging people to make the shift out of agriculture means 'providing them economic opportunities that are consistent with a modern economy', including 'initiatives ranging from education to incubators that allow entrepreneurship to mature'. These cannot be future promises. 'As the protests over land acquisition grow across the country state governments that want to avoid social turmoil will have to recognize that people have to be drawn out of agriculture before their land is acquired and not the other way round' (Pani 2006).

The third argument relates most directly to this book's central purpose to explore connections between the various dimensions of India's 'great transformation'. The link between SEZs and the rise of Hindu nationalism, a key component of this transformation, is mainly indirect. It is nevertheless notable that when defending SEZs as necessary, some BJP politicians have spoken of SEZs' role in projecting India's economic power – a means of preparing Indian firms for operating within the global markets and overseas jurisdictions in which they increasingly will have to do business.

At least one BJP spokesperson also advanced the argument that SEZs would facilitate cultural preservation by providing an alternative to the emigration of India's skilled professionals (Ranjan 2006). The implication is that India is creating its own 'abroad' within its borders – a hybridized space that can serve as a functional equivalent of foreign territory. Far from being scars on the nation's sacred geography, SEZs might represent a symbolic absorption of the world beyond India. SEZs could even shield India's cultural core from what some Hindu nationalists decry as the corrupting foreign influences of consumerism and western lifestyles by quarantining these, to the degree possible, within defined enclaves where they can do less harm.

Is there a link between India's experience with SEZs and what has been called India's 'second democratic upsurge'? Arguably the most direct connection is of a negative variety: visions of unaccountable governance within SEZs paint a grim picture of what India's economic modernizers consider necessary to promote prosperity. If SEZs are a harbinger of what is to come, the democratic gains realized for historically oppressed groups through one set of institutions could well be reversed through others. And, yet, critics who stress the democratic deficit seemingly built into the SEZ model of governance may have misread the relationship between SEZs and the continued democratization of India's democracy.

While SEZ developers and the businesses that will operate within them seek to evade India's burdensome regulations, so do many of the people who will flock to the SEZs. A good proportion of those who will reside in SEZs, or aspire to do so, will be members of India's middle class. It is for technological and managerial professionals that the extensive 'social amenities' are being constructed. These zones of relative affluence will offer not merely economic privileges, but (for some) a form of desirable political exile as well. The idea of the multipurpose SEZ, where large numbers of people will reside as well as work, is premised on a belief that many people are eager to escape from India's democracy as currently constituted. SEZs provide a means for a privileged (but growing) segment of India's polity to avoid the tumult that characterizes contemporary India, both the politicization of religious identity and the second democratic upsurge.

This does not imply that SEZ residents will not desire the civil rights or political voice associated with liberal, representative government. They may, however, be highly price-conscious consumers of democracy. A great many upwardly mobile, professionally qualified, globally connected people consider India's form of politics too chaotic (and indeed corrupt) to deliver the benefits classically associated with democracy. The entry into mainstream politics of previously marginalized groups – people regarded, even by first-generation members of the middle class, as socially backward, easily manipulated by populist demagogues, and too often willing to sacrifice progress at the altar of equality – has made living amidst India's current democratic dispensation an unattractive proposition for its emerging elite. SEZs offer a form of partial political secession – much as access to privatized health and education allows better-off people to opt out of public provision. Moving to an offshore haven located onshore may thus constitute the next best thing to emigrating abroad – better, in fact, because of the ability to do so while remaining in India. If forfeiting some of the procedural benefits of democracy is the price of admission, this is a cost that many Indians may well be willing to pay.

This is perhaps the most disturbing aspect of what amount to 'special governance zones'. It is not difficult to imagine political leaders making the case that India's decentralized, representation-obsessed, procedure-encumbered form of democracy had become unworkable – and that SEZs demonstrate a model for the nation at large: a streamlined version of governance in which officials and business elites collaborate to provide effective public services in the service of a long-term vision of India's economic place in the world. A kind of South Korea in South Asia.

Notes

1 Various meanings of second-generation reforms are discussed in R. Jenkins, (2004), 'Labor Policy and the Second Generation of Economic Reform in India'. In R. Jenkins and S. Khilnani, eds, *The Politics of India's Next Generation of Economic Reforms*, Special Issue of *India Review*.
2 The SEZ Act explicitly altered several existing laws, including the Banking Regulation Act, the Income-Tax Act, the Insurance Act and the Stamp Duties Act.
3 China's four original SEZs were Shenzhen, Shantou, Zhuhai, and Xiamen (Crane 1990).
4 One account that sees 1980 as the crucial watershed is A. Kohli, 2006. 'Politics of Economic Growth in India'. *Economic and Political Weekly*.
5 In the same article, Anand Jain, a partner in the Maha Mumbai SEZ, asks: 'Why do they worry about my bloody SEZ? ... Why not have ten SEZs and solve all Mumbai's problems?'
6 These terms appeared in 'Revoke the SEZ Act', a petition signed by representatives of 37 activist organizations, 28 June 2007.
7 A relatively balanced account is 'Sovereign States', *Business World* (2006a).
8 He used this term at a 'Parliamentarians' Forum on Economic Policy Issues', Council for Social Development, 3 May 2007, New Delhi. Bajaj received support from other Rajya Sabha members.
9 Personal communication with a reporter who covers Gurgaon for the real estate trade press, 15 June 2007.
10 This is true in other areas of reform as well. See A. Sinha (2005), *The Regional Roots Of Developmental Politics In India: A Divided Leviathan*, Bloomington, IN: Indiana University Press.
11 Interestingly, the controversy surrounding SEZs spurred action on resettlement and rehabilitation legislation and amendment of the Land Acquisition Act. Neither had been enacted at the time of writing, but both were priorities of the UPA government, which won re-election in May 2009.
12 Personal communication, 12 August 2007.
13 These were the words of a senior manager at PricewaterhouseCoopers (*Business Standard*, 2007).

5 The contested geographies of federalism in post-reform India

Stuart Corbridge

Introduction

It is widely believed that the deeper structures of Indian federalism are centralizing while many of the social practices that animate these structures have worked to disperse power and resources. The original federal design for the post-colonial state was informed by the Government of India Act of 1935, which arrogated considerable powers to the imperial capital, New Delhi. But the Constitution of India also had close regard for the experiences of the nationalist movement, and especially the Indian National Congress, which had been compelled over several decades to balance 'centralizing and regional forces within its fold' (Kohli 2001: 11, summarizing Dasgupta 2001; see also Brass 1982). It should come as no surprise, then, that in the first 20 years after independence India was both made to hang together – notably by Sardar Patel in his dealings with the Princely States, but also in Kashmir, Nagaland and Goa – and yet endowed with sufficient latitude that regional elites could press important claims for resources, patronage and identity against the central government, 'the Centre'. To put matters more formally, although the Constitution of 1950 provides for the dismissal of elected state governments in favour of President's Rule (Article 356), and while the states have always been made to depend on grants-in-aid from the Centre (under Article 275, reflecting a prior bias in the allocation of tax powers to New Delhi under the Seventh Schedule), the deepening of democracy in India, when allied to the demise of the hegemonic powers of the Congress Party, have ensured that Centre–state relations are more often a terrain of negotiation than of simple fiat. The fact that Hindi never became the official and exclusive language of state, as provided for in the Constitution, albeit after a period of 15 years, is just one case in point. The Centre was unable to impose this on the South, or indeed in Bengal.

What might be called existing federalism in India is brought to life by a range of political actors – including political parties, trade unions and bureaucrats, but also extending to major corporations, caste associations, social movements and criminal gangs – which are compelled to deal with one another in the context of constantly changing pressures and incentives, economic as well as political (Manor 2001). Nevertheless, there is a sense, perhaps, that the practical workings of federalism in India from 1950 to 1990 were less complex than they are today. Or that, at any rate, they were more obviously dominated by one political party, the Congress,

The contested geographies of federalism in post-reform India   67

and the contrasting political skills of its two major leaders, Jawaharlal Nehru and his daughter Indira Gandhi. Understandably enough, the focus in these years was on the Party's strategies for managing Centre–state relations, including through various Finance Commissions, and on its changing electoral fortunes. Particular attention was devoted to the question of maintaining unity in diversity, and to the Congress Party's considerable achievements in negotiating what Selig Harrison (1960) suggested would be India's 'most dangerous decades'.

What is less evident in this literature, obviously, are the sorts of issues that have dominated discussions of federalism since about 1990, and in particular the interlocking relationships between existing federalism in India and the sometimes competing claims made by economic reformers, cultural nationalists and popular social movements.[1] How are these claims being presented and negotiated? How far has the process of economic reform provoked policy decentralization by virtue of abolishing licensing and location controls once held by the Centre? How far has the process of economic reform been strengthened by the emergence of competition states led by Chief Ministers acting as *de facto* CEOs? How far has it been held back by a lack of progress in dealing with state-level fiscal deficits and security problems? Relatedly, how is the federal system linked to the emergence of coalition politics in the Lok Sabha, and to the particular electoral trajectories since 1980 of the Bharatiya Janata Party and various caste-based and regionalist parties? How is it being changed by a more activist judiciary? And where is opposition to these 'elite revolts' (Corbridge and Harriss 2000) being mounted, particularly if, as seems to be the case, the willingness of state governments to challenge an ongoing process of economic reform dissipated sharply in the second half of the 1990s and into the 2000s, the rhetoric of certain Leftist parties notwithstanding?

Some of these questions will be taken up here, but mainly in regard to a second area underplayed in discussions of Indian federalism. This has to do with basic geography. There has been a good deal of work on changing governance relations in federal India, most of it produced by political scientists. We also have important studies of the economic performance of India's states in the post-reforms period, and of Centre–state engagements with international bodies like the World Trade Organisation.[2] And of course there is work on the continuing crises in Kashmir and the north-east.[3] Rather less focus, however, has been placed on such apparently mundane matters as the joining together of India with roads, railways and airports, or staffing and equipment levels in the 'trenches' of the federal state, including the Block Development Office.[4] And yet this is now beginning to matter a great deal, as the inequalities brought about in part by economic liberalization become more visible and as state absence looms more sharply into view. New questions are being raised about the forms of space- and place-making proposed by economic reformers, on the one hand, and by cultural and religious nationalists, and also India's dispossessed, on the other.

This paper works slightly to recast Rob Jenkins's (1998a, 1999) important arguments for seeing India's federal system as a (net) facilitator of economic reform in the country.[5] Its focus is on those states left behind in the rush to create what Lawrence Saez (2002) calls 'federalism without a centre'. At the end of the day, a functioning state has to control the territory it makes claims upon. It has to provide security and gain some measure of legitimacy. This is true of unitary and federal states alike. What must be of concern in India today are not only the ongoing crises in Kashmir and the north-east, but also the spread of Naxalism from Nepal down to some districts of Tamil Nadu. The spread of underground Left forces may not index the failures of economic liberalization in India – it signifies its absence far more than its presence – but it does point out place-making practices (red bases, liberation zones, other challenges to the state and market) that stand in opposition to efforts by government and business to create new and stronger spaces for the expansion and more rapid circulation of private capital. Following Henri Lefebvre (1976), we might say indeed that both Naxalite groups and religious nationalists continue to be engaged in making geographies that don't always conform to the drive for 'abstract space' that economic reform generally demands and which India's federal system has partly helped to create.

Competition states and the circulation of capital

Post-Independence India's ambitions to promote a vibrant federal democracy took shape with reference to two more mythologies of rule, those of socialism and secularism. If the central ethos of the Nehruvian years – or those of the Nehru-Mahalanobis years (the Second and Third Five Year Plans, 1956–66) – was not quite 'high modernist' in James Scott's terms (Scott 1998), it was nonetheless committed to a model of modernization that proposed some dramatic changes to India's landscapes and in the production of Indian citizens. At the heart of this venture was a drive for import-substitution industrialization (ISI) that would rapidly build up the capital goods capabilities of the post-colonial nation. Most of the planned new growth would come from the resource-rich and yet also economically backward regions of the country: notably (Bihar)/Jharkhand (home to Bokaro Steel City and the Heavy Engineering Corporation at Ranchi-Hatia), Orissa (Rourkela), Chhattisgarh (Bhilai) and Andhra Pradesh (Visakhapatnam). Private sector-led growth would feature more strongly in Gujarat and Maharashtra, although even these States pressed demands for 'national projects' that would be located within their borders.

In practice, efforts at industrial decentralization were undone by policies of freight equalization, which ensured that the price of minerals taken from the resource triangle of eastern India was more or less the same across the country. Hugely discounting the importance of transport costs in this way did little to encourage the establishment of resource-processing industries in eastern India, as opposed to the extractive industries, which seem to have imposed on the region a version of the 'resource curse' noted more frequently in sub-Saharan Africa (Collier 2007). Instead, it is the argument of scholars including Rob Jenkins, Aseema Sinha and Lawrence Saez that the possibility of creating a more even economic geography of India had to await the removal of various Freight Equalization Acts, and that this in turn was bound up with a much broader re-crafting of Centre–state relations that both followed and facilitated an ongoing project of economic reform.

Jenkins' major arguments are fourfold and they make this case with particular clarity. First, he says, India's economic reforms *have* been far-reaching, not least in the areas of trade and industrial reform and in regard to the liberalization of foreign direct and portfolio investment regimes. (Aseema Sinha reminds us that 80 per cent of all investment in the Indian economy in 1978 was in the public sector, and thus largely under the control of the Centre, which 'dominated anything related to industrialization' [2004b: 28]; by 1998 the public sector accounted for about 40 per cent of total investment). Second, this might surprise us. Political rhetoric before the reforms began was strongly anti-market. Populists preferred to talk vaguely about the empowerment of the poor through caste-based struggles around *izzat*, or honour, and political and economic elites were believed to have much to lose from downsizing the rents that followed from their command of an over-developed state. What was in it for them? Third, India's federal arrangements were widely considered to be 'sub-optimal, in terms of both equity and efficiency' (Jenkins 1998a: 3). On the one hand, the Centre controlled too much of the revenue base to promote efficient levels of decentralization. On the other hand, the willingness of the Centre to bail out India's states with grants-in-aid ensured that the latter faced neither a hard budget constraint nor consistent pressures to be innovative, competitive or market-preserving. Fourth, notwithstanding the insights offered in the second and third arguments (above), the reform process in India *has* snowballed precisely because key political actors have been able to capture new and expanded rents from private sector development, and because 'the impact of liberal economic reform varies from state to state' (ibid.: 9).

Innocuous as it might seem this last contention is key. Jenkins maintains that reforming states have benefited significantly from increased employment growth, foreign investment and more buoyant tax bases, and have few reasons to challenge New Delhi's agenda. The Chief Ministers (CMs) of Gujarat and Maharashtra, for example, have strong incentives to chase foreign funds, including those of Non-Resident Indians (NRIs), and to pose as Chief Executive Officers (CEOs). Chandrababu Naidu was the very model of a CM as CEO in Andhra Pradesh, and he was famously rewarded by the World Bank and other major donors – including by Clare Short for the UK's Department for International Development (DFID), who declared he was a man that Britain could do business with. (Short left office at about the same time that Naidu was removed from office by Andhra's voters). In contrast, politicians 'from states that suffer relative declines in economic performance (or autonomy in determining economic policy) have both less clout and fewer allies (among their counterparts in states that perceive themselves as beneficiaries) with which to mount a serious challenge to liberalization' (ibid.).

In short, India's federal system has facilitated economic reform and economic growth, at least in net terms. For all its centralizing tendencies and imperfections, Indian federalism has helped to promote a set of competition states that are working hard to outdo one another in their courtship of inward investment. Having set the table, the Centre has been able to sit back and allow various experiments to take place in the states that advance its reform agenda. Pro-business legislation follows, and with it what some are now calling a process of accumulation by dispossession (referring to illegal land acquisitions rather more than tax-avoidance schemes). At the same time, what Jenkins calls an emerging 'pattern of provincial Darwinism' (ibid.: 10) ensures that potential opponents of liberalization find it hard to solve collective action problems. Classically, the trade union movement in India is becoming 'more regionally fragmented' (ibid.: 15) as it is compelled to use its scarce resources to challenge new labour laws in one state after another. Facing pressures from middle-class voters and consumers even the Communist governors of West Bengal have chosen to court foreign direct investment and to prioritize urban-industrial over rural-agricultural development. In doing so they are turning their backs on a long history of confrontation with the Centre on development policy issues (Sinha 2005). In the last three years Bihar has got in on the act, with the new Chief Minister, Nitish Kumar, making strenuous efforts to promote the state as a haven of good governance, as witness his freedom of information initiatives. NRIs from Bihar have responded in good measure, at least through their own version of virtual reality, the web, where they have been keen to bid an unfond farewell to the dark days – *kali yuga* – of Lalu Prasad Yadav.

There is more to Jenkins on federalism that I can convey here. The gist of his case, however, is that India's federal system has been more market-preserving than many theorists had anticipated. National political elites have relied on the system 'to create intra-state rivalries capable of promoting resistance to their policy agenda, and on state-level political systems to reduce interest group potency' (ibid.: 20). To the extent, too, that 'the political trends associated with liberalization' ... have deepened 'the regionalization of Indian politics' (ibid.), as Jenkins believes to be the case, the costs of drifting back to either a *dirigiste* economy or a polity ruled from on high have correspondingly been increased.[6]

This is surely right. Jenkins' work – like that of Saez and Sinha – has helped us rethink the entwined political and economic logics of federalism in India, and we are the richer for it. At the same time, however, the fact that there is now widespread elite support for the reforms across the Centre and the states does not mean that the expanded role of private capital is assured equally across the country or that it faces no opposition from non-elite groups. What is truly remarkable about India's infrastructure – the basic geographies that support and hinder liberalization – almost 20 years after the reforms began is its patchiness and poor quality. Proponents of the idea of 'India Shining' like to point to the technopoles in Bangalore and Chennai, or to the gleaming glass office complexes in Gurgaon and Bandra Kurla (Mumbai). They also point out the rapid growth in land and mobile telephone connections since 1990, and a parallel rise in airplane passengers carried by the likes of Jet, Sahara, Kingfisher and Air Deccan.[7] The country has moved on from Doordarshan and Indian Airways, and was in 2009 in the process of completing a road system based around the Golden Quadrilateral of four- and six-lane highways that will link Delhi, Mumbai, Chennai and Kolkata. Even rail passenger and freight transport figures seemed to be on an upward curve under the stewardship until recently of Lalu Yadav.

But we must keep things in perspective. This is not China, where airport facilities are already world-leading in many more cities than Beijing, Hong Kong and

Shanghai, and where road networks are routinely maintained to the highest standards even in inland areas. Delhi's airport is still hindered by air traffic control problems, not all of which are caused by winter fogs, and many leading airlines continue to be un- or under-represented in India. More to the point, consider how India's geography might look even to the middle classes of the eastern states, never mind those in the north-east. Two flights a day from Ranchi to Delhi with Indian Airlines (IA) in 2007 was a 100 per cent improvement on the service offered by the same airline in 2002, and remained the only credible alternative to a 24-hour train journey. The situation in Raipur was slightly better with 18 flights a week to Delhi shared by three carriers (IA, Jet and Air Deccan), but here too the alternative rail journey runs to a day. Even on the better-established Patna–Delhi route there were only five planes a day in mid-2007 (Indian Airlines, Jet and Sahara), although this also was a distinct improvement on the situation in 2000. Driving to the national capital from any of these cities is still not a realistic option.

It can reasonably be argued that this poor level of connectivity is a legacy of the pre-reforms era, and that, in any case, not only is the volume of air passenger and road traffic slowly increasing from the 'east to the rest', but the urban middle classes of Bihar, Jharkhand, Chhattisgarh, Orissa, Madhya Pradesh and so on now also have access to the internet. But this sanguine view overlooks the fact that such internet access is often powered by domestic generators, the level of publicly guaranteed electricity provision being poor in cities like Patna, Ranchi and Raipur.[8] It also looks past two legacies of post-reform federalism that are more troubling than those highlighted by Jenkins.

The first of these has to do with India's fiscal deficits. According to a recent World Bank survey, 'India must invest around 3–4 per cent more of GDP on infrastructure to sustain growth of around 8 per cent, address existing gaps and meet policy-driven coverage goals' (2006: xv). Some of this investment will come from the private sector, including in the form of public–private partnerships. Nevertheless, the implications for public spending are considerable and will have to be borne at a time when India's general government deficit is creeping upwards again to 9 per cent of GDP (it was 9.9 per cent of GDP in 2001/2) after four years of significant fiscal reductions in both New Delhi and the States. Just as India gained from favourable conditions in the world economy for much of the period 1991–2008, it suffered during the global turndown of 2008–9 (albeit far less than most of its competitors).

This bears on a second observation. Although there are reasons to be optimistic about the long-term buoyancy of Indian revenues (Rao and Singh 2005), and while Jenkins is right to observe that many western/southern states will not turn their backs on the reform policies they embraced in the 1990s, the electoral arithmetic has been different in some eastern states. Even after the formation of Uttaranchal (now Uttarakhand) and Jharkhand in 2000, the share of Bihar and Uttar Pradesh (UP) in India's total population remains close to one quarter. And the reform process is not much advanced in either state, save perhaps by various private sector interests in western UP. Until the election of Nitish Kumar – and then, one suspects, still rather more in word than in deed – neither state provided a reforming Chief Minister, or even a substantial opposition politician committed to economic reform.[9]

The 'provincial Darwinism' that Jenkins refers to has barely been seen. Instead, the first-past-the-post electoral system that governs India's federal polity worked for two decades in Bihar to entrench a political regime that solved the 'collective action problems' that Jenkins also refers to simply by ignoring demands for development, never mind economic reform. Lalu Yadav's Janata Dal (JD)/Rashtriya Janata Dal (RJD) secured power in Bihar by providing Yadav and Kurmis, at first (later just Yadavs, and later still just some Yadavs) with state patronage and a very real sense of their improved social standing, and by providing Muslims with a hugely welcome sense of security. The Chief Minister of Bihar (later, the husband of the Chief Minister of Bihar) twice told this author that he was opposed to 'development' on the basis that it would worsen 'the hole in the ozone layer'. He then suggested, more candidly, that there were few votes in development (especially *gram vikas*), which unlike empowerment he could not expect to deliver any time soon.

Now, there is a degree of idiosyncrasy here that must be remarked upon. It is possible that the JD/RJD government could have won more votes by providing both a politics of empowerment and a minimal politics of development and better governance. The sheer incompetence of Bihar's government, and its crass disregard for the livelihood/security needs of ordinary people, was sharply picked up by N. C. Saxena in 1998, when, as Secretary of Rural Development in the Government of India, he sent an open letter to the Chief Secretary of Bihar, declaring that: 'The State of Bihar is being treated like a private property by those at the top ... [and run by] a lower-level bureaucracy [that] has no work ethic, no feeling for the common cause, no involvement in the nation ... they have only a grasping, mercenary outlook, devoid of competence, integrity and commitment' (quoted in Thakur 2003: 146). He went on to note that while his Ministry had set aside more than 1,000 crore rupees for rural development schemes in Bihar in 1997–8, 'Not a single rupee has been sanctioned by our department for drinking water schemes this year because the Bihar government has not been able to finalize procedures for buying pipes for the last one year' (ibid.: 146–7).

But while all this was horribly true, it was mirrored in significant degree in the 'patronage democracy' to Bihar's West (Uttar Pradesh), and led in both states to the out-migration of many urban professionals and business people, the point I want to make here is that the damaging outcomes of a politics based on 'ethnic headcounts' (Chandra 2004) were rooted directly in the structures of India's federal polity. Nothing in those deeper structures of rule – not the prospect of a harder budget constraint, not the existence of the All-India Services, not the demonstrated success of many Western States, not even the threat or use of President's rule – has so far compelled leading politicians in Bihar or UP to embrace economic reform as a matter of Darwinian survival. From 1990 onwards, the Backward Classes that have come to power in these two States have used their offices mainly to fight wars with those seen as their erstwhile tormentors (in Bihar, the Bhumihar-Rajput-Brahmin-Lala [Kayastha] upper castes: those targeted by Lalu as *Bhurabal*).[10] In neither State has the Centre been able to inculcate a determined politics of economic reform. One sees signs of growing consumerism even in Patna, where often ill-gotten gains have been ploughed into shopping malls, including by leading politicians and their families. But just as the dominant image one might take from Mayawati in UP is the writing into public space of portraits, bust and statues of Dr Ambedkar, so the image from Bihar is the extraordinary decline of public education institutions (including the AN Sinha Institute on the banks of the Ganges in Patna) and of public spaces (the huge *maidan* in Patna), and the just as visible decline of many state institutions and government offices. Exceptional as Bihar might still be, what is truly significant there after nearly 20 years of economic reform is not the bias of the government for or against liberalization, but the difficulty that the states has faced until very recently in acting at all, let alone in circulating capital.

Federal spaces of opposition

Just as we will never reach the end of history, so too we will never reach the end of geography. It is reasonable to suppose that time–space relations are becoming stretched or disembedded in an age of 'globalization'. But the notion that we are approaching a 'flat world', as Thomas Friedman (2005) has it (drawing on Nandan Nilekani), is no more plausible than the claim that capitalism will achieve its lofty goal of annihilating space by time. If Marx taught us anything it is that processes of capitalist development are necessarily uneven, contradictory and crisis-ridden. Henri Lefebvre once remarked that capitalism survived in the twentieth century 'by occupying space, by producing space' (quoted in Harvey 2001: 376). He further argued that the space ideally produced by capital was abstract space, a dull, homogenized space that facilitated the circulation of capital and which was progressively emptied out of social meanings that might challenge its hegemony. Its organising practices are calculative, bureaucratic and violent. Its production is made possible by dispossession (Lefebvre 1991).

The production of abstract space is necessarily an important goal for many of India's political and business elites. And yet Gurgaon and Bandra Kurla are almost too iconic in this respect. The formation of better-functioning stock markets, the installation of a Metro system in Delhi, the building of the Golden Quadrilateral, the damming of the Narmada river, the garishly named Operation Sunshine in Kolkata (the forcible eviction of street-side stalls by the ruling Left Front government in 1996 [Chatterjee, P. 2004b: 61]), all these are more representative of what Lefebvre had in mind. As another great student of space (the geographer, David Harvey: 1982) has pointed out, however, while processes of capitalist accumulation appear to work in the direction of spatial entropy – capital finding new openings for profit in the same way that water finds its level – they do so by first freezing space. Capital can only circulate by producing fixed spaces – mainly urban spaces, but also regional, national and international assemblages of just that which was being highlighted in section II: infrastructure or fixed capital. Oil has to be taken to the United States from the Middle East by pipeline and tanker; even the circulation of electronic monies and complex derivatives depends on the building up and supposedly close regulation of financial centres (New York, London, Hong Kong, Tokyo, Dubai and so on) that are anything but dispersed (*vide* Wall Street and the City). Even worse, from the point of view of today's boosters of globalization, the production of abstract space also contains within it the production of counter-spaces of opposition, or what Lefebvre called 'differential space'. Precisely because of the problem of spatial fixity, capitalism cannot develop evenly or produce flat landscapes of abstract space. Rounds of investment take place with reference to the built environments produced by previous rounds of investment. In the process, some people and places are bulldozed out of existence, or get left behind as others pull ahead.

And some will resist. Some will object to space being produced in such abstract and utilitarian terms. They will insist on its other meanings, as the Sangh Parivar has done with respect to India's 'sacred geographies': the land that is holy from the Indus to the seas, as Veer Savarkar put it, with its cardinal points, mountain abodes of the Gods, the city of light (Kashi) produced for Lord Shiva by the cosmogonic austerities of Lord Vishnu (Parry 1994), Ayodhya, and so on. One can reasonably argue that if the BJP government in New Delhi (1999 to 2004) sent signals to foreign and domestic investors that India was open for business, the actions of some BJP-led state governments – UP in 1992, Gujarat under Narendra Modi – sent very different messages.[11] Modi's regime, sadly, has not been punished for its complicity in the Gujarat genocide of 2002. Capital continues to pour into the state, including from NRIs in the US and the UK, a large number of whom are active supporters of the Vishwa Hindu Parishad and militant Hinduism more broadly. Still, an image gets lodged in the wider world that is not consistent with India Shining, or with what DFID (Government of United Kingdom 2007) has now taken to calling Global India (as opposed to Developing India and Poorest India).

Capital has shown itself to be indifferent to democracy at the global scale. But what it does covet is good public relations and stable governance. Riots in Bombay or Ahmedabad to make those cities more 'Hindu', including through land grabs; Muslim 'terrorism' in the same cities or elsewhere; the wholesale production of public space in the name of one community (much more so than the sponsorship of Hindu temples by affluent business people: see Fuller 2003, Harriss 2003b) – these forms of counter-spatial practice can sometimes pose problems for agendas of economic reform and liberalization, and are partly incubated by India's federal system of rule. The same argument might be made of caste-based politics across the Gangetic plain, only more so. Ashutosh Varshney (1999) maintains that the Rao-Singh government of the early 1990s was able to push ahead with its reform policies because it won the support of coalition partners that were initially sceptical or hostile: they supported the Congress Party because their greater fear was that the BJP would seize power at India's Centre. On balance, then, we can agree both that the BJP acting in power in New Delhi, and the fear of the BJP coming to power in New Delhi, advanced the reform agenda, at least in net terms. In the case of the JD/RJD in Bihar, however, or the Bahujan Samaj and Samajwadi parties in UP, national fears could not trump state-level policies or anxieties. In these cases, the capture of power at the state level led to policies that were unsupportive of the broader agendas of capitalist development and the production of abstract space. As already explained, it is likely that capital was disinvested, or only minimally invested in net terms, from eastern UP and Bihar over the period from 1990 to c.2005, as business people found it impossible to do business in the absence of a minimally capable state: one that would provide basic property rights, electricity, water and security with at least as much vigour as it provided statues of Ambedkar or huge cardboard cut-outs of a smiling Lalu.

And then there is 'Poorest India'. DFID's production of a tripartite geography of India is hardly innocent. The UK's aid agency is flush with money and needs to spend a rapidly expanding budget. At the time of writing (2008) it invests about £350 million on India annually, and the prospect of India being declared a Middle Income Country by 2010, '11, '12 or '13 elicits mixed emotions. Still, the agency has a point when it notes that the number of 'absolutely poor' people living in India – those surviving on less than one dollar a day – was somewhere between 250 and 300 million 60 years after the country achieved independence. The prime minister, Manmohan Singh, also made a point of highlighting this in his speech to the nation from the Red Fort on 15 August 2007. In other words, aid could be justified for the India that had been left behind, or which had left itself behind. *Sotto voce*, the suggestion was that aid might be spent in that growing number of districts and states where the state was being challenged by the Maoist or Naxalite movement(s).[12] Significantly, too, the Naxalites were singled out by Manmohan Singh as one of the greatest threats facing India at the time that he became prime minister, the other beings rural poverty and international terrorism.

The connections between the spread of Naxalism in India since about 2000 and the progress of economic reform are anything but clear – whatever the claims made in some Naxal blogs. There is some truth in the claim that parts of eastern India have served as 'internal colonies' for capitalist development elsewhere in the country, and that the Maoist movement has mainly taken hold among *Dalit* and *Adivasi* communities in regions where capital accumulation has been largely extractive and/or based on coercive labour regimes. But this is not an argument that I want to develop here. In relation to the changing structures and practices of federalism in India the more important points are these: (a) processes of economic reform have widened the gap between India's richer and poorer states (by making the former richer still); (b) this widening gap will prompt a range of exit and voice options in the poorer states, including migration, resistance/rebellion, and demands to be included in the virtuous circle of growth and reform; and (c) these different options will be mediated by patterns of state presence/absence (which can themselves be linked to prior geographies of fiscal federalism in India), differential rates of population growth, and the dominance or otherwise of ethnic headcounts in determining political settlements in the provinces.

On the question of India's uneven development between c.1990 and 2005 the basic facts are well known, although their relationship to the process of economic reforms is unclear. Per capita net state domestic product at constant 1993/94 prices actually fell in Bihar from Rs. 4,474 in 1990/1 to Rs. 3,396 in 2003/4 (probably because of the loss of Jharkhand), while the residents of Uttar Pradesh, including the richer western parts of that state (but not Uttaranchal), saw their real incomes rise from Rs. 5,342 in 1990/91 to a meagre Rs. 5,975 in 2003/04.[13] Matters were slightly better in Orissa and Madhya Pradesh, where per capita net state domestic product increased from Rs. 4,300 to Rs. 7,176 in the former state, over the same time period, and from Rs. 6,350 to Rs. 8,038 in the latter. In Maharashtra, meanwhile, the corresponding figures show more than a 60 per cent increase in real terms over 13 years, from Rs. 10,159 and Rs. 16,765. In Gujarat the rate of economic expansion was even greater, with a per capita net state domestic product of Rs. 8,788 nearly doubling in 2004/5 to Rs. 16,878.[14]

These differences in economic performance are also picked up in human development indicators, albeit to a lesser degree and with some evidence of a closing gap in literacy figures, as would be expected. Reported literacy rates increased from 37.49 per cent in 1991 to 47.00 per cent in 2001 in Bihar, and from 40.71 per cent to 56.27 per cent in UP over the same period. In Gujarat and Maharashtra the corresponding figures show 1991/2001 literacy rates of 61.29 per cent/69.14 per cent and 64.87 per cent/76.88 per cent respectively. Nevertheless, in 2005, the infant mortality rate in Madhya Pradesh was as high as 76 per 1,000 live births, and in Orissa 77 per 1,000; in Maharashtra and Tamil Nadu the corresponding figures were 36 and 37, while that for Kerala was 14 per 1,000 live births (Government of India, 2007, Table 9.1). Not without reason has the World Bank recently noted that, 'Parts of India [now] have poverty rates similar to those in many sub-Saharan African countries, while other regions of India resemble richer Latin American countries' (World Bank 2006: Figure 1.12). Rural Bihar falls into the first category, south Delhi very much into the second.

In terms of specifying the links that might obtain between these development gaps and local patterns of exit and voice (or even loyalty), there is clearly need for caution. Standard economic theory suggests that capital will flow to Poorest India once the wage gap between Global and Poorest India opens sufficiently wide. But standard theory also accepts that wage gaps must be understood in relation to productivity gaps and the provision of key public goods, including minimally acceptable levels of infrastructure and security. And herein lies the rub. These public goods are hugely undersupplied in many parts of eastern India, in part in consequence of India's federal politics. Bad governance in states like Bihar has not been adequately punished by the Centre. The same might be said of UP or Jharkhand. Nor is it clear that politics in these states must become more pro-business in the near future, or even in the medium term.[15] To the extent that professional people continue to be driven from parts of eastern India, and to the extent that the highest rates of population growth in India today are to be found in these states, and particularly among the Backward Classes, it is just as likely that a populist politics based around ethnic headcounts and the looting of the state will continue, or even deepen. It is even possible that the relative weight of what I have called 'eastern India' will increase in the Lok Sabha, where its voice might be raised more loudly against the agendas of economic reform and the production of abstract space. This is unlikely, but not impossible – especially if the national rate of economic growth plunges for any reason.[16]

Finally, in Bihar and Jharkhand, the two states I know best, but also in large parts of Chhattisgarh, and in significant parts of Orissa, Madhya Pradesh, Uttar Pradesh and Andhra Pradesh, the state is simply not an effective ground presence in some blocks and *panchayats* (Corbridge et al. 2005).[17] This is what some discussions of federalism in India seem to miss. Government is not remotely joined up because government is missing. (Take a look at the Block Development Offices of Sahar Block, Bhojpur District, Bihar, one of the epicentres of the Naxalite movement in India in the 1980s and 1990s, or Lapong Block, Jharkhand, where Naxalites of a different stripe have gained ground only in the past few years. Government – offices, files, the police, metalled roads, district engineers, teachers and other public servants – is barely present). And into the gap, of course, providing some form of security, come various Naxalite groups, and with them in central Bihar the *senas* (private armies) of the Forward Caste landlords. (These are mirrored now in Chhattisgarh by *Salwa Judum.*)

It is still the case that many more people are exiting the eastern states in search of work in the richer western states than are actively involved in India's extreme Left movements. It is perhaps also the case, as Joan Robinson once said, that 'the only thing worse than being exploited by capital is not being exploited at all' (or by semi-feudal landlords, we might add). The tragedy of large parts of eastern India, to repeat, is that capital is too often absent. All that said, it would be foolish to ignore the recent rapid growth and diffusion of what increasingly is an organized Maoist presence in eastern India. India is not Nepal. It has not laboured recently under monarchical rule, and it is continuing to provide very significant rates of economic growth at the national level. But then again, eastern India is not 'India', and these aggregate statistics count for rather little in its constituent states. Where the state is largely absent, parts of eastern India resemble Nepal more closely than many politicians in New Delhi would care to admit.[18]

Conclusion

This paper has not sought to argue that India is about to split up, or that a strong central state cannot yet impose its will on the 170 (of 602) districts of India that are reported as having a Naxalite presence (or infestation as it sometimes called).[19] Transport connections between eastern India and the rest of the country have been improving since c.2005 and can be quickly improved much more.[20] Nor does this essay dispute the claim that federalism in India has worked strongly to support the economic reform agenda that has taken hold in New Delhi and most western and southern states. Instead, I have tried to advance the following points. First, if we want to draw up a balance sheet linking India's federalism to its developmental ambitions it might be necessary to draw back a little from the positive assessment made by Rob Jenkins. If India's federal system has helped produce competition states in the likes of Gujarat, Maharashtra and Tamil Nadu, and has in the process become more 'horizontal' (in Aseema Sinha's terms), it has also helped some eastern states to ignore these same logics in favour of domestic political considerations that are less pro-growth. Second, one consequence of the political settlement that exists in parts of eastern India has been widespread and deepening state failure, sometimes to the point of near absence. This in turn is linked to the production of a Maoist movement that *can* be challenged by the state, but which will not *easily* be challenged. Here again we see the legacies of state absence as geographical absence, of remoteness and a lack of infrastructure and security. Lastly, in reinforcement of this point, it is helpful to recognise the materiality of actually existing federalisms. Rob Jenkins' arguments about provincial Darwinism highlight one role of what we can call 'relational space': of key agents in one locality or jurisdiction acting in regard to the actions of agents elsewhere. To this we need to add a stronger sense of the ways in which abstract space in India is being produced alongside the countermanding spaces of absent infrastructures, uneven development, cultural and religious nationalisms, and in the limit, liberation zones and other areas of contested rule. It is in relation to these interlocking accounts of the production of space, place and politics that we can hope to make better sense of federalism's role in the reinvention of India.

Notes

1. An important exception is Vanaik (1990).
2. On the former, see Ahluwalia (2000) and Sachs et al. (2002); on the latter, see Jenkins (2003).
3. On Kashmir, see Bose (2003) and Chandhoke (2005); on the north-east, see Baruah (2005).
4. Joel Migdal (2001) usefully describes the translation problems that must arise between the commanding heights of government and its field offices and trenches, or those sites of rule dominated in India by Block Development staff, forest guards and police constables. On the wider question of elite versus vernacular understandings of the 'state idea', see Kaviraj (1991).
5. Important parallel arguments have been made by Lawrence Saez and Aseema Sinha, among others (see also Schneider 2004), but they are not discussed in detail here. Saez (2002) contends that economic liberalization has provoked a more effective decentralization of policymaking powers in India than any number of institutional changes, including those – like the Inter-State Council – prefigured by the Report of the Sarkaria Commission on Centre–state Relations (1988), or those that might yet emanate from the Commission on Centre–state Relations set up in April 2007 under the leadership of (retired) Justice Madan Mohan Punchhi. A system of 'cooperative federalism' in which state finances were largely determined by the Centre has mutated into one of 'inter-jurisdictional competition' in which states attract funds from private investors on the basis of market-friendly policies. Aseema Sinha (2004b, 2005), for her part, has paid more attention to the re-emergence of 'strong federalism' after a long period in which the relative powers of the Centre were greatly enhanced. She agrees with Jenkins and Saez that India's states are now competing with each other for far more than centrally determined resources (what she calls vertical competition); key today is horizontal competition for 'resources from a greater variety of actors' (2004b: 26). Significantly, however, Sinha shows how 'Leading states in the reform process (Gujarat and Maharashtra, for example) have utilized their previous linkages and institutional skills developed under the old regime to leverage crucial advantages in the new policy regime' (ibid.: 27). Her work is distinguished by its close attention to questions of *how* political claims are made, and *how* political coalitions are built up and reshaped – and the path dependencies of both. Finally, it is worth noting that a Supreme Court ruling in 1994 insisted on the applicability of judicial review to proclamations of President's Rule under Article 356 – a clear example of structural changes in Centre–state relations taking place outside the 'reform route' so strongly emphasized by Saez: on this, see Rudolph and Rudolph (2001b).

6 On the regionalisation of Indian politics, see Weiner (1999).
7 The total number of telephones in India in 2004/5 was about 125 million, and was targeted to reach 250 million (or about one quarter of the population) by the end of 2007 (Government of India 2006a: 182–3. The same source (p. 195) notes that 68.9 per cent of all airline flights in April–December 2005 were with private carriers.
8 Internet usage in India in 2007 was reported as being 3.7 per cent of the population, up by 620 per cent since 2000. In China, the percentage of the population using the web in 2007 was reported as 12.3 per cent and in Pakistan as 7.2 per cent (data from www.internetworldstats.com/stats3.htm). A recent World Bank report also draws attention to the miserable state of piped water supply in Indian cities. Whereas the residents of Jakarta, Dakar, Colombo, Kuala Lumpur and Durban can expect 24 hours of piped water supply each day, the figure for Chennai is quoted as 1.5 hours per day in 2005–6 (as compared to 10–15 hours per day in the early 1980s), while in Udaipur and Bangalore the supply runs for 2.5 hours, in Delhi for 4 hours and in Mumbai for 5 hours (World Bank 2006: 13–14). Although the report fails to make this clear, the figures cited here presumably refer to the average or median urban citizen.
9 I discount here the fact that Lalu Yadav visited Singapore in 1995 to advertise the merits of Bihar, or that Mulalyam Singh Yadav and Mayawati in UP have each tried on occasions to present their state as pro-prosperity as well as pro-equality. I am referring to a concerted agenda for economic reform that would be distinguished, at a minimum, by state provision of key public goods (water, electricity, roads, security) and significant investments in institutions and policy regimes that would aim to secure high levels of inward investment.
10 Lalu Yadav made frequent references to '*bhurabal saf koro*' when he came to power in 1990. He later explained that he meant this to refer only to Bihar's governing 'deadwood', but the caste references were obvious and plainly intended. It is perhaps unnecessary to add that the politics of the Backward Classes in Bihar have been dominated by the 'creamy layers' of the Other Backward Castes; only recently have different leaders from within this group found it necessary to build more vertical coalitions that incorporate Scheduled Caste communities like the Paswans (much less so the Musahars). In UP politics, in contrast, the Bahujan Samaj Party of Kanshi Ram and Mayawati was formed chiefly to advance the interests of *Dalits*; the primary vehicle for OBC communities has been the Samajwadi Party under the leadership of Mulayam Singh Yadav. Following the 2007 State Assembly Elections, Mayawati was returned as UP's Chief Minister for a third time, replacing Yadav.
11 On the Modi regime's extraordinary attention to place-making in the wake of the earthquake that hit Kachchh in 2001, see Simpson and Corbridge (2006). On militant Hinduism and the politics of space more generally, see Krishna (1997) and Corbridge (2002).
12 There is no space here to comment on the rivalries between different extreme-Left groups, or on an emerging literature that discusses the development of what might be called quasi- or shadow-Naxalite groups, often featuring local youth in a bid for state funds. For more, see Bhatia (2004), Shah (2006) and Kunnath (2006).
13 Government of India 2007: 110, Table 10.4. The table does not explain why per capita net state domestic product in Bihar drops from Rs.4,474 in 1990/1 to Rs.3,338 in 1996/7, before climbing slowly to Rs.3,773 in 2004/5 (provisional). A logical assumption is that this reflects the loss of Jharkhand, for which corresponding figures are backdated only to Rs.5,647 in 1996/7.
14 These differences in performance were evident long before the reforms of 1991/93, of course. As ever, there is a danger of losing track of some important continuities in India's growth trajectories (on this, see Rao et al. 1999; also Corbridge and Harriss, 2000; Kohli 2006; and Kochar et al. 2006). The point I wish to make here has to with the politics of these trajectories, and the fact that economic liberalization has not led to greater regional convergence in per capita net state domestic product.

15 'Who will invest in Bihar? If they invest in Bihar, they will be finished!' Laloo Yadav, in response to Nitish Kumar's initiative to attract businesses to Bihar (according to the entry for Lalu Prasad Yadav on Wikipedia).
16 Much will also depend on how the 'agrarian crisis' deepens in eastern India, as elsewhere. Atul Kohli is surely right to maintain that almost regardless of how that crisis plays out, the scale of the gaps that are now being opened up between urban and rural India, as between west and east India, is already so great that we must anticipate an extraordinary movement of people to India's swelling towns and big cities over the next 20–30 years. In this sense, at least, India in the late 2000s was just on the cusp of its 'great transformation'. (Comment made at LSE-Columbia conference, September 2007. I am also grateful to Atul for comments on an earlier draft of this paper).
17 Again discounting Kashmir and the north-eastern states, the total population of which in 2001 ran to almost 50 million people.
18 It is worth remembering too that the rise to power of an organized Maoist movement in Nepal, certainly outside Kathmandu (and Manjushree Thapa [2005] urges us to *Forget Kathmandu* in her beautifully written book of that title), happened rather quickly – in important respects between 1996 and 2006, during the time of the armed uprising. The merging of the Maoist Communist Centre of India and People's War in September 2004 as the Communist Party of India (Maoist) drew inspiration from the Communist Party of Nepal (Maoist), itself founded in 1994 by Pushap Kamal Dahal, better known as Prachanda.
19 Figure quoted in *The Economist*, 17 August 2006, 'India's Naxalites: a spectre haunting India'. A map produced as part of the same article refers to 165 'conflict-affected districts'.
20 To put it another way, 'bad geography' can be tempered by good or better institutions and public policy, as Dani Rodrik and others have maintained more broadly, notably in debate with Jeffrey Sachs and his colleagues (Rodrik et al. 2004; Sachs et al. 2001). It is surely unwise, however, to assume that past and present geographies (natural or constructed) have no bearing on the shape of present institutions and policies.

6 Patterns of wealth disparities in India
1991–2002[1]

Arjun Jayadev, Sripad Motiram and Vamsi Vakulabharanam

Introduction

Researchers writing on Indian growth and distribution have tended almost exclusively to study the evolution of consumption. Given the considerable theoretical and empirical advances in analyzing consumption surveys, the intense controversy surrounding the methodology of collecting survey data and the relevance of the findings for the political validation of reforms, this is completely understandable. In maintaining an exclusive focus on consumption and income however, they have by and large overlooked an important aspect in which changes in the economy appear to have manifested themselves – in the growth and distribution of asset holdings across households, regions and groups.[2] This remains the case despite the availability of relatively reliable and sophisticated national level wealth data. Wealth ownership may be correlated with income/consumption, but is a conceptually distinct and valid (if incomplete) measure of welfare. Wealth is ultimately the source of non-wage income and can be critical to the accumulation of advantages and for human welfare, whether in terms of capabilities, status, dignity or indeed through much more direct political influence.[3] Moreover, some economic reform measures in India have had their effects primarily on altering the relative value of assets and therefore on household wealth, a change that may not be reflected in equal proportion in income or consumption trends. A ready example is the fact that increased foreign direct and portfolio investment has resulted in large and rapid capital gains on real estate and financial holdings, a process that has certainly contributed to urban growth in many areas but which may not be adequately reflected in consumption data. Given these kinds of alterations in the value, structure and ownership of household assets, certain questions arise. For example, as India undergoes its great transformation, how are the new dynamics of the economy reflected in the evolution of the country's wealth? What are the observable patterns of wealth accumulation that have plausibly been created by the process of engagement with the global economy? How have patterns of wealth accumulation altered the political economy?

In order to examine these questions more closely, we examine the wealth distribution in India in 1991 and 2002 – years that bracket the first decade of economic reforms. Given the fact that there is virtually no secondary literature on this subject, our account is primarily descriptive in that it assesses average changes across individuals and groups in these two years. Further, it is primarily an examination of inequality for the country as a whole, and does not focus on regional narratives, which may be of great interest. It is also – in the case of some of our hypotheses – a speculative account. We suggest that despite the substantial complexities in the data, it is difficult to observe any convergence – the data are more consistent with growing interpersonal, inter-class and spatial divergence of wealth accumulation during the period. We note certain highlights of this story at the outset. First, the interpersonal wealth distribution was substantially unequal in 1991 and is now more unequal (if only marginally so) in a period where wealth has also grown substantially across most groups.[4] While the interpersonal examination shows the entrenchment of existing inequalities, there are striking class disparities that are observable. Specifically, the data illustrates the rise and consolidation of two important sociological groups in the political, economic and cultural life of India – an urban elite (roughly the Indian middle class/white collar workers/new middle class) and a section of the rural population, primarily the landed and those involved in non-agricultural activities, who are increasingly recognized as dynamic socio-economic groups within the rural sector. The urban sector has certainly seen phenomenal growth but there is little evidence of convergence within the urban sector among classes, again consistent with the idea that inequalities remain entrenched. Urban groups, taken as a whole, have been the largest gainers in the period and have benefited most strongly from the economic reforms while the poor, especially in rural areas, have seen much slower rates of asset accumulation. Although a more nuanced analysis is needed, these developments, we speculate, are consistent with the phenomenon of elite ascendancy or "elite revolt" (Corbridge and Harriss 2000), wherein the notion of elites needs to be expanded to include a rural elite whose political ties and engagement with urban opportunities have stood it in good stead. Finally, we note that there has been a pattern of divergence in wealth outcomes by state and region with the poorer (northern and eastern) states witnessing slower and lower wealth accumulation than the middle and upper income (southern and western) states, reflective of the growing sub-national variation in development paths.

In section 1 we discuss our data and the (considerable) difficulties involved in its use. In section 2 we provide snapshots of and discuss the interpersonal distribution of assets in 1991 and 2002. Section 3 elaborates on the rise of the two elites and the implications of this ascendancy for Indian political economy. It also provides a speculative discussion of the links between patterns of wealth accumulation and political transformations. Section 4 discusses the distinct regional and state-wise patterns. Section 5 concludes.

1 Data

In our paper, we focus on household per-capita net worth and household per-capita assets. The NSS Survey defines total household assets as comprising of

> physical assets like land, buildings, livestock, agricultural machinery and implements, non-farm business equipment, all transport equipment, durable household goods and financial assets like dues receivable on loans advanced

in cash or in kind, shares in companies and cooperative societies, banks, etc., national saving certificates and the like, deposits in companies, banks, post offices and with individuals

(NSS 2005c: 5)

At the outset, however, it is important to provide a caveat to the use of these data and the inherent difficulties faced by researchers. Some of these problems have been summarized in Subramanian and Jayaraj (2006a) and Jayadev et al. (2007a and b), but bear repeating. First, a common feature of wealth distribution is the tendency for large concentrations of wealth at the top end. It has been pointed out (Brandolini et al. 2004) that unless conscious efforts are made to over-sample the very wealthy, wealth concentration tends to be under represented in the sample. This is problematic since a few very large values at the upper tail of the distribution can impact the summary measures significantly. This is an issue that NSS needs to pay particular attention to.

A second problem that has been identified and reiterated in the Indian case by Subramanian and Jayaraj (2006a) is the presence of a general tendency among respondents to under-report their wealth. This problem is compounded further given that this bias tends to increase with wealth, i.e. under-reporting is more at higher wealth levels.

A third problem is incorrect valuation of reported assets, due to the difficulty in obtaining market prices for various kinds of assets. Even if the reported prices are based on recent transactions, they tend to be underplayed and hence are lower than market values. Also, given the absence of explicit wealth-based deflators (Vaidyanathan 1993), to make comparisons among real wealth holdings at different points in time, consumption-based deflators need to be used. If we utilize the only commonly available price deflator, the CPI (rural or urban), real wealth may be biased in 2002/3. Compounding the problem, such estimates may not be able to fully capture rates of change across different income/wealth groups, because we are deflating based on the consumption of relatively poorer groups. Given the impossibility of obtaining appropriate price deflators across asset categories, most of our analysis here refers to yearly distribution of assets.[5]

There are other problems, such as the prevalence of illegitimate but effective ownership (e.g. encroachment of common properties, and *benaami* land ownership), which leads to under-counting of the assets owned by the wealthy. Moreover, as Subramanian and Jayaraj (2006a) and Davies et al. (2006) argue, there is strong evidence to suggest that liabilities are severely underreported in India (by a factor of nearly 3). The fact that the correlation between net worth and total assets is very high (at over 0.995), suggests that this may be the case, and as such, considerations of asset valuation aside, net worth values are probably overstated. Given all these difficulties, we believe that the measures of inequality that we are presenting below underestimate the true extent of wealth inequality in India.

We begin by examining the interpersonal wealth distribution at the per-capita level. Focusing on per-capita instead of household has the advantage of taking household size into account. This approach is not without limitations,[6] but as pointed out by Sierminska and Smeeding (2005: 4), ignoring household size

> implies that households are assumed to have perfect returns to scale in the use of wealth or that access to wealth of one member of the household has no effect on the access of other members, as wealth is a public good within the unit.
>
> Moreover, it is important to treat the individual as the unit of reference, since welfare ultimately resides in individuals and not in households.
>
> (Deaton 1997: 153)

This is not of course to deny that there is some "public good" content to wealth in that all household members benefit from the possession of wealth, e.g. in terms of status. Rather, it is to suggest that ignoring the substantial differences in household size in a developing economy such as India may lead to perverse and misleading results.

II Interpersonal wealth distribution

For most Indians who possess some wealth, asset holdings are concentrated in land and buildings. Table 6.1 shows the proportion of overall per-capita assets disaggregated by the main categories of holdings for rural and urban areas (land, buildings and durables) in both 1991 and 2002. There are important differences according to the sector, with durables accounting for a much larger proportion of the asset holdings of urban, as compared to rural, individuals in both periods. Likewise, land is the primary asset of rural individuals, accounting for nearly half of total per-capita assets for both periods. Other assets (the sum of non-farm equipment, agricultural machinery, transport vehicles, deposits, loans, shares, etc.) constitute only about 10 percent of total per-capita assets.

Table 6.2 provides an indication of the ownership rates (proportion of the population owning an asset) of these assets. Ownership rates for the biggest categories – land

Table 6.1 Major categories of total assets

| | 1991 | | | 2002 | | |
	Overall	Rural	Urban	Overall	Rural	Urban
Land	43.4%	49.4%	24.7%	43.1%	48.6%	26.9%
Buildings	29.7%	29.5%	30.7%	32.8%	32.7%	33.2%
Durables	15.2%	10.4%	29.9%	13.5%	9.8%	24.2%
Others	11.7%	10.7%	14.7%	10.6%	8.9%	15.8%
Total	100%	100%	100%	100%	100%	100%
N	301658	200179	101479	709291	456571	252720

Table 6.2 Ownership rates by asset

	Ownership Rate (1991)	Ownership Rate (2001)
Total	99.88	99.97
Land	86.92	89.61
Buildings	88.21	89.45
Livestock	60.86	49.95
Agricultural Machinery	68.64	64.66
Non-Farm Assets	15.58	20.12
Transport	50.34	58.62
Durables	99.75	99.86
Shares	9.15	7.33
Deposits	23.29	90.48
Loans	2.10	2.38

and buildings – have remained roughly the same. By contrast, there is an increase in ownership of livestock and agricultural machinery and a decrease in ownership of non-farm assets, perhaps reflecting a movement of the rural rich away from agriculture (to non-agriculture) as it becomes relatively less profitable over this period. Several researchers (e.g. Lanjouw and Stern 1998) have pointed to the increasing role of rural non-agricultural activity in raising incomes in rural India and this finding may be seen as some further support for this position. The most striking rise has been in the ownership of deposits, with over 90 percent of the respondents having some deposits in 2002 compared with less than 25 percent in 1991. A puzzling feature of the data is the fact that the ownership rates of shares has actually declined, from 9.15 percent to 7.33 percent of the population, a finding that runs contrary to both the received wisdom and other studies (e.g. SEBI-NCAER 2000 and 2003) which have found that share and debenture ownership in India has expanded considerably. While these studies cannot be used to benchmark the All-India Debt and Investment Survey, this divergence suggests that one should be cautious when drawing conclusions on share ownership and distribution when utilizing either of the surveys.

Turning now to summary measures of inequality, there is a small increase in the degree of an already high level of inequality. The Gini coefficients for total per-capita assets and per-capita net worth (assets less debt) are presented in Table 6.3. The Gini coefficients for per-capita net worth and per-capita assets have seen an increase of about 2 and 1 percentage points, respectively. It should be noted that for reasons stated above, these levels and increases are almost certainly underestimates since the extremely wealthy are not properly sampled.

Table 6.4 provides Gini coefficients for each type of asset. We can see that inequality of these assets has been largely stable. Hence, there is no single asset

Table 6.3 Distributional measures

Distribution	1991 Overall	Rural	Urban	2002 Overall	Rural	Urban
Gini Coefficient (Total Assets)	0.64	0.61	0.70	0.65	0.61	0.69
Gini Coefficient (Net Worth)	0.64	0.61	0.70	0.66	0.62	0.69

Table 6.4 Gini by category

	Gini 1991	Gini 2002
Per-Capita Assets	0.64	0.65
Per-Capita Land	0.73	0.73
Per-Capita Livestock	0.72	0.77
Per-Capita Building	0.71	0.68
Per-Capita Agricultural Machinery	0.93	0.93
Per-Capita Non Farm	0.98	0.97
Per-Capita Durable	0.67	0.64
Per-Capita Transport	0.92	0.93
Per-Capita Deposits	0.93	0.92
Per-Capita Shares	0.99	0.99
Per-Capita Loans and Others	0.99	0.99

(or subset of assets) that is driving the overall pattern of changes in inequality. One point bears mentioning however. As is evident, the ownership of shares and loans (what one might broadly call financial assets and liabilities) is highly concentrated with Gini coefficients in the order of 0.99. This suggests that the tremendous focus given to the health of the stock market and to the movement of corporate assets in the media, as well as to its political importance, reflects the interests of a very narrow constituency. Although there is evidence that there is a larger and more widespread holding of corporate assets, it is still a component of very few portfolios.[7] Even if one were to impute indirect holdings of shares and debentures, the concentration would likely continue to be very high.

Two striking features of the data are the huge disparities in wealth concentration and the relative stability of the wealth shares over the decade. Since we are unable to track individuals or households across time (and thus cannot measure wealth mobility), we examine the shares and cumulative shares by decile for both total per-capita assets and per-capita net worth for both years. Table 6.5 shows that the top 10 percent of individuals possess a little over half of the total wealth (whether measured

Table 6.5 Share of assets and net worth by decile

Wealth Decile	1991 Total Assets Share (%)	1991 Total Assets Cumulative Share (%)	1991 Net Worth Share (%)	1991 Net Worth Cumulative Share (%)	2002 Total Assets Share (%)	2002 Total Assets Cumulative Share (%)	2002 Net Worth Share (%)	2002 Net Worth Cumulative Share (%)
0–10	0.37	0.37	0.22	0.22	0.40	0.40	0.21	0.21
10–20	1.07	1.44	1.00	1.23	1.08	1.48	1.01	1.22
20–30	1.86	3.30	1.80	3.02	1.79	3.26	1.72	2.94
30–40	2.78	6.08	2.72	5.75	2.62	5.88	2.57	5.51
40–50	3.91	9.99	3.87	9.61	3.67	9.56	3.64	9.15
50–60	5.37	15.36	5.34	14.96	5.06	14.62	5.02	14.17
60–70	7.37	22.73	7.35	22.3	7.02	21.63	7.00	21.17
70–80	10.47	33.20	10.47	32.77	10.22	31.85	10.22	31.39
80–90	16.41	49.61	16.44	49.21	16.64	48.49	16.67	48.06
90–100	50.39	100.00	50.79	100.00	51.51	100.00	51.94	100.00

in terms of assets or net worth) in the country, while the bottom 10 percent possess a mere 0.4 percent of the total wealth. The bottom 50 percent of the population own less than 10 percent of the total wealth. The wealthiest have tended to consolidate between the two surveys (the top 10 percent owned 51.94 percent of wealth in 2002 versus 50.79 percent in 1991), while the asset-poor (i.e. the bottom 10 per cent) have only lost their share (0.21 percent in 2002 versus 0.22 percent in 1991).

Table 6.6 performs a similar exercise, by looking at the average wealth holdings by decile of mean per-capita monthly expenditure.[8] The growth rate in asset accumulation is highest in the top decile. By contrast, the growth rate of assets in the bottom decile is the lowest. In other words, there is a stronger picture of divergence in asset holdings as the rich have pulled away from the poor in asset accumulation.

This narrative is further strengthened when one examines the very top end of the wealth distribution. Table 6.7 provides an indication of sharply increased holdings at the very top end of the distribution. The ratio of assets held by the individual at the 95th percentile to those held by the median individual rose from 758 percent to 814 per cent, while the corresponding ratio for net worth rose from 766 percent to 824 per cent. When we examine these figures with the reference point of the individual at the 99th percentile, the ratio rose from 1,851 percent to 1,958 percent for assets and 1,886 percent to 2,012 percent for net worth. It should be noted that the idea of rapidly increasing wealth at the very top end of the income/wealth distribution is broadly in agreement with another examination of the very rich in India (Banerjee and Piketty 2005).

Table 6.6 Average per-capita wealth by expenditure decile

Monthly Per-Capita Expenditure Deciles	1991 Average Per-Capita Assets	1991 Average Per-Capita Net Worth	2002 Average Per-Capita Assets*	2002 Average Per-Capita Net Worth*	Implied Annual Growth Rate	
0–10	8257	8075	8982	8691	0.8%	0.7%
10–20	10197	9965	12151	11814	1.6%	1.6%
20–30	11187	10956	15052	14639	2.7%	2.7%
30–40	13362	13106	17428	16913	2.4%	2.3%
40–50	16116	15817	19859	19272	1.9%	1.8%
50–60	17955	17578	24119	23518	2.7%	2.7%
60–70	22898	22459	29539	28698	2.3%	2.3%
70–80	27536	26982	35011	33938	2.2%	2.1%
80–90	36287	35493	51109	49722	3.2%	3.1%
90–100	76683	75175	111007	107801	3.4%	3.3%

* = deflated values.

Patterns of wealth disparities in India 89

Table 6.7 Increasing concentration of wealth at the upper end of the wealth distribution

Percentile	1991 (as % of median)		2002 (as % of median)	
	Total Assets	Net Worth	Total Assets	Net Worth
90%	479%	482%	515%	522%
95%	758%	766%	814%	824%
99%	1851%	1886%	1958%	2012%

In sum then, the interpersonal distribution of wealth shows only a minor increase in inequality using a summary measure such as the Gini. It is possible and likely that this measure misses interesting divergences at the very top end of the distribution. While examining the overall interpersonal distribution of wealth is a useful exercise in itself, it provides little indication of political and social processes that may be underlying or influenced by these changes. We now turn to an attempt at examining this.

III Sociological character of wealth disparities

Between 1991 and 2002, there has been rapid asset growth in the urban areas and we speculate that there has been a consolidation of an urban and a rural elite, which is reflected in the wealth surveys at these two points in time. Constructing readily agreed-upon measures of classes or other social formations is fraught with various difficulties (Wright [1997] discusses some of these). In the Indian context, these measures can quite legitimately differ along lines of ownership, management, career prospects, income, caste and kinship status, education or other such categories. We wish to consider a division that is indicative of significantly different positions with respect to occupation and resultant opportunities in the age of economic reforms. We are aware that our measure of status will elide some important differences within and among groups, but believe that these categorizations are nevertheless valid and useful to understand broad trends.[9]

We derive the status variable by using the NCO classification of 1968 (available for both the 1991 and 2002 surveys) as well as details on landholdings and the household type (whether self-employed or working for others) to categorize urban and rural households. We separate rural and urban areas as we believe that the wealth accumulation and income generation dynamics vary significantly between the two. We have seven categories: urban elites, urban lower service workers, urban manual workers, rural elites, rural middle groups, rural workers and rural non-agricultural groups. The NCO category for each household is the principal occupation (occupation of the primary earning member) of the household. Those occupied in white-collar employment (professional, managerial, technical and administrative occupations in urban areas, NCO first digit: 0–2) are classified as elites. Those occupied in sales and clerical occupations (NCO first digit: 3–4) are classified as lower service workers. Those working in low-level, typically informal service occupations (e.g. hotels and households, urban agriculture, factories, construction and other manual occupations) are the urban manual workers (NCO first digit: 5–9).

The rural occupations are subdivided into agricultural and non-agricultural occupations. People involved in agricultural occupations are further classified according to the landholdings they possess. Those who possess more than 10 acres of land are classified as rural upper class or rural elite. Those between 2 and 10 acres are classified as rural middle class. Those with less than 2 acres are combined with the landless workers and classified as rural working people. As in International Crops Research Institute for the Semi-Arid-Tropics (ICRISAT) studies, a factor of 1.98 is used to convert wetland into its equivalent dry land. The choice of cut-offs for this categorization is admittedly arbitrary and by international standards 10 acres might seem too low to qualify for membership to rural upper classes. However, an examination of the data shows that only 10 percent of the rural population claim to own greater than 8.8 acres, which provides some legitimacy for the notion that 10 acres of land puts the owner in a relatively privileged category. Of the non-agricultural population, those that are self-employed (working in non-agricultural occupations) as well as any residual population are considered part of the rural "others." The justification for this is that some people working for the government and other established occupations and those that are self-employed cannot be easily classified as possessing the characteristics of any one of the above mentioned categories. Finally, those households that do not report their occupation are dropped.

Before presenting our comparative results across these categories, it is useful to examine the sociological composition of our two elite categories if only to buttress our prior about these groups. The first – the urban elite – may be said to correspond broadly to the social formation that has been described in accounts of middle class resurgence and elite ascendancy (Corbridge and Harriss 2000). The rural elite group as a whole is led by OBCs and forward caste Hindus. Table 6.8 summarizes the status variables by religion and caste. Independent analyses provide corroboration for the upper-caste dominance of the urban elite. Sheth (1999) finds in a survey from 1996 very similar numbers as our own. Table 6.9 reproduces his findings.

There is by now a voluminous and rich literature describing the 'new' urban middle class in India. This work has examined the manner in which this social formation has shaped and in turn been shaped by emergent processes such as liberalization, cultural nationalism and democratic mobilization (Varma 1998; Corbridge and Harriss 2000; Sridharan 2004a; Fernandes 2006; Fernandes and Heller 2006). Many of these researchers catalog a significant overlap between upwardly mobile middle class support for liberalization (a fact that is often articulated through the discourse of increased opportunities for wealth accumulation), new forms of urban activism and of course an inclination towards Hindutva, even if all these relationships are complexly constituted. Our analysis cannot add much to these accounts, except perhaps to underscore how much the urban middle class is – to borrow Fernandes' phrase – the "representative citizens" of the liberalized Indian economy.

Table 6.10 provides some insights into the dynamics of wealth accumulation across status categories. Three points bear noting. First, both urban and rural elite are considerably wealthier than the other groups. Second, urban groups as a whole

Table 6.8 Sociological breakdown of status variables

	Urban Elite	Urban Middle	Urban Manual	Rural Elite	Rural Middle	Rural Lower	Rural Non-Agricultural
FC	46.77	40.50	23.72	37.99	25.18	11.86	28.63
OBC	29.74	32.83	39.32	44.78	44.74	40.91	39.41
Others	13.91	14.00	13.43	6.56	6.96	8.52	9.09
SC	7.56	10.38	20.42	4.48	11.45	28.46	17.12
ST	2.01	2.29	3.10	6.19	11.68	10.25	5.76
Buddhist	0.36	0.55	0.84	0.30	0.36	0.63	0.60
Christian	3.64	1.94	2.50	0.40	1.70	2.13	3.16
Hindu	78.71	76.67	75.45	89.73	88.04	82.88	82.00
Jain	1.25	1.52	0.20	0.27	0.03	0.04	0.15
Muslim	13.05	17.54	19.42	4.76	7.89	12.63	11.81
Other	0.02	0.25	0.09	0.12	0.53	0.26	0.29
Parsee	0.09	0.00	0.00	0.00	0.00	0.00	0.00
Sikh	2.88	1.53	1.49	4.41	1.45	1.42	1.99

Table 6.9 Sociological breakdown of white collar employment (from Sheth 1999)

Social Group	Proportion of Social Group in Sample	Occupation in White Collar Employment
Upper Castes	24.8%	53.3%
Backward Castes	39.3%	26.6%
SC	19.7%	9.2%
ST	9.7%	2.4%
Muslims	6.5%	7.5%

have seen more rapid growth in asset accumulation. If one looks at mean values, the two elite categories continue to dominate in absolute terms, but the growth rates of asset ownership tell a more complex story. In urban areas, there is very little difference in the growth rates of these three groups, which is perhaps more indicative of the low levels of initial wealth than large welfare increases. Note for example that the wealth of the urban manual group in 2002 was less than the same for the urban elite in 1991. In rural areas, the rural elite and the rural non-agricultural groups have seen their wealth grow most rapidly, consistent with the notion of a divergence in that sector. Third, if one examines medians as a different, perhaps more robust measure of central tendency for wealth (which, as we mentioned above, is highly unequally distributed), the divergence between the elites and the rest in both the

Table 6.10 Mean and median wealth breakdown by status category

Status Category	Mean 1991	Mean 2002	Ratio 2002 to 1991	Median 1991	Median 2002	Ratio 2002 to 1991
Urban Elite	65397	186328	2.85	32149	91010	2.83
Urban Middle	31477	91943	2.92	17075	45692	2.68
Urban Manual	18612	53232	2.86	9501	25120	2.64
Rural Elite	64727	190512	2.94	51328	147529	2.87
Rural Middle	30529	75136	2.46	23775	58359	2.45
Rural Lower	9807	25118	2.56	6726	16567	2.46
Rural Non Agricultural	21583	66277	3.07	13893	35924	2.59
Urban Total	30505	92908	3.05	14363	36672	2.55
Rural Total	20352	53501	2.63	12599	26039	2.07

urban and rural sectors is more evident. As such, although the interpersonal wealth distribution does not show considerable divergence of outcomes, a class-analytic perspective suggests a potential narrative about the underlying dynamics of wealth distribution and the divergence between elite groups and others.

Just as much as the distinction within the urban, the differentiation within the rural sector is worth elaborating on. Our finding of a striking divergence in outcomes within the rural sector for the rural elite and the rural non-agricultural sector vis-à-vis others has been corroborated by other sources. Consumption surveys show that the top quintile of the rural sector has seen its income expand substantially with the rural rich seeing their per-capita consumption increase considerably since 1989/90, while there was much slower growth in the lower end of the distribution (see Vakulabharanam and Motiram [2007] for a *précis* of this argument).

The growing wealth in these pockets of the rural sector has also been remarked upon in a recent National Council for Applied Economic Research (NCAER) (2006) report. A prominent feature of this report is the identification of rural elites, who have pulled far away from the rest of the rural population in terms of wealth and aspirations.[10] It is worth quoting Srivatsava (2006) on the reasons for this:

> Good monsoons and rising productivity have fattened farmer incomes, while the rapid increase in rural land prices due to spreading urbanization has brought windfall gains. Food processing and backward linkages established by many large multinationals and Indian companies, as well as access to good private education that has allowed people to work in the rapidly growing services sector (tourism, hospitality, banking, information technology, retail and business outsourcing) and send money back home, have also played an important role ... According to NCAER, more and more affluent farmers are investing in the education of their children so that they can find employment opportunities, which are readily available now. Just as the state of Kerala has benefited immensely from remittances from people who have sought work in the Middle East, children from rural areas migrating to urban employment opportunities are contributing to the welfare of their family's back home.

These processes have been identified earlier by Balagopal (1987) in his description of the rising 'provincial propertied class' in Andhra Pradesh. Banaji (1994) has elaborated on this and suggested that this class exists elsewhere too. These groups, which were early beneficiaries of the green revolution, he argues, have found ways to diversify into the urban sector. This is true at the household level, wherein migration of some members of the household happens to urban areas. This also happens for the class as a whole wherein there are close interlinkages between those members who migrate to urban areas and invest their surplus capital in urban ventures (e.g. cinema halls, real estate, small-scale IT firms). Similar arguments have been made by Sharma and Poleman (1993) and Jodhka (2006) (for Punjab). The findings remarked upon earlier, viz. relative decline in importance of livestock in wealth, and the increase in the importance of liquid deposit holdings may perhaps be a reflection of this process, as farmers diversify into non-agricultural activities.

While there is no rigorous way of identifying rural elites from the NSS survey as commensurate with the agrarian middle class or new agrarian capitalists, as they have variously been referred to, there are certainly compelling overlaps. The top end of the rural elite is substantially different from the rest of the group, in terms of social composition. The top 10 percent of the rural elite are predominantly "others" and are dominated by forward castes (and wealthy Sikhs in the north). Geographically, they are concentrated in Punjab, Haryana, UP and Maharashtra, not coincidentally states which benefited most from the Green Revolution.

The political and economic ties of this group have been subject to some research. As the rural elite becomes wealthier and more diversified, its political power heightens. Baru (2000) for example has written about the contestation between a regional capitalist class and a more established urban capitalist class over new markets. Also the regional capitalist class has utilized regional politics to project its interests into further domains.[11]

The fact that the urban white-collar elites and some rural elites are primarily the major gainers in terms of asset accumulation in this period helps to clarify the nature of labor market segmentation and exclusion in the modern Indian economy. Access to stable white collar employment is limited and is reflected in the small proportion of the sample involved in such activity (about 5 percent). Similarly, the fast-growing section among the rural elite is also small and inaccessible, perpetuated through kinship networks and corresponding to the upper end of the rural elite wealth distribution. The extent to and manner in which these groups accommodate entry in the years to come will therefore have significant political implications. The growing debate on reservations in the private sector for example will center on the fact that despite the promise of equality, access to the most dynamic sector is limited for lower castes. Similarly, debates on the manner in which the state will promote the rural sector will consider the political importance of the successful rural elite.[12]

While noting the fact that liberalization and economic development may be creating new patterns of inequality in wealth holdings across sociological groupings, we have had little to say about the relationship between caste and religious politics and wealth disparities. This is largely due to the fact that our data allow for a useful break up on caste and religious lines only for 2002. Yet, these processes are not unlinked and merit some attention, albeit speculative.

First, despite the "second democratic upsurge" of the 1990s whereby traditionally marginalized political groups began to make greater inroads into political space (Yadav 2000), entry into the new economy – perhaps the single most important source of the rapid growth in personal wealth that is evident in urban India – remains fairly limited for backward castes. Upadhyay (2007) argues that the IT industry, which is the *sine qua non* of the new economy displays a remarkable social homogeneity – it is "largely urban, middle class, and high or middle caste." Backward castes remain excluded by a variety of means, including educational stratification and the pervasive influence of networks. One could possibly make a similar argument for other "elite" service industries like finance, private banking, etc.

Madheswaran and Attewell (2007) argue that discrimination alone can account for a large proportion of wage differences in the salaried urban labor market, with unequal access to jobs being considerably more relevant than wage discrimination to understand this division. In an overview paper in the *Economic and Political Weekly* on the differential experiences of *Dalits* and Non-*Dalits* in the urban labor market, Thorat and Newman (2007: 4124) conclude that the "problem of discrimination remains a serious one – even at the very top of the human capital hierarchy." They cast some doubt on whether the natural operation of the market will be sufficient to correct this inequity and inefficiency in labor allocation. The natural extension for the politics of Mandal has therefore been the extension of a demand for reservations into the private sector and elite educational institutions of the country (the IITs and IIMs). These remain the conduits of entry into the new economy and the obvious disparities between those who have access to these networks and those who do not, will only serve to intensify these demands.

Second, the links between Hindutva and wealth accumulation are much less self-evident. When in 2004, after its ill-fated 'India Shining' campaign, the BJP ceded power to a coalition involving the Left parties, perhaps for the first time, the fall in the value of the stock market was invoked as a barometer of the feelings of the country.[13] As such, the link between the beneficiaries of India's pattern of growth and their political affiliations was evident. Four years on, the continued pattern of growth with perhaps even more rapid increases in wealth under a different government has disturbed this strong identification. As such, interesting new patterns of political support are being drawn. For example, in its most important state-level electoral success in recent times, the BJP's victory in Karnataka was built on varied associational ties with the rural hinterland, with newly rich commodity producers and vastly enriched urban landed elites. The Congress by contrast emerged as the choice favored by urban middle classes in its display of its "pro-corporate, pro-metropolis alliances" (Vasavi 2008). Such new patterns of politics are almost certain to develop through the country and as such will determine the manner in which Hindutva and the right-wing agenda come to be shaped.

IV Sub-national variations

There is a large and growing literature that has considered the political economy of the liberalization experience at the sub-national level.[14] Sinha (2005), one of the more recent examples, makes a compelling case for example that the Indian development experience is one best understood as animated by different sub-national polities and that the overall experience of liberalization should be understood as effected and shaped by "diverse regional industrial orders." The decentralized nature of growth and competition of states is certainly a phenomenon of the 1990s, in which states began to adjust to the opportunities provided by liberalization and the freeing of private capital. As Rudolph and Rudolph (2001a) have noted in their examination of Chandrababu Naidu, states have found greater autonomy in setting their development agendas under the new opportunities and frameworks provided by a more market-oriented economy. These opportunities are unevenly available and accessed. Purfeld (2006) for example shows that capital allocation continues to go primarily to the richer states, with the five richest states receiving over half the capital flows within the country. Foreign direct investment is similarly concentrated. These imbalances have critical importance for growth of course, but also for the accumulation of assets.

Table 6.11 depicts growth rates by an often-used classification of the 14 major states as "poor" (Bihar, Orissa, Uttar Pradesh, Madhya Pradesh and Rajasthan), "middle-income" (Andhra Pradesh, Kerala, Karnataka and West Bengal) and "rich" (Tamil Nadu, Haryana, Gujarat, Punjab and Maharashtra). The numbers tell a stark story. The middle-income states such as Karnataka, Andhra Pradesh and Kerala, with their phenomenal urban growth, seem to have witnessed impressive accumulation of household assets, although this process needs to be understood more clearly through further disaggregated analysis. These states, together with the middle-income and rich states, are experiencing much faster asset-growth rates than the poor states. While we do not undertake any formal tests of divergence because of the fact that we do not have an adequate time series, it is useful to note that the finding is roughly in keeping with the substantial literature on divergence among states that has been amassed in recent years (Rao et al. 1999; Sachs et al. 2002; Aghion et al. 2005; Purfeld 2006; Kochar et al. 2006). This finding may perhaps reflect greater incentives and ability to save and invest and consequently more rapid accumulation in the middle- and high-income states.

It is interesting to note the distinct regional nodes of growth. For example, growth in asset holdings has been fastest in the urban areas of the middle-income states. These regions include dynamic urban centers such as Hyderabad and Bangalore, which have been important foci for international and national capital (as indeed has West Bengal, another state in the category). At the other end, asset growth has been slowest in the poor states, both in urban and rural areas, despite starting at average levels of wealth around the same as middle-income states.

Another often-used categorization is geography. Grouping and examining states by the geographical categorization of North, South, East and West points to a significant if not unexpected divergence. The southern and western states have seen faster asset growth than the other states, and are now significantly wealthier on average (Table 6.12). This is in keeping with the findings from other studies on the relative strength of the south and the west in their experience with liberalization and globalization.

A more thorough analysis of these sub-national changes may address the relationship between the rise of the regional elites and the manner in which asset ownership has grown within the corresponding regions. It might also consider more closely the nature of exclusion from wealth accumulation within regions of low and high growth and the economic changes and political movements that have led to these outcomes. Such analyses require much closer examination and are at this juncture beyond the purview of this paper. We speculate, however, that the fragmented and uneven nature of asset growth by region and by state, indeed within states, will continue to generate various pressures on the state for redress. Thus for example, in Bihar, we witness Nitish Kumar's attempt to promote Bihar's desirability as a location for investment perhaps in order to "catch up" with other states; in Andhra Pradesh, we observe strong protests around the preferential treatment of

Table 6.11 Mean of assets by state income categorization

	Mean 1991	Mean 2002	Ratio	Rural Mean 1991	Rural Mean 2002	Ratio	Urban Mean 1991	Urban Mean 2002	Ratio
Poor States	21346	52295	2.4	20290	47340	2.3	26145	73774	2.8
Middle Income States	19218	59577	3.1	17034	46696	2.7	25673	96392	3.8
Rich States	29964	90515	3.0	28367	85131	3.0	33318	101889	3.1

Table 6.12 Mean of assets by regional categorization

Region	Mean Wealth 1991	Mean Wealth 2002	Difference	Ratio
East	12973	36643	23670	2.8
North	24804	61920	37116	2.4
South	20969	65772	44803	3.1
West	28439	81732	53293	2.8

coastal Andhra Pradesh in irrigation projects, in Karnataka we see the voting out of S. M. Krishna's perceived Bangalore-centric government; in West Bengal, a confrontation between the urban middle class and the agricultural populace, played out through pressures on the state over development projects, and so on. Perhaps, most critically, a "red corridor" where Naxalite activity is reported is often linked to disparities in wealth outcomes. As the process of development continues to move away from direction or guidance by the center, these pressures on the states and regions will become more insistent.

V Conclusion

In anecdotal accounts and popular imagination, a striking feature of Indian growth over the last 15 years has been the opportunity for the large-scale accumulation of assets. Liberalization and engagement with the global economy have unleashed the potential for the hitherto unimaginable accumulation of wealth. What our analysis shows is how unequally this prosperity has been shared. The liberalization period reflects a trend of consolidation of already concentrated wealth among the wealthy who continue to possess asset levels of orders of magnitude much higher than other groups. As such, this study throws independent light on the process of growth and distribution.

Other features from our examination stand out. Perhaps most importantly from the point of view of understanding the political and economic formations of the post liberalization period, the asset data shows the strengthening of what we have termed the urban and rural elites. Spatial divergence is also evident with winners and losers forming distinct regional/geographical blocs.

The overall picture that emerges can be described (for want of a better term) as the entrenchment of multiple Indias, with vastly different expectations, opportunities, patterns of consumption, sources of wealth and levels of welfare among regions, groups and individuals. Urban middle classes form one such India that has consistently diverged away from the urban poor over the last 15 years. Similarly, rural elites (especially the upper brackets of these) have managed to consolidate their position relative to the rest of the population. That this is a concern is evident from the contours of current political debate (the renewal of the Naxalite movement, the question of reservations in the private sector, the question of agrarian welfare, the rhetoric of inclusive growth and so on). The last 15 years has seen the

Patterns of wealth disparities in India 99

unshackling of market forces, which has brought with it vast opportunity as well as deep and unsettling levels of disparity in welfare for India's citizens, demonstrated in our analysis of asset ownership. By all accounts and indications, these trends only threaten to intensify in the coming decades.

Notes

1 For their valuable comments, we would like to thank Dilip Mookherjee, Sanjay Reddy and other participants at the conference. The usual caveat applies.
2 Recent exceptions are Subramaniam and Jayaraj (2006a and b) and Jayadev et al. (2007a and b).
3 The Karnataka state elections of 2008, which saw the BJP come into power for the first time, is instructive in this case. These polls were distinguished from previous ones by a large number of newly wealthy real estate developers and mining magnates standing for election with enormous wealth derived from the gains in land valuation in the state and in the appreciation of commodities. For example, *The Hindu* (2008) reported that: "a realtor and first-time candidate of the Congress in Bommanahalli, has assets of over Rs. 180 crore. M. 'Layout' Krishnappa, Congress nominee from Vijaynagar, has assets worth over Rs. 94 crore. The BJP candidate in Bommanahalli, G. Prasad Reddy, has assets valued at over Rs. 313 crore, and Anil Lad, a mine owner who is contesting on Congress ticket from Bellary city, is worth over Rs. 147 crore."
4 Of course, the notion of what constitutes a high level of inequality in wealth is something that needs qualification. It is certainly true that within the country there are vast disparities in the possession of wealth. Comparing across countries however, the Indian wealth distribution, like the income distribution, appears to display low-to-middling levels of inequality. As far as we are aware, there is only one attempt (Davies et al. 2006) to compare household wealth inequality across countries, according to which Indian household wealth inequality is greater than the same for countries like China, Japan, South Korea and Bangladesh, but considerably lower than the same for countries like Brazil, Mexico, Indonesia, Argentina, Turkey, Thailand and the US.
5 In a previous paper (Jayadev et al. 2007a), we look at actual means and medians using the CPI deflator and find that there have been increases in wealth across virtually all axes, and that the interpersonal wealth distribution has become somewhat more unequal. Regional and other group-wise indicators show sharp divergences. Nevertheless, the problem with our estimates in that paper is unsolved.
6 Heterogeneity within the household is ignored. For instance, adults and children are treated as equivalent. Economies of scale within the household are inadequately captured and might lead to underestimation of the welfare of larger households (Sierminska and Smeeding 2005). The per-capita approach can be thought of as using the simplest possible equivalence scale. Unfortunately the literature on wealth inequality does not provide better equivalence scales that can be used in the Indian context.
7 The Society for Capital Market Research and Development carried out three surveys of household investors from 1990 to 1997, showing an increase in the total number of share owners from about 10 to 20 million over the period (or about 1–2 percent of the population). In another survey (SEBI-NCAER 2000 and 2003) the proportion of all households in India who invest in the stock market was about 7.5 percent, with about 15 percent in urban areas and 4 percent in non-urban areas investing in shares. The percentage of the population that invested in mutual funds was higher, at about 10 percent of all households.
8 These data are also available in the wealth surveys.
9 While a longitudinal comparison cannot be made among religious and detailed caste groups because of the unavailability of data for the 1991 survey, the picture of stark

and continuing disparities among these groups is evident in examining the 2002 data, for which these groups are categorized. These data point to a strong social basis for economic exclusion and perpetuation of poverty among the asset poor communities such as Scheduled Castes and Tribes, Muslims, and the uneducated. See Jayadev et al. (2007a) for details.
10 The report finds that the rural rich are 1,000 times more likely than rural poor to own a motorbike, 100 times more likely to own a color television and 25 times more likely to own a pressure cooker.
11 This is perhaps most strongly the case in Andhra Pradesh, where the rise of Telugu Desam Party is closely tied to the emergence of the provincial propertied classes that have been pushing for greater visibility and strength at the national level. There are also other, less stark cases, of an intertwining between regional party and provincial propertied classes such as the Akali Dal in Punjab.
12 One blatant case wherein the state takes care of its rural elites happened in the state of Andhra Pradesh. While the regions of Telangana and Rayalaseema have been demanding higher investments in irrigation vociferously, the region of coastal Andhra (one of the beneficiaries of green revolution), which is already high on water resources, got a huge project called the Polavaram project. In a general anti-agrarian sentiment that has prevailed in this state, the granting of this project happened primarily through the lobbying of the rural elites and the preferential treatment of the state.
13 For an insightful analysis of this election outcome, including its effect on the stock market, see the op-ed piece by P. Chatterjee (2004a) in the *Telegraph*.
14 Thus for example Sachs et al. (2002), Rudolph and Rudolph (2001a), Ahluwalia (2002) etc. examine the different effects of the state from the move towards market orientation and the actions of the state polity.

7 Political economy of agrarian distress in India since the 1990s[1]

*Vamsi Vakulabharanam
and Sripad Motiram*

Introduction

Several studies have pointed out that Indian agriculture has performed poorly since the 1990s, especially after 1994–5 (e.g. Dev 2004; Reddy 2006; Vaidyanathan 2006; Radhakrishna et al., 2007). This claim is made along two axes. First, growth in agriculture after 1990 has declined relative to the 1980s (Government of India 2007). Second, small cultivators have witnessed a reduction in their welfare.[2] We discuss welfare declines below, but one manifestation of this is the increase in farmer suicide rate in some regions of the country, for example in Telangana and Vidarbha.[3] The economics literature that has attempted to explain these outcomes is sharply polarized. One group (Gulati and Kelley 1999; Gulati and Narayanan 2003) has held the slow pace of agricultural liberalization responsible, and has advocated an increased role for markets. The other group (Sen 2003; Patnaik 2003) blames the withdrawal of state support of agriculture and the integration of agriculture into global markets, and advocates an increased role for the state. While drawing significantly on the latter strand, our paper offers an explanation based on long-term structural changes, changes in policy framework, and a realignment of classes in rural India.[4]

We claim that the changes in outcomes between the 1980s and the period after 1990 have a complex explanatory structure. First, they have to be traced back to an event of central significance: the introduction in the mid 1960s of green revolution technologies and practices for foodgrains in select pockets of India. While this was done to provide a solution to the pressing problem of food shortages and near-drought, it allowed a departure from the earlier efforts to institute a more egalitarian asset structure (e.g. redistributive land reforms) in rural areas. This policy package led to the achievement of national food security (as defined by the policymakers) by the late 1970s, while also unleashing other broad changes. It led to a gradual diffusion of green revolution technologies across the country ("lagged" green revolution), especially into the semi-arid regions that comprise more than 40 percent of the total cultivated land (Harriss-White and Janakarajan 2004). These technologies spread into non-food cultivation too, and into the practices of small-scale and marginal farmers, having a broader impact than was initially envisaged (Vakulabharanam 2004). By the 1990s, most of the farming households had been brought into the orbit of markets (for outputs and inputs). At the same time, introduction of these technologies led to the development of capitalist class relations in certain pockets of the country, and in others, it led to a perpetuation of peasant agriculture that had become market-oriented. In this paper, we focus on the period after 1990, to examine the impact of this central event on contemporary agricultural processes.

Second, the green revolution was premised on sustained support from the state in various ways, a position that the state has attempted to withdraw from in a haphazard way since 1990. The state had offered various input subsidies, especially for fertilizers, electricity and credit. It had provided infrastructural support (primarily in irrigation and electricity), extension services and minimum support prices to cultivators. In the realm of consumption, the state had supported the poor through an extensive network of its Public Distribution System (PDS). An ad hoc set of policies after 1990, inspired by the general wave of liberalization across the country, has attempted, unevenly, to withdraw this support (Patnaik 2003; Vakulabharanam 2005). Insofar as the pre-liberalization policies had come to benefit the poorer agricultural groups, the withdrawal of this support has meant greater distress for farmers, and indirectly, adverse effects on the wages of agricultural workers.

Third, mobilization within rural areas has itself undergone considerable transformation. Even as sections of the elite farming groups and agricultural market intermediaries have found ways to incorporate themselves into the faster-growing urban economy, other sections of these classes have rooted themselves in agriculture, extracting rents and shaping agricultural policy to benefit them. In interesting, but uneven ways, Hindu nationalism has tended to penetrate primarily rural elite mobilization. On the other hand, increasing distress in agriculture has had significant reverberations, with various democratic mobilizations across the country pushing for, and succeeding in slowing down liberalization policies in agriculture and in some cases being able to introduce policies such as the National Rural Employment Guarantee Act (NREGA) that explicitly go against the grain of liberalization.

To summarize, we document three interrelated phenomena in the 1990s: slowing down of agricultural growth, improved performance of large farmers relative to the 1980s and a decline in the performance of small farmers and agricultural laborers relative to the 1980s. We explain the first and third phenomena through the interplay of lagged green revolution and liberalization processes and the second through interaction between liberalization processes and rural mobilizations. Disentangling the effects of these three processes (liberalization, lagged green revolution and mobilization) through a *ceteris paribus* analysis would have been insightful, but is impossible with the available data, and hence not attempted.

The remainder of the paper is organized as follows. Section I describes agrarian distress, focusing primarily on growth and distribution. Section II addresses the relation between liberalization in the context of a green revolution that is slowing down, and agrarian distress. Section III addresses the question of rural class mobilizations and agricultural policy. Section IV concludes.

I. Unequal growth since the 1990s

Indian agriculture has been going through a crisis since the mid-1990s, as reflected by several indicators. Before going further, it is worthwhile to present the broad findings.

(i) The rural sector, and agriculture in particular, has seen a downturn on several dimensions: growth, distribution and poverty reduction. Agriculture has grown at a much slower pace, rural poverty continues to be very high, the rate of poverty reduction has reduced and rural inequality has increased. These trends have been reversed from the previous decade, when there were substantial improvements.
(ii) While the rural scenario has worsened, the impact has been felt unevenly, with certain classes, castes, and regions[5] faring worse than others. For instance, while large farmers have witnessed higher growth rates (of average consumption), other groups have seen the opposite result.
(iii) Rural–urban inequality, which was high to begin with, has increased. The urban sector has lower poverty and higher average consumption compared to the rural sector. Within rural areas, the non-agricultural sector has fared better than the agricultural sector.

I.1 Growth

Agriculture has been growing at a much slower pace since 1990/1 as compared to the previous decade (see Table 7.1). The average agricultural growth rate during the period 1990/1 to 2004/5 was 1.96 percent per annum (p.a.), much lower than the corresponding figure for the 1980s (3.45 percent p.a.). Both foodgrains and non-foodgrains grew at faster rates during the 1980s.

Agricultural growth can be achieved through increase in either inputs or productivity. In post-independence India, both channels have been used (Rao and Storm 1998). However, comparing the period since 1990/1 with the 1980s, agriculture seems to have run out of steam on both fronts (Table 7.2). The area under cultivation

Table 7.1 Agricultural output growth in India

	Foodgrains	Non-Foodgrains	All
1980s	3.33%	3.89%	3.45%
1990–1 to 2004–5	1.64%	2.81%	1.96%

Source: RBI India Statistical Year Book.

Table 7.2 Area and land productivity growth in India

Area/Cropping Pattern	Foodgrains	Non-Foodgrains	All
1980s	-0.02%	1.10%	0.24%
1990–1 to 2004–5	-0.07%	1.03%	0.25%
Productivity			
1980s	2.88%	2.24%	2.57%
1990–1 to 2004–5	1.27%	1.39%	1.29%

Source: RBI India Statistical Year Book.

has increased by 0.25 percent during the period 1990/1 to 2004/5, whereas the corresponding figure for the 1980s is almost the same (0.24 percent). In both periods, the area under non-food crops has grown (1.10 percent and 1.03 percent for the 1980s and 1990/1 to 2004/5, respectively) whereas the area under foodgrains has decreased (growth rates of –0.02 percent and –0.07 percent for the 1980s and 1990/1 to 2004/5, respectively). More alarmingly, productivity has grown at a much smaller rate (1.29 percent p.a.) during the period 1990/1 to 2004/5 as compared to the 1980s (2.57 percent p.a.).

I.2 Distribution

The above analysis reveals that agriculture has not done well in terms of growth. Growth has also not been shared evenly among all groups. To get a disaggregated picture, we look at various classes and caste groups in India. We conceptualize the rural economy in terms of eight classes: large farmers, medium farmers, small farmers, marginal farmers, agricultural laborers, self-employed in non-agricultural

Table 7.3 Average monthly per-capita expenditure for various classes (2005–6 values)

Class	38th Round (Rs.)	50th Round (Rs.)	61st Round (Rs.)	Growth 38–50 (%)	Growth 50–61 (%)
Large	627.46 (1.83%)	739.33 (1.30%)	906.06 (0.65%)	1.65	1.87
Medium	523.55 (18.39%)	606.23 (14.83%)	661.80 (12.01%)	1.48	0.80
Small	451.42 (13.09%)	537.11 (12.21%)	588.87 (11.22%)	1.75	0.84
Marginal	436.45 (12.75%)	527.57 (15.47%)	566.70 (15.51%)	1.91	0.65
Agri Laborer	340.13 (27.63%)	408.50 (28.34%)	432.99 (24.89%)	1.85	0.53
Total	444.60	525.21	581.87	1.68	0.94

Source: Authors' computations from NSS unit level data. The Consumer Price Index for Agricultural Laborers (CPIAL) from the RBI database on the Indian economy is used to convert to 2005–6 values.

Note:
a. Large farmers (self-employed in agriculture, land possessed more than 10 hectares), medium farmers (self-employed in agriculture, land possessed between 2 and 10 hectares), small farmers (self-employed in agriculture, land possessed between 1 and 2 hectares), marginal farmers (self-employed in agriculture, land possessed between 0 and 1 hectare), agricultural laborers (self-employed in agriculture with no land or who define themselves as agricultural laborers);
b. figures in parentheses are the shares of various classes. They do not add up to 100% because the non-agricultural classes are excluded. The "total" figure refers to the average for all classes (both agricultural and non-agricultural).

sector, non-agricultural laborers and others.[6] The first two groups are net labor-power buyers (i.e. the capitalist class process dominates production). Small farmers use mostly household labor or reciprocal labor among themselves. Marginal farmers and agricultural laborers are net labor-power sellers. This classification scheme helps us conceptualize the class position of a household and is also similar to other schemes (e.g. of the Indian government). We apply this classification to the National Sample Survey (NSS) 38th (1983–4), 50th (1993–4), and 61st (2004–5) rounds. Average consumption[7] (Table 7.3) has increased for all classes.[8] However, except for large farmers, average consumption was growing at a much faster rate for all classes between the 38th and 50th rounds. We can also see that the class structure itself has changed between the 50th and 61st rounds: there is a higher share of marginal farmers and agricultural laborers and a lower share of other agricultural classes, reflecting both a process of peasantization/proletarianization and demographic changes (e.g. population growth, breakdown of joint families causing fragmentation of landholdings). Also, a higher proportion of the rural population is now engaged in the non-agricultural sector.[9]

The poorest class in India comprises of agricultural workers. Table 7.4 presents data on real wage rates for the period 1990–1 to 1999–2000 for 15 major states. Real wages fell in four of these states and even in the states where they increased, they have grown sluggishly, with only two states recording a growth rate higher than 3.5 percent per annum (implying doubling of wages in roughly 20 years). Moreover, in states where wages have increased, they have fluctuated and in fact shown a decline in some years.

Moving from class to caste, NSS did not enumerate the Other Backward Classes (OBCs) in 38th and 50th rounds. We therefore adopt two caste schemes (Table 7.5). In the first, OBCs are included in other Hindus, Muslims or non-Hindus, whereas in the second they are explicitly enumerated. Irrespective of the scheme, in terms of average consumption, STs have fared the worst in all rounds, whereas other non-Hindus have fared the best. Using scheme 2, we can observe that OBCs have fared better than SCs and STs. All groups, except other non-Hindus, have seen a reduced growth rate of average consumption, with the STs being the biggest losers.

Rural poverty has been declining since 1983 (Table 7.6). However, the rate of poverty reduction was higher in the period 1983–94 as compared to the period 1994–2005.[10] Given the unprecedented growth that India experienced in the latter period, one would have expected and liked to see a higher rate. Moreover, given population growth, a lower rate of poverty reduction implies a smaller reduction in the number of poor.

Both rural and agricultural inequalities have risen between the 50th and 61st rounds (Table 7.7), reflecting a trend reversal – they were falling between the 38th and 50th rounds. Land inequality decreased, reflecting a fragmentation of landholdings, as discussed above.[11]

The already high rural–urban disparity (Table 7.8) has increased between the 50th and 61st rounds. The ratio of the average rural to urban consumption has been increasing since the 1980s. Rural poverty continues to be higher than urban poverty

Table 7.4 State-Wise Wage Rates of Agricultural Labor for Kharif Crops in India (Rs. per Man Day)

States	1990–1	1991–2	1992–3	1993–4	1994–5	1995–6	1996–7	1997–8	1998–9	1999–2000	Growth 1990–2000
Andhra Pradesh	2.8	2.48	2.52	2.7	2.81	2.77	2.81	2.93	2.83	2.94	0.49%
Assam	2.94	2.68	2.7	2.54	2.48	2.53	2.59	2.65	2.63	2.61	-1.18%
Bihar	2.24	2.14	2.04	2.16	2.19	2.18	2.08	2.36	2.22	2.14	-0.46%
Haryana	3.78	4	4.49	4.26	4.28	4.33	4.47	4.68	4.75	5.17	3.18%
Gujarat	2.57	2.46	2.65	2.72	2.76	2.82	2.99	3.42	3.67	4.05	4.65%
Karnataka	1.92	1.67	1.47	2.02	1.7	1.53	1.89	2.21	2.15	2.33	1.95%
Kerala	3.65	3.8	4.17	4.07	4.27	4.95	5.53	6.4	7.55	6.39	5.76%
Madhya Pradesh	2.03	1.95	2.19	2.28	2.14	2.25	2.28	2.29	2.31	2.4	1.69%
Maharashtra	2.51	2.14	2.15	2.7	2.69	2.4	2.4	2.92	2.76	2.46	-0.20%
Orissa	1.74	1.68	1.86	1.86	1.79	1.79	1.8	1.84	1.85	1.85	0.61%
Punjab	3.99	4.15	4.31	4.39	4.33	4.1	3.93	4.05	3.93	3.9	-0.23%
Rajasthan	2.85	3.02	2.91	2.69	2.72	3.06	3.53	3.71	3.11	3.63	2.45%
Tamil Nadu	1.8	1.87	2.12	2.36	2.39	2.48	2.67	3.02	3.1	3.26	6.12%
Uttar Pradesh	2.22	2.25	2.41	2.25	2.2	2.52	2.46	2.78	2.79	2.63	1.71%
West Bengal	3.07	2.88	3.58	3.35	3.17	3.15	3.22	3.62	3.5	3.53	1.41%

Source: India Statistics.

Table 7.5 Average monthly per-capita expenditure for various castes (2005–6 values)

Caste	38th Round (Rs.)	50th Round (Rs.)	61st Scheme1 (Rs.)	Round Scheme2 (Rs.)	Growth 38–50 (%)	Growth 50–61 (%)
ST	346.30	437.45	443.89	443.89	2.36%	0.13%
SC	372.77	445.90	494.32	494.32	1.81%	0.94%
OBC				579.72		
Other Hindu	475.33	563.97	624.08	737.99	1.72%	0.92%
Muslim (Non SC, ST, OBC)	423.31	498.25	568.61	554.02	1.64%	1.21%
Other Non-Hindu	628.71	796.60	1152.66	1147.64	2.40%	3.42%
Total	467.81	522.15	591.09	591.09	1.11	1.13

Source: Authors' computations from NSS unit level data. 2005–6 values are derived, as in Table 3.

Table 7.6 Rural poverty and poverty reduction rates in various regions

38th Round (%)	50th Round (%)	61st Round (%)	Rate (38–50)	Rate (50–61)
46.73	37.21	28.29	–0.95	–0.81

Source: Authors' computations from NSS unit level data. We use the national poverty line.

Table 7.7 Inequality in rural and urban India

	38th Round	50th Round	61st Round
Agricultural Gini	0.3045	0.2780	0.2807
Rural Gini	0.3091	0.2859	0.3045
Agricultural Land Gini	0.6709	0.6724	0.7310
Urban Gini	0.3353	0.3333	0.3766

Source: Authors' computations from NSS unit level data.

Note: Agricultural Gini – Gini of Monthly Per-Capita Expenditure for those involved in agriculture; Rural (Urban) Gini – Gini of Monthly Per-Capita Expenditure for the entire rural (urban) sector; Agricultural Land Gini – Gini of land possessed for those involved in agriculture.

Table 7.8 Comparison of mean monthly per-capita expenditure in rural and urban sectors

	38th Round	50th Round	61st Round
(1) Rural	111.19	281.40	558.80
(2) Urban	162.98	458.04	1052.35
Ratio of (2) to (1)	1.47	1.63	1.88

Source: Authors' computations from NSS unit level data.

(Himanshu 2007). Similarly, the non-agricultural and agricultural sectors have been diverging – the ratio of average consumption in the non-agricultural sector to the same in the agricultural sector, increased from 1.06 (50th round) to 1.10 (61st round).[12] Increasing rural–urban inequality is not necessarily a problem and can be argued (along with rural–urban migration) to be a part of the development process. However, as we note elsewhere (Motiram and Vakulabharanam 2007), the most recent rural–urban migrants are not being absorbed into labor-intensive (or other) manufacturing and are swelling the ranks of slum dwellers, who make their living in the urban informal sector. Moreover, agrarian distress is a significant factor in their decision to migrate. This is not in the spirit of the arguments of Arthur Lewis and other development economists of his era.

To conclude this section, although output growth rate has declined compared to the previous decade, it is still positive. However, the growth rate of consumption in the 1980s was broad-based (with small cultivators and agricultural workers doing as well as or better than other groups), whereas the 1990s have seen a sharp decline in the growth rate in consumption of especially the poorer groups. This is coupled with an improved performance for richer farmers. We call this phenomenon "unequal growth." In the next two sections, we explain these empirical phenomena.

II. Lagged green revolution, liberalization and agricultural outcomes

In this section, we explain the output slowdown and distress outcomes for the poorer agricultural classes since the 1990s, analyzing the linkages between policy changes, changes among technological and production practices, market relations, and consumption patterns. We also show how certain classes have strengthened at the expense of others, mainly due to the introduction of liberalization policies.

II.1 Technology, investment and production

Since the 1970s, technology and production processes that were brought into foodgrains during the green revolution in fertile regions diffused to less fertile regions, non-food crops and to poorer cultivators. High yield variety (HYV), and more recently, genetically modified (GM) seeds, intensive fertilizer and pesticide use, tubewell irrigation with the concomitant use of electric motors, and tractors for ploughing (where available), have been the basic means of production that are now diffused across the country. Since this method of cultivation is capital-intensive, it leads to high dependence on credit (formal or informal). Labor input is used mainly in sowing, weeding, fertilizer and pesticide application, and harvesting. This model that emphasized yields as opposed to extensive or intensive cultivation was premised on state support in the provision of inputs, marketing, infrastructure, credit and extension, before the advent of liberalization policies (Rudra 1992).

The period since 1990s witnessed only a deepening of this model of production. It is useful to identify a few of the changes that occurred during this period. Newer varieties of HYV and GM seeds have been introduced, increasing market dependence and financial burden of farmers. Fertilizer application has increased from 0.19 tonnes/hectare in 1990–1 to about 0.25 tonnes/hectare by 2003–4 (Table 7.9). Given a rise in fertilizer prices, and a continuation of subsidy for a particular variety (the N among the N, P and K varieties) of fertilizers, there has been a distortion in the mix that is employed. This can and has hurt yields significantly (Harriss-White and Janakarajan 2004). While net-irrigated area grew at about 1.1 percent per annum, tube wells grew at more than 4 percent per annum during this period, contributing to roughly 44 percent of all irrigated land by 2001–2. This figure was

Table 7.9 Fertilizer consumption in India

Year	Fertilizer Consumption ('000 Tonnes)	Net Sown Area (million hectares)	Fertilizer Consumption/ Hectare
1990–1	27806.59	143.00	0.19
1991–2	27790.90	141.63	0.20
1992–3	26350.87	142.72	0.18
1993–4	27346.20	142.34	0.19
1994–5	29877.16	142.96	0.21
1995–6	30888.47	142.20	0.22
1996–7	31599.24	142.81	0.22
1997–8	35428.22	142.08	0.25
1998–9	36586.94	142.58	0.26
1999–2000	38556.76	140.96	0.27
2000–1	35547.65	141.16	0.25
2001–2	36541.98	141.42	0.26
2002–3	33965.69	132.66	0.26
2003–4	35386.97	140.88	0.25

Source: India Statistics

Table 7.10 Irrigation trends in India ('000 hectares)

Period	Canals Govt	Canals Private	Canals Total	Tanks	Wells Tubewells	Wells Other Wells	Other Sources	Total
1970–1	11972 (38.49%) (1.90%)	866 (2.78%) (−0.28%)	12838 (41.28%) (1.76%)	4112 (13.22%) (−2.53%)	4461 (14.34%) (7.89%)	7426 (23.88%) (0.95%)	2266 (7.29%) (1.19%)	31103 (100.00%) (2.21%)
1980–1	14450 (37.32%) (1.62%)	842 (2.17%) (−5.46%)	15292 (39.49%) (1.33%)	3182 (8.22%) (−0.77%)	9531 (24.62%) (4.11%)	8164 (21.08%) (2.49%)	2551 (6.59%) (1.40%)	38720 (100.00%) (2.18%)
1990–1	16973 (35.34%) (−0.98%)	480 (1.00%) (−6.33%)	17453 (36.34%) (−1.09%)	2944 (6.13%) (−3.15%)	14257 (29.69%) (4.14%)	10437 (21.73%) (0.47%)	2932 (6.11%) (−0.49%)	48023 (100.00%) (1.06%)
2003–4	14941 (27.11%)	205 (0.37%)	15145 (27.48%)	1943 (3.53%)	24169 (43.86%)	11096 (20.14%)	2752 (4.99%)	55105 (100.00%)

Source: India Statistics.

Note: Figures in the first set of parentheses are the shares for a particular source. Figures in the second set of parentheses are the growth rates during the decade; for 1990–1, this is post-liberalization growth rate.

about 30 percent in 1990–1 and 14 percent in 1970–1 (Table 7.10). Other sources of irrigation (canals and tanks) have registered negative growth rates during this period. Despite these increases in input use, there has been a significant slowdown in output growth (as noted above).

Why has output growth slowed down? In our opinion, the slowdown in output growth is due partly to decreasing returns over time accruing to the green revolution technologies, and partly to the liberalization framework adopted towards agriculture. Separating these two effects is not possible due to data limitations, so we provide an analytical discussion of the two effects and how they feed into each other.

The lagged green revolution has primarily been implemented in less fertile, semi-arid regions, and in the mono-cropping of non-food crops like cotton, leading to undesirable effects such as soil erosion, steadily increasing pest resistance and the increasing ineffectiveness of fertilizers (which are increasingly applied based upon price, rather than productivity). The continued exploitation of groundwater has also thrown up serious problems for sustained output growth given the gradual erosion of this resource. Several studies have pointed to the steadily decreasing returns to green revolution technologies since the 1980s.[13] The decline in yields that we pointed to between the 1980s and 1990s is evidence of this phenomenon.

In this context, one issue that has to be addressed concerns short- versus long-run implications. Why did farmers adopt technologies that gave high payoffs in the short run, but turned out to be somewhat ineffective in the long run? Of course, one can argue that farmers (like other economic agents) cannot be expected to anticipate the future perfectly. But other reasons are also plausible – groundwater use can be construed as a classic case of a negative externality that farmers did not internalize, and state support (especially in irrigation) fell short of requirements.

Liberalization processes have also contributed to this output slowdown in a significant way. In particular, public investment in agriculture (usually facilitating yield improvements) declined slightly in nominal terms, from Rs. 4,395 crores (1990–1) to Rs. 4,221 crores (1999–2000) (Table 7.11). This slack has been taken up only partially by private investment, which grew from Rs. 10,441 crores (1990–1) to Rs. 13,083 crores (1999–2000). A look at total investment as a share of GDP is more revealing – it fell from 1.92 percent (1990–1) to 1.37 percent (1999–2000) and kept declining through the 1990s (Figure 7.1). In recent years, it has picked up, but is still comparable to what it was in 1990–1. One important area in which investment has occurred is irrigation, which is crucial for agricultural growth in many parts of India. However, as we can see from Table 7.10, since 1990–1, growth rate in irrigation has been much lower than the same in previous decades. Also, much of the investment into tube wells is private, which (through groundwater) had adverse implications for sustained output growth.

Table 7.11 Agricultural investment in India

Year	Total (Rs. crore)	Public (Rs. crore)	Private (Rs. crore)	Public Share (%)	Private Share (%)	Share of GDP (%)
1960–1	1668	589	1079	35.30	64.70	
1970–1	2758	789	1969	28.60	71.40	
1980–1	4636	1796	2840	38.70	61.30	
1990–1	14836	4395	10441	29.60	70.40	1.92
1995–6	15690	4849	10841	30.90	69.10	1.57
1996–7	16176	4668	11508	28.90	71.10	1.51
1997–8	15942	3979	11963	25.00	75.00	1.43
1998–9	14895	3870	11025	26.00	74.00	1.26
1999–00	17304	4221	13083	24.40	75.60	1.37
1999–00	43473	7716	35757	17.70	82.30	2.20
2000–1	38735	7155	31580	18.50	81.50	1.90
2001–2	47043	8746	38297	18.60	81.40	2.20
2002–3	46823	7962	38861	17.00	83.00	2.10
2003–4	45132	9376	35756	20.80	79.20	1.90
2004–5	48576	10267	38309	21.10	78.90	1.90
2005–6	54539	13219	41320	24.20	75.80	1.90

Source: Economic Survey of India.

Note: 1960–81 figures are for base year 1980–81; 1990–00 figures are for base year 1993–94; 1999–06 figures are for base year 1999–00. Percentage share of GDP is at constant prices.

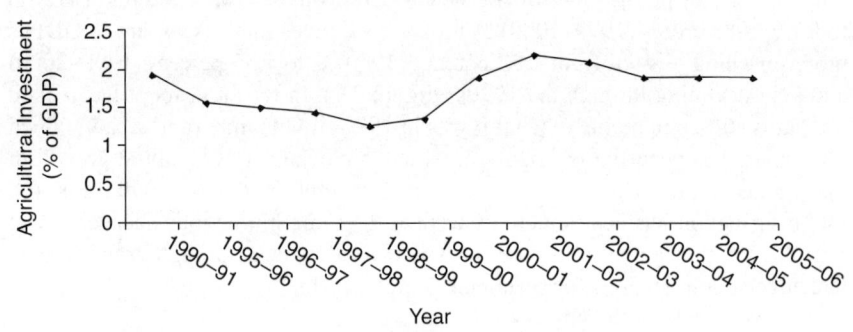

Figure 7.1 Agricultural investment as a percentage of GDP (1990–2006).
Note: The base year changed in 1999–00, so the best way to look at the above figure is to consider 1990–00 and 2000–06 as two different series.

II.2 Agricultural markets

Agricultural liberalization policies have been attempted mostly in the realm of markets, both external and internal. The simple dictum of "getting prices right" is the main imperative for pushing reforms in this arena, so that producers supposedly have the correct incentives (Schiff and Valdes 1992; Krueger 1992). There are two aspects to this story. First, the differentials between domestic and international prices ought to be erased. Second, input prices ought to be governed by the market logic. These policies have been motivated along the lines that there had been an anti-agriculture bias in developing countries, and that domestic agricultural prices had been kept artificially low in order to promote industry.

The implications of this understanding are that government subsidies in various input markets should be gradually eliminated, and that Indian agriculture should be opened to the external sector. The actual implementation of policies has been somewhat uneven, regionally as well as in terms of the extent. Pressures from various rural groups[14] (elite and non-elite), and the level of enthusiasm of state-level leaders[15] have determined the degree of implementation. A summary of measures implemented so far is presented in Table 7.12.[16]

The main effects of the implementation of liberalization policies are as follows. First, both agricultural exports and imports have increased substantially (Government of India 2007; Government of India 2006–7). Second, domestic and international market prices of non-food crops have begun to show considerable convergence (Vakulabharanam 2004), even as international prices are heavily influenced by subsidies given to first-world farmers and agribusinesses.[17] Third, the "price scissors" effect has come into play, especially for non-foodgrain producers. Given the sharp decline after the 1990s in the global prices of non-food crops, while the cultivated area of these crops has been growing, cultivators have been facing falling output prices. This is the case even though the domestic terms of trade (TOT) between agricultural and non-agricultural sectors up to the late 1990s moved in favor of the agricultural sector, after being consistently in favor of manufacturing during the 1980s. From about 1998 onwards, however, there has been a reversal of this relation with agriculture losing more than 5 percent between 1998–9 and 2004–5 (Government of India 2007). The growth rate in yield for non-food crops during the 1990s, although higher than the same for food crops, has declined relative to the 1980s. At the same time, with increased use of inputs (as discussed above) and rise in input prices, the costs of production have tended to rise. One factor that has contributed to the rise in input costs in some years is the decline in input subsidies. Input subsidies per hectare of gross cropped area (Figure 7.2) have been erratic in the 1990s, dipping twice – in 1991–2 and 1996–7. Moreover, the trend rate of growth in the 1980s was much higher than the same in the 1990s.

Why did consumption growth rates fall steeply for small and marginal farmers? One of the important factors behind this phenomenon is that institutional credit provided at affordable interest rates has not kept pace with the growing needs of small and marginal farmers, who have moved into more market-oriented cultivation. This is partly a result of the approach that the state should withdraw from

Table 7.12 Summary of Liberalization Measures Introduced in the Agricultural Sector

Area of Liberalization	Policy Changes and Measures of Implementation
I. External Trade Sector	In tune with the WTO regime, since 1997 all Indian Product lines placed in Generalised System of Preferences (GSP).
	In 1998, Quantitative Restrictions (QRs) for 470 agricultural products dismantled. In 1999, further 1,400 agricultural products brought under Open General Licensing (OGL) and canalization of external trade in agriculture almost reversed.
	Average tariffs on agricultural imports reduced from 100% in 1990 to 30% in 1997.
	Though India is in principle against Minimum Common Access, it is actually already importing 2% of its food requirements.
II. Internal Market Liberalization	
1. Seeds	Since 1991 100% foreign equity allowed in seed industry. More liberalized imports of seeds.
2. Fertilizers	Gradual reduction of fertilizer subsidies since 1991.
3. Power	Since 1997 Power Sector reforms were introduced at the behest of the World Bank in states like Andhra Pradesh and power charged increased. Power sector opened for private sector.
4. Irrigation	Water rates increased in some states. Participatory water management was sought to be introduced through Water Users' Associations (WUAs). States like Andhra Pradesh made new large irrigation projects conditional on 'stakeholder' contribution to part of investment.
5. Institutional Credit	Khursro Committee and Narasimham Committee (1992) undermining the importance of targeted priority sector landing by the commercial banks. The objectives of Regional Rural Banks' (RRBs) priority to lending to weaker sections in rural areas diluted since 1997.
6. Agricultural Marketing	Changes in the provisions of Essential Commodities Act. Relaxation of Restrictions on the inter-State Movement of farm produce. Encouragement of Contract Farming. Agricultural Commodity Forward Markets.

Source: Reddy (2006).

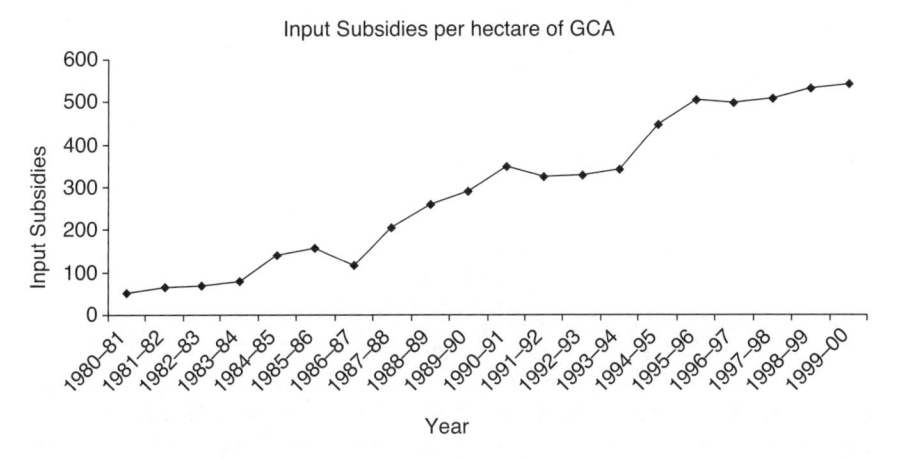

Figure 7.2 Input subsidies per hectare of Gross Cropped Area (GCA).
Source: Gulati and Narayanan, 2003.

social banking (Pande 2007), which was posited as highly inefficient, with unacceptable recovery rates.[18] With rising fixed costs due to tube-well irrigation and associated technology, and rising variable costs due to increased input costs, state withdrawal in this area has meant two things. First, farmers (especially small farmers) have become more dependent on informal sources of credit (moneylenders).[19] Outstanding debt to moneylenders as a proportion of total debt has increased from about 20 percent in 1991 to about 35 percent in 2002 (Table 7.13). Second, there is a very high incidence of indebtedness among small farmers. In 2003, more than 83 percent of all farm households that have outstanding debt are "small." While small farmers (more than 60 percent of total farmers) commanded less than 40 percent of cultivated area, they carried about 60 percent of debt in 2003 (Misra 2007, Appendix 3a). Also, interest rates charged by these moneylenders are high – 24–60 percent (government banks charge 15–18 percent) depending upon the urgency of the need. This indicates that small cultivators have faced the greatest burden of reforms in terms of institutional credit.

Apart from increased dependence on moneylenders, farmers have become dependent upon networks of market intermediaries who work in interlinked and colluding markets.[20] This implies that the market power of these agents has increased considerably, as has been documented in various studies.[21] In the absence of a clearly defined land collateral, this class uses various other forms of collateral, chief among them being crop collateral through the interlinking of credit and product markets. This means that farmers have to sell their crops to moneylender-traders whom they borrow from, which creates incentives for moneylenders to closely monitor cropping patterns (e.g. in the Telangana region of Andhra Pradesh, the collateral is in the form of non-food crops. See Vakulabharanam 2004). Gradually, small farmers are losing their autonomy in the determination of cropping patterns. To conclude, there is a sharp increase in the economic power of moneylenders and a corresponding decline in the power of small and marginal farmers.

Table 7.13 Main sources of household credit and debt

	Banks	Moneylenders	Relatives	Government	Traders
1991	35.61%	20.20%	9.45%	3.66%	2.56%
2002	30.37%	33.24%	9.98%	1.66%	2.26%
Growth	−1.44%	4.63%	0.50%	−6.94%	−1.12%

Source: Authors' computation from NSS All India Debt and Investment Surveys.

II.3 Consumption: policy and patterns

In this section, we focus on how liberalization policies have altered consumption patterns in rural areas, but also address the question of consumption declines for agricultural workers and other net buyers of foodgrains. This has occurred in two ways. First, liberalization policies in agricultural markets have increased the relative price of foodgrains, thereby adversely affecting the vast majority of the rural population, which is a net buyer of foodgrains.[22] Second, the PDS has been altered and the government's intent seems to be complex – it is caught between wanting to phase out PDS over time and its obligation towards the poor.

It can be observed (Table 7.14) that foodgrain prices have shown an upward trend relative to non-food prices, partly due to trade liberalization policies that have imported deflationary global prices into the domestic economy. Foodgrain producers were shielded from this by the government through minimum support prices, especially for rice and wheat. Since small and marginal cultivators switched from foodgrains to non-food crops, this had adverse effects on these cultivators, as they

Table 7.14 Wholesale price index of food and non-food articles

Year	Food	Non-Food	Ratio of (1) to (2)
1995–6	122.2	135.4	0.90
1996–7	137.3	134.2	1.02
1997–8	141.4	137.5	1.03
1998–9	159.4	151.8	1.05
1999–2000	165.5	143.0	1.16
2000–1	170.5	146.5	1.16
2001–2	176.1	152.9	1.15
2002–3	179.2	165.4	1.08
2003–4	181.5	186.3	0.97
2004–5	186.3	187.6	0.99
2005–6	195.3	179.1	1.09

Source: Ministry of Industry.

Political economy of agrarian distress in India since the 1990s 117

have become net buyers of foodgrains. As we argue below, the grain procurement policies of the government in the context of a declining trend of global commodity prices also contributed to making foodgrains dearer for working groups.

Far-reaching changes have been made to the PDS. We do not give the details here in the interest of space and since these are discussed elsewhere (see Chapter 8, this volume). This has created several problems and has led to the curious situation where foodgrain stocks were rising in the early years of this decade, even as the cereal intake of a vast population has taken a tumble. There has been hunger amidst plenty.[23]

To conclude this section, we were able to establish linkages among lagged green revolution, liberalization and two of the three empirical phenomena outlined in Section II. In the next section, we present the political economy of these empirical observations and explain the third empirical phenomenon (improved performance of large farmers after 1990), by focusing on the period 1980–2005 to get a contrast between pre- and post-liberalization decades.

III. Rural mobilizations and economic outcomes

As discussed above, adoption of green revolution technologies and practices in selected parts of India and their spread to other regions of the country had serious implications for agricultural productivity and consumption patterns. This also altered the agrarian class structure and influenced farmer mobilizations in the country. These mobilizations help explain both the improved performance of capitalist farmers and the contested arena that agricultural liberalization policies have become.

III.1 Elite mobilizations: "new" farmer movements and Hindutva

The initial phase of green revolution (in the 1970s) resulted in the creation of rich capitalist farmers and a agricultural proletariat (Patnaik 1997; Rudra 1992). The creation of the proletariat happened both through the eviction of tenants and the increased use of hired labor. As the green revolution spread to other regions and crops, a similar process of proletarianization occurred since these other crops (e.g. hybrid cotton) require high levels of supervision, irrigation, fertilizers and pesticides. Two other important effects occurred. First, farmers with even small amounts of land got access to a marketable surplus. Second, the green revolution embedded both large and small farmers in a process of "commoditisation," wherein they became sensitive to market prices because both output and inputs became commodities for them (Lindberg 1994). All the above factors provided the basis for the "new farmers" movements that emerged in various parts of India[24] in the 1970s and became powerful in the 1980s.[25]

Unlike earlier agrarian movements, these eschewed a demand for land redistribution and instead fought for higher output prices, lower input prices, lower taxes and loan waivers (Lindberg 1994). Although scholarly literature is divided on the issue of the class basis of these movements: whether they largely represent the interests of rich large farmers (Assadi 1994; Banaji 1994; Dhanagare 1994;

Hasan 1994) or middle farmers and petty commodity producers (Lennenberg 1988; Omvedt 1993),[26] in our opinion, two arguments can be made. First, these movements provided a conduit through which the class of large farmers that emerged in the post-green revolution phase articulated its interests. Second, by forcing the state to adopt certain measures (e.g. loan waivers, increases in procurement prices) they influenced agricultural outcomes, especially for large farmers.[27] Since these movements were largely unconcerned about agricultural laborers,[28] the question arises as to who was representing them. Left parties and *Dalit* organizations largely did this, although in some contexts, the farmers' organizations made alliances with these groups.[29] Ironically, the Left's strategy to organize agricultural workers separately from peasants in the early phases of green revolution provided an impetus to the farmers' movement in the green revolution belt in North India (Gill 1994).

How did the various agricultural groups fare in the 1980s when farmers' movements were strong? As we can observe from Table 7.4, between the 38th and 50th rounds, we can see that large farmers showed good growth rates and the concessions that they were able to obtain from the state undoubtedly contributed to this. However, other agricultural groups (in particular small and marginal farmers) did equally well or better than large farmers. This can be explained by the fact that large farmers were starting from an already high base and ran into the limitations of the green revolution, whereas other groups started from a relatively low base and were still exploiting the early benefits of green revolution.

After scaling unprecedented heights in the late 1980s, the farmers' movements have been in relative decline since the 1990s. Apart from penetration of Hindutva ideology (discussed below), liberalization has exposed the deep ideological fissures existing within these movements – the Shetkari Sanghatana and the Gujarat Khedut Samaj have taken a position openly supporting the World Trade Organization (WTO) and the entry of multinationals into agriculture, whereas the Karnataka State Farmers' Association (KRRS) and the Bharatiya Kisan Union (BKU) have taken the opposite position. While the former have legitimized their arguments on the basis of comparative advantage, farmers' right to choose and the rural sector's need for modern technology, the latter (especially KRRS) have relied on Gandhian ideas to critique the corrosive effects of multinational capital. This lack of a united front, something that these movements were able to at least partly present in the 1980s has allowed the state to push through policies (discussed above) that are inimical to the agricultural sector as a whole, although large farmers continue to protect their interests.[30]

Given that in the 1990s the limitations of green revolution were starkly exposed and farmers' movements were weakened, the continued superior performance of large farmers is puzzling. Surely, rising procurement and support prices offers only a partial explanation. Four additional explanations suggest themselves. First, the withdrawal of the state from certain spheres, in particular institutional credit, has hurt the lower classes, but has left large farmers unaffected (Ramachandran and Swaminathan 2002). To the extent that large farmers are also involved in other roles (e.g. trading, moneylending), this has benefited them. Second, large farmers have used their prosperity to straddle both the rural and urban sectors and have diversified their sources of income (e.g. real estate, trading, etc.). Despite the reduced profitability in agriculture, they have managed to protect themselves. This is essentially the "provincial propertied classes," argument made by Balagopal (1988).[31] A recent NCAER report (Srivastava 2006) discusses in detail the consolidation of the rural rich and their linkages through family to the fast growing urban economy. Third, even where large farmers have relocated to the urban areas, they have ensured that their kith and kin, who still reside in rural areas, are protected, through government policies or otherwise. Fourth, a significant part of the growth in the 1990s for these groups owes itself to either foodgrain cultivation (which has seen rising prices during this period) or a transition to high-value crops such as fruits and vegetables, which have seen growth in cropping areas as well as prices during this period. Two further observations can be made about this class. First, over the last two or three decades, this regional capitalist class has emerged to compete with the more established capitalist classes in urban areas (Baru 2000). Second, this regional capitalist class has also utilized the domain of regional politics to further its ends.[32]

What is the relation between these farmer movements, new class alignments, and Hindutva? Since the late 1980s, Hindutva politics has spread to many parts of India and has considerably eroded the power and influence of the farmers' movements. Initially, there was a belief that these movements would resist the tide of Hindutva and in fact provide a bulwark against it. However, these beliefs were quickly belied by reports of BKU members participating in the demolition of the Babri Masjid, alliances between BKU and Bharatiya Janata Party (BJP), and Sharad Joshi's inability to prevent Shetkari Sanghatan's members from campaigning for Shiv Sena or BJP (Brass 1994; Hasan 1994; Lindberg 1994). This vulnerability can be explained partly by the major antagonism in the countryside (which to a certain extent these movements embody), which is between upper-caste Hindu farmers and *Dalit* laborers. The rise of BJP has pulled the upper-caste farmers into its fold (Hasan 1994; Brass 1994). More importantly, the new farmers' movements project an undifferentiated rural India (taking as given, the existing class and caste cleavages) pitted against an urban other (Brass 1994; Hasan 1994; Lindberg 1994). While this ought to unite Hindus and Muslims in an undivided rural bloc, this construct has tended to become open to colonization by the notion that an authentic India is rural (as opposed to the urban culture that is compromised with the west) and Hindu.[33] This then provides the basis for an alliance with an urban Hindu India that craves a strong sense of authentic nationhood in the wake of the flux that has characterized it after the 1990s. The provincial propertied classes are one of the constituent sociological bearers that bridge the barriers between the rural and the urban mindscapes of the undivided authentic India.

III.2 Democratic mobilizations

New caste configurations?

Tables 7.15 and 7.16 present class composition and shares of various castes and caste composition of various classes, respectively, based upon the NSS 61st round.

Table 7.15 Class composition of various castes (2003–4)

Class	ST (%)	SC (%)	OBC (%)	Other Hindu (%)	Muslim (%)	Other Non-Hindu (%)
Large	0.26	0.12	0.69	1.40	0.26	2.49
Medium	14.83	3.46	12.72	20.17	5.83	25.27
Small	14.95	5.72	11.81	14.61	9.99	12.06
Marginal	12.27	11.96	16.86	17.68	18.16	13.23
Agri Laborer	33.75	41.14	21.27	11.92	21.28	7.93
Non-Agri Self-Emp	6.76	15.42	18.76	14.93	25.75	14.32
Non-Agri Labor	11.58	15.29	9.46	6.39	9.81	12.70
Others	5.60	6.89	8.43	12.90	8.92	12.00
Total	100	100	100	100	100	100

Source: Authors' computations from NSS 61st Round unit level data.

SCs and Scheduled Tribes (STs) are overrepresented among the laboring agricultural classes and underrepresented among the landed classes. They make up the bulk of the laboring population. Therefore, to a large extent, their mobilization mirrors the problems that the mobilization of agricultural laborers has encountered in recent times (as discussed above). Despite this, *Dalit* organizations and Left groups have been involved in mobilizing them.

Some insights about the realignment of caste power in rural India can be garnered from the evidence that the NSS data provide. First, some of the new farmers' movements had tended to mobilize other castes (e.g. *Jats* in UP),[34] and this had at times thrown up tensions between them and the OBCs, as witnessed for example in the response of the farmers' movements to the recommendations of the Mandal commission (Hasan 1994). While this contradiction (between OC and OBC) is still acute in certain parts of the country, it is probably becoming increasingly less important at an aggregate level in rural India. There is an observable acceleration of rural–urban migration rates among the OCs during this period (broadly the provincial propertied classes). On this issue, it is worthwhile to point out that based upon our computations from the NSS 55th round Employment and Unemployment Survey we found that the caste composition of recent (within the past 10 years) male rural–urban migrants is as follows: 5.19 percent (ST), 13.67 percent (SC), 33.64 percent (OBC) and 47.50 percent (others).[35] Second, another observation that we can make from Tables 7.15 and 7.16 is that OBCs have the highest representation among dominant agrarian groups. The electoral gains that the OBCs have made (especially in UP and Bihar) have further consolidated their power in the

Table 7.16 Caste Composition of Various Classes (2003–4)

Caste	Large (%)	Medium (%)	Small (%)	Marginal (%)	Agri Laborer (%)	Non-Agri Self-Emp (%)	Non-Agri Labor (%)	Others (%)
ST	4.28	13.02	14.05	8.34	14.31	4.32	11.71	6.82
SC	3.83	6.02	10.67	16.13	34.59	19.55	30.68	16.63
OBC	45.72	45.21	44.94	46.44	36.5	48.52	38.75	41.54
Other Hindu	37.73	29.34	22.75	19.92	8.37	15.79	10.71	26.00
Muslim	2.70	3.27	5.99	7.88	5.76	10.49	6.33	6.93
Other Non-Hindu	5.74	3.14	1.61	1.27	0.48	1.29	1.82	2.07
Total	100	100	100	100	100	100	100	100

Source: Authors' computations from NSS 61st Round unit level data.

everyday matters of villages. On the other hand, as the OC castes migrate to the urban sector, and the OBCs have consolidated their position in the rural economy, the SCs and STs remain trapped in the rural sector. The new contradiction in rural India seems to be between the more numerous and labor-power hiring (at least to a certain extent) OBCs and the labor-power providing SCs (and STs). This manifests itself not only in the everyday struggles over work, wages and land, but also in the electoral domain, where large-scale mobilizations of these groups contest each other.[36]

Anti-liberalization struggles

The post-liberalization period has been dominated by the focus on the urban economy, especially the high-end services sector. By all indications, the state has come under the sway of the urban capitalist and middle classes and the provincial propertied classes. As the dependence of industry and services on agriculture weakens, it appears as if agriculture has become de-linked from the overall high growth process that India has been experiencing (Chandrasekhar 2007). This is certainly true in terms of overall output growth and consumption growth rates for a majority of the agricultural population.

In this context, it does seem that the small peasantry, in a significant departure from its earlier forms of protest/resistance, has shown its precariousness and desperation after the 1990s, in choosing the act of suicide as its most visible form of protest or response. This sustained desperate response over a period of about ten years (1997 to 2007) has prompted reactions from different groups. First, different Indian governments are worried about getting re-elected, and therefore pay some attention to the issue of increasing rural distress. Also, at a time when Indian governments (almost all political parties) are keen on promoting India internationally as an economic competitor to China, the phenomenon of farmer suicides does not present an alluring image to the international investors. These have prompted some of the governments (central and state) to take note and introduce ameliorating policies. Second, smallholders who are broadly in the same economic status as the ones who have died, have taken up various struggles in different parts of the country to obtain greater control over markets i.e. to reduce input (e.g. power) prices or increase output prices. Third, the old parliamentary Left, the radical Left groups and some of the farmers movements (like KRRS) have re-energized themselves around issues of agrarian distress and in turn have intensified their struggles around the issues of affordable credit, remunerative prices for small farmers and what they term as policies toward globalization. These struggles have certainly had an impact on the state over the last few years. In some states, power subsidies have been re-introduced in a big way. Large-scale irrigation projects have been taken up.[37] In a grand opening act calculated to both satiate the demands of the Left as well as to alleviate popular discontent, the government introduced a significant welfare measure – the National Rural Employment Guarantee Act (NREGA). The government also set up a high-powered debt committee to make recommendations about rural credit structures.[38] At this juncture, the state and the dominant capitalist classes in the urban sector cannot afford to ignore the agrarian crisis. At the same time, there is no concerted effort to strengthen smallholder agriculture.

To conclude this section, agricultural elites reveal an inclination to move towards a capitalist model of agriculture and are quite comfortable with the integration of sections of their classes into the non-agricultural sector as well as the urban economy. Democratic mobilizations are quite complex. On the one hand, in caste terms, there may be an emerging new configuration with the OBCs displacing the Hindu upper castes from their elite spaces in the everyday functioning of villages, while *Dalits* find themselves fighting yet another battle to improve their economic and political status. Smallholders have to deal both with a slowing green revolution and a state that pursues policies toward liberalization, although in an ambivalent fashion.

IV. Conclusion

Indian agriculture faces a contested future. On the one hand, the vision of certain groups of policymakers, economists, multilateral agencies, multinational capital and to an extent that of the provincial propertied classes is that capitalist agriculture (in different forms) should replace the current form of smallholder agriculture. One variant of this model that has found extraordinary support even among progressive-minded economists (Banerjee et. al. 2002) is that of contract farming, a system wherein capitalist firms enter into contracts with small farmers to advance capital and collect the produce at the end of the year. In the short term, this would seem to solve the problems of marketing and credit, which are at the heart of the crisis that has beset Indian agriculture today, even if the peasants increasingly lose control over the process of production as well as the product. As Marx defined it, this is "formal subsumption of labor to capital," which may well be a proto-capitalist form of agrarian organization.

On the other hand, a vast majority of the agrarian population is that of smallholders, who want to retain their autonomy over the production process and the product. This vast majority has now been dragged into the green revolution model that is slowing down even as the state unevenly tampers with its support structures. They come increasingly into the orbit of informal credit markets that further exacerbate their distress. It is important to observe that these informal lenders are not as interested in evicting indebted peasants from their land, as they are in continued surplus extraction. Is there a way for smallholders to emerge out of this trap? While increasingly the aspiration of villagers of different classes might be to escape into an urban space, the new urban capitalist sector in India (unlike China) is simply not creating jobs at a pace that can accommodate huge numbers of rural migrants.

For a while to come, it may even be in the interests of the dominant urban classes to support agriculture in the current form that can employ a majority of Indian workers. The recently tested strategy of the state to substitute various non-governmental strategies for its pre-liberalization roles of being a welfare provider has apparently not worked very well.[39] It is clear that the state has to continue to play a central role in order for smallholder agriculture to survive. In addition, certain creative solutions such as finding alternatives to the green revolution model on a gradual basis so that food security does not get instantly threatened, and promoting forms of cooperation among peasants that would allow them to get credit and market their crops on their terms, and re-emphasizing old imperatives such as land reforms.[40] The one thing that seems to be working in favor of smallholder agriculture at this time is its strength in numbers. In a land of electoral democracy, this is no small strength. Indian smallholder agriculture, it appears, will continue to survive in the near future, if ever more precariously.

Notes

1 For their comments on a previous version, we thank Sanjay Reddy, Sanjay Ruparelia and other participants at the Columbia-LSE-New School conference in New York in September 2007.
2 In the analysis below, we will continue to make this distinction between changes in the growth rate and changes in levels of welfare, consumption, etc.
3 See the special issue of *Economic and Political Weekly* (2006b). Misra (2007) and K. Nagaraj (2008) present suicide rates for farmers and non-farmers. The latter study highlights the important role that the agrarian crisis has played in this phenomenon.
4 This is somewhat similar to the framework adopted in Harriss-White and Janakarajan (2004).
5 In the interest of space, we have omitted a detailed regional analysis. This is available on request.
6 The procedure is as follows. We take all the households that are self-employed in agriculture (household type 4 in NSS surveys) and divide them into four classes based upon the land possessed by the household: large farmers (greater than 10 hectares), medium farmers (between 2 and 10 hectares), small farmers (between 1 and 2 hectares) and marginal farmers (between 0 and 1 hectare). We define agricultural laborers as either those who are self-employed in agriculture but with no land, or who define themselves as agricultural laborers (household type 2). The non-agricultural sector is comprised of self-employed in non-agriculture (household type 1 in NSS surveys) or non-agricultural labor (household type 3 in NSS surveys). The category "others" is a residual one.
7 We looked at both the mean and the median since both are valid measures of central tendency. Since these give roughly the same inferences, we discuss the mean only.
8 In the interest of space, we present results only for agricultural classes. The results for non-agricultural classes are available upon request.
9 We can see this by computing the share of population that is not in agriculture. For the 38th, 50th and 61st rounds, the figures are 26.31 percent, 27.85 percent and 35.62 percent, respectively.
10 A similar result has been obtained in other studies, e.g. Sen and Himanshu (2004 a and b) and Himanshu (2007). To be consistent with these studies, we compute the rate of poverty reduction in a particular period by dividing the fall in poverty rate in this period by the length of the period.
11 This result is consistent with NSS findings on land and livestock (NSS 2006, chapter 3).
12 This picture does not change if we include the residual category "others," the members of some which could be construed to be within the non-agricultural sector.
13 See e.g. www.twnside.org.sg/title/bioc2-cn.htm (accessed 29 March 2007), the statement of the FAO's regional representative for the Asia Pacific.
14 This is discussed in the next section in greater detail.
15 Agriculture is a state government subject in India. The center only makes broad guidelines, but the actual implementation depends upon the state governments, e.g. the Andhra

Pradesh government in the 1990s and until 2004 has been one of the most active proponents of agricultural reforms.

16 We include Water User Associations here both because in many cases they involve user charges and since they are part of a paradigm wherein other/newer kinds of organizations are given key roles instead of state agencies or democratically elected government bodies.

17 On this issue, it is worthwhile to point out that subsidies per farmer in 1999 in the European Union, Japan, US and OECD countries are $17,000, $26,000, $21,000 and $11,000, respectively. The corresponding figure for India is $66! (source: India Stat). The question of a level playing field is important as organizations like WTO fail to persuade the first world states like EU or the US to reduce subsidies to their farmers. This betrays hypocrisy on part of the multilateral agencies, which advocate trade liberalization for the developing countries.

18 On institutional credit pre- and post-liberalization, see Ramachandran and Swaminathan (2002), which also presents results from fieldwork in rural Tamil Nadu.

19 NSSO collects occupational data in their consumption and wealth surveys according to the NCO classification. We discovered that moneylenders in rural areas are beginning to appear in ever-larger numbers in the latest consumption surveys compared to the 1980s, although compared to the entire population, their numbers are still small. The big jump seems to have happened in the early 1990s. Moreover, we believe that there is an underestimation of this phenomenon for two reasons: (i) some moneylenders from whom farmers borrow could be in the urban sector (i.e. in the nearby town or city) and (ii) some of the moneylenders can be expected to hide their identity from government enumerators since they do not want the government to enquire about the interest rates and recovery practices.

20 Motiram and Robinson (2010) show how interlinking of markets can increase market power by facilitating collusion. On interlinking, see Bardhan and Udry (1999), chapter 9.

21 For an excellent conceptual discussion of agrarian power, especially in the Indian context, see Desai et al. (1984). In several articles in *The Hindu*, noted journalist Sainath has documented the rise in the power of these intermediaries, e.g. see Sainath (2005). Also see Misra (2007) and NSS (2005).

22 This is definitely true in the short run, although the long-run effects are not clear and are hotly debated among scholars. See Varshney (1995), chapter 5.

23 Many of these problems have been analyzed by a high-level committee appointed by the Indian government. See the report at http://fcamin.nic.in/dfpd/EventListing. asp?Section=High per cent20Level per cent20Committee per cent20Report&id_pk=12& ParentID=0 (accessed on 29 March 2010). Also see Harriss-White and Janakarajan (2004).

24 Some important groups are the Bharatiya Kisan Union (BKU), led by Mahindra Singh Tikait in UP and Ajmer Singh Lakhowal, Balbir Singh Rajwal and Bhupinder Singh Mann in Punjab, Shetkari Sanghatana (Sh S), led by Sharad Joshi in Maharashtra, Karnataka Rashtra Ryota Sangha (KRRS), led by Prof. Nanjundaswamy in Karnataka and Tamilaga Vyavasavavigal Sangham (TVS), led by Narayanaswamy Naidu in Tamil Nadu.

25 In specific contexts, there were other factors, e.g. in the green revolution belt (Punjab, Haryana and Western UP) some of these are: a long history of politicization of farmers, a discontent fuelled by the drying up of high incomes that farmers saw in the initial phases of green revolution, a caste-based solidarity among farmers due to the fact that they mostly belonged to the *Jat* community (Gill 1994).

26 For a discussion, apart from the above studies see Brass (1994) and Varshney (1995), chapters 4 and 5.

27 Both higher procurement prices and loan waivers are likely to yield higher benefits to large farmers since they have higher marketable surpluses and outstanding loans

to institutional sources. On the issue of loan waivers, especially during the Janata Dal government, see Varshney (1995: 143–5).
28 Sh S in the 1980s included their demands too but with a weak commitment.
29 Varshney (1995: 133–8) discusses the awkward position that laborers find themselves in relation to the farmers' movements. On the one hand they cannot antagonize large farmers, who provide them employment and credit, while on the other hand their awareness of their position pulls them towards agitation for higher wages and non-participation in agitations for higher prices.
30 This can be seen from procurement and support prices, both of which have been rising.
31 This class has been observed in other contexts too (Banaji 1994).
32 For instance, the rise of TDP in Andhra Pradesh is closely tied with the emergence of the provincial propertied classes that have been pushing for greater visibility and strength at the national level.
33 Hindutva ideology has also tended to succeed among the subalterns too in certain regions. For instance, for the role of *Adivasis* in the Gujarat genocide of 2002, see Balagopal (2002).
34 This is not true for Maharashtra. The Shetkari Sanghatana has tended to be more open about its mobilization. See Gupta (1997) for an interesting contrast between BKU and Sh S.
35 The all-India percentages of these groups are 8.81 percent, 19.72 percent, 35.84 percent and 35.63 percent, respectively.
36 NREGA can potentially benefit the SCs and STs since a bulk of them are laborers and because some states (e.g. Andhra Pradesh and Orissa) have as a part of NREGA given high priority to development of SC/ST lands. This can also have implications for the local political economy.
37 Ironically, the issues over which the small farmers and the Left groups are fighting over today are broadly the same issues that were highlighted in the "New" Farmer movements. With the diffusion of green revolution, these have become the central issues for small farmers today. That the introduction of subsidies may truly cause perverse changes is further ironic. For instance, power subsidies may only further exacerbate the exploitation of groundwater in rural India.
38 The massive debt waiver for farmers announced in the 2007 budget is another instance.
39 This is especially true in the area of providing credit to farmers through micro-credit groups. In our fieldwork in Andhra Pradesh, we observed that micro-credit is neither adequate nor affordable for agriculture. This is corroborated by evidence from other parts of the country (Ramachandran and Swaminathan 2002). NGO developmental activity seems somewhat scattered, democratically unaccountable and idiosyncratic. It seems as if the extensive Indian developmental state cannot be substituted easily.
40 Cooperatives have seen mixed success in developing countries. In the Indian context, while some (e.g. Operation Flood dairy cooperatives) have been very successful, others have failed. One reason for failure has been rent-seeking by powerful members (e.g. in sugar cooperatives in Maharashtra). These issues have been discussed in detail in Motiram and Vakulabharanam (2007).

8 How far have India's economic reforms been 'guided by compassion and justice'?
Social policy in the neoliberal era[1]

John Harriss

> It is hard to imagine how midday meals could have been extended to 100 million children without the firm intervention of the Supreme Court [but] the fact that it took public interest litigation to get political leaders to focus on children's nutritional rights is a telling reminder of the lopsidedness of Indian democracy
>
> Jean Dreze[1]

It was Yashwant Sinha who, as Finance Minister, spoke of 'reforms guided by compassion and justice', in his Budget speech in 2000. This is just the most succinct of any number of statements by Finance Ministers along similar lines. This essay enquires about the extent to which these claims have been translated into practice, and about the politics that lie behind such moderation of neoliberal policies as has occurred.

The theory of the neoliberal state, as David Harvey has argued in his *Brief History of Neoliberalism* (2005), holds that its essential function is to use the monopoly of violence to preserve fundamental freedoms, most importantly those of private property rights, together with maintaining the rule of law, freely functioning markets and free trade. Individuals, meanwhile, should take responsibility for their own welfare: 'Individual success or failure are interpreted in terms of entrepreneurial virtues or personal failings ... rather than being attributed to any systemic property (such as class exclusions widely attributed to capitalism)' (2005: 66). If, as is often the case according to a lot of evidence, the flexible labour markets that are essential to a neoliberal economy reduce the various resources that people derive from employment, then they will be hit very hard in the context of this determination to transfer all the responsibility for their well-being to individuals. At the same time neoliberals are profoundly suspicious of democracy, tending to favour 'governance' by experts and elites – a shift that may also be favoured by middle classes (see Harriss 2006) – and oppose as vested interests strong collective institutions such as trade unions. Then, as Harvey says, 'Faced with social movements that seek collective interventions ... the neoliberal state is itself forced to intervene, sometimes repressively, thus denying the very freedoms it is supposed to uphold' (2005: 69). Exactly as Polanyi feared, the utopian project of neoliberalism is ultimately sustained only by resort to authoritarianism.

This is the theory. In this essay, however, I aim to examine evidence about the practices of the Indian state in the context of liberalizing economic reforms and of India's increased integration into the global economy. The contemporary history of India presents a much more complex picture. There certainly are aspects of this history that may be explained by the theory of the neoliberal state, but the neoliberal project in India is tempered by India's constitutional design and state tradition, as well as by social movements that have transnational dimensions, and by popular democracy. Neoliberalism attempts to make a reality of what Polanyi famously characterizes in *The Great Transformation* (1944) as the myth of the self-regulating market economy. Such an economy, in his view, can never be fully realized because it depends upon the reduction of 'labour', which means people, 'land', which means the natural environment, and money, to commodities. In his analysis of the history of the nineteenth and early twentieth centuries he shows the existence of a 'double movement' as people resist being treated as commodities, and he argues that the turmoil of the first half of the twentieth century can be understood as the outcome of the double movement – which is the push on the one hand to realize the self-regulating market economy (the goal of neoliberalism), and the protective countermovement that emerges to resist it on the other (Block 2001: xxviii). In contemporary India the neoliberal drive is taking place in the context of a society in which, for all the manifest imperfections of Indian democracy, and the persistence of elements of the hierarchical *ancien regime* of caste and kingship, democratic ideas are by now deeply rooted.[3] The advocates of neoliberalism have had to contend with organized opposition in India's fractious and turbulent electoral democracy. The neoliberal drive is taking place, too, in the context of a society in which very strong expectations of the responsibilities of the state in regard to social welfare persist and are generally widely shared across social classes (Chandhoke 2005). It is also a state in which the constitutional design sets up many veto points that act as a brake upon abrupt changes and make for systemic stability (Kapur and Mehta 2005). Resistance to the neoliberal project has been built especially by social movements that have been able to use instruments of the state, achieving positive results when they have successfully appealed to the Supreme Court. What Polanyi described as the 'double movement' can be discerned in contemporary India. This phase of the continuing project of establishing the self-regulating market economy is taking place, too, in a very different political context. As Chandhoke argues, at the moment when neoliberal policies aimed to relegate the state to the sidelines, transnational movements in the sphere of civil society drawing on the rights discourse, have sought to reinstate the centrality of the state. As she says: 'The state is caught between the Scylla of economic globalization and the Charybdis of political globalization and heightened activity in civil society' (Chandhoke 2008).

I do not mean to advocate what, from the viewpoint of critics of neoliberalism, might be held to be a panglossian view – that all is well because the people have mobilized democratically against the onslaught of neoliberalism and of globalization. There are of course very powerful opposing forces. The Indian state is also repressive, frequently having to resort to action by a police force that is still organized primarily – as it was in the colonial period – to be the coercive agent of social control (Verma 2005). Police action is often supportive of what Harvey (2006) refers to as accumulation by dispossession – as the state seeks to take away rights to land and to natural resources in the interests of capital (see Jenkins, in this volume, on resistance to 'enclosures' for SEZs; and Kalshian 2007). Popular democracy, meanwhile, is regularly betrayed by unprincipled political leaders who seek the spoils of office or otherwise pursue the claims of particular social groups, defined by caste or by religion, at the expense of others. The collective organization of labour, never very powerful (Chibber 2003, though see also Teitelbaum 2006), has been further weakened. The Supreme Court has often not been supportive of labour rights. The social movements to which I have referred are not, with certain exceptions, popular mobilizations at all but more like lobby groups with a strongly middle-class character – and the middle class, fearful of the 'politics of din' (Alam 2004), is not necessarily supportive of popular democracy. In what follows, therefore, I am concerned to try to capture the tensions and contradictions that are evident in contemporary India.

The essay begins with a brief review of evidence on the social impact of the pursuit of neoliberal policies in India. I then examine trends in social policy before turning finally to the social movements and political mobilizations that reflect the double movement.

Trends in employment, wages and well-being

It has been widely argued that India is experiencing 'jobless growth' – a view supported by National Sample Survey (NSS) data showing that the rate of growth of the labour force as a whole, in the 1990s, fell below the rate of growth of population, and well below its rate of growth in the 1980s.[4] This notion is contested, however, in some interpretations of more recent NSS data that show acceleration of employment growth in 2000–5, within both urban and rural areas and amongst both men and women.[5] Not only is the 'jobless growth' thesis refuted but it is also argued by Sundaram (2007) that there has been a marked increase of 'good quality employment'. The essential points in this case are that self-employment has grown markedly in urban non-agriculture, especially amongst women; casual employment generally has declined; and regular salaried non-agricultural employment has increased, especially for women – at over 5 per cent per annum in the recent decade. For Unni and Raveendran (2007), however, this apparently rosy picture has to be qualified by recognition that some of the increase of regular salaried jobs is in a subsidiary capacity, indicating part-time working; while the increase in female participation is of women mainly at lower levels of education, implying that their access to employment is either in self-employment or at the bottom of the wage/salaried employment hierarchy. There is evidence, too, from the NSS that the extent of home-working has increased quite significantly especially amongst women. Most significant of all, the average daily real wages of regular workers declined in 2004–5, by comparison with 1999–2000 (particularly for females), indicating the growth of poorly remunerated jobs in urban areas in regular-salaried employment. Unni and Raveendran conclude from these observations that 'while there has been a growth of employment particularly in urban areas, the nature of this growth and the quality of the employment generated needs probing ... (there being many indications) ... of the informalization of work, which has implications for the levels of incomes and security of the workers' (2007: 199). The increased employment of women in particular in subsidiary, part-time occupations, some of them involving home-working, and large numbers of them being poorly remunerated, are developments that have been characteristic of economies that have participated in economic globalization (see, for example, Castells 1997).

'Informalization' of employment is of course greatly to be desired according to the advocates of economic liberalization, for labour market regulation beyond an absolute minimum is held to give rise to inflexibility and this in turn to reduce employment, because it increases labour costs. Besley and Burgess conclude from comparison across Indian states that those 'which amended the Industrial Disputes Act in a pro-worker direction experienced lowered output, employment, investment, and productivity in registered or formal manufacturing' (2004: 91). Their arguments have been subjected to significant criticism (for example by Bhattacharjea 2009), but it is on the basis of analyses of this kind that it is very commonly argued that labour market inflexibility is one of the most significant problems constraining India's economic growth. Both theoretical and empirical work, however, in relation to India and to other countries, does not lead to unequivocal conclusions regarding the impact of employment protection legislation (Sharma 2006, and Bhattacharjea 2009). There is also substantial evidence that 'employers have been able to find ways to reduce the workforce even with "restrictive" provisions in place' (Sharma 2006: 2081) – such as that on the retrenchment of workers – using the mechanism of the voluntary retirement scheme in the later 1990s (Nagaraj 2004), or in the indications of the increase in the numbers of contract workers in the total number of workers in manufacturing (from about 12 per cent in 1990 to 23 per cent in 2002 according to Sharma 2006: 2081).

Informalization/'flexibilization' has certainly been taking place, and its negative consequences for workers are attested to in a number of case studies. It is not necessarily the case that total household incomes decline, partly because of increased workforce participation on the part of women, and in some cases of children, but livelihoods have become much more vulnerable. Breman's analysis (2001) of the impact of informalization in Ahmedabad makes this point very forcefully; and it is shown up as well in Gooptu's studies (2007) of once permanently employed jute mill workers in Kolkata.

Given the trends in employment and wages the extent to which poverty has declined in India over the past 20 years might be found surprising. There can be few more earnestly debated topics than that of the trends in poverty in India over the past quarter century, partly because their measurement has been complicated by methodological changes. Now there are at least four alternative figures on the current 'headcount' of rural poverty from different official sources: 28 per cent from the Planning Commission; 42 per cent from the Tendulkar Committee report; 50 per cent from the Saxena Committee report; and 80 per cent from the National Commission for Enterprises in the Unorganized Sector.[6] There is some agreement that there was little poverty reduction in the 1990s, while the evidence of stagnation and crisis in the agricultural economy (see Vakulabharanam and Motiram, in this volume) shows the likelihood of widespread rural distress. If the incidence of rural poverty has declined since 2000 – as it appears to have done, according to several authorities – it may have been because of factors such as lower inflation and low increases in food prices, as both Himanshu (2007) and Dev (2008) argue. Subsequently the trends in both indicators have moved very rapidly in the opposite, adverse direction (and at the time of writing, in March 2010, increasing prices are causing great concern).[7] Datt and Ravallion, of the World Bank, conclude their most recent study of poverty trends very cautiously, saying that there 'signs', only, of 'an emerging trend towards a faster decline in the fraction of the poor in the country' (2010: 59), and reporting that there are indications, too, that 'the growth process may have become less pro-poor' (2010: 57). Some non-income indicators of poverty, too, for the recent period, present a disturbing picture[7]. The National Family Health Surveys[8] show little if any progress with regard, for instance, to malnutrition amongst children – the proportion of underweight children in India remains as high as 42 per cent (compared with 20 per cent in sub-Saharan Africa) – while the incidence of anaemia has been increasing.

In summary, then, while it clearly cannot be claimed that the pursuit of neoliberal policies is to be blamed for the continuing prevalence of ill-being in India, it is also clear that recent very high rates of economic growth have not been translated into comparably high rates of growth of productive employment, or of improvements in well-being. We consider now how, if at all, the state has responded to these trends.

Trends in social policy

Here we consider both the 'social sector' as conventionally understood (that is as including the budgetary categories of 'social services' and 'rural development' – which has included major poverty alleviation and employment programmes) and the safety net that is supplied through the Public Distribution System (PDS), intended to make staples available at low prices, and programmes such as the Integrated Child Development Scheme (ICDS), Midday Meal Scheme, and other social security measures. Scholars who have studied social policy and expenditure in India have sometimes excluded food policy and subsidies for the perfectly sensible reason that it is difficult to determine 'which component of that subsidy benefits the poor and which component benefits the food grain producers' (Mooij and Dev 2004: 104). Reasonable though this argument is, it surely is essential to take account of the functioning of the Public Distribution System (PDS), since this plays an essential part in the social safety net – given evidence on the strong relationship that holds between the relative success of major states in reducing poverty, and their support for the PDS (Harriss 2003a).[10]

Mooij and Dev have examined social policy and trends in expenditure on the social sector through the 1990s (Dev and Mooij 2002 and 2004), considering both the rhetoric of successive governments as this has appeared in budget speeches

– which are still significant policy statements in the Indian context – and the actual trends in expenditure. They show that Finance Ministers throughout the 1990s continued to offer strong commitments to the goals of addressing poverty and of social development, though always with the assumption that economic growth is the prior condition for poverty reduction. They trace shifts in the ways in which poverty has been conceptualized, explicitly or implicitly in the statements, and in the ways in which it is proposed that the problem should be addressed, noting through the decade a move towards a broader, multi-dimensional concept of poverty and 'a shift away from income and employment programmes to human development' (Mooij and Dev 2004: 97). They note a consistent silence on the issue of employment in the regular economy ('It would be no exaggeration to state that, as far as one can judge from these budget speeches, India in the 1990s had no employment policy' [2004: 103]), and a systematic neglect of the problems of economic inequality and redistribution. They conclude – following their analysis of the trends in expenditure, on which more below – that 'the human development framework [to which India moved in the later 1990s], sympathetic as it may be, helped to divert attention from the more structural characteristics of poverty' (2004: 117). But then, social policy in India has never been deployed as a redistributive measure, but has always treated the symptoms of poverty, not its structural causes.

How were resources actually allocated in the 1990s? Perhaps the most important point to stress is that throughout the 1990s and to the present, in spite of commitments that have been made by governments, public expenditure on both education and health in India (in the 1990s expenditure on education hovered at around 3 per cent of GDP, that on health only a little above 1 per cent)[11] is well below international norms, and even below what obtains in some poor developing countries (Dev and Mooij 2002: Tables 22 and 23). Social expenditure as a share of GDP has also been lower than in the 1980s, though its share in aggregate expenditure increased from the mid 1990s, probably reflecting – more than anything else – increased expenditure on wages and salaries following the recommendations of the Fifth Pay Commission of 1997. Mooij and Dev conclude that 'despite all the lip-service being paid, anti-poverty policies and social development do not get the priority they deserve ... The difficulty is to cut down on other expenditures, and other things get priority. This bias is not surprising given the social background and urban lifestyle of India's policy elite' (2004: 118). They suggest that the rising middle class has little interest in supporting universal provision of social security, not least because it has largely withdrawn from public education and withdrawn pretty much altogether from the public health care system.

Mooij and Dev's conclusion about the lack of real as opposed to rhetorical priority given to poverty alleviation and social development is borne out by what happened to the PDS in the 1990s and at the beginning of the new millennium. The introduction of the economic reforms led to pressures to contain India's fiscal deficit and to concern over the cost of food subsidies. It was argued that subsidies could be cut back and the PDS maintained if it were better targeted. The Targeted PDS was introduced in 1997. Households had to be classified as either 'Below Poverty Line' (BPL) or 'Above Poverty Line' (APL), then prices were to be kept low for the BPL but APL prices were raised substantially. The supply of foodgrains to the PDS was also reduced, and the consequence of the different measures was that offtake from the Food Corporation of India declined in the context of increasing stocks. It was also recognized by researchers that there were entirely understandable and predictable but still very serious problems associated with the definition and identification of BPL households, and that large numbers of people who should have been entitled to cheap foodgrains were denied their entitlements. The most egregious example of the failures of targeting came from Dharavi, supposedly Asia's largest slum, with a population of half a million, where only 151 families had been issued BPL cards (Swaminathan 2000: 97). But these problems were then compounded by the BJP-led government in 2001 when it sharply increased prices in the Fair Price shops, effectively removing the APL households altogether from the PDS. It was true that the monthly allocation to BPL families was increased from 10kg to 20kg but the requirement for the purchase to be made at one time put it beyond the reach of many poor families. The changes that were introduced at this time also linked increases in procurement prices to increase in issue prices to ration card-holders.[12] Madhura Swaminathan correctly anticipated, in an article written at the time, that the new scheme would leave the FCI with even larger stocks of grain. 'Are the stocks going to rot in warehouses?' she asked (*The Hindu* 2000). This was exactly what did happen in the succeeding years. There was really no more eloquent testimony to the subordination of the needs of poverty reduction and of social development to the dictates of neoliberal fiscal rectitude. The undercutting of what is probably the most important single component of social security provision in India has continued, outside the state of Tamil Nadu, which continues to run a universal system (see note 10). Data from the 61st round of the NSS show very high rates of exclusion of the most needy from the system (at least 50 per cent of BPL households do not have ration cards) – even though, contrary to the arguments of politicians – the costs of the food subsidy as a share of GDP have actually been falling (Swaminathan 2008).

There were some modest changes in the policy rhetoric in the early years of the new millennium, but the first Finance Minister of the United Progressive Alliance government that came to office in 2004, P. Chidambaram, reverted in his policy statements and in his budgets to a strongly neoliberal line, albeit wrapped in a lot of reference to the social objectives laid out in the Common Minimum Programme of the UPA, and to the importance of poverty elimination ('the whole purpose of democratic government', as he put it in 2005). These characteristics have not changed under a new Finance Minister, Pranab Mukherjee, in 2009–10.[13]

As it has evolved the policies pursued by the UPA in office have emphasized what, in the budget speech of 2006, Chidambaram described as 'flagship programmes', intended to realize the social objectives of the CMP: the National Rural Employment Guarantee Scheme, launched only after vigorous debate in 2006; the Bharat Nirman programme, launched in 2005–6 for building infrastructure and basic amenities in rural areas; the Mid-day Meal Scheme; the Rajiv Gandhi National Drinking Water Mission; the National Rural Health Mission, launched in 2005, and intended to provide accessible and affordable health care to the poorest rural households; the

Sarva Siksha Abhiyan, the initiative for the universalization of elementary education first introduced by the NDA government in 2001; the Total Sanitation Campaign; the Integrated Child Development Scheme, which is of long-standing but is supposed to be being extended and strengthened; and the Jawaharlal Nehru National Urban Renewal Mission, launched in 2005–6. The objectives of these programmes are all very worthy but Chidambaram was reluctant, in the practice both of his approach to taxation and raising of revenues, and of budgetary allocations, to resource them adequately, stinting the National Rural Employment Guarantee Scheme[13] – though this is the most important social policy innovation that has been implemented – and, in spite of small increases in allocations for education and health, encouraging private sector provision rather than providing for the universal access that he had seemed to promise.[15]

Primary responsibility for the social services, and for rural development, lies with the states rather than with the centre. Much depends, therefore, in practice, both on the allocation of financial resources by the centre to the states, and the efficiency with which the states are able to utilize budgeted funds. An important trend in the period with which we are concerned has been the introduction of programmes – such, notably, as the 'flagship programmes' – by the centre, but the resources devoted to these have tended to substitute for the allocation of funding by the states. The proportion of central government (Plan and Non-Plan) expenditure allocated to social services and rural development in the early years of the present century continued the trend of the later 1990s. It stood at a little over 10 per cent from 1996–7 (Dev and Mooij 2002: Table 8) through to 2005–6 (the first full year in office of the UPA government) when it rose to 13.75 per cent. There was a further increase to 15.48 per cent in 2007–8, and further projected increases to 19.46 per cent according to the Budget Estimates for 2009–10. Though the increased allocations of 2005–6 to 2007–8 were accounted for in part by increases for education and health, latterly these have fallen back again. The recent increase in all 'social' allocations is accounted for by increased expenditures for rural development, and by special allocations for north eastern areas (Government of India 2010: Table 11.3). Expenditure on social services as a share of aggregate expenditure by central and state governments combined stood at around 23 per cent in the later 1990s (Dev and Mooij 2002: Table 5), but this figure dipped down to around 20 per cent in 2002–3 through to 2005–6, at which point it began modestly to increase again. The Revised Budget Estimates for 2008–9 have it standing at 24.0 per cent, and the Budget Estimates for 2009–10 at a fraction less than this (Government of India 2010: Table 11.4.). As a share of GDP social services expenditure remained stuck at around 5.5 per cent (with that on education about 2.6 per cent and that on health about 1.2 per cent) through to 2008–9 and 2009–10 – when an increase to 7.23 per cent is projected. It has been reported that social sector spending by all the states has declined (it stood at 38.6 per cent of total expenditure in 1990–5 and at 35.9 per cent in the budget estimates for 2007–8).[16]

The broad figures show that the share of social services in total expenditure has hardly increased under the UPA regime, in spite of the increases in the budgeted allocations of the central government, to which the Finance Minister has drawn much attention in his speeches. There is a plethora of schemes designed to provide social safety nets, and social security for unorganized sector workers, most of them introduced since the inception of India's economic reforms (listed in Dev 2008, Appendices 6 and 8), but is known that most of them, in most states, actually reach very few of their intended beneficiaries. The National Commission on Enterprises in the Unorganized Sector, for example, estimates that only 6 per cent of unorganized workers (who make up 93 per cent of the labour force, remember), are getting some kind of social security benefits (Dev 2008: 216). There has been no great change in the priority being accorded to social development, in spite of Chidambaram's reference to 'universal access to education and health' – in which spheres, it is generally recognized, people have turned increasingly to private sector providers (see note 14). It is true that in his first budget, in 2004, Chidambaram introduced a 2 per cent cess on all taxes, to raise money specifically for education (increased to 3 per cent in 2007, with the additional 1 per cent being dedicated for secondary education). But in practice this has been used to substitute for other outlays rather than to supplement them, and it is estimated that the education cess now accounts for about 60 per cent of the total outlay on education (Himanshu 2008). The accent in UPA budgets has been on classic neoliberal concerns: tax-cutting, reducing the fiscal deficit and cutting back regulation. Beneath the rhetoric of the budget speeches it appears that concessions have been made to the achievement of the objectives of the Common Minimum Programme, rather than these having been made the core purpose of policy. 'Targeting' and 'privatization' are key themes; and though increases in expenditure on education and health have been budgeted for they have been way below what would be required to achieve the stated targets in the CMP of raising expenditure on education to 6 percent and that on health to 2–3 per cent of GDP. The combined expenditure of centre and states, as a proportion of GDP, remained below 3 per cent for education and 2 per cent for health through to 2008–9, when the Revised Budget estimates show expenditure on education creeping fractionally above 3 per cent of GDP. The problem is not that the Indian state invests less in the social sector in this time of liberalization, but that historically state spending has been so low. Dev and Mooij's conclusions from their analysis of social sector expenditure in the 1990s, concerning the lack of priority given to social services and to social security, still stand, in spite of the commitments made in the Common Minimum Programme.

The limitations of social provisioning in India are clear, yet there have also been significant innovations in public policy in recent years that reflect the kind of 'double movement' of which Polanyi wrote, and the pressures upon the state. The Government of India has latterly 'enacted laws that upgrade the status of social welfare coded in Part IV of the Constitution, to that of fundamental right, in response to campaigns launched by civil society organizations (and) interventions of the Supreme Court' (Chandhoke 2008). In all of this the role of the middle class has been decisive and it is altogether more complex than Mooij and Dev suggested in the conclusions of their analysis of social policy.

Mobilizations around social and economic rights

Several important social and economic rights have been legislated for in recent years:

(i) *Right to Education*: Thanks in part, at least, to the engagement of the National Alliance for Fundamental Right to Education (which was supported by CRY, an NGO funding agency), in November 2001 the 93rd Constitution Amendment Bill was passed by the Lok Sabha, and a new sub-clause has been entered into the Constitution guaranteeing that the state shall provide free and compulsory education to all children aged 6–14. The Bill long awaited implementation, however, because of mobilizations by civil society groups over the neglect of early childhood development and failure to provide for those aged over 14, and a clause that introduces compulsion of parents or guardians of young children. The legislation was stimulated in the first place by a ruling of the Supreme Court in 1993 to the effect that 'though right to education is not stated expressly as a fundamental right, it is implicit in and flows from the right to life guaranteed under Article 21'. In August 2009 the Lok Sabha passed the free education bill, and it came into effect in April 2010. Criticisms concerning the failure to address the needs of early childhood development, and the disparities between well-funded private schools and state-run schools continued to be expressed (Jha and Parvati 2010).

(ii) *Right to Information*: The Freedom of Information Act was notified in January 2003, in response to a campaign launched first in 1996 by the Mazdur Kisan Shakti Sangathan (MKKS) in Rajasthan, which also invoked a ruling of the Supreme Court.

(iii) *Right to Food and Right to Work*: The National Rural Employment Guarantee Act was enacted by parliament in September 2005, and extended to all districts in the country in April 2008, providing for up to 100 days of guaranteed wage employment to rural households. This was the outcome of a campaign initially for the Right to Food, which was launched in 2001, stimulated by the filing of public interest litigation by the Peoples Union for Civil Liberties demanding that accumulating stocks of food in government warehouses be used to meet endemic conditions of scarcity and deprivation.[17] The Supreme Court subsequently issued notice in September 2001 directing government to provide for midday meals in all schools, and to extend the ICDS. Later the Campaign began to press the UPA government to deliver on its commitment to the Common Minimum Programme (CMP). The CMP included a commitment to a national employment guarantee, and key activists with the Right to Food campaign, who were also members of the National Advisory Council (appointed to monitor the implementation of the CMP), presented a draft bill at its first meeting. There was subsequently considerable conflict between different government departments over the bill, and the further, considerably diluted draft brought eventually before parliament by the Ministry of Rural Development was subjected to fierce criticism by civil society actors. Together they formed a campaigning organization, People's Action for Employment Guarantee (PAEG), which – amongst other actions – organized a 'bus yatra' through ten states to mobilize popular support. The Act that was finally passed reflected the success of the PAEG in securing the restoration of most of the provisions of the original proposals. Early studies of the implementation of the NREGA show up the considerable difficulties of implementation, but also that it has led to increased popular awareness of rights.[18]

The campaigns that have driven all this legislation, invoking the language of rights, have been led by middle-class intellectuals, deploying a wide repertoire of political strategies, making use of transnational networks and deriving funding from international NGOs, and latterly involving the support of the Left parties on which the UPA government depended for support from the outside[18]. With the exception of the campaign on the right to information, however, they have not been concerned with raising popular consciousness, but have rather lobbied policymakers; and they have achieved notable results only when they have successfully appealed to the Supreme Court. Jean Dreze wrote tellingly of the Right to Food Campaign in 2004:

> The 'leaders' almost invariably come from a privileged social background. However sensitive they may be to the viewpoint of the underprivileged, they cannot but carry a certain baggage associated with their own position. The bottom line is that, with few exceptions, social movements in India (or for that matter elsewhere) are far from democratic. This lack of internal democracy jars with the values we claim to stand for, and creates a deep inconsistency between means and ends.
>
> (2004: 128)

The democratic limitations of the counter movement against neoliberalism in contemporary India are also reflected in actions, or intended actions, against labour rights. The Second National Labour Commission, which reported in 2002, sought to enhance the rights of employers to close establishments and to legitimize the use of contract labour, whilst expressing criticism of 'the increasing tendency on the part of trade unions to get together in *ad hoc* struggle committees' (Rajalakshmi 2002:101). In 2003 the Supreme Court, in responding to litigation over the Government of Tamil Nadu's dismissal of large numbers of public employees, ruled that government employees had no 'fundamental, legal, moral or equitable rights to strike'. This was part of a series of verdicts on democratic rights and labour issues that went against the interests of labour (Venkatesan 2003) – though more recently judges in the Supreme Court and in the Madras High Court have emphasized the need to protect the rights of workers in the context of liberalization and globalization.[20] The most striking incident of police repression of labour rights took place in July 2005 against workers in a Honda plant in Gurgaon; and this was in a context in which lockouts by employers have come to account for a much higher proportion of person-days lost than strikes by employees.[21]

On the other hand there have been important moves toward the organization of some groups of unorganized sector workers, such as construction workers and women employed in rolling bidis (Agarwala 2006). Agarwala suggests that these mobilizations amongst unorganized sector workers have contributed to making government take up their needs by establishing the National Commission for Enterprises in the Unorganized Sector (in September 2004). The Commission prepared two draft bills: (a) Unorganized Sector Workers Social Security Bill, 2006; and (b) Unorganized Sector Workers (Conditions of Work and Livelihood Promotion) Bill, 2006. These were, however, set aside by the UPA government in May 2007, and substituted by a single bill (passed into law in December 2008), much watered down by comparison with the NCEUS proposals. Still, the sheer fact of so much official policy interest in the unorganized sector (adumbrated by Dev 2008) is remarkable, and shows how far the Indian state has been pushed away from the neoliberal model.

Conclusions

The single clear conclusion that emerges from the preceding analysis is that in so far as successive governments of India have pursued 'reforms guided by compassion and justice' it has been as a result of pressures from within civil society, usually supported in parliament by the Left parties. Governments have enacted lots of social security legislation, a large part of it since the introduction of economic reforms in 1991 (see Dev 2008, appendices), but have rarely backed it up with adequate financial allocations. The historic failures of the Indian state to allocate sufficient resources for public education and health services are not being corrected in the way that it was claimed they would be by the UPA government, and in many ways they are being compounded by the encouragement of privatization. In spite of the rhetoric of budget speeches, priority has been given to neoliberal economic policies. No sector of public policy shows this more clearly than does the public distribution system, which provides the single most important component of publicly provided social security in India. It has been under continuous threat through most of the period since the introduction of the economic reforms. Nonetheless, the compulsions upon Indian governments to provide for social security have ensured that the Indian state continues to depart quite significantly from the neoliberal model. The Indian state tradition persists, and even if the character of the state is changing, as Rudolph and Rudolph have argued (2001), from an interventionist to a regulatory state, there remain significant checks upon and moves away from state support for social welfare. The Supreme Court did, after all, intervene in response to public interest litigation to check the moral offence of allowing foodgrains to rot in government godowns.

The counter-movements in India that have brought about some tempering of neoliberal policies are not, however, popular mass movements (with the partial exception of the right to information campaign), but rather are coalitions of local NGOs and advocacy groups, drawing on transnational networks, led by middle-class intellectuals. We should recognize, as Pratap Bhanu Mehta has argued, that the Indian middle class is 'now struggling to articulate new conceptions of social justice'.[22] But as Mehta also said, the middle class is 'not an unalloyed carrier of virtue', and in others of their actions members of the Indian middle classes show both their mistrust of democracy and their support for measures directed at the disciplining of the urban poor. Even progressive citizens' organizations are not notably supportive of the struggles of the urban poor for living space and for livelihoods, and they tend to favour technocratic solutions to public problems as against representative democracy (Fernandes and Heller 2006; Harriss 2006). They are not generally supportive of the collective organization of working people, towards which the Indian state has been increasingly repressive. The 'lopsidedness' of Indian democracy, of which Jean Dreze speaks in the epigraph to this essay, has been very much in evidence.

Notes

1 This paper owes a great deal of stimulation and draws some empirical material from Neera Chandhoke's so-far-unpublished report on 'Globalization and the Indian State'. I am very grateful to Neera, and also to Madhura Swaminathan for giving me access, before its publication, to her recent paper on food security.
2 *Frontline*, 11 March 2005, 22(5), 52.
3 See Javeed Alam, *Who wants Democracy?* (2004).
4 Different scholars provide different estimations of these growth rates, but there is agreement on the trends. Dev (2008), Himanshu (2007) and Unni and Raveendran (2007) all estimate the growth rate between 1993–4 and 1999–2000 as having been a little less than 1 per cent per annum, compared with a rate of around 2 per cent per annum in 1983 to 1993–4. Sundaram (2007) gives estimates of 1.45 per cent annum in 1993–4 to 1999–2000, as compared with 1.71 per cent in the earlier period.
5 Dev (2008: Table 7.5) estimates the growth rate over this period to have been 2.86 per cent per annum; Sundaram (2007) gives 2.7 per cent and Unni and Raveendran (2007) and Himanshu (2007) rates of just under 3 per cent per annum.
6 See Jean Drèze 'Poverty Estimates vs Food Entitlements', *The Hindu*, 24 February 2010.
7 The fact that the government should have announced that 40 per cent of the population are eligible for food subsidies to provide for one meal per day (BBC News report 20 April 2010) seems to bear out these arguments and to cast doubt on the more optimistic assessments of poverty reduction.
8 Utsa Patnaik has shown that if poverty is measured directly, in terms of calorie intake, it is seen to have increased very sharply in rural India (Patnaik 2007).
9 These surveys have been conducted in 1992–3, 1998–9 and most recently in 2005–6, corresponding fairly closely, therefore, in terms of timing, with the 50th, 55th and 61st rounds of the NSS.
10 Visits to villages in Tamil Nadu in the summer of 2008 most strongly confirmed this argument. The state is unique in continuing to have a universal PDS, and ration rice was available at that time at the rate of Rs. 2 per kg (and more recently at Rs. 1 per kg). This quite clearly makes a crucial contribution to the livelihoods of poor people, and in combination with the availability of even only a few days of employment under NREGS, helps to empower labourers.
11 The UPA government, under the Common Minimum Programme that it agreed with its allies, made commitments to devoting 6 per cent of GDP to education, and 2–3 per cent to health services.

12 A major policy change at this time was that the price at which the Food Corporation of India sells grain for the PDS to state governments was set at half the 'economic cost' incurred by the FCI for BPL and at full economic cost for APL.
13 See articles by C. P. Chandrasekhar and R. Ramakumar, *Frontline*, 26, 15 for 31 July 2009, on Mukherjee's first budget in July 2009; and by Subrat Das and Yamini Mishra, 'What does Budget 2010 imply for the social sector?, in *Economic and Political Weekly*, March 27 2010, xlv(13), 64–8, on the 2009–10 Budget.
14 In the budget of 2006 the sum of Rs. 10,170 crores was allocated to NREGS, but at the same time expenditure on other rural employment programmes was cut by Rs. 9,000 crores. In the following year the scheme was extended from 200 to 330 districts of the country, but this was backed by only a 3.5 per cent increase in budgeted expenditure. And the proportion of budget expenditure devoted to rural employment declined from 2.56 per cent in 2005–6, before the introduction of NREGS, to 1.92 per cent in the budget for 2008–9 (Himanshu 2008).
15 The drive toward privatization is reflected in the *Approach Paper to the Eleventh Plan*, which emphasizes targeting of social services, user charges, and the importance of parental 'choice' in education (Athreya 2006). Private spending accounts for around four-fifths of health expenditure in India, one of the highest ratios in the world. This is a telling indication of the extent to which even very poor people turn to private providers (Ghosh 2007).
16 These data from a Reserve Bank of India report commented upon in *Financial Express*, 14 January 2008.
17 The website of the Right to Food Campaign (www.righttofoodindia.org) is very informative. The Campaign's work has extended to Midday Meals, universalization of the ICDS, revival of the universal PDS, and campaigning for land and forest rights.
18 See articles in *Economic and Political Weekly*, 2008, 43(19); and – for reports of evaluative studies conducted in 2008 – *Frontline*, 2009, 26(1).
19 This was until the tensions between the Left and the government over its nuclear deal with the United States led to the withdrawal of Left support in July 2008.
20 See S. Dorairaj, 'Verdict for the worker', *Frontline* 2010, 27(7).
21 Praful Bidwai notes that 'In the three-year period of 1994–6, lockouts on average claimed 85 per cent more person-days than did strikes. That disproportion further increased in the three years 2002–04 to 218 per cent'. (*Frontline* 22(17),110).
22 From an article in *Indian Express*, 7 June 2006.

9 The transformation of citizenship in India in the 1990s and beyond

Niraja Gopal Jayal

Contemporary citizenship discourses and the idea of the citizenship regime

Even as scholars and philosophers contemplate a post-national world of cosmopolitan citizens, the idea of citizenship in the Western world has already been dramatically transformed in a way that is at odds with the attractive image proffered by the votaries of cosmopolitanism. Historically mature states, confident of their place in the world, have recently been observed searching frenetically for ways of defining their national identities and 'national values' to better cement ties between citizens, and also to ensure that new citizens adduce sufficient proof of subscribing to the shared values of the nation. New citizenship tests in the United Kingdom, the United States, Australia and the Netherlands testify to this.

This transformation has, of course, occurred after 9/11 and the debacle of multiculturalism in Western societies. It was, however, preceded by another moment of transformation that occurred in the 1980s, when ascendant neoliberalism triggered a questioning of the welfare state on the grounds that it had encouraged a lazy parasitism and discouraged civic sentiments. That economic turn delegitimized social citizenship and was also accompanied by a curiously celebratory rediscovery of the virtues of civic republicanism.

If the first moment of neoliberal transformation affected the *content* of citizenship in terms of both social citizenship and the identity dimension, the second moment has been chiefly concerned with the question of *who is or can be a citizen*. Until recently, the preoccupation with the substance of citizenship, and the acceptance of the nation-state as its operative framework, had led theorists to presume that citizenship-as-legal-status is on the whole, and for the most part, a settled issue (Kymlicka and Norman 1995). The imperilled project of multiculturalism, and the renewed contentiousness of legal aspects of citizenship, now forces a rethinking of the fundamentals and parameters of the normative theory of citizenship.

These essentially northern transformations convey a message that has resonance even in the south. They suggest that practices of citizenship remain contentious, bound up as they are with the two abidingly contentious questions of, first, national identity and membership of a political community; and second, the attribution of social and economic rights to citizens. This paper seeks to understand, in the Indian context, the impact of the 'three central transformations' of the last decade and a half in terms of precisely these two dimensions of citizenship: the relationship between national identity and citizenship; and the future of social citizenship. It situates the discussion of these themes in the context of the foundational conception of Indian citizenship, which has been decisively altered by the three distinct forces of social, political and economic transformation in the last 15 years, viz. Hindu nationalism, backward caste mobilization and economic reform.

In doing so, the paper deploys the concept of 'citizenship regime' (formulated by Jenson and Phillips [1996] in relation to Canada, and developed by Yashar [2005] for Latin America)[1] in a contextually useful way, encompassing questions such as: who is a citizen and what are the terms of inclusion and exclusion? What is the nature of the identification of citizenship with nationality or cultural identity? What is the recognized unit of citizenship – individuals or groups – especially for the articulation of effective citizenship claims? What is the substance of citizenship rights, including and especially the rights of social citizenship? What is the role of the state in stabilizing or undermining a particular citizenship regime? How do state and societal discourses and policies – of recognition or redistribution – shape citizenship?

While the paper does not comment on each of these questions, it does argue that the three central transformations that are the concern of this volume have definitively altered the nature of the citizenship regime (CR) defined by the constitutional vision. It is obviously not the claim here that these three transformations alone, or at one fell stroke, accomplished this shift, or even that they cohere with each other. However, that a decisive shift has taken place between CR c.1950 and CR c.2000 is irrefutable, and these three transformations have indeed played a central role in mediating them. The next section of the paper outlines the major shifts that have occurred, not least the implicit abandonment of the project of social citizenship. Additionally, it reflects on the need to problematize the implications of these shifts and suggests other developments that also have an impact on the citizenship regime. The third and final section of the paper presents a case study that ironically demonstrates how the claims of denizens struggling for legal citizenship are articulated in the language of social citizenship. This is contrasted with the radically different approach of the state to claims of 'dual citizenship' emanating from emigrants from India now living in the countries of the North.

Citizenship regimes: before and after the central transformations

Citizenship regime c.1950

There would be little disagreement about the main features of the citizenship regime c.1950, though it is not in the articles of the Constitution relating explicitly to citizenship that these are to be found. The deliberations of the Constituent Assembly on the question of citizenship were prolonged and vexatious, with Dr. P. S. Deshmukh arguing that Article 5 'has been the most ill-fated article in the whole Constititution'. (CAD 1949a: 351) Nehru echoed this view, saying that this article had received more consideration in the past few months than any other article in the Constitution (CAD 1949b: 398). What lay at the heart of the debate on this article was not any contention about the *philosophy* of citizenship, but the mainly technical question of determining who is an Indian, defined almost exclusively in the context of the migration to and from Pakistan. The debate on Articles 5–11 (and 5 and 6 in particular) was thus conducted in the shadow of questions of descent and domicile.[2]

It is therefore outside of Articles 5–11 that the substantive constitutional vision of universal citizenship is to be found. The chief preoccupation of the founders of the republic was the creation of a society whose citizens shared a strong sense of national identity despite cultural diversity. The founding idea of India was of an intrinsically diverse and plural nation-state, and though national identity was defined in 'national-civic' rather than 'national-ethnic' (Beiner 1995:8) terms, it remained a rather wobbly construct, a complicated 'national-civic-plural-ethnic' combination that curiously did not seem to its sponsors to be chaotic or untidy, much less inconsistent.

The project of Indian modernity – and its approach to cultural diversity – is perhaps nowhere better exemplified than in Jawaharlal Nehru's *Discovery of India*, the *locus classicus* of the unity-in-diversity approach. His understanding of communal conflict between the Hindus and Muslims was irreproachably Marxist (Nehru 1989: 466–7) and, therefore, poverty, backwardness, caste, region and religion were all viewed as different faces of the same retrograde phenomenon, which would be transcended by the alliance of science, reason and economic development. Modernization, on this account, would provide an impetus to processes of secularization, and the conflict between universalist and particularist citizenship would be negotiated and ultimately resolved on this terrain.[3]

Within a democratic political framework, universal citizenship should translate into universal adult franchise. Though some members of the Constituent Assembly supported an educational/literacy qualification for political rights, Ambedkar argued forcefully that the suffrage itself would serve as an education, especially for the hitherto excluded 'untouchables', and therefore no educational or property qualification was acceptable (Ambedkar 1989). The Sapru Committee came to similar conclusions, though from rather different premises. The risk of enfranchizing the entire adult population, it stated, should be taken to prevent the concentration of power in the hands of a powerful few. Hence, though the average voter's 'judgement may be faulty, his reasoning inaccurate, and his support of a candidate not infrequently determined by considerations removed from a high sense of democracy, he is yet no better or worse than the average voter in many parts of Europe where adult franchise has been in force for some time' (quoted in Austin 1999: 147) Together with adult suffrage, the adoption of direct elections was justified by the argument that they made possible the creation of a new national identity superseding the parochial and caste identities of people (ibid.: 46–9).

Citizenship in the modern Indian nation-state was thus presented as the biggest of the 'Chinese boxes' (to use Walzer's metaphor): a primary, architectonic and essentially secular civic identity that transcends all ascriptive identities. The mythology of the nation-state invested the attachment to national identity with moral superiority over the attachment to primordial identities of religion, language or caste affiliation. This obscured, of course, the rather obvious fact that *both* types of identity are social and political constructs.[4] More importantly, it obscured the tensions and contradictions inherent in what Rudolph and Rudolph have described as the '*simultaneous* commitment to communities and to equal citizenship' (1987: 178, emphasis added).

The institutions of governance were intended to conform to the liberal-individualist conception of equal citizenship, encompassing equal rights for all individual citizens and upholding the principle of equality before the law. The only significant exceptions to this were (a) the recognition of certain categories of rights for which (cultural) communities rather than individuals would be the bearers of rights; and (b) the provisions for compensatory discrimination for historically disadvantaged groups.

How these exceptions were justified is important. In the normative argument that underpinned the departure from the principle of equality, the underlying assumption in respect of religious minorities was that the democratic principle of equality is an insufficient guarantee for minorities who will, in the presence of a dominant majority, always be insecure in the enjoyment of their cultural rights.[5] In relation to members of the scheduled castes and scheduled tribes, the normative justification was that equality of opportunity would be effectively denied to these groups as they could not, given their histories of marginalization, compete on really equal terms, and hence required special guarantees as enabling background conditions of equality.[6] As such, the reservation of seats in public institutions was not, as it seemed to be, a denial of equality; on the contrary, it was a measure designed to promote *effective* equality. In both cases – separate personal laws and policies of compensatory discrimination – these were viewed as *interim* measures on the path to a society in which greater social equality and processes of secularization would eventually lead to the universalist norms of citizenship becoming firmly entrenched.

The conception of national identity on which the Indian idea of citizenship rested was actually quite amorphous,[7] which may explain its fragility in the face of the first systematic attempt to give concrete shape to the nation, viz. the project of Hindutva. This finds reflection in the political discourse of the early years after independence, in the ironic but unmistakable resemblance between the qualities attributed to, on the one hand, the Congress Party in the nationalist movement, and carried over into the Indian nation after independence, and, on the other, the features attributed to Hinduism. The adjectives employed (rightly or wrongly) to describe the Hindu religion – absorptive, assimilative, accommodative, eclectic, tolerant – were treated as accurate descriptions of society itself, and therefore as attributes of the 'umbrella' nationalist party that claimed to represent all its members.

Universalist citizenship conceptualized as national-civic identity was complemented by the constitutional vision of social citizenship, expressed in the welfare-orientation of the state, which assumed primary responsibility for development. In addition to the fundamental rights of citizens (interpreted generously by the Courts), the Directive Principles of State Policy, though non-justiciable, provided the framework for a just and egalitarian society.

The transformation of citizenship in India in the 1990s and beyond 145

In sum, then, the Indian citizenship regime c.1950 conceptualized the individual as the basic unit of citizenship, whose inclusion in the polity was on equal terms with every other citizen. Groups and cultural communities found recognition in the form of special compensatory provisions, but they were not in the first instance viewed as the locus of the primary membership of the individual; nor were they recognized as the mandated mediators of group interests vis-à-vis the state. In terms of the substance of citizenship rights, these were interpreted comprehensively and expansively, even if the state capacity to provide these was wanting. However, the state remained not only the locus of the primary loyalty of the citizen, but also the agency entrusted with maintaining and upholding the citizenship regime.

Citizenship regime c.2000

The standard narrative of India's Great Transformation translates rather easily into a plausible, but disquietingly predictable, narrative about citizenship. First, the ideology of Hindu religious nationalism sponsored by the BJP and its affiliates in the Sangh Parivar invented *new forms of exclusion*, which were backed with grotesque violence. The genocide against Muslims in Gujarat (2002) and the killings of Graham Staines and other Christian missionaries a few years earlier, are evidence of the venomous anti-minorityism that is the hallmark of the Parivar's exclusionary ideology.[8] From Golwalkar and Savarkar, to Advani and Vajpayee, the Parivar has argued that Bharat, the Indian nation, is essentially a 'cultural unit'. Religious minorities, on this argument, are acceptable only because they share in this historical and cultural legacy by virtue of having been born on this soil.[9] As such, the blood in their veins is still Hindu, which is what their ancestors were: 'Even today, we are not one because we are citizens of one State. Rather Bharat is one State because we are one.' (Vajpayee 1969 [2007]: 315).

By contrast, the caste-based political parties of north India invented *new forms of inclusion*, expressed in higher levels of representation for members of the backward castes in legislative bodies and a presence in the institutions of governance. Of course, the claim of empowerment through such political mobilization relates primarily to the promise of these parties to give dignity and respect to the social lives of their voters/constituents. Driven by the mobilization and heightened participation of the subordinate castes, this phenomenon has been famously described as 'the second democratic upsurge' (Yadav 2000)

It is true that by the early 1990s, the OBCs, whose representation in India's first parliament was of the order of 5 per cent, had achieved a representation of 25 per cent, which has been more or less sustained since. These numbers were, in the main, the contribution of the northern states, which witnessed what Jaffrelot has called 'India's Silent Revolution'. Backward caste representation in the Lok Sabha from these states increased from 16.31 per cent in 1991 to 22.17 per cent in 2004 (Jayal 2006: 135). Likewise, the earlier dominance of upper castes in Union Cabinets between 1947–90 was eroded, with a trend towards greater backward caste representation beginning in 1984, reaching its highest point – 53 per cent and 58 per cent respectively – in the two United Front governments of 1996–8 (ibid.: 157–8). The acceptance, and later the implementation, of the 1980 recommendations of the Mandal Commission created guaranteed representation for the OBCs in public employment as well. In 2008, similar quotas were extended to admissions to institutions of higher education, after a good deal of popular contention finally adjudicated by the Supreme Court. In addition, the regionalization of the party system also brought with it new opportunities for even the smallest regional (often OBC) parties to participate in coalition governments at the federal level, and sometimes to exercise critical bargaining power.

Finally, there is the great economic transformation wrought by the process of economic reform and the liberalization of the economy, and the consequent widening of disparities, generating *new types of exclusion* based chiefly on class (though also on regional north–south differences in the pace of development as well as the widening rural–urban divide) and expressed in the form of exclusions from the patterns of consumption of the middle and upper classes, as also from the aspirational lifestyles of the upwardly mobile and the wealthy, as seen in a range of media representations from the popular cinema to television advertising.[10] The rise of the new middle class, as Fernandes argues, has not only shaped societal responses to liberalization, it has also begun to assert agency as a distinctive social group. Some of its claims to, and activities on, urban public spaces – such as neighbourhood beautification programmes – represent ways of constituting civic life in profoundly exclusionary ways (Fernandes 2006: 211–13). There is also arguably some coherence between the expanding middle class (with its predominantly Hindu and upper-caste character[11]), its consumerism, diasporic links and receptivity to cultural chauvinism.

Concurrently, neoliberal policies and fiscal deficits have forced cutbacks in public spending, which directly affect the provision of social citizenship. Service delivery increasingly involves donor funding (such as the World Bank-funded District Primary Education Programme, for instance) and the implementation of these programmes increasingly involve the participation of non-governmental organizations. The reinvention of the citizen as consumer in the domain of the market is paralleled by her reinvention as a client vis-à-vis public service delivery.

The big changes of the 1990s have thus clearly played a central role in redefining the nature of inclusion and exclusion in India's society and polity. The old exclusions practised by the politics of Hindutva – against the Muslim community – have become more deeply entrenched through a wider dissemination of Hindu nationalist ideology in society. New exclusions have been created by economic liberalization. It is only democratic mobilization that can be credited with effecting new inclusions. However, while inclusion is the hallmark of backward class mobilization, it has in turn engendered its own exclusions – notably, that of the Most Backward Classes (MBCs).

Though it presents a broadly accurate picture, the unambiguousness of this narrative of the transformation of citizenship regimes must be qualified and problematized in two ways: first, by examining the multiple patterns of inclusion and exclusion that have been unleashed by it, the ambiguities and contradictions internal to subordinate groups, and also the conflicts between them; and second, by bringing into view some other transformations of consequence that have occurred during the same period.

Take the democratic mobilization of the backward classes first. It is well known that the domination of particular caste groups within this broad category of OBCs has led to a simmering resentment in those – such as the Most Backwards – notionally included, but effectively excluded, from the privileges conferred by such membership. The agitation against the implementation of the Mandal Report in 1989, and again in 2006 against its extension to institutions of higher education, are taken as among the defining moments of the popular democratic mobilization, because the participants in these agitations were mainly upper-caste youth. It is, however, interesting to examine not merely the familiar response of the upper castes but also that of the *Dalits*. It is well known that the relationship between these communities in rural India is fraught with conflict, and that OBCs are commonly perceived as oppressors of *Dalits*. As far as quotas in employment or education are concerned, the *Dalits* have long enjoyed the benefit of reserved seats and these need not logically be arenas of conflict. But leading *Dalit* intellectual Chandra Bhan Prasad explained his opposition to a political unity between *Dalits* and OBCs thus:

> Shudras play with Dalit sentiments – they will point to the social monster called Brahmans, rob Dalits' support, come to power, and then turn to Dalits to oppress them. Every ruling group looks for subjects. And the Shudras, once in power, treat Dalits as subjects as they cannot treat Brahmans as subjects ... Dalit-OBC unity is theoretically most undesirable, as the fruits of unity will go to Upper OBCs or Upper Shudras, who tend to practice Brahmanism of the medieval era. The Shudras' aim is to dislodge the Brahmans, and continue with the Chatur-Varna Order, while Dalits want to destroy the Order itself. So, when both the categories have different aims, where is the theoretical basis for unity?
> (Prasad 2001)

Many such conflicts, of course, have already played out politically. The *Malas* and the *Madigas*, both *Dalit* castes in Andhra Pradesh, have been locked in conflict over the *Madiga* claim to a sub-quota on grounds that the larger share of the scheduled caste quota has been appropriated by the *Malas* (Balagopal 2000). Likewise, the violent agitation by the *Gujjars* in Rajasthan (which peaked in 2007) showcases the high stakes involved in labelling. Feeling marginalized by other dominant groups among the OBCs, and registering the mobility experienced by the *Meenas* as a Scheduled Tribe, the *Gujjars* have been demanding a ritual downgradation, though a secular upgradation to the status of Scheduled Tribe. Clearly, the monolithic feel-good narrative of inclusion and empowerment effected by popular democratic mobilization is more complicated than it would appear at first sight.

Likewise, it is important to observe not just those excluded by the march of the market, but also those newly included by it. It is obvious that the middle classes have been the chief beneficiaries of the economic reforms, and their culture of consumption has been viewed as defining the 'group identity' of the 'new middle class'. On the other hand, large numbers of the poor are excluded not just from access to the market, but sometimes also from their already precarious livelihoods. What about the groups that occupy the segments of the spectrum between these two extremes? In his ethnographic study of just such a group, Tim Scrase shows how the lower middle classes – a class fraction rather than a class – respond to the new economic policies. Women belonging to this class group, he suggests, experience a new feeling of freedom by being able to enter the employment market.

> The crucial difference between an earlier generation and the contemporary situation for lower middle-class women is the firm belief that this class fraction is taking the lead in defying the conventional stereotypical jobs that are open to women and entering these occupations. For example, the explanations are couched in terms of 'women in our kind of families' are taking up previously unacceptable jobs such as medical sales representative, shop keeper and even bus driver or tram conductor. This is qualitatively different from the upper middle-class women entering male-dominated high-status jobs ... This is not to claim the demise of gender hierarchies within families. However, these representations do challenge some aspects of traditional femininity ... and they demonstrate the powerful significance of going out to work and the meaning it has for the women.
> (Scrase 2006: 7–8)

Unlike the economic transformation, which is inherently depoliticizing, the first two transformations – Hindu nationalism and OBC politics – are curiously similar in their strategy of deploying the political to entrench or transcend the social. The politics of Hindutva seek out the political domain to consolidate Hindu identity (BJP), while the backward caste assertions have been chiefly preoccupied with providing the people with *samman* and *izzat* through representation in governance institutions. Another important similarity between them is they both reject the idea of a civic community that is not inflected by particularistic identities. The idea of universal citizenship enjoys little purchase within these political arguments, as cultural citizenship has acquired pre-eminence, and social citizenship is compromised.

While the project of social citizenship has, for the most part, been a casualty of the economic reforms process, it could be argued that each of the three central transformations has contributed to its marginalization. The apparent support for it in the political programme of backward-caste mobilization is in fact misleading. To the extent that the backward-caste agenda goes beyond providing *samman*, it is about job and education quotas; and to the extent that these (quotas) can be seen as forms of entitlement to social and economic rights, they entail a departure from the universalistic character of social citizenship, as they are necessarily predicated upon a fragmentation of the citizenry into groups that have entitlements and groups that do not.

It is undeniable that the change wrought by the three central transformations in the citizenship regime c.1950 has been compelling and consequential. However, the last decade and a half has also witnessed other transformations, with significant implications for the practice of citizenship. It will suffice here briefly to mention only three of these. The first is the Seventy Third Amendment to the Constitution, which mandated the creation of *panchayats* and reservation in these institutions for women and members of disadvantaged caste and tribal groups. Despite the well-known resistance of local society to *Dalits* and women elected to *panchayats*, and the abuse of technicalities such as no-confidence motions by local upper-caste notables to subvert their functioning, the *panchayats* have often proved to be institutional spaces for the effective practice of citizenship. Women *sarpanches* have, in the face of intimidation and threats, asserted their constitutional right to chair (literally from a chair rather than a corner on the floor) *gram panchayat* meetings despite being told to make tea or go home. They have asserted their right to hoist the national flag on Independence Day, on occasion wresting it through a court decision. The *panchayat ghar* provides an institutional public space in which discrimination cannot be practised as blatantly as elsewhere. For elected representatives, and equally for their constituents, it provides an enabling, though by no means uncontested, space for the exercise of the rights of equal citizenship, in a way that transcends, instead of entrenching, particularistic identities.

A second important transformation may be attributed to the various claims – mounted chiefly by popular campaigns and sometimes through public interest litigation – that have demanded the rights associated with social citizenship, such as rights to housing, education, food, information and employment. Some of these have been interpreted into existing provisions of the Constitution by the Supreme Court, others have attracted a policy response, while yet others have been given a statutory basis. The Right to Information Act and the National Rural Employment Guarantee Act, both enacted in 2005, are examples of how popular mobilization, along with political commitment to welfare, can translate into effective initiatives for social citizenship. As Neera Chandhoke has argued, the conditions for transition to social democracy include a competitive party system, political parties and trade unions committed to social welfare, civil society activism to put welfare issues on the policy agenda and, perhaps uniquely in the Indian context, a pro-active judiciary (Chandhoke 2005c: 36). Most recently, in April 2010, the Right to Education for children between the ages of six and fourteen was enacted as a fundamental and legally enforceable right.

A third, and less encouraging, shift can be seen in the area of what Nikolas Rose and Carlos Novas, building upon Giorgio Agamben's thesis of the biologization of politics, have called 'biological citizenship' (Rose and Novas 2002). The idea of biological citizenship provides a new post-Marshallian way of reading the politics of race and nationality, as it has done for the fallouts of Chernobyl and Bhopal. In India in the 1990s, one challenge of biological citizenship may be seen in the claim that caste discrimination is equivalent to racial discrimination. Here, however, we take the example of sex-selective abortion, a practice that acquired disturbing proportions through the 1980s and 1990s.

In 1997, a (United Nations Population Fund) UNFPA report estimated India's 'missing women' as between 32 and 48 million (Srinivasan et al. 1997). The Census of 2001 documented a sex ratio of 933 females per 1,000 males. Though marginally better than the 927 of the 1991 Census, this is much lower than the global average of 990. While 'son preference' in Indian society has, for several hundred years, encouraged female infanticide, the recent availability of sophisticated technologies of sex-determination has made possible sex-selective abortion or female foeticide. Economic prosperity is no inhibitor of such practices, as the abysmal sex ratios in the states of Punjab and Haryana show. A correlation has also been established between the higher availability of clinics providing ultrasound sonography and a lower sex ratio in Maharashtra, where almost 80 per cent of these clinics are located in the five richest districts of the state, whose sex ratio also happens to be the lowest (Chandran 2006).

The Medical Termination of Pregnancy Act 1971 legalized abortion to safeguard the health of pregnant women. The subsequent introduction of amniocentesis – to detect foetal abnormalities – also made possible sex-determination, and so came to be used as a sex pre-selection test, resulting in widespread misuse of the MTP Act. It was to check this rampant abuse that a new law was enacted in 1994, and subsequently amended in 2003: the Pre-Conception and Pre-Natal Diagnostics Techniques (Regulation and Prevention of Misuse) Act (PCPNDT), banning sex-determination tests and providing for punishment of up to three years' imprisonment for offenders. The ban is believed to have driven the tests underground, making them more expensive rather than less common. In December 2007, a BBC Asian Network hidden-camera investigation of a reputed gynaecologist in New Delhi provided irrefutable proof of this (BBC News South Asia 2007).

Meanwhile, a recent attempt to enforce the law by a police crackdown on clinics offering sex-determination tests in Punjab has resulted in a sudden increase in the number of girl children being either killed or abandoned in garbage dumps and fields. This has provoked the Shiromani Gurdwara Prabandhak Committee (the apex body that administers Sikh shrines) to put cradles outside the Sikh temples to encourage the parents of unwanted female infants to leave them there instead of killing them (Dogra 2008). The continuing practice of female foeticide – in economically prosperous regions more than in backward ones, in urban areas more than rural, and even amongst the Indian diaspora in the UK – is testimony not only to the resilience of patriarchal ideology and culture, but also to the gendering of biological citizenship.

This phenomenon is reflected also in access to health care. Maternal mortality in India is estimated at 301 per 100,000 live births, which puts the risk of a woman dying, each time she becomes pregnant, at 1 in 330. This in turn means that if a woman gets pregnant three times in her life, the chance of her dying is 1 in 101. (Radkar and Parasuraman 2007: 3262) Despite an overall decline in the rates of fertility, birth and infant mortality, the National Family Health Survey (NFHS-3) establishes the greater vulnerability of rural women and their lack of access to antenatal, natal and postnatal medical facilities. Anaemia, wasting and malnutrition continue to rise among both children and adult women.[12]

These transformations are arguably as important and defining of contemporary India as the 'three central transformations'. They suggest that the shift from one citizenship regime to another may be contested and politically negotiated, and that interaction between state institutions, state policies and societal initiatives shapes and influences the evolution of the citizenship regime.

Non-citizens in search of (social) citizenship

Ironically, the ideal of social citizenship survives where it might be least expected, among those excluded from the formal legal status of citizenship. This section of the paper presents some narratives on citizenship from migrant settlements in the border districts of Jodhpur and Jaisalmer in Rajasthan.[13] These are mostly *Dalit* and *Adivasi* communities, which migrated from the Sind and Punjab provinces of Pakistan in the wake of the demolition of the Babri Masjid. They include some who have been denizens of the country for several years, and are still awaiting the grant of formal citizenship, and also some who *have* been granted legal citizenship but remain disappointed with its inability to afford them access to basic needs and rights.

These refugees lead a precarious existence. Visibly poor and dependent upon daily wage labour, they wistfully compare their work in the fields across the border with the hard labour of breaking and carrying stones that they now have to do. Why then did they migrate? The answer is usually presented in terms of an escape from the insecurities of minority status. It is hard to discern a strong sense of the idea of India, or of belonging to it. To the extent that there is a sense of belonging, it is occasionally defined in terms of the Hindu faith, but more often in terms of family roots, as many of them had ancestors who once owned land here and almost all have extended families on both sides of the border. It appears that while minority identity is a significant factor in the decision to leave Pakistan, it becomes rather less important on arrival as a refugee. Here, there are two crucial aspects of quotidian life that have to be confronted: first, the fulfilment of basic needs and livelihoods; and second, the hostility of the host population. In the face of these challenges, religious identity has little purchase and hence becomes much less relevant. If anything, there is a sense that they are penalized for their identity on both sides of the border.

> In Pakistan, they say we are Indians (Bharatiya) because we are Hindus, here we are called Pakistanis and all our actions are suspect.
>
> (Field interview)

Nevertheless, comparisons are inevitably offered between the quality of life in Pakistan and in India. Physical insecurity, especially the vulnerability of women to rape and abduction, appears to be of paramount importance. Religious persecution and efforts at religious conversion are also frequently mentioned, as is the destruction of temples in the period following the destruction of the Babri Masjid in Ayodhya. The present is preferred in terms of better conditions of law and order and freedom from religious persecution, but in terms of livelihood, almost all compare their life as agricultural labourers working in the fields favourably with their current insecurity and the hard labour they now have to do.

What is most striking is the fact that almost every individual – regardless of caste, tribe and gender – defines citizenship in terms of the '*suvidha*' it is or was expected to provide. *Suvidha* is a Hindi word that loosely translates as 'facilities'.

In this context, it suggests a meaning closer to the fulfilment of basic needs, which are asserted as entitlements and spelt out as land, livelihood, government school, water and electricity. It also implies a range of official documentation such as ration cards, caste certificates and Below Poverty Line (BPL) cards that would provide access to various governmental poverty-reduction programmes.

Both for those who do not yet have it, and also for those who do, citizenship remains the architectonic aspiration under which are subsumed all their dreams and hopes for a better quality of life and greater security. For those who do not have it yet, the magic key to all these goods is citizenship. For those who do, there is acute disappointment at the promise of citizenship remaining unfulfilled. This explains why many people speak of citizenship as an *instrument*: 'citizenship is the key to everything. Even to apply for a water or electricity connection, you need citizenship'.

Indeed, it is notable that the argument of shared culture does *not* form a prominent part of the citizenship or even recognition claims of these people. If they mention their identity as Hindus, it is in the context of their experiences of religious discrimination in Pakistan. When they speak about citizenship in India, it is in terms of *social* citizenship. Even as the deficiencies of citizenship in the Pakistani context are signified by the insecurity engendered by religious difference, the presumed security of religious freedom is not viewed as a satisfactory substitute for the expected *content* of citizenship in India. Here, it is social security rather than freedom of religious practice that becomes important.

As far as the content of citizenship is concerned, these claims do not invoke identity or any affective dimension. Identity is not relevant either in the making of citizenship claims or in the state's response to these claims. The arguments offered are not those of blood and belonging, or even voting rights, but rather of land, livelihood and basic services. It is the meagre entitlements to subsidized foodgrain, job quotas and development schemes that are at stake, along with the *accoutrements* of official poverty: caste certificates, the Public Distribution System and BPL cards. As such, citizenship is instrumental – a formal qualification for access to certain material opportunities. Indeed, one could even say that citizenship is the form taken by claims of what are little more than rights to the fulfilment of basic needs, for those who are citizens in purely juridical terms, but also for those who are not yet citizens even in the minimum juridical sense.

How does the case of the Rajasthan migrants speak to the two debates that I identified as having dominated theorizing about citizenship in recent times? First, it draws our attention to the sterility of the civic universalism versus cultural particularism way of casting the citizenship debate. The hegemony of the idea of citizenship interpreted purely in terms of identity and belonging is clearly being interrogated by alternative narratives of citizens and proto-citizens. A conception of citizenship that is centered on identity not only precludes the recognition of material inequalities, it also ignores the important overlap between different types of inequality such as the cultural and the economic. It is no accident that the claimants of citizenship in Rajasthan are, for the most part, poor *Dalits* and *Adivasis* whose condition is marked by the twinning of social exclusion and economic marginalization. The more prosperous upper-caste groups that migrated are comfortably settled, while those who stayed on enjoy reasonable social relations with Muslims of the same social class as themselves. Unlike the *Rajput* and Muslim elites who could deal well together, it is the *Dalits* and *Adivasis* that have suffered marginalization and exclusion on both sides of the border.

Second, it is clear that the neoliberal assumption that social citizenship encourages passivity, discourages civic participation and renders citizens into passive recipients of welfare, needs to be questioned.[14] The fieldwork suggests that social citizenship does not necessarily encourage a depoliticized notion of citizenship, or of passive dependence on the state. With the political parties keeping their distance, the migrants have mobilized under the leadership of an NGO, the Pak Visthapit Sangh. This mobilization entails collective action in terms of hitherto unfamiliar categories. Neither caste nor religion, but displacement and statelessness become their primary identity, the basis for a new collectivity. This, along with the robust assertions of rights that we encounter in the field – articulated with passion and even in the absence of the franchise – may be viewed as forms of 'insurgent citizenship' (Isin 2002: 273).

Even as the legal conception of citizenship in India has unmistakably moved from a *jus soli* (birth-based) to a *jus sanguinis* (blood or descent-based) conception, and even as these interviews seem to invoke the argument of *jus sanguinis*, the claims of the Rajasthan migrants clearly do not command the same respect in the state as those of the persons of Indian descent who are now citizens of countries in the global North. The claim to legal (and impliedly social) citizenship of the stateless Rajasthan migrants contrasts sharply with the claims to dual (purely legal) citizenship mounted by those who are already citizens of other states but wish to enjoy the *additional* privileges of Indian citizenship. The claimants of dual citizenship are the educated and prosperous professionals who migrated to the US and other developed countries in search of better professional opportunities after the mid 1960s. The attitude of the Indian state towards this older diaspora was summed up in Jawaharlal Nehru's injunction to these people to maintain their allegiance to their adoptive homelands. This attitude began to undergo a change around 1998 when, at a conference of Global Indian Entrepreneurs, Prime Minister Vajpayee announced his government's intention of setting up a committee to go into the issue of dual citizenship for Non-Resident Indians (NRIs). The explicitly stated justification for this was the government's desire to attract investment by the diaspora. Meanwhile, all persons of Indian origin holding foreign passports would become eligible for Person of Indian Origin (PIO) cards, which would give them the same benefits in respect of ownership and transfer of property and visa-free entry as NRIs. The High-Level Committee on the Indian Diaspora, headed by L. M. Singhvi, submitted its report in 2000, recommending the grant of dual citizenship through an amendment of the Citizenship Act 1955.

In 2003, parliament amended the Citizenship Act of 1955 providing for persons of Indian origin to apply for the status of 'overseas citizens of India'. This was, however, restricted to PIOs in 16 countries, ostensibly countries which recognized dual citizenship, but not surprisingly all located in the advanced industrial societies of the west. It excluded not only the countries to which nineteenth-century emigration from India had taken place, but also the countries in West Asia to which labour has migrated in large numbers in the last few decades. The Congress-led UPA government continued the previous BJP-led government's policy of holding an annual Pravasi Bharatiya Divas convention. At one of these occasions, Prime Minister Manmohan Singh announced the government's decision to grant dual citizenship, though the Citizenship (Amendment) Ordinance that followed in June 2005 provided for the status of Overseas Citizen of India (OCI) rather than dual citizenship. The OCI card excludes persons of Indian origin from Pakistan and Bangladesh. It confers various benefits including a multipurpose, multiple entry visa for life, and other rights in consonance with those enjoyed by NRIs. The OCI is not given an Indian passport, is not eligible for political office or for public employment, does not have the right to vote, and correspondingly has no duty to pay taxes. Indians in West Asia, however, continue to complain about the manifestly partisan attention of policymakers to Indians in Europe and America, who acquire disproportionate privileges including separate and easier queues at Indian airports. The contrast is obviously even sharper when we consider the case of the Rajasthan migrants.

Conclusion

It has been argued here that the citizenship regime c.2000 bespeaks the virtual abandonment of the two substantive projects that defined the citizenship regime of the founding phase: that of a political community defined in national-civic (rather than national-ethnic) terms and that of social citizenship. The first must be explained with reference to *both* forms of identity politics – Hindu nationalist as well as backward caste – notwithstanding the exclusionary thrust of the first and the broadly inclusionary tendencies of the second. Despite this apparent difference, they have both contributed to the creation of a social and political consensus that citizens enter the public sphere pre-constituted by their identities, and that mediation by ascriptively defined communities constitutes the legitimate form of interaction between citizen and state. The abandonment of the second project of social citizenship is, of course, more easily explained by the shift in economic policy. However, it is also confirmed and fortified by the obsession with cultural identities – whether of religion or of caste – which have supplanted the idea of social citizenship with the primacy of cultural citizenship.

Concurrently with the three central transformations, other transformations have also occurred that have arguably had a modest but promising expansionary impact on citizenship. These include the emerging new public spaces for the assertion of citizenship claims (viz. the *panchayats*) as well as the recognition, by the state, of some claims of social citizenship articulated by popular campaigns. Of course, the citizenship regime c.2000 remains contested not only by people's campaigns but also by more violent articulations of protest, from the Special Economic Zones to Naxalism in central India and beyond.

Notes

1 The concept of the citizenship regime draws upon neo-institutionalism and political economy to identify patterns of change in the relationship between the state, the market and communities in Canada. In times of economic and political turbulence, such as neoliberal reform, it is argued, citizenship regimes undergo change as the role of the state, the division of labour between the state and the market, and the relationship between state and civil society, are fundamentally restructured. (Jenson and Phillips 1996: 113) In the Latin American context, the resistance of indigenous movements in five countries of that region to neoliberalism has been explained through the concept of a citizenship regime that is a composite of boundaries (who has citizenship), form (of interest intermediation) and content (of rights and practices) (Yashar 2005: chapter 2).

2 The chief preoccupation was with determining the cut-off date for persons migrating from Pakistan to India; the time within which persons who had left India were entitled to return; whether people who left did so for genuine fear and insecurity or whether evacuee property was a consideration; whether incoming 'refugees' who were 'deemed to be citizens' should have a lower status than others; and so on.

3 Minoo Masani's *Our India – 1953* – a book for young people that has sold 500,000 copies since its first edition was published in 1940 – was a manifesto of the new India as it embarked on the ambitious project of what was then called 'nation-building'. It proudly detailed the diversity of India in every sphere, from the natural and physical to the economic and social, and recommended the harnessing of this diversity in the cause of planned economic development, which would lead to enhanced productivity and eventually the conquest of poverty. The new India was to be constructed, rather like the Soviet utopia on which it was modelled, through a variety of economic activities. Cultural differences, however, were cheerfully swept under the carpet, and a centralizing model of political and economic development was assumed to be the appropriate instrument through which the idea of India would, willy-nilly, get fashioned. On this view, the primordial identities of caste and language would gradually wither away as economic modernization and its concomitants – widespread literacy, urbanization, modern bureaucratic and managerial structures and social mobility – struck roots. It was, of course, intended that these processes would be facilitated by a strong interventionist state.

4 For if the articulation of sub-national identities – on the bases, variously, of language, religion or region – is explicable in instrumentalist terms, the construction of 'national' identity too arguably occurred through processes of political mobilization against colonial rule.

5 This resulted in guarantees for the freedom of religion, including the freedom to practice and propagate it, as well as through providing for separate personal laws for members of minority communities, alongside a universally applicable criminal law.

6 This took the form of constitutional provisions for affirmative action for the scheduled castes and tribes, both in public employment as well as in the central and state legislatures.

7 Walzer has argued that the commitment to national liberation does not always survive the liberation struggle: 'nationalists are not bound by a body of authoritative law or a set of sacred texts. Beyond liberation, they have no program, only a vague commitment to continue a history, to sustain "a way of life"' (Walzer 1995: 161).

8 These were incidents of violence against Muslims and Christians that were perpetrated by mobs mobilized by Hindu organizations, some of these affiliates of the BJP. The complicity of the state government, especially in the Gujarat violence, is well established. The BJD government in Orissa, then an ally of the BJP at the Centre, also did not act to stop or prevent further violence against minorities. As the party leading the coalition at the Centre, the BJP's attitude towards the violence ranged from casual acceptance to justification.

9 This recalls the distinction between two alternative principles in citizenship law: *jus soli* (place of birth) and *jus sanguinis* (line of descent). By the first principle, which is typically seen as more inclusive, the primary mode of acquiring citizenship is by birth (as in the United States); by the second, the right of citizenship is acquired through the nationality of one's parents (as in Germany). It is notable that in Vajpayee's usage, *jus soli* becomes a hegemonizing and homogenizing category, far removed from its historical association with inclusion.

10 Challenging the liberal myth that markets further the project of inclusion, Solinger's study of urban China shows that the migration of peasants to the cities threatens the entitlements of urban citizens, the beneficiaries of the erstwhile socialist system of *hukon* (or household registration) that brought with it access to free education, health care, employment and exemption from conscription. The peasant migrants, Solinger argues, become objects of resentment and institutionalized discrimination, as they threaten the 'exclusivity' of these citizenship privileges. Markets thus block rather than enable citizenship (Solinger 1999).

11 Cf. Lakha 1999.

12 Between the last such survey (NFHS-2), conducted in 1998–9 and the present one, conducted in 2005–6, anaemia in married women has gone up from 52 to 56 per cent, and in pregnant women, from 50 to 58 per cent. Anaemia in men, by contrast, is 24 per cent (International Institute of Population Sciences and Macro International 2007: 310).

13 Fieldwork conducted in April 2007.

14 This refers to the neoliberal critique of the social-democratic welfare state, as it is believed to constitute citizens as recipients of state-provided goods.

10 Making citizens from below and above

The prospects and challenges of decentralization in India

Patrick Heller

Democratic deepening and local government

In recent years the literature on participatory democracy has grown exponentially. Driven in part by important theoretical developments in normative democratic theory the interest in participatory democracy has grown apace with the increasing recognition of the deficits of representative democracy, especially in the context of low-intensity citizenship (O'Donnell 1993).

The challenge of democratic deepening has both a vertical and horizontal dimension. The vertical problem is essentially a Weberian problem: many new democracies suffer from poor institutionalization and in particular weak forms of integration between states and citizens. The problem is twofold. On the one hand, there is the issue of how citizens engage the state. State–society relations tend to be dominated by patronage and populism, with citizens having either no effective means of holding government accountable (other than periodic elections) or being reduced to dependent clients. In the absence of clear and rule-bound procedures of engagement, citizens cannot engage the local state *qua* citizens, that is, as autonomous bearers of civic and political rights. On the other hand, there is the problem of *where* citizens engage the state, that is, the problem of the relatively narrow institutional surface area of the state. Given that local government is often absent or just extraordinarily weak in much of the developing world, there are in fact very few points of contact with the state for ordinary citizens.

The horizontal problem refers to the Tocquevillian view of democracy, which focuses on the quality of associational life. Tocqueville argued that democracies function well when citizens make use of their associational capacities and recognize each other as rights-bearing citizens. If Indian democracy has endowed citizens with formal rights, pervasive inequalities within society limit the capacity of certain categories of citizens to act on their rights effectively. This distorts the associational playing field and produces a wide range of exclusions (Mahajan 1999). Taken together, the vertical problem of state–society relations and the horizontal problem of perverse social inequalities undermine the associational autonomy of citizens, the *sine qua non* of any effective democracy (Fox 1994). Under these conditions, a critical question arises: Citizens can vote, but beyond punishing incumbents, how can they actually engage with and influence the state?

But why should we accord so much importance to non-electoral participation? This question has received extensive attention in the literature, and I will only summarize key points here. There are essentially five types of claims that have been made. First, meaningful forms of participation can serve as "schools of democracy," allowing citizens to use and develop their civil and political rights. This is the Tocquevillian point, and has informed much of the civic engagement and social capital literature. The general point is that the more often citizens engage each other and state institutions as rights-bearing citizens rather than as clients, supplicants, subjects or dependents, the more likely they are to support and respect democratic rules and norms, including resolving conflicts through rule-bound mechanisms. Varshney's (2002) argument about how dense and cross-cutting associational ties reduces ethnic conflict in India is a case in point. A thickening of civic ties can in turn have very positive spillover effects, such as increased trust and lower transaction costs in economic and social life.[1] Second, participation can help strengthen the accountability of democratic institutions by increasing the intensity and quality of ties between citizens and officials, and exposing state institutions to more continuous and noisier forms of scrutiny. In other words, it can help remedy the principle-agent problem. In turn, state actions that are seen as responsive to broad-based inputs will enjoy much higher legitimacy and stakeholder buy-in. Third, more direct forms of participation can have direct developmental benefits by providing decision-makers with better information about needs and problems (leading to better targeting) and better feedback on the effectiveness of interventions. Fourth, when participation has a pro-poor bias it not only gives the poor or historically marginalized a voice that is otherwise often lost through the aggregative logic of elections, but it can also give state reformers key allies to work with circumventing or otherwise neutralizing traditional powerbrokers (Tendler 1997). The fifth argument has received much less attention in the literature on participation and decentralization, and yet in some respects may have the most profound implications for the quality of democracy. Theorists of deliberative democracy, most notably Habermas, draw a direct link between the quality of participation and the validity of preferences in democratic societies. No one has made this case more eloquently than Amartya Sen:

> Public debates and discussions, permitted by political freedoms and civil rights, can also play a major part in the formation of values. Indeed, even the identification of needs cannot but be influenced by the nature of public participation and dialogue. Not only is the force of public discussion one of the correlates of democracy ... but its cultivation can also make democracy itself function better ... Just as it is important to emphasize the need for democracy, it is also crucial to safeguard the conditions and circumstances that ensure the range of and reach of the democratic process. Valuable as democracy is as a major source of social opportunity ... there is also the need to examine ways and means of making it function well, to realize its potentials. The achievement of social justice depends not only on institutional forms (including democratic rules and regulations), but also on effective practice ... This is a challenge

that is faced both by well-established democracies such as the United States (especially with the differential participation of diverse racial groups) and by new democracies.

(1999: 158–9)

There are two key ideas here that need to be highlighted. The first is that Sen, in keeping with other theorists of participatory democracy, is arguing that we must not just have democracy, but that we must also *practice* democracy. Second, he moves beyond the traditional political science focus on how preferences are aggregated and represented to argue that democracy is first and foremost about how preferences are *formed*. And the key to how preferences are formed has to do with the quality and inclusiveness of public debate.

Local government looms large as the key terrain for developing these participatory dimensions of democracy. This is true both at a general level as well as in the specific circumstances of India. In a general sense, all these participatory dynamics of making citizens, both in terms of enhancing associational capabilities and improving the nature of citizen engagement with state, have their most immediate and palpable expression in local arenas. It is at the local level after all that citizens are most likely to first engage in public deliberation, to see and experience the state, to develop democratic norms and to form associational ties. Political theorists and political sociologists have often lost sight of this simple fact in part because theories of citizenship have all too often simply been equated with histories of the nation-state. Yet, as Margaret Somers has shown in her critique of Marshall's (1964) stage theory of the evolution of civic, political and social rights in England, social rights in some regions of England were effectively claimed and secured by workers well before the advent of the labor movement and the modern welfare state. Thus, as early as the seventeenth century, in those local communities where councils were not dominated by landed interests, subordinate groups were able to use local public spheres to claim and secure a range of social rights. She concludes that "Recognizable popular citizenship rights have only emerged historically in the participatory spaces of [local] public spheres in tandem with 'relationally-sturdy' civil societies" (1994: 589).

The democratic and developmental significance of local government takes on added importance in the Indian context because local government has been the weakest link in the chain of state–society relations. Three points need to be underscored. First, at the local level, development has been experienced as a largely top-down, bureaucratic affair, over which ordinary citizens enjoy little if any say. Second, the local incarnation of the state has, with notable exceptions, been dominated by elite interests, and linked to society largely through patronage. Third, the actual presence of local government has been so thin both institutionally and financially, that it has not provided a usable platform for public deliberation or action.[2] In sum, the form of the local state and the mode of its interface with society has been so circumscribed by social power and extra-legal authority that it has tended to subvert rather than nurture the actual practice of citizenship by subordinate groups.

The problem of civil society in India

Much of the literature on civil society rests on classic liberal assumptions that view associational life as largely spontaneous, constrained only by overbearing state authority. The recent emphasis on participation in policy and donor circles thus often slips into a form of boosterism that fails to acknowledge the extraordinary challenges that participation faces in any societal context, but particularly in societies marked by poorly formed civil societies and weak public authority. Any serious discussion of democratic deepening must begin with the sociology of actually existing civil society.

First, recent work in sociology has underscored just how resilient and durable inequality is. The term "durable inequality" comes from Tilly (1999) who has argued that most inequalities are organized around binary or hierarchical categories such as male/female, black/white, or in the case of hierarchical inequalities, class and caste. The point is that distributions of resources and opportunities are often organized around these categories, and the mechanisms of exclusion are mobilized or operationalized through the use of categories. The various forms of capital that groups mobilize to reproduce their positions in society – economic, social and cultural capital – are hoarded and deployed within the boundaries defined by the categories. These boundaries are of course not airtight, but groups, and especially dominant groups, expend tremendous energy and time in patrolling boundaries. And in hoarding privileges, dominant groups ensure ongoing exclusion. This includes not only reproducing caste, class and gender differences through daily practices, but also instrumentalizing institutions and governance in general to serve those interests. The weapons of the rich – to inverse James Scott's famous line – represent a vast and powerful repertoire of techniques (material and symbolic) to reproduce inequality.

The more general point is that inequality is relational – that is it is constituted through struggles between groups. In this sense, inequality is not given, but produced. This point bears emphasis because in much of the literature and especially in the policy world, inequality is usually treated not in relational terms, but in residual terms. That is inequality is seen as an unfortunate by-product of imperfect markets, bad policies or historical legacies that can be removed through good policy, more complete markets or changes in attitudes. The problem is that such views fail to recognize that because inequality is produced, better policy or more enlightened attitudes will do little to change inequality until the question of power is addressed.

The more careful analyses of civil society in India have provided very skeptical accounts. At a general theoretical level, Mahajan and Chatterjee have both questioned the viability of the very concept of civil society in India, and especially its democratizing character. Mahajan (1999) argues that because communities and group identities in India remain strong – and even have legal sanction – participation along group lines can often produce demands that are contrary to the principles of legal, individual equality. Chatterjee goes even further, arguing that civil society is a terrain of engagement with the state that has been dominated by elites and goes on to assert that most Indians "are not proper members of civil society and are not regarded as such by the institutions of the state" (2001: 8). And some recent empirical work by John Harriss has shown that the space of civil society is primarily populated with middle class groups that have crowded out lower class/caste groups (2006).

But one has to be very careful here. While we should be attentive to the kind of critical perspective Mahajan develops and note that there are indeed historically rooted forms of inequality in India that preclude any spontaneous associational life and make civic engagement a rather exclusive affair, we also have to recognize that there is a tremendous amount of variation in local civil societies. Let me provide two sets of examples: the first points to historically formed civil societies, the second points to a new churning of associational life.

First, Varshney has shown that there are places in India, specifically cities, where intercommunal associational ties have produced civic spaces where (1) a wide range of actors can participate in public life; (2) engage in more or less reasoned discussion about highly emotive issues such as communal conflict; and (3) resolve problems through cooperation. Second, as is well known, the history of anti-Brahmin movements in the south has fundamentally transformed caste relations, opening up a range of political spaces and associational practices that simply do not exist in much of the north. Also, as I have argued elsewhere (Heller 2000), the extensive social rights that have been secured in Kerala can be tied directly to its historical pattern of civil society formation.

Second, there is enormous churning taking place among subordinate groups in India. The most remarkable expression of this has been in electoral patterns, and in particular in what Yadav (2000) has dubbed the "second democratic upsurge." But below the surface of electoral politics, many have also noted a new effervescence of associational life. As Corbridge et al. write, "power is leaching steadily, and in some respects ineluctably, to the lower castes, and has been claimed by them in terms which often resist the presumptions of a benign and disinterested state" (2005: 83). From fieldwork in Bihar, Jharkhand and West Bengal they conclude that it is "the indirect effects of a discourse of participation that have been most effective in carving out spaces of citizenship for poorer people, however small and disappointing these spaces might seem to be" (2005: 122). In his work on urban movements in Mumbai, Appadurai (2002) has pointed to a similar dynamic by showing that new forms of civic agency are fundamentally challenging dominant discourses and practices. One could point to many more examples, but I want to highlight two based on very recent, innovative fieldwork. The first comes from Sanyal's (2009) research on micro-credit schemes in West Bengal. Drawing on 400 interviews with poor women, she finds that making small loans to women is having none of the desired economic effects, since men still, for the most part, end up controlling the capital. But she does find that for many of the women she interviewed, participation in women's groups has very significant effects in terms of expanding their associational capabilities. Women who had very limited if any associational life – that is contacts and social intercourse outside the extended family – found themselves attending village gatherings (and even extra-village meetings) and in the process developing a range of new capabilities, including critiques of patriarchal power, new solidarities and expanding what Appadurai calls their "culture to aspire." A second notable example of this churning is Agarwala's research (2006) work on informal sector women workers in the *beedi* and construction industries. Across three different states, she has documented new forms of organizing in what historically have been extremely difficult arenas for collective action. What is notable about the types of mobilization she documents is that they have taken place outside of traditional union- or party-dominated structures, and despite not being linked to each other, have all developed forms of claim-making that revolve around their identities as citizens demanding rights and recognition. In light of these examples – and there are many more – it is clear that even as access to civil society remains highly circumscribed by social power, this has hardly prevented many subordinate groups in India from using their rights. What makes this churning all the more interesting and possibly transformative is that it is taking place in a rapidly changing political and institutional field.

Panchayati Raj: the silent revolution?

The significance of Panchayati Raj is that it represents a potentially very significant expansion of the political opportunity structure. The 1992 73rd Constitutional amendment mandates that states constitute *panchayats* as self-regulating governments, hold elections every five years and devolve power and resources to *panchayats*. As is always the case in federal India, the actual powers and functions devolved are for states to decide. (Among other things this sets up a unique natural experiment: a single treatment – creation of democratic institutions where none existed before – but with actual take-up left to states.) However, even in its threadbare form, Panchayati Raj is a watershed.

Much as was the case with liberalization, decentralization was initiated by state elites at the Centre. Indeed, even as state elites were working ever more closely with an increasingly narrow dominant class-base (Kohli 2007), state elites also led the process of reforming the local state. And the diagnosis that fed into the reforms is itself telling. On the one hand, there was a recognition that the Nehruvian developmental state had failed to transform agrarian social relations and that in particular the problem lay with command and control line department modes of delivery, which had proven to be heavy-handed (even authoritarian) and inefficient, a point of view famously expressed in Rajiv Gandhi's apparently improvised comment that only 15 paise of every rupee ever reached the intended beneficiary. On the other hand, there was a clear recognition that entrenched rural power structures had thwarted local development. Thus Panchayati Raj was specifically conceived as an instrument for leveling the playing field in favor of lower classes and lower-caste actors.[3]

So what do we actually know about the impact of Panchayati Raj, 18 years after the legislation was introduced? First, it quite simply but dramatically expanded the surface area of the state. To borrow from Corbridge et al. (2005), sightings of the state in rural India can be rather intermittent and when sighted, it is experienced more as top-down bureaucracy than as democratically accountable authority. With the exception of West Bengal, which has held local elections since 1978, most states have not held elections on a regular basis, and development has been the affair of silo-like departmental bureaucracies. With a firm constitutional mandate to hold elections,[4] the states now at least have a local democratic incarnation. In effect, the reforms have created 232,278 voter-accountable institutions (499 at the district level, 5,905 at the block level and 232,278 at the village level) where none existed before. Second, a whole new political class of some 3 million elected representatives has been created, which in principle includes a third of seats set aside for women and proportional representation for Scheduled Castes (SCs)/Scheduled Tribes (STs). Not surprisingly, many states have fallen short of the mandated representation of minorities, but a majority have achieved one third representation for women, and a majority has close to or higher proportional representation of SC/STs (Chaudhuri 2006: 174).

Third, while the actual amount of power devolved to local governments is hard to assess, and could only be done through very careful state-by-state analyses, there clearly has been some devolution of funds. Average annual funds available to local *panchayats* between 1990–5 and 1995–8 rose by nearly 60 percent (Chaudhuri 2006:182).

But beyond these very broad observations, we actually know surprisingly little about the overall progress that has been made. What evidence we do have is at best fragmentary. Most studies focus on single states and only rarely look at a representative sample of *panchayats*. And those that have looked at multiple states (e.g. Besley, Pande and Rao 2006; 2007) tend to focus on a limited set of measurable variables from which it is difficult to draw larger lessons about changes in democratic governance. Chaudhuri (2006) has, however, provided a useful overview of comparative achievements in institutional terms.

Drawing on data from the eleventh finance commission, he constructs an index of performance that tracks political, financial and functional devolution. As observers of Panchayati Raj reforms might have predicted, Kerala and West Bengal are the highest performers. What is more surprising is the second tier of performers. This group includes Maharashtra and Karnataka, which already had solid track records of decentralization before the constitutional amendments. But it also includes Madhya Pradesh and Rajasthan, two states that are usually lumped in with the low-performing BIMARU (Bihar, Madhya Pradesh, Rajasthan, Uttar Pradesh) states. The achievements in West Bengal have been well documented by the careful work of Bardhan and Mookerjee (2004). West Bengal's efforts in building local government, however, predates Panchayati Raj reforms, and is politically somewhat of an anomaly given the uninterrupted rule of the CPM (Communist Party of India, Marxist). To try and tease out some of the possibilities and limitations of Panchayati Raj, I turn to two very different cases, Kerala and Madhya Pradesh, both of which had very weak institutions of local government before the reforms.

The people's campaign for decentralized planning

The design and impact of Kerala's decentralization reform – officially the People's Campaign for Decentralized Planning – have been well documented. Here I present a brief overview of two research projects that examined data from all 990 *panchayats* in Kerala and a survey of 862 key respondents conducted in 72 randomly selected *panchayats* (Chaudhuri and Heller 2003; Heller, Harilal and Chaudhuri 2007).

In terms of its basic design, the Campaign in Kerala represents the most ambitious decentralization initiative in India. The scale of financial devolution has been very significant (30 percent of plan expenditures) but just as importantly decentralization in Kerala has been marked by full functional devolution and the creation of a comprehensive, nested, participatory structure of local integrated planning and budgeting.

A number of studies have already established that in institutional terms the Campaign has resulted in a significant reorganization of the state and governance, and that the level and scope of decentralization surpasses what has been achieved in any Indian state since the 1993 constitutional amendments (Thomas Isaac and Franke 2002; Véron 2001; World Bank 2000; Aiyar 2009). The increase in the discretionary portion ("grant-in-aid") of *panchayat* budgets has been dramatic, jumping from Rs. 1,000 million in 1996–7 (the year before the campaign) to 4,204 million in 1997–8, and over 5,000 million in each of the three years following (Government of Kerala 2001) and has been sustained at an average of 27 percent of the state planning budget in every year since (Government of Kerala 2008). A World Bank report found that Kerala has the greatest degree of local expenditure autonomy and is the most fiscally decentralized state in India, and second only to Columbia in the developing world (2000: 28–2).

The second decisive impact of the Campaign has been on the level and social composition of participation. Data collected by the State Planning Board from all 990 *panchayats* for the first two years of the campaign shows that 10.3 percent of the electorate participated in the first annual Gram Sabhas in 1996 and 10.6 percent in 1997. The social composition of the campaign improved drastically in the second year. If in the first year of the campaign SC/ST participation was well below the average rate (relative participation was 0.53 with 1.0 = participation rate of the general population) by the second year it was 1.44, meaning that SC/STs were participating in greater proportions that non-SCs. Similarly, women's relative participation increased from 0.57 to 0.82, with women constituting 40 percent of all participants in 1997–8. These findings are confirmed by data collected from a random sample of 72 *panchayats*, which shows that while overall participation has declined (falling to 4.7 percent of total population in 1999 from 7.8 percent in 1997), its social composition has stabilized (Heller, Harilal and Chaudhuri 2007). In 1999–2000, women accounted for 41 percent of participants, and SCs accounted for 14 percent of participants, well above their proportion of the general population and their 11.5 percent representation in the sample. It is also important to note that the task forces – which were given the responsibility of actually designing and budgeting projects for different sectors – were also relatively inclusive. Women represented 30 percent of task force members, and SCs were proportionally represented. Moreover, 75 percent of all task force members were from civil society.

The high levels of participation appear to have ensured that the inputs of the Gram Sabhas and the task forces were incorporated into final budgets. In a survey of over

862 respondents from the 72 *panchayats*, an overwhelming majority reported that the "felt needs" expressed in Gram Sabhas and the projects designed by task forces were integrated into the final *panchayat* budget (Heller, Harilal and Chaudhuri 2007). Respondents also reported increased accountability of officials. The developmental impact of the Campaign was also marked. Over 80 percent of respondents reported that across 13 different areas of development, the performance of the *panchayat* was an improvement over the past. The performance of *panchayats* was, however, uneven across areas. The Campaign's most marked successes were in building roads, housing for the poor and *anganawadis* (child services) where almost two thirds felt the difference was "significant." In contrast, less than one fourth of respondents felt that *panchayats* had made a "significant" difference in economic development (employment, agricultural support and irrigation). What makes these survey findings especially robust is that the response rate did not vary significantly across respondent categories (politicians, civil society and government officials).

There have been significant problems with the Campaign. The "big bang" approach that was adopted in Kerala and that consisted of devolving resources and functions before building the necessary local institutional capacity was politically effective, has left significant problems of system stabilization. *Panchayats* have found it difficult to manage and spend funds, *panchayat* plans are more often lists of demands rather than carefully integrated proposals for promoting development, and local plans were never effectively coordinated with block and district plans. Having said this, the Campaign has irreversibly re-scaled the political geography of the state by creating substantial, well-resourced and democratically accountable local governments were none existed before. It is notable that this new institutional architecture and distribution of resources has survived two changes of government and now enjoys support from all political formations. Thus, even critics have concluded that the Campaign has not only created a "public platform for a vigilant civil society" but has also ensured an "enabling environment for development" (Kannan and Pillai 2004: 39).

Of course, many will simply argue that these outcomes are just another example of Kerala's unique history and social structure. It is certainly the case that with its high levels of literacy and comparatively lower levels of social inequality, Kerala presents a more inviting environment for democratic decentralization than most states. But a structuralist account completely misses the inherently political nature of such reforms. On the one hand, the Campaign represents a very decisive rupture with the past. Indeed, looking at Kerala in the 1980s one would not have thought it a likely candidate for decentralization. In the post-independence period, Kerala has benefitted from some of the most effective top-down governance institutions in India. Thus traditional line departments have successfully provided universal education and healthcare and an effective public food-distribution system. The public employee unions in Kerala moreover are extremely strong and have long resisted decentralization. Neither party in Kerala has historically supported decentralization: the Congress because it has a weak local organizational infrastructure compared to the CPM, and the CPM because it has long been wedded to democratic centralism and to exerting direct party control over local units. Given these *a priori* conditions, the Campaign's success must be explained not imputed from favorable structural conditions.

On the other hand, the explanation for the adoption and success of democratic decentralization can be found in shifting political alignments and opportunities, and in particular the relationship of the political field to civil society and changing social and economic circumstances. What made decentralization in Kerala possible was a complex set of political interventions, and what made implementation successful were key strategic choices and careful institutional design. To begin with, though the reforms were pushed through by the CPM, it was not the CPM as a whole that championed decentralization, but rather a reformist faction within the party that had the support of the late E. M. S. Namboodirpad, the party's most respected and authoritative leader at the time. That faction itself had very close ties to the KSSP (Kerala Sastra Sahitya Parishad), a powerful and autonomous mass-based organization that had a long history of promoting development through grass-roots initiatives. In other words, it was the influence of a civil society organization that pushed a key faction in the party to embrace a new vision of development and to support decentralization. Second, there was a widespread recognition that something had to be done to preserve Kerala's advanced social-welfare state in the face of liberalizing reforms and an endemic fiscal crisis. The traditional line department command-and-control state that has produced Kerala's universal services was poorly equipped to improve upon those services. Decentralization emerged as an attractive strategy of pushing forward a second generation of public sector interventions to promote economic and social development. Third, decentralization held the possibility of reaching out to new constituencies – women and youth – to extend support for the party beyond its traditional constituencies of organized labor. Finally, these factors coincided with the passage of the 73rd Amendment, giving the CPM both opportunity and political cover to push through reforms (Heller 2005).

Madhya Pradesh

That political contingencies can open up significant spaces for reform is underscored by the case of Madhya Pradesh. Madhya Pradesh could not be more different than Kerala. In addition to having among the highest levels of poverty in India, the state is marked by entrenched structures of dominant caste power at the state and local level, and with the exception of the Narmada Dam movements, has not been home to a very active civil society.

Despite this, Madhya Pradesh is widely viewed as having made significant progress in promoting decentralization and greater participation by traditionally marginalized groups, most notably *Dalits* and *Adivasis*. James Manor has provided the most nuanced and detailed account of how the Chief Minister Digvijay Singh, who served two terms (1993–2003), was able to push through a number of decentralization reforms. During his tenure he shifted power and resources downward by empowering local *panchayats* to spend money, introduced numerous single-sector user-committees in education, forestry and water management;

encouraged the formation of over 250,000 self-help groups encompassing millions of people, mostly women; formed para-professionals to provide help to councils; and launched mass mobilization campaigns, most notably a literacy campaign (Manor forthcoming: 29).

The data on Madhya Pradesh is not as rich as what we have for Kerala or West Bengal, so we must be careful in drawing conclusions. In comparative terms, Madhya Pradesh's performance has been solid, if not spectacular. Average per capital expenditures for all local bodies increased 227 percent between 1990–5 and 1995–8 (surpassing all Indian states except Kerala) and when combined with other measures of devolution Madhya Pradesh ranks second among the new adopters of decentralization (Chaudhuri 2006: 186).

The area where decentralization has by all accounts had its greatest impact is in primary education. The Education Guarantee Scheme (EGS) was the first dedicated program to be carried out through the new decentralized structures. The goal of EGS was "to provide community-centered and rights-based primary education to all children in a quick and time-bound-manner" (Anderson 2006). The scheme specifically empowered any *panchayat* that did not have a school within one kilometer to request a school from the government. The government was mandated to respond within 90 days by providing the necessary funding. The *panchayat* was tasked with identifying a teacher from the community and forming a PTA (parent-teacher association).

Manor (forthcoming) describes the EGS as an example of the government stimulating demand. The response, in Manor's evaluation, was "patently massive." By 1998, the scheme had achieved its target of almost complete access to primary education by drawing in 2 million children with over 31,000 villages getting new schools in a two-year period (McCarten and Vyasulu 2004). Drawing on a repeat household survey, McCarten and Vyasulu report that for the poorest 40 percent the probability rate for completing the 5th grade increased by 21 percent between 1992–3 and 1998–9, compared to 5 percent at the national level (2004: 736). By 2001, the primary education system in Madhya Pradesh was entirely decentralized, with *gram panchayats* charged with recruiting and monitoring teachers. A nationwide study of teacher absence in India found that Madhya Pradesh had the third lowest rate at 17 percent, well below the national level of 24.8 percent (Kremer et al. 2005). By one assessment, EGS has led to the "actualization of [individuals'] rights to elementary education from the State government" (Anderson 2006). The literacy rate in Madhya Pradesh jumped 20 percent overall (including 22 percent for women) between 1991 and 2001, the second largest decadal growth record in India ever.

What was the political equation that made all this possible? As Manor argues, at the most basic level it was a pragmatic effort to build a new electoral base for the Congress party. Because of increased electoral pressure from the BJP, Digvijay Singh had to break with the party's old reliance on the rural dominance of the *Rajput* caste and political bosses and to reach out to *Dalits* and *Adivasis*. And in response to the rising tide of Hindu chauvinism and caste-based politics, Singh opted to make a drive for development. But he knew he could not work through the traditional bureaucracy since it was corrupt and beholden to dominant caste interests. So instead he opted to stimulate demand from below by devolving resources and authority to the local level, bypassing the traditional patronage channels of local bosses and directing resources to elected councils and user committees. In doing so he worked with a close, hand-picked cadre of young bureaucrats and insulated the new development bureaucracy from patronage politics by creating special-purpose delivery vehicles – Rajiv Gandhi Missions – in areas ranging from tackling illiteracy to watershed development and iodine disorders. Thus, even during a period when state downsizing was the order of the day, Manor points out that during Singh's tenure "major progress [was] made in extending the downward reach of the state" (forthcoming: 26).

There are three dimensions of the Madhya Pradesh story that need to be highlighted. First, the political configuration that made change in Madhya Pradesh possible was not as idiosyncratic as a focus on Singh's leadership might suggest. What transpired in Madhya Pradesh was a classic instance of the pincer strategy in which a determined executive bypasses traditional intermediaries to link directly with grass-roots actors. This is for example what happened in Tendler's (1997) influential analysis of successful poverty reduction in the northeastern Brazilian state of Cerea. Second, Singh took advantage of a shifting electoral scene to reach out to historically marginalized groups. Without the loosening effect of the "second democratic upsurge," it is unlikely that any Congress leader would have staked their electoral fortunes on the direct mobilization of *Dalits* and *Adivasis*. Third, Singh strategically took advantage of opportunities that the Centre had created. Much as in the case of Kerala, opposition to decentralization was somewhat tempered by the fact that the Centre had provided the legal setting, some resources and a lot of symbolic capital for reform.

The limits of a top-down process of reform should be emphasized. Many critics, including Singh, have complained that *panchayats* in Madhya Pradesh have been dominated by *sarpanches*. Gram Sabhas moreover have been found to be ineffective in holding elected officials accountable and concerted resistance by the bureaucracy and local elites has blocked the expansion of *panchayat*'s institutional capacity for development planning (Behar and Kumar 2001). This underscores the limits of intervention from above and the pincer strategy. In the absence of organized civil society partners and the synergistic state–civil society ties that sustained reform in Kerala, the dangers of political backlash and elite capture remain acute.

Taking stock

The jury is still out on Panchayati Raj. From our limited knowledge we can say that most states have done little, some have done a bit, and a few either already had strong track records that they have extended (West Bengal, Karnataka) or broke new ground and made important headway (Madhya Pradesh and Kerala). The reforms have, however, been significant on three counts. First, the initiative itself points to the existence and activism of a faction of state reformers. Even as the Indian state is being increasingly restructured in a pro-business direction (Kohli 2007),[5] there are also significant pockets of reformers within the state dedicated to improving the accountability and effectiveness of the state in promoting development (the genesis of the National Rural Employment Guarantee Act is another case in point). Those officials at the national level who support decentralization have significant and often very enterprising allies in the states. Second, new spaces and new rules of engagement have been created. Ordinary citizens have been afforded opportunities to engage public authority in ways that simply did not exist before (Sanyal 2009, and Jalal in this volume). Whether such opportunities for engagement translate into the effective making of citizens depends on a host of factors, not least of which are local power configurations and local histories of civil society formation. Third, the participatory thrust of the reforms has lent new legitimacy and credibility to calls for mobilizing citizens. As Corbridge et al. (2005) point out, even if the mandated structures of participation never quite function on the ground as prescribed, the very language of participation resonates with popular aspirations and can readily be turned against a non-performing state. Whether or not these patterns will converge into more robust and sustainable arrangements remains to be seen, but there is certainly an urgent need for more detailed and careful tracking of how decentralization is actually being implemented across different states and how it is impacting participation on the ground.

From the review of the two cases of Kerala and Madhya Pradesh it is possible to draw out some analytic observations. First, participation is more plastic than we generally assume. The conventional wisdom in political science is that participation is stratified and that stratification is driven by stock variables (literacy, race, income, etc.). Much of this literature is based on the US, but maybe the US is the outlier. We already know that in the electoral arena in India this simply does not hold true. The social composition of participation – as Yadav (2000) has shown – has changed dramatically. Just how plastic participation can be is underscored by the Kerala case. In the first year of the Campaign, participation mirrored social structure. But by the second year of the Campaign, women and *Dalits* were well represented. And Kerala is not unique in this respect. Alsop et al. (2000) found that in Rajasthan and Madhya Pradesh participation in Gram Sabhas was not stratified by caste, and Krishna (2002) has carefully documented how in the past two decades a new stratum of middle-caste, educated activists have come to play a new role in local politics, displacing the traditional upper-caste powerbrokers. If the extension of the franchise has provided subordinate groups with new avenues of political engagement, albeit with a significant lag, the creation of local participatory spaces is also certain to provide new opportunities for ratcheting up agency.

Second, if the plasticity of participation is in part a function of changing social structures – including various kinds of political empowerment from below – it can also be a result of state intervention. Associational life is artifactual – that is, an artifact of how the state structures political and civic life. In Kerala, the increase of women and *Dalit* participation was a direct result of new incentives and new fora created by the state. In Karnataka, Singh's Education Guarantee Scheme triggered a tremendous response from the rural poor.

Third, institutional design matters. In its rush to celebrate associational life, the literature on participation often fails to recognize the complex ways in which institutions structure incentives for participation and can favor or block pro-reform alliances. Much of Madhya Pradesh's success can be attributed to the creation of parallel delivery structures and of the careful manner in which Singh built linkages to new constituencies while isolating or at least neutralizing traditional intermediaries. This has by definition not resolved the problem of entrenched powers, but it did allow for new and more effective forms of state intervention. In Kerala, the challenge was different. The patronage system had less to do with traditional social power than highly competitive electoral politics. The Campaign was designed specifically with the intent of incorporating politicians and officials while at the same time reducing the opportunities for patronage. Delivery was structured through existing institutions, but the complex set of nested participatory structures increased transparency and reduced opportunities for elite deal-making (Heller, Harilal and Chaudhuri 2007).

Conclusion

Because inequality is produced, it is durable. Because inequality is produced, it is plastic. Institutional reforms can change the transaction costs that the poor and the marginalized face in engaging the state. In this respect, Panchayati Raj represents an important step in the direction of deepening democracy. But those reforms will only be as effective as the type of politics through which they are constructed. What even the very fragmentary evidence I have reviewed here points to is that the politics of reform comes in many shapes and configurations. Developing better typologies of these configurations and understanding how and why such favorable opportunity structures emerge calls for much more research. Having said this, there are clear signs of a Great Transformation. Even as rural power structures remain intact and a new urban dominant class secures its power, what has undeniably changed in post-independence India has been the slow but increasing capacity of subordinate groups to voice their grievances, or to paraphrase Habermas, to redeem the unredeemed citizenship claims of a democratic society. This is tangibly and unmistakably evident in the "second democratic upsurge." The intriguing possibility that I would like to close with is that if the power shifts associated with the Panchayati Raj and the many stirrings of civil society converge, this may yet produce an upsurge of even far greater significance for strengthening citizenship.

Notes

1 Not all forms of associational life have such positive effects. As Bourdieu (1984) always emphasized, social capital can be the basis of exclusionary practices and Riley (2006) and Berman (1997) have all shown how under certain political-historical circumstances, associational life can become the basis for very illiberal politics. The RSS in India also comes to mind.
2 At Rs. 45 per capita in 1990–5, Chaudhuri describes the resource base of local government before Panchayati Raj as "laughable."

3 de Souza (2003) quotes K. C. Sivaramakrishnan – one of the drafters of the Bill and secretary of Ministry of Urban Development – to this effect.
4 As of 2002, all states had held two local elections, except Bihar and Punjab, which had held only one election (Chaudhuri 2006: 171).
5 Mani Shankar Aiyar, the architect of the reforms and the first Minister of Panchayati Raj, has been a very vocal and articulate advocate of decentralization, and a prominent critic of the distributional consequences of liberalization (2009).

11 Hindutva's ebbing tide?

Radhika Desai

The Lok Sabha elections of 2004 defeated Hindutva in the moment of its greatest 'Shining India' hubris and those of 2009 saw an even worse performance on the part of the Bharatiya Janata Party (BJP).[1] The BJP descended into crisis as the Rashtriya Swayamsevak Sangh (RSS) attempted to reassert control over, and force stock Hindutva themes back onto, the BJP. Hardly likely to yield electoral dividends – the focus on the economy and terrorism in 2004 and 2009 respectively had probably been justified – these moves were made amid a critical leadership transition. L. K. Advani, the party's Prime Minister designate in 2009, resigned and the party of Hindutva was, for the first time since the 1960s, bereft of the Vajpayee-Advani leadership. While both the party and the RSS seemed agreed that leaders in their 50s such as Arun Jaitley, Sushma Swaraj, Rajnath Singh, Narendra Modi and Venkaiah Naidu should succeed, older leaders – Jaswant Singh, Yashwant Sinha and Arun Shourie – still hungry for power, attacked their younger colleagues for causing the 2009 defeat (Vyas 2009; Noorani 2009). While tensions around RSS control and the exact dose of Hindutva in the BJP's political message have persisted from the very moment the erstwhile Bharatiya Jana Sangh (BJS) sought power in alliance with other parties – in the non-Congressism of the 1960s and the JP movement and the Janata government of the 1970s – the possibility that they could become unmanageable in the new circumstances could be discounted. No wonder then that the BJP was billed as being electorally in 'retreat' and organizationally in 'crisis' and 'decline' (*Economic and Political Weekly* 2009, Lokniti 2009, Noorani 2009, respectively).

This chapter argues that while the internal crisis of Hindutva will surely unfold in interesting, and possibly momentous ways, whether or not it turns out to be terminal depends equally on the fortunes and actions of rival parties and political forces. More is needed to analyse and understand this than the idea that Hindutva's policies of 'divisiveness and intolerance' could never work in 'diverse and tolerant' India. Such a view fails to explain Hindutva's recent successes and specify the developments that facilitated it. I have long argued (beginning with 1999a) that the tendency to attribute Hindutva's rise to changes in party and Sangh Parivar strategy alone was always limited and calls for a wider perspective. This applies equally to its present arrest and possible decline.

The 2004 and 2009 general elections could turn out to mark the ebbing of Hindutva's political tide; they may equally merely prolong the political flux of recent decades. The BJP's trajectory can only be understood as part of the evolution of India's political system since the shift to economically liberal policies in Indian agriculture in the late 1960s (Desai 2004a and 2004b). This was the decisive point at which the crucial component of independent India's early development strategy – the social transformation of its agriculture as the basis of a sustained, broad-based and domestic capitalist industrialization in India – was pronounced a failure. The consequent turn to progressively more market-driven policies in this sector set off the 'slow-motion counterrevolution' that was neoliberalism in India (Desai 2008). The social forces it produced, the provincial propertied classes (Balagopal 1987), re-shaped Indian politics. Originally regionally distinct agrarian bourgeoisies taking the form of farmers' movements, these groups soon acquired interests in the urban and industrial sector and emerged as regional, rather than specifically agrarian, propertied interests and sponsored regional parties seeking all-round development in their respective states. These parties drove the long and slow-moving political earthquake that worked itself thorough the Indian political system over the next decades, fracturing it. Regional parties were formed as agrarian bourgeoisies and then provincial propertied classes defected from Congress, resulting in its decline. While regional parties from some states became part of the National Democratic Alliance (NDA) at the centre and, often allied with the BJP in state governments, the provincial propertied classes boosted the fortunes of the BJP elsewhere by supporting it directly. Congress decline, regional party proliferation and the BJP's rise have reshaped the Indian party system *together*.

While, *prima facie*, the Indian political system could come to rest in a scenario of the two national parties competing for power in coalition with its own distinctive set of regional parties, the elections of 2009, in which, for the first time in 40 years an incumbent government was re-elected after a full term in office, confirm a fundamental problem with this scenario: the neoliberalism shared by India's political classes is rejected by its electorate and even a slight mitigation of it – like that imposed on the UPA by the Left after the 2004 victory – can make the difference between defeat and decline and victory (however tentative) and the possibility of revival. I show this in what follows by first fleshing out this point in a discussion of the verdicts of 2004 and 2009 and then backing it up in an outline of the three major political developments named above and their effect on Hindutva's fortunes. Distinct combinations of these three trends in the states produce India's new political geography, accounting *inter alia* for Hindutva's differential advance in different parts of the country. The conclusion returns to the question of what, if anything, can pull the plug on the Hindutva tide.

The 'great transformation' of Indian politics through cultural nationalism, popular democratic mobilization and economic liberalization (see also Corbridge and Harriss 2000) envisaged in this volume overlaps substantially with my account though two critical differences may be noted. First, the 'great transformation' framework dates the onset of economic liberalization at 1991. Focused on industrial liberalization, its 'urban bias' cannot comprehend the economic drivers of political change in the countryside where elections are still won and lost. This chapter dates the most politically relevant economic shift at 1969. Second, 'popular democratic mobilization' echoes Yogendra Yadav's (2000) 'democratic upsurge' and confounds two quite distinct, indeed, opposite phenomena. While the upsurge of the lower castes and classes in parties like the BSP might constitute a democratic upsurge – underprivileged groups' increased participation (however flawed, see Mendelsohn and Vicziany 1998) – that of the middle-caste propertied, which expanded the number of middle-caste members of the state Vidhan Sabhas and the Lok Sabha, signified the rising political power of a new layer of the propertied amid accelerated caste-class polarization since the late 1960s. It was considerably more plutocratic than democratic.

A party system treading water

Lokniti and associates (Lokniti 2009; Yadav and Palshikar 2009), see the BJP as a party in retreat. Although the BJP made 'some mistakes during the campaign – attacking a prime minister with a clean image, bringing up Narendra Modi's name halfway through the campaign, supporting Varun Gandhi, and so on ... the BJP was not the only party making such mistakes. On balance, the BJP's selection of candidates and campaign strategy was, as always, a shade better than that of the Congress' (Lokniti 2009: 2). This, despite the considerable internal problems the BJP suffered since losing office in May 2004. The right-wing party made a major policy gaffe in opposing the proposed nuclear deal with the United States, landed on the same side as the Left, underwent further bouts of the perennial tussles with the RSS, suffered organizational disorientation when one of its more promising younger leaders, Pramod Mahajan, died, then Vajpayee bowed out of political life and Advani's adventuresome remarks about Jinnah in Pakistan caused confusion.

Lokniti traced the reasons for the BJP defeat to arrest or reversal on all fronts of its advance hitherto: new areas, new social groups and alliances. Not only did BJP lose allies, it stopped expanding into new areas (except Karnataka) and lost votes among the poor, lower castes and minorities, it also lost parts of its core constituency among middle-class urban voters. The BJP was now a party with

> a smaller catchment area, a declining capacity to reach out to newer groups, and a lower "coalitionability". It takes an exceptional situation, such as Kargil, an extraordinarily accommodative leadership, as that of A. B. Vajpayee, and an extra large coalition such as the NDA of 1999 to carve out a victory from this base. Otherwise, it faces a permanent disadvantage.
>
> (Lokniti 2009: 2)

This may yet turn out to be too smug an assessment on all three counts.

Lokniti's own analysis shows that the Congress/UPA victories and the BJP/NDA defeats appear more dramatic than they are. Both Congress and the BJP lost vote shares in 2004. And, though only the BJP lost them again in 2009, taking a further step downwards from its 1998 peak of 25.59 per cent to come to 18.8 per cent, the

Congress gain, going from 26.53 per cent in 2004 to 28.55 percent in 2009 made its vote just a little higher than in 1999 when it was 28.3 per cent. These small changes in vote shares were exaggerated into the great changes in seat shares: in 2009 the BJP lost 22 seats on a 1.2 per cent vote-share reduction and the Congress gained 61 seats on the strength of a 2.02 per cent vote-share increase. The regional parties retained most of their collective share of votes and seats and the Left lost far more seats than votes. Overall, none of the three trends – Congress decline and regional parties' and Hindutva's rise – that had fractured the party system by 1989 such that it no longer yielded single party majority governments altered decisively.

Though twice defeated nationally, the BJP remains in power in Chhattisgarh, Gujarat, Himachal Pradesh, Karnataka and Madhya Pradesh. And it shares power with regional parties in Bihar, Jharkhand, Nagaland, Punjab and Uttrakhand. Congress, meanwhile, rules in Andhra Pradesh, Arunachal Pradesh, Delhi, Rajasthan, Haryana, Mizoram and Manipur while sharing power in Assam, Goa and Maharashtra. Whether the BJP can make this state-level electoral record into a base for the 'comeback' depends on developments on two fronts – its ability to harvest sufficient votes from the lower classes/castes and minorities and its 'coalitionability'. And they depend on Congress's performance. For the BJP can win the votes in lower socio-economic strata that make the difference between office and opposition because they

> have known nothing but populist promises, and their repeated betrayal, from the other main political force in the country, the Congress. The vast majority of India's poor have had no real—consistent and principled—political representation at all and the Left remains regionally quarantined. But they have registered their dissatisfaction with neoliberalism nevertheless: all the governments since the mid 1980s have pursued the neoliberal agenda, and all have been rejected by the electorate.
>
> (Desai 2004b: 57)

The Congress-led UPA has been able, for the first time since 1984, to win re-election due to the pro-poor policies the Left forced on it. Congress can advance electorally primarily by going further along this path to secure the constituency of the poor for itself and deny the BJP those of their votes that have hitherto carried it to power in New Delhi and may yet do so again.

Congress gained 5 per cent of the votes of the rich, though it lost votes among the middle classes and gained 3 per cent among its core electoral constituency of the lower classes and the poor, while losing votes among the very poor (Yadav and Palshikar 2009: 40). These gains, however, work in opposite directions. The former, electorally less weighty, gain was reliant on pursuing the very neoliberalism on whose dilution the latter achievement, which made the larger contribution, relied. Such dilution as Congress allowed could only be attributed to the Left's insistence on schemes such as the National Rural Employment Guarantee Scheme (NREGS), which gave Congress' neoliberalism the 'human face' that was indispensable in 2009.

> The evidence is that the beneficiaries of the schemes rewarded the UPA in this election. Among them, it was a crucial issue and the UPA vote on the basis of this issue was three percentage points higher than its overall voting percentage. A gap of three percentage points may appear narrow, but it is significant because it still shows the beneficiaries of these schemes were numerically huge.
>
> (Rai 2009: 82)

Clearly the Left made the difference between loss of vote share in 2004 and the gain that reaped such a harvest of seats in 2009. The Congress that was ushered into office in 2004 was pulled in opposite directions by its 'electoral base among the poor and its desire for the approbation of the upper- and middle-caste Hindu propertied groups' and it was clear that

> [o]nly if the Congress manages to become in government what it has not been hitherto – a party able to secure its hold over the classes and groups which provided the electoral arithmetic of its power – will it acquire, *ex-post facto*, the legitimacy that will make it difficult to topple and which may yet give it further terms in power.
>
> (Desai 2004b: 64 and 67)

However, events since then also confirm that, free of Left pressure, Congress is once more free to indulge in its electorally counter-productive pursuit of the approval of the upper and middle classes and castes to the exclusion of securing its real electoral base. That much was plain in the government's first new budget in March 2010.

Moreover, Congress electoral consolidation may also be crucial to its ability to attract regional allies. The BJP certainly had the initial coalitional advantage, having adjusted to the necessity for coalitions first in 1998: after all the non-Congressism of the 1960s, the JP movement and the Janata Party of the 1970s had been important dress-rehearsals. In contrast, 2004 was the first election in which Congress finally gave up pretending that it could govern alone. Congress's coalitional strategies have been less effective than the BJP's: unlike the NDA, the UPA governments have been minority governments. Developments since 2004 have thrown both national parties' alliances in flux. The 2004 UPA minority government lost Left support and that of some other UPA constituents by 2008. While the NDA also suffered defections as the Left organized the Third Front and a smaller Fourth Front of Hindi heartland regional parties emerged in the 2009 campaign, and while the BJP's poor performance does increase the incentive for the more successful among its regional allies to fly the coop, there is no clear evidence of lower BJP 'coalitionability', only of a smaller coalition, for the moment. The future of the Third and Fourth Fronts is hardly secure.

Whether and how much this changes depends on how well Congress performs on this front. On the one hand, Congress electoral advance clearly makes it more attractive for some regional parties. Congress made the largest contribution to the UPA's increased seat share, and the reshuffling of coalition partners proved fortuitous for it: the Trinamool Congress, the single biggest gainer among regional parties, came over from the NDA and, with stable vote-getters like the DMK, regional allies contributed an additional 19 seats. The BJP, by contrast was not only solely responsible for the NDA's reduction in seats, the gains of other parties such as the JDU in Bihar reduced the NDA's losses. While BJP losses might further shrink the NDA, the UPA is not without its troubles. Congress' shorter experience with coalition is not co-incidental. The regional parties represent precisely those social forces whose ambition the Congress could not contain and there are fractures of interest between these forces and the Congress electoral base among the lower classes and castes. That these problems are far from resolved is clear in recent developments. Though Fourth Front parties gave the UPA their unconditional support, complications by the spring of 2010 involving price increases and the women's reservation bill put that support into question.

The Congress can best contest and contain the BJP not by attempting to snatch the latter's constituency among the upper caste propertied, as it intuitively thinks, but by consolidating its support among the broader and lower part of India's social pyramid by genuinely representing its interests. Only this can end the BJP's ability to skim off enough votes among this constituency and make it unelectable. If Congress can achieve this, the upper- and middle-caste propertied – the core constituency of the BJP and/or the regional parties depending on the state in question – may also learn that their interests are best re-articulated along rather than athwart those of the lower classes, a development that will affect the BJP more adversely than the regional parties.

Were Congress to choose this path, it could close the Hindutva chapter of Indian politics. If it does, that chapter will ironically have been bookended by two Left initiatives, one which tried and failed to keep the BJP out of power and another, eight years later, which used its all-too-brief moment of vicarious power to put its imprint on national policy. In 1996, the Left famously put together the United Front (UF) coalition designed specifically to keep the BJP out of power. Based on the illusory idea that the middle-caste-based regional parties were somehow bulwarks against the upper-caste politics of the BJP, that they were 'profoundly opposed to saffron, represent[ed] a pluralisation of regional aspirations and populisms ... on the whole anti-brahminical in [their] caste politics [and] without the stridencies and caste opportunisms of a Kanshi Ram' (Ahmad 1996), the coalition not only broke up, but most of the important regional parties outside the Hindi heartland choose to ally with the BJP after its even stronger showing in the 1998 elections, inaugurating the BJP's six-year stint in power. Economic policies it foisted on a reluctant UPA in 2004 to mitigate rural distress, however, made the critical difference that turned Congress decline into advance and a second defeat for Hindutva, inadvertently showing how to pull the plug on the Hindutva tide.

Three political trends

Caste/class polarization after 1969 led upper castes/classes from Congress to the BJP, and the middle-caste propertied groups, the provincial propertied classes, to form regional parties. While the first process contributed to Hindutva's expansion beyond the north Indian upper-caste petty bourgeoisie, the latter process gave the BJP political muscle in the critical countryside. Provincial propertied classes' regional parties everywhere (except the Hindi heartland, on which see below) have been part of the NDA at some point. Where they did not form regional parties, as in states such as Gujarat, they supported the BJP directly by becoming part of its core constituency.

Congress decline

An upper-caste conceit conflates the middle castes with the lower castes and sees middle-caste political power as relatively recent. Actually, it dates back to the moment Gandhi transformed Congress into a mass organization. At the time middle-caste landed groups became Congress 'link men' in the countryside. Their dominance over local areas and communities delivered rural votes in the required numbers to win elections for Congress time after time (Kothari 1967; Kochanek 1968).

Ongoing commodification, commercialization and the penetration of capitalism in the countryside increased the economic power of these landed groups and this had a paradoxical effect on their relationship with Congress. On the one hand, anxious to translate their greater economic clout into political power, they now chafed at upper-caste dominance within Congress and the 1967 General Elections showed that in many parts of the country, these groups were willing to leave the Congress and assert themselves against it (Kamat 1979).

On the other hand, these very processes made their utility to Congress dubious. After the 1967 defeat Mrs Indira Gandhi first moved left to the further chagrin of propertied groups, both rural and urban. The Congress split in 1969 with the Congress-O (Organization) parting company, thinking it represented the 'organization' of the party among the middle castes in the countryside. If the splinter party really had represented the middle castes, the split would have left Mrs Gandhi with no means of winning elections. But perhaps Mrs Gandhi knew what Congress-O leaders did not: that the disloyalty of dominant caste groups mattered less than before. That, as a consequence of the spread of capitalism and commercialism in the countryside, the very processes that increased the economic power of the dominant caste agricultural bourgeoisie also diminished their ability to dominate their local areas politically. The cash-nexus increasingly edged out older fealties, making them significantly less effective as vote-getters (Lele 1995). A populism that spoke over the heads of such (no longer) link men directly to the poor electorate was more likely to win votes. (These processes are central to Frankel 2005, Frankel and Rao 1989).

Thanks to Congress' massive dominance and the political wilderness beyond, the exit of the middle castes from Congress did not become clear until the 1990s. Now ebbing and now flowing, however, the process, combined with the loss of urban upper caste elites to Hindutva, left Congress with an electorate almost entirely composed by lower-caste and -class groups and minorities. After the 1967 debacle, the Congress was back in power in 1971 with a seat tally that compared well with the best of Nehru's, and 1980 reversed the ignominious post-Emergency defeat. If that were not enough, the 1984 General Elections, which took place after Mrs Indira Gandhi was assassinated, gave Congress its highest seat tally yet, practically suffocating all opposition. Who would have predicted then that this was the last Congress majority government for a quarter century and counting?

Congress was displaced in some states that featured an entirely regionally specific party system – Tamil Nadu and UP being the most important – or was reduced to being one of two major parties, facing either the BJP or a regional party as its main opponent in state politics or competing for state power in alliance with one or more regional parties often against the BJP allied to other regional partners.

As the new century opened, Congress had lost any hope of regaining the dominance it once enjoyed. At best it could be one of two national parties contesting elections in alliance with regional and other parties, possibly alternating in power. While by 2009 a definite chance of Congress revival could be glimpsed, it was not clear that the party leadership was willing to read the electoral data and draw the necessary policy inferences. Moreover, the political alignment of the regional parties, for the moment indispensable for winning power in New Delhi, remained in flux with new party groupings such as the Third and Fourth Fronts suggesting important tensions within the party system that needed to work themselves out. The two most important – that between Congress' electoral base and its economic policies and that between Congress and the regional parties which constitutes its coalitional weakness – have already been mentioned.

Regional parties

Out of Congress, the regionally diverse middle castes, in most states the most numerous caste category, mobilized on issues of linguistic rights and state reorganization in the 1950s and 1960s and they really came into their own as the politics of the agrarian bourgeoisie and later those of the provincial propertied classes emerged. By the 1970s, with more and more of them outside Congress, dominant-caste capitalist farmers and rich peasants formed non-party farmers' movements, demanding more generous state policies towards agriculture: subsidies for inputs such as fertilizer and electricity, and higher state procurement prices for grain. Their complaints about adverse terms of trade for Indian agriculture against industry were generally ill-founded, except for a brief period of adversity in the mid 1970s (Mitra 1977). Nevertheless arguments about 'urban bias' were successfully deployed in their populism or 'new agrarianism', celebrating a harmonious and pristine 'Bharat' menaced by urban and industrial 'India' (Vidyasagar 1996, Bharadwaj 1995, Byres 1974). It obscured how the costs of adverse terms of trade for agriculture were borne by agricultural labourers in their meagre wages, while prosperous and capitalist farmers reaped huge cost-plus surpluses on procurement prices geared to the lower productivity of medium and small farmers (Patnaik 1995). Former 'state boss' of the Congress in Western Uttar Pradesh, Charan Singh, went further and floated a regional political party of the agricultural bourgeoisie in North-Western India, the Lok Dal. Its power was perhaps best demonstrated at an immense rally in New Delhi in 1979, which massed rural power in the heart of the capital and delivered the unmistakable message that it could only be short-changed at great political price. The Lok Dal became a major component of the five-party merger, the Janata Party, which ousted Mrs Gandhi's Congress party from power in the post-Emergency general elections of 1977.

The next major milestone in the development of these forces was the creation of the National Front government in 1989 at a time when the ongoing decline of Congress and the still nascent rise of the BJP created room for a coalition government of regional forces. Their attention was already, however, fixed on horizons beyond agriculture alone as the main plank of the National Front government became the implementation of the Mandal Commission Report recommending reservations for middle castes (confusingly known as 'backward castes', or officially as 'Other Backward Classes') in government educational institutions and employment. The regionalization of Indian politics, reflecting the states-focused power base of this new segment of the bourgeoisie, became a settled pattern by the 1990s. It revolved as much around demands for more industrial development in the regions, as greater support for agriculture (Sathyamurthy 1997).

The emergence of regional parties was uneven in one critical respect. Whereas regional parties emerged in many states, in others the provincial propertied classes either divided their support between a regional party and the BJP or supported the BJP directly. When that happened, the states in question featured straight Congress–BJP contests. The pattern of regional parties' advance can, however, only be understood in conjunction with that of Hindutva's advance, with which it is closely linked.

Hindutva

The popular account of the rise of the Hindutva begins in the late 1980s when, having been reduced to two seats in the 1984 general elections, the organizations of Hindutva – the RSS and its fraternity of organizations including the notorious Vishwa Hindu Parishad (VHP) – decided to counter middle-caste political mobilization around the implementation of the Mandal Commission report for reservation of government jobs and places in educational institutions for the middle castes with the campaign – frequently violent – to build a temple to the Hindu deity Ram at the site of a sixteenth-century mosque in Ayodhya. With 'Mandir' pitted against Mandal, Hindutva had arrived with a vengeance. BJP politics revolved around aggressively asserting Hindu identity and Hindutva as the basis of Indian civilization and culture. In 1989 the BJP seat count went steeply up to 87.

To see this steep rise in seats as the result of the Mandir campaign alone is, however, to leave the party's history prior to the mid 1980s completely out of account. While that campaign certainly paid dividends, the seat tally of 1989 was also a restoration to the BJP of a right-wing constituency that had been in the making over previous decades, a constituency in which, moreover, other parties of the Right progressively lost ground to the BJP. This was the powerful undertow that first culminated in the formation of the Janata government in 1977 in which the BJS was the largest component with over 90 seats, a third of the total. During the 1980s this constituency found its way back to Congress, but only temporarily. By the late 1980s, it was once again precipitated out of the Congress and its new culmination came with the formation of the NDA governments of 1998–2004.

The smaller Hindu parties first ceded ground to the BJS in the first decade of independence. When, in the 1960s, Congress' upper-caste constituency also began to bleed away to the Right both the BJS and secular Right parties like Swatantra benefited. Over the next decade, however, the constituency of the latter was also absorbed into the BJP, as was, eventually, that of the Congress-O. Of all the parties on the Right, the BJP had the flexibility to offer the combination of economic liberalism and social authoritarianism (which took the form of majoritarian cultural nationalism) that became the hallmark of the new Right practically everywhere (Desai 2006b and 2004a). At the same time, the BJP's ability to form governments relied on a remarkable, and little understood, relationship to regional parties. This relationship too needs to be put in a longer historical perspective if the politics of the Right – that is, the politics of property – are to be fully understood in India today.

The growth of a national, largely upper-caste and upper- and middle-class constituency of the Right was never enough to form a government and, in the event, the agrarian/regional propertied classes became the indispensable complement. The Janata experiment – the combination of Right parties, the BJS and Congress-O, and parties of the middle-caste propertied, the Lok Dal, and the Socialists – blazed the trail. Itself the culmination of decades of 'non-Congressist' electoral and parliamentary cooperation between the opposition parties, and of extra-parliamentary cooperation during the JP movement, the Janata party rested on *mutual* ideological accommodation between the BJS and its allies: the BJS deemphasizing the overt upper-caste elements of its Hindu politics and its allies adapting their 'secularism' to the cultural privileges of a Hindu identity shared with the upper castes, all for the greater good of the propertied they represented.

Such political alliances appear incongruous only as long as the middle castes are confounded with lower castes and jointly considered anti-brahmanical and anti-upper caste. To be sure the middle castes were central to several anti-Brahmin movements of the early twentieth century. And they campaigned for the implementation of the Mandal Commission Report and faced upper-caste ire in an episode generally considered critical to the rise of the BJP in the late 1980s and early 1990s. However, historically they also shared with the upper castes common interests in the exploitation of the lower castes (which usually included lower ranks of the middle castes) and, as they grew into substantial and capitalist farmers, and then provincial propertied classes, other economic and cultural interests. When the regional parties showed themselves willing, nay eager, to enter into coalition with the BJP, no more was heard about their middle-caste anti-Brahmanism and Left and liberal commentators dismissed this turn as merely opportunist. But these political alliances had the longer and sounder history traced here. Indeed, the right-wing character of the politics of the middle castes and the status of the regional parties as parties of provincial propertied classes is not fully appreciated.

The 1980s brought disarray in regional as well as right-wing politics. The party of Hindutva, freshly out of the Janata party sought, like all its other former components, to claim its true legacy. It dropped the word 'Sangh' from its name, taking a distance from its parent organization, proclaimed a commitment to 'Gandhian socialism' and remained distant from the RSS until the late 1980s. Ironically, the BJP's way back to Hindu themes and identity in the 1980s may well have been prepared by Mrs Indira Gandhi and Congress. For their part they entered the 1980s having relinquished the Left populism that had culminated in the Emergency, and had faced that great middle-class revolt that was the JP movement. With their more sensitive political ears to the ground, they sensed the caste/class polarization of the Indian social formation and concluded, correctly it would seem in retrospect, that the expansion of the middle and propertied classes – rural and urban – and their consolidation in the form of the Janata party required appeals to their Hindu identity and to more economically liberal policies. So, it was Mrs Gandhi who first flirted with Hindu religious leaders in the early 1980s, and Congress was rewarded with RSS support in the Delhi elections and the 1984 Lok Sabha elections that brought the party its highest vote ever (Frankel 2005: 708). While it is widely recognized that Mrs Gandhi emphasized issues of national unity in these years, the extent to which this conception of the nation was already inflected towards Hinduism is usually ignored. And she succeeded in absorbing the right-wing constituency that had been consolidated by Janata, into Congress – a process furthered by Rajiv Gandhi with his economic liberalization programme.

Only when these experiences were digested by the BJP leadership did it return to the RSS fold and to Hindutva themes in the late 1980s. This return certainly yielded electoral dividends among the more fanatical Hindus. However, they were always a minority. Far weightier was the return of the constituency of the broader Right to the BJP: the Bofors scandal and the Rajiv Gandhi government's fumbling over minority and majority 'appeasement' over Muslim Personal Law and Babri Mosque issues respectively helped loosen them from their decade-long adherence to Congress. The BJP now began to garner votes from upper caste Hindus and increasingly also from middle-caste Hindus who, while they were not particularly fanatical, saw Hindutva as a means of asserting their cultural superiority as a complement to their economic and social ascendance, and who increasingly indulged in forms of religiosity which connected with politics and business (McKean 1996). This was the logic which expanded the BJP's own social basis among the upper castes outside the Hindi heartland and among the middle caste propertied in many states, while in others, the parties of the provincial propertied classes were able and willing to ally with the BJP (Desai 2004c).

However, even this expansion was not enough. After all, this upper- and middle-caste/class constituency could never be a numerical majority and no amount of Hindutva campaigning and no number of RSS shakhas could conjure up more where no more existed. As in the 1960s and 1970s, the party of Hindutva found that it was necessary to make wider appeals among social groups lower down the class/caste scale if they wished to pursue office seriously. *Prima facie*, getting and stabilizing an electoral base among these groups for a party of Hindutva and neoliberalism should have been as easy as the proverbial camel going through the needle's eye. Few among the *Dalits* or the *Adivasis* had much to gain from such a politics. It was only in a context where, given cross-party agreement on neoliberal economic policies that became evident in the 1990s, and which left the lower castes and classes with no political representation other than populist forces, that the BJP could at least hope to skim off enough votes among these groups by means of a combination of material inducements for tiny elites, and intimidation and merely psychological rewards – appeals to Muslims to 'Indianize themselves' or invitations to *Dalits* and *Adivasis* to enter the Hindu fold – to the rest. Incredible as it was, this phenomenon spawned an academic cottage industry trying to explain Hindutva's appeal among subaltern groups in their own right (e.g. MacLean 1999, Patel 2005, Teltumbde 2005). Inevitably, these electorally necessary appeals caused tensions between the RSS and the BJP over strategy and ideology, which erupted periodically.

By the late 1990s these logics had brought the BJP to power in New Delhi, but they also, as now seems clear, may well have given it all the votes and seats they could give. Amid continuing liberalization of economic policies and the caste/class polarization it fostered, coalitions between the BJP and regional parties became a new form of the necessary political alliance between the industrial and the (formerly) landed classes, spanning formerly significant rural–urban and upper-middle caste divides in the interests of property. Hindutva succeeded in becoming the party of the industrial bourgeoisie and the predominantly upper-caste and middle-caste urban professional, salaried and business classes. In many parts of the country it also succeeded in attracting the middle-caste provincial propertied classes in one of two ways. Either through coalitions between the BJP, the party of the upper-caste urban, professional, salaried and industrial interests on the one hand and the regional parties of the middle-caste provincial propertied interest on the other, or through a class coalition of these two segments within the social basis of the BJP itself. In the latter states, the BJP is already what it hopes to be in the country as a whole: a social coalition of the upper-caste and middle-caste propertied.

The advance of the BJP and the associated decline of Congress and rise of regional parties have not been uniform across the country. Indian states evince at least four distinct patterns of political competition depending on whether the middle caste propertied have their own regional parties, and on how they relate to the national parties. As already mentioned, in states with no regional parties, upper and middle-caste/class propertied groups are the mainstay of BJP support while lower-caste and -class groups and minorities support Congress in straight Congress–BJP contests. Typically, also, these states are economically better off than the rest of the country and the BJP tends to do better than Congress. An important exception to this rule is Madhya Pradesh, where relative backwardness is combined with straight two-party competition, but with a greater numerical advantage to Congress than in other states. Other states in this category include Chhattisgarh, Delhi, Gujarat, Haryana, Himachal Pradesh, and Rajasthan.

A second category consists of states where the major regional party allies with the BJP or the Congress, more often with the former than the latter. These include Andhra Pradesh, Assam, Bihar, Jharkhand, Karnataka, Orissa, and Punjab.

Maharashtra falls into a third category as a state that features two major regional parties, or groupings of regional parties each of which allies with one or the other national party, both of which also have a substantial presence in the state. Tamil Nadu constitutes a fourth category in which only regional parties are in contention and are grouped around two major regional parties, each set allied with one or the other national party. Kashmir, and the states that the Left dominates or in which it has a substantial presence – West Bengal, Kerala, and Tripura – and UP, constitute exceptions to this pattern of the politics of class-caste polarization.

Since 2004 Congress has made considerable inroads into the BJP's and some regional parties' constituencies among the propertied classes but they remain uncertain. To the extent that the policies favoured by these classes have to be compromised under Congress thanks to its core electoral base among the lower castes and classes and minorities, they remain fair weather friends. On the other hand, Congress stands to lose even its core electoral base through the pursuit of the policies favoured by the propertied – economic policies that favour the rich, and social and cultural policies that compromise the interests of the lower castes, Scheduled Tribes and minorities. That electorally Congress should devise and pursue policies that are capable of securing and extending this core social base is a no-brainer. And, as long as the Left remains regionally quarantined, this constituency remains the Congress' to lose: it is not as if there are other parties clamouring to represent the interests of these groups. Moreover, Congress expansion in this sector of the electorate will deny the BJP and its regional allies those crucial votes among that sector that give the BJP support beyond their core constituency, which parties of the propertied cannot do without. Of course, as long as Congress fights shy of taking this plunge of political and electoral acceptance, as long as it continues to seek the support and approval of the propertied, both they and the lower castes and classes and the minorities will remain uncertain of their loyalties, and leak critical votes to the BJP which may yet bring it back to power. This will especially be so for as long as neoliberalism remains the unchallenged paradigm of economic policy.

There is one scenario that has entered the realm of possibility since the onset of the world financial and economic crisis that must be mentioned before closing. A central factor in the consolidation of the constituency of the propertied in India has featured the role of (Non-Resident Indians) NRIs among whom those based in the US were ideologically the most important. Close ties with the US were pursued by all governments over recent decades and support for neoliberal policies was to a significant extent based on an uncritical approval of the US economy and the US's world role. The Pew Global Attitudes survey of 2006, which found anti-Americanism rampant in every other country outside the US itself, found India bucking this trend with 71 per cent of the exclusively urban respondents expressing approval of the US. Can the present crisis, which is simultaneously the crisis of neoliberalism and US hegemony, finally break this infatuation? In one sense a break is probably already here: until the crisis the US was the only country in the world with which India ran a substantial export surplus. The drying up of the US market will certainly re-direct trade elsewhere and the economic slowdown in the West more broadly will also increase the importance of expanding the domestic market.

Of course, objective developments can only accomplish so much and a great deal depends on India's political elites reading the writing on history's wall. If they do, however, there are likely to be new fissures among the propertied classes among those who will and those who will not go along with a new set of economic policies – policies which, like those of the early years of independence, will require greater egalitarianism and will focus on expanding the purchasing power of the poor to create out of them the market that can power India's economic and industrial growth. In that scenario, it will be easier for Congress to choose the economic policies that will also help consolidate and expand its core electoral constituency and deny the BJP and its allies the votes that make the difference between winning and losing.

Conclusion

This analysis of the rise of Hindutva has placed it in the context of the contradictions of Nehruvian development planning and the progressive economic liberalization to which it had already succumbed by the end of the 1960s. The ensuing pattern of class/caste polarization in which the emergence of the provincial propertied classes took centre stage explains the emergence of a constituency for Right politics that Hindutva consolidated from the late 1980s onwards. At the same time, the different regional combinations of liberal economic development and caste/class dynamics give political developments in India, including the rise of Hindutva, a distinct geography.

Was the development of Hindutva in India inevitable once the country had abandoned development planning and started on the path towards economically liberal policies? Perhaps, perhaps not. The politics of the new Right worldwide has featured some combination of economic liberalism and socially authoritarian politics – whether articulated in terms of religion, national culture or by some other ordering of social privilege. In this Hindutva is just the Indian version of forms of socially authoritarian ideologies that have accompanied the new Right everywhere – religious politics, racism, national chauvinism, etc. It could have been less powerful, but only in a context where bourgeois culture had other secular forms of expression. This, on the whole, the culture of the expanding Indian middle class did not have.

Note

1 I would like to thank the editors for their comments, which greatly improved this chapter. Remaining errors and omissions are, of course, my responsibility.

12 Expanding Indian democracy
The paradox of the third force

Sanjay Ruparelia[1]

Introduction

In 1989, a seven-party coalition named the National Front (NF) defeated the Indian National Congress in the country's ninth general election. The new governing coalition encompassed the lower castes and rural elites of the Janata Dal (JD), a successor to the Janata Party (1977–80), the first non-Congress government to rule New Delhi since independence. It also included the burgeoning commercial interests of ascendant regional parties, which demanded greater cultural recognition and political devolution. To capture power, the NF had to rely upon the external parliamentary support of the communist Left Front (LF) and the Hindu nationalist Bharatiya Janata Party (BJP), staunch political rivals that agreed to support the fledging minority administration in order to oust the Congress. Conflicts within the NF led to its premature demise and allowed the Congress to return to power.

Nevertheless, the election of the NF constituted a watershed in modern Indian democracy. According to India's pre-eminent psephologist, Yogendra Yadav, it signalled the beginning of India's 'third electoral system' (see 1999a and 1999b). The rising electoral participation of historically subordinate groups, emergence of distinct party systems in the states, and implementation of liberal economic reforms, lower-caste assertion and growing Hindu nationalism, had ushered in a 'post-Congress polity' in which state-level dynamics would determine the face of government in New Delhi. The regionalization of the federal party system heralded the end of the Congress' dominance and single-party majority governments at the Centre. More: the 'second democratic upsurge' of various subaltern groups, and their desire for equality, respect and self-rule, symbolized the radical promise of a new politics. The NF represented the possibility that a 'third force' would emerge as a catalyst of and vehicle for these rising democratic aspirations.

Subsequent events seemed to confirm these expectations. The Congress returned to office following the collapse of the NF. But then India's eleventh general election in 1996 saw the United Front (UF), a coalition of 15 state-based parties, capture national power. Its lower-caste, communist and regional parties sought to provide a counterpoint to the traditionally dominant Congress and ascendant Hindu nationalists. In many ways the new ruling coalition embodied the most distinct manifestation of the third force.

In hindsight, however, the UF was its apogee. Like its predecessor, the UF was a short-lived minority Union government that succumbed to the Congress' machinations. The willingness of the BJP to moderate its Hindu nationalist agenda enabled the party to craft a rival multiparty coalition – including several erstwhile members of the UF – and capture national power following India's twelfth general election in 1998. The first, short-lived, tenure of the BJP-led National Democratic Alliance (NDA) (1998–9) led Yadav (1999a) to retain hope in the second democratic upsurge. But the return to office of a larger BJP-led coalition after the thirteenth general election in 1999, and the unravelling of ties within and between former third-force parties during its second incarnation (1999–2004), narrowed the 'third space' in national politics. The Congress' decision to pursue federal coalition-making during the fourteenth general election in 2004, allowing its United Progressive Alliance (UPA) to unseat the BJP, deepened the sense of defeat amongst proponents of a third force. According to Yadav (2004), it signified the 'closure' of the third electoral system.

What explains the vicissitudes of the third force since 1989? To what extent have economic liberalization, popular democratic mobilization and ascendant cultural nationalism shaped and been shaped by the agendas, strategies and judgements of its main constituents? Does the failure of lower-caste, communist and regional parties to forge a durable national coalition represent the impossibility of a viable third force in contemporary Indian democracy?[2]

In general, scholars offer two perspectives to explain the chronic political instability of the third force. The first essentially sees its parties as factions of disgruntled former Congressmen, who come together to capture power for its own sake, with little to distinguish their policies (see Brass 1990). The single-point agenda of these inherently expedient coalitions explains their tumultuous disunity. The second camp attributes the volatility of various third-force alliances to their distinct caste, regional and class interests, diverse state-level bases and provincial outlooks. Hence the inability of these coalitions to imagine, pursue and achieve a distinctive vision of how to govern the country (see Khilnani 2004). Either way, the short life spans of the Janata, NF and UF appear to be reiterations of a theme.

Although well taken, these critical perspectives overstate the case in several ways. First, despite their minority parliamentary status, each of these governing coalitions pushed various initiatives in economic policy, Centre–state relations and foreign affairs against great odds. Second, many of their initiatives resembled proposals and tendencies as opposed to fully developed programmes, reflecting mentalities rather than clear political ideologies (Corbridge and Harriss 2000: 176). Nonetheless, they depict a complicated reality that warrants greater scrutiny. Finally, the dominant explanations of the third force are static, deeply structural and overdetermined. Thus we need to examine its trajectory through the agendas, strategies and judgements of its chief protagonists through multiple conjunctures. To do otherwise would be to ignore their impact – as if these parties had little to do with the 'reinvention' of India since 1989 (Corbridge and Harriss 2000), and as if the latter failed to affect them in turn.

Accordingly, this essay explains the trajectory of the third force over several phases: its crystallization (1989–91), culmination (1996–8) and dissolution (1999–2009). Three interwoven processes shaped its prospects over the years. First, despite their initial opposition, the decentralizing political logic of rapid economic liberalization after 1991 compelled most third-force constituents – including the Left – to push similar measures in their states. Economic liberalization also caused intra-party rifts, exacerbated inter-state disparities and deepened the regionalization of politics (see Jenkins 1999; Rudolph and Rudolph 2001a). Second, the main constituents of the third force opposed militant Hindu nationalism through much of the 1990s. But the BJP's decision to moderate its official political agenda in the late 1990s, its growing third-party status in several key states (see Sridharan 2004c) and the deepening effects of neoliberal economic reform exacerbated the centrifugal tendencies of the third force. Finally, many parties of the third force spearheaded popular democratic mobilization in the 1990s through a politics of recognition, especially amongst middle- and lower-caste groups and non-Hindi speaking regions. Yet ground-level distributive conflicts within the JD, and the fixed, indivisible and zero-sum conception of power that informed its politics, undermined power sharing within the party and tore it apart. A related conception of power informed the Left, which led to its refusal to share power with other parties, undercutting the wider political alliance. Taken together, the tensions created a grand paradox. The third force epitomized the idea of 'federal nationalism' (see Arora 2004).[3] Yet the practices of power that distinguished its parties, combined with the increasingly divergent compulsions of a federal market polity, undermined its capacity to survive.

The crystallization of the third front

The National Front (1989–91)

The NF was a seven-party coalition that ousted the Congress, following the ninth general election in 1989. The parties campaigned over corruption, inflation and the Congress' alleged incompetence (Kohli 1990: 4). Yet the polls occurred amidst rising communal tensions following the Shah Bano affair and the demand by militant Hindu nationalists to build a Ram Mandir (temple) on the site of the Babri Masjid (mosque) in Ayodhya in Uttar Pradesh. Indeed, the 1989 polls proved to be critical. The rising electoral participation of various subaltern groups, and the growing significance of states as the key electoral arenas for voters, would lead to two-party or bipolar competition in the states and parliamentary fragmentation in New Delhi (Yadav 1999a). The fractured electoral verdict in 1989 produced the first minority federal coalition government at the Centre since independence.

The NF was a complex multiparty alliance. Its inner ring comprised pre-poll allies. The core was the JD, which consisted of three main groups: the Jan Morcha of V. P. Singh and other Congress dissidents; factions of the Lok Dal led by Devi Lal and Ajit Singh; and the Janata Party of Ramakrishna Hegde, Chandrasekhar and George Fernandes. Three regional parties – the Telegu Desam Party (TDP) from Andhra Pradesh, Asom Gana Parishad (AGP) of Assam and Dravida Munnetra Kazagham (DMK) from Tamil Nadu – formed the second dimension of the inner circle. All these parties had worked together in a series of opposition-led regional conclaves in the 1980s that sought to reorganize Centre–state relations. The final member of the inner circle was the Congress (Socialist).

The outer ring of the NF comprised two formations that agreed to avoid electoral contests with its inner circle in order to defeat the Congress. They shared an intense mutual enmity, however, and had differences with the other parties too. The first was the Left Front, led by the Communist Party of India (Marxist) (CPM). The Left opposed V. P. Singh's willingness to accommodate the BJP, which it perceived as a major threat to the nation. It also feared that Singh would continue to deepen the liberal economic reforms that he had begun as the Congress' Union finance minister in the mid 1980s (Chatterjee 1997: 185–7). The second outside supporter was the BJP. It agreed numerous seat adjustments with the JD in northern India, which paid off handsomely (see Sridharan 2005). According to observers, the BJP high command wanted to join the inner ranks of the NF. But the Left objected to its participation, prompting V. P. Singh to devise state-level seat adjustments to ensure that neither party shared an electoral platform (Chatterjee 1997: 161–3, 185–7).

For some, the governing coalition lacked a viable political organization and a feasible alternative programme (Chatterjee 1997: 171–3). Others thought that its prospects of compromise, while not 'insurmountable', were fair at best (Kohli 1990: 21–3). It was easy to see why. Unlike the pronounced 'rural bias' of the Janata in the 1970s (see Corbridge and Harriss 2000: 80–90), the NF's economic policies were not too dissimilar from the Congress. The government financed its expenditures through heavy borrowing at home and abroad while continuing to liberalize trade and investment (Corbridge and Harriss 2000: 127, 151). Singh had left the Congress over the issue of corruption, not economic liberalization, which he had helped to initiate under Rajiv Gandhi (Kohli 1990: 15–21). The Left criticized these economic policies. Its stance involved internal tensions, however. The West Bengal chief minister, Jyoti Basu, had introduced several liberal measures in the mid 1980s to cope with industrial stagnation and labour strikes (Chatterjee 1997: 185–7). These contradictions would gradually intensify.

Still, the NF was arguably more attuned to the country's traditional economy policy of industrial support and external protection (Adams 1990: 97). It also increased agricultural subsidies. The power of propertied middle castes in the JD was a result of their previous departure from the Congress. Their growing investment and holdings in the urban and industrial economy transformed these middling agricultural groups into provincial bourgeoisies with their own parties (Desai 2004b: 55). The NF thus represented the continuing electoral ascent of the *kisans* (farmers) in national politics.

The orientation of the NF towards Centre–state relations and foreign affairs was more distinct. It established the Inter State Council, a body to enable chief ministers of the states to address federal issues. Despite the mounting political crisis in Kashmir V. P. Singh and his new foreign minister, I. K. Gujral, sought to improve bilateral relations in the subcontinent (see Rose 1990: 67–74), and the NF employed softer rhetoric regarding Pakistan. Gujral renegotiated bilateral treaties with Nepal regarding trade and transit, and sought to improve ties with Sri Lanka following the exit of the Indian Peace Keeping Force (Ganguly 1994: 156). And the government made positive overtures towards China. All these initiatives revealed a more pacific, cooperative and positive outlook towards Centre–state relations and the subcontinent.

But the downfall of the NF, due to conflicts within the JD and vis-à-vis the BJP, thwarted its possibilities. A leadership tussle between V. P. Singh, Devi Lal and Chandrasekhar mired its workings from the start. It evoked the 'single-mindedly self-destructive' struggles within the 'squabbling gerontocratic triumvirate' of Moraji Desai, Jagjivan Ram and Charan Singh during the Janata in the late 1970s (Corbridge and Harriss 2000: 88–9). The inability of anti-Congress formations to 'act in unity' reflected the 'ambitions of [their] leaders for senior posts' and a 'mercurial politics' where 'power-first principles' prevailed (Kohli 1990: 21–3).

There were important differences, however. First, whereas the Janata championed the agrarian populist dreams that threatened the urban, commercial and industrial interests of the historic ruling bloc (Chatterjee 1997: 71–2), the battles within the JD during the NF represented the clash between '*kisan* politics' and 'quota politics' (Jaffrelot 2000: 87). In August 1990, V. P. Singh implemented the recommendations of the Second Backward Classes Commission (also known as the Mandal Commission Report), which extended reservations in elite administrative services and central public enterprises to Other Backward Classes (OBCs) on the basis of caste. Devi Lal had objected to the Report prior to the 1989 polls and resigned upon its implementation. The policy created a horizontal interest group of backward castes, providing Singh with his own large, newly mobilized, electoral constituency. But Devi Lal's hostility to it was wider (see Jaffrelot 2000: 87–97). The Mandal Commission excluded the rich Jat farmers of northern India to which he belonged, beneficiaries of the Green Revolution in the 1970s, who enjoyed dominant caste status. In contrast, the relatively prosperous Yadavs were not excluded, thanks to successful political lobbying by the charismatic JD leader in Bihar, Lalu Prasad Yadav (Jaffrelot 2000: 100–1). Moreover, the mantra of 'social justice' employed by V. P. Singh to justify expanding reservations threatened to undercut the *kisan* political front led by Devi Lal by emboldening weaker agricultural groups – tenants, sharecroppers and labourers – belonging to the OBCs. Indeed, Lal had objected to naming the party the Samajwadi Janata Dal, which would have emphasized its socialist commitments, and to Singh's proposal to reserve 60 per cent of the party apparatus for the 'weaker sections' of society (Jaffrelot 2000: 95). In the end, however, quota politics prevailed (Jaffrelot 2000: 106).

Second, unlike the state-level mergers between parties that led to the Samyukta Vidhayak Dal (SVD) of the 1960s and to the Janata after the Emergency, the NF was a genuine multiparty coalition based on inter-state alliances (Sridharan 2004b: 500). Furthermore, the inclusion of the TDP, AGP and DMK, despite their poor electoral showing in 1989, gave it a distinctly regional face. V. P. Singh wished to undermine the image of regional political formations as 'anti-national', which Indira Gandhi had recklessly sown, and to demonstrate that such parties could govern at the Centre (see Manor 2004c). In short, their participation in the NF signified political learning (Kohli 1990: 8–9), and distinguished its disposition towards Centre–state relations and, to a lesser extent, foreign affairs.

Yet the greatest difference between the NF and its predecessor concerned its eventual stance toward Hindutva (Hindu cultural nationalism). The implementation of Mandal antagonized the BJP, threatening the interests of its high-caste urban base, and instigated social conflicts across northern India. The hawkish BJP leader L. K. Advani launched the Ramjanmabhoomi, a modern chariot journey across the country to mobilize support for a Ram Mandir in Ayodhya. Mounting communal violence led Lalu Prasad Yadav, then JD chief minister of Bihar, to arrest Advani in October 1990. The decision prompted the BJP to withdraw its external parliamentary support to the NF government. It exposed a simmering division between the Hindu nationalists and their more secular lower-caste allies that had originated after the Emergency. On the one hand, the Lok Dal of Charan Singh had opposed Hindu nationalist Bharatiya Jana Sangh (BJS) parliamentarians having 'dual membership' with the Rashtriya Swayamsevak Sangh (RSS) (Jaffrelot 1998: 282–314).[4] On the other, the BJS had resisted the appointment of the Mandal commission by Moraji Desai (Jaffrelot 2000: 94). These two conflicts had compelled the BJS to quit the Janata and rechristen itself as the BJP in April 1980. The two sides entered various electoral alliances after 1984. But the implementation of Mandal ten years later, combined with the participation of various regional parties in the NF, helped to crystallize the idea of a third force vis-à-vis the BJP and the Congress.

The fall of V. P. Singh's ministry led to another minority Union government led by Chandrasekhar, now the leader of the Janata Dal (Socialist) (JD[S]), with the Congress' outside support. But it only lasted a few months. The Congress accused Chandrasekhar of spying on Rajiv Gandhi and toppled his government, triggering the tenth general election in 1991 and enabling a minority Congress administration to return to power.

Congress in minority (1991–6)

The JD was the main casualty of the failure of the NF. Its three main groupings split into competing forces in the Hindi heartland, partly as a result of its fall from office. More importantly, the gradual popular acceptance of the Mandal Commission Report and its implementation by the Supreme Court in 1992 dissolved the unity amongst OBCs that opposition to the Report had initially created (Jaffrelot 2000: 101). Ironically, however, its official terms and subsequent operationalization created future difficulties for the JD. In Uttar Pradesh, the Ajit Singh faction of the Lok Dal, 'susceptible to Hindu chauvinist appeals' (Frankel 2005: 665), left the JD after the 1991 polls to support the minority Congress government. In contrast, the rising OBC leader Mulayam Singh Yadav stuck with Chandrasekhar and his JDS, now rechristened the Samajwadi Janata Party (SJP). But Mulayam Yadav's desire to form his personal organization, and patronize his own community, led to the establishment of the Samajwadi Party (SP) in 1992. Finally, in 1994, George

Fernandes and Nitish Kumar created the Samata Party (SAP), due to micro-level vertical conflicts amongst the OBCs. As chief minister of Bihar, Lalu Yadav had directed considerable patronage towards his own community, excluding the Kurmis and Keoris who supported Fernandes and Kumar. The two Yadav leaders had 'instrumentalized' the empowerment of OBCs for their particular castes. The emergent power of the OBCs, reaching its zenith as a horizontal interest group due to politics of the Mandal, weakened at its moment of triumph (Jaffrelot 2000: 104–6).

In some ways, the break-up of the JD reflected previous divisions. The party was principally an amalgamation of the Lok Dal, which privileged the interests of rich capitalist farmers, and the Janata Party, whose socialist leanings favoured extending reservations in public institutions. The implementation of Mandal exacerbated these disagreements. Yet these material conflicts and ideological differences could not explain the fierce leadership disputes within these groupings. Explanations diverge. Many commentators lamented the desire for short-term political aggrandizement. Others claimed that such self-destructive internecine struggles reflected a failure of these leaders – who frequently established new political groups based on their self-proclaimed personal charisma (see Kumar 2004b) – to grasp that long-term political success required organizational discipline and personal self-restraint. But these practices suggested, in turn, an underlying belief: of power as a fixed, indivisible, zero-sum good. In particular, the manner in which these leaders exercised their newly acquired strength resembled the techniques of resistance, insubordination and defiance practised by genuine subaltern groups.[5] It was a conception of power essential for the governed, but self-liquidating for its elites.

The immediate beneficiaries of the collapse of the NF, of course, were the Congress and the BJP. Yet neither could turn back the tide. Despite the sense of disorder surrounding V. P. Singh's administration, and a wave of sympathy for the Congress following Rajiv Gandhi's assassination by the Liberation Tigers of Tamil Eelam (LTTE) during the tenth general election, the Congress failed to acquire a parliamentary majority upon returning to office.[6] It also had a crisis of leadership. The party stalwarts urged Rajiv's widow, Sonia Gandhi, to assume the mantle of rule. Her refusal allowed Narasimha Rao, an aging congressman from Andhra Pradesh, to become the prime minister of a minority Union government. He took the helm amidst growing economic turbulence, driven by unchecked fiscal deficits and a mounting balance-of-payments crisis. Rao and his newly appointed finance minister, Manmohan Singh, responded by introducing the most sweeping liberal economic measures the country had seen, dismantling India's 'permit license raj'.

Economic liberalization reduced the opposition to Mandal by creating new avenues of prosperity and status for historically advantaged groups (Jaffrelot 2000: 101). Yet neither it, nor the return to office, failed to reverse the Congress' deteriorating fortunes. Structural adjustment created a federal market economy with two distinct consequences (see Jenkins 1999; Rudolph and Rudolph 2001a; Sinha 2004b). On the one hand, fiscal restraint in New Delhi gradually led to a decline in public investment and central economic assistance to the states and raised the cost of greater commercial borrowing. On the other, the decision to 'liberalize from above' forced every state to compete for scarce private investment, exposing them to new constraints imposed by the Centre, credit-rating agencies and international financial institutions. Thus economic liberalization intensified the centrifugal political logic of the third electoral system. The two previously independent causal processes became mutually reinforcing (Rudolph and Rudolph 2001a: 1548). These devolutionary processes both embedded the reforms and spurred the rise of the third force. But it would test the unity of the latter as well.

The second immediate beneficiary was the BJP, which emerged as the second largest party in the Lok Sabha after the 1991 polls. It made important gains in Rajasthan, Delhi and Gujarat at the expense of the JD. The BJP also strengthened its position in Maharashtra through a coalition with the Shiv Sena, whose regional nativist concerns increasingly reflected an anti-Muslim ideology (see Katzenstein, Mehta and Thakkar 2004). The furore created over Mandal, particularly in urban north India, galvanized the privileged high-caste votaries of Hindu nationalism.

But the brutal reductive logic of 'Hindu, Hindu, Hindustan' – which informed the BJP's resolve to abrogate Article 370 of the Constitution granting Jammu and Kashmir special asymmetric rights, and to implement a uniform civil code nullifying personal religious laws – also stiffened the resolve of its opponents. The formation of a BJP state government in Uttar Pradesh, aided by the increasingly charged rhetoric of the Ramjanmabhoomi and passivity of the minority Congress government in New Delhi, ended with the demolition of the Babri Masjid in Ayodhya on 6 December 1992. The ensuing communal violence brought losses for the BJP in state assembly elections between 1993 and 1995. The party emerged stronger in Delhi and Rajasthan but lost its incumbency in Himachal and Madhya Pradesh (Corbridge and Harriss 2000: 131). It faced an emboldened JD in state assembly elections in Karnataka in 1994 and in Maharashtra and Bihar in 1995. And it encouraged the SP and Bahujan Samaj Party (BSP) to join hands in Uttar Pradesh, creating a lower-caste coalition of *Dalits*, OBCs and Muslims that deposed the BJP in the 1993 state assembly elections. Granted, the *dalitbahujan* alliance ended in acrimony after two years. Personal animosity between Mulayam Yadav and Mayawati, its respective leaders, leading to violent partisan conflicts; the marginalization of Kurmis, a lower OBC community that largely supported the BSP, in the state bureaucracy (Jaffrelot 2000: 103); and deeper material conflicts in the countryside, between dominant Yadav castes and landless *Dalit* labourers, were to blame. Nevertheless, excessive communal violence isolated the BJP. They encouraged the party high command to ally with parties that appealed to lower-caste voters ('indirect Mandalization') and to promote lower-caste leaders within the party structure ('direct Mandalization') (Jaffrelot 2000: 104–6). The second democratic upsurge of historically subordinate groups, despite its strong internal contradictions, began to constrain the politics of Hindutva.

The culmination of the third force

The United Front (UF) (1996–8)

The UF was a diverse coalition of 15 state-based parties that came together following the highly fractured verdict of the eleventh general election in 1996. Its principal aim was to stop the BJP, which had emerged as the single largest party in the Lok Sabha, from coming to national power. The new coalition was a complex political entity. The inner circle of the UF comprised four partisan blocs. Its leading protagonist remained the JD. Although electorally diminished, its presence alongside the SP reflected the steady political clout of intermediate and lower-caste groups, enabling the JD Karnataka chief minister H. D. Deve Gowda to become its first prime minister. The stronger electoral performance of the TDP, AGP and DMK granted these regional parties greater voice. The appointment of the TDP chief minister of Andhra Pradesh, N. Chandrababu Naidu, as the convenor of the UF symbolized the rise of the regions. The third component was the Communist Party of India (CPI), which broke ranks with its Left Front allies and decided to participate in a Union government for the first time.[7] Lastly, a series of newly fashioned parties joined the coalition. Several were Congress factions disaffected with Narasimha Rao: the Tamil Maanila Congress (TMC), Indian National Congress (Tiwari) INC (T) and Madhya Pradesh Vikas Congress (MPVC). The most significant was the TMC, led by G. K. Moopanar and the former Union commerce minister Palaniappan Chidambaram, who became the UF's finance minister.

Like the NF, the UF was a minority governing coalition. It required allies to survive. The larger and smaller allies of the CPI in the Left Front – the CPM, Revolutionary Socialist Party (RSP) and All India Forward Bloc (FB) – constituted the first. The CPM helped to craft the UF and devise a common minimum programme and participated in a steering committee that it had partly established. But the party rejected an offer to make Jyoti Basu the prime minister, and formal cabinet participation more generally – a decision the West Bengal chief minister would later call an 'historic blunder'.

The CPM's stance ignited controversy. The party central committee argued that the presence of stronger regional parties – with their 'agro-barons' and 'kulaks' – in the newly formed coalition heralded greater economic liberalization (see Ahmad 1996). Participating in government would force it to accept responsibility for policies that it opposed. The minority parliamentary status of the UF made it unstable as well. Thus the CPM preferred to play the role of 'honest broker', arguing that its renunciation of office represented its 'accumulated moral hegemony' rather than a 'lost historic opportunity'. Many political opponents accused the party of exercising power without responsibility, however. Others charged it with hypocrisy. The new industrial policy introduced by the Left Front government in West Bengal in 1995 reflected a neoliberal policy dispensation (see Sinha 2004a). Finally, some argued that the CPM's refusal to enter government revealed a party beholden to 'textbook solutions' offered by 'high theory', eager to trade the 'messy practical realities' of multi-party democracy for the 'pure space' of critique (see Nigam 2000; Menon and Nigam 2007).

Each view had its rationale. On the one hand, the logic of the post-1991 reforms compelled every ruling party to pursue economic liberalization in the states where they governed. In this regard, the CPM's decision to provide outside support was a shrewd political strategy. It enabled the party to fight Hindu nationalism at the Centre and protect its state-level bastions without forsaking its right to dissent. Yet the refusal of the CPM to join the government betrayed a 'politics of self-reproduction' that began in the 1980s (see Chatterjee 1999). Arguably, it also revealed a static, moralistic and total conception of power that militated against power sharing with its socialist counterparts and diminished its possibilities of realizing a broader social transformation.

The second prop to the government, the Congress, was larger and far less reliable. The party was the principal rival of most UF constituents. Moreover, it had previously taken advantage of splits in both the Janata and the NF, only to topple their remnants. The diversity of the UF and its dependence on the Congress led an editorial in *Economic and Political Weekly* to declare:

> What purpose can such a patchwork creature of doubtful longevity serve in terms of the objectives that the so-called Third Front is said to be pursuing, except to invite even more popular cynicism in the face of incessant internal bickering and eventual collapse?
> (1996: 1099)

As sceptics feared, personal struggles, sectional rivalries and ideological conflicts beset the short-lived tenure of the UF.

Yet in many ways the UF represented a culmination of the idea of the third force, illuminating its promise and limits. In economic policy, it pushed reforms in industry, trade and investment. It set up a Disinvestment Commission to examine the performance of state-owned enterprises. And it continued to devolve economic power to the states. This pro-liberalization thrust was largely due to prime minister Deve Gowda, the staunchly neoliberal finance minister P. Chidambaram and the support of the regional parties, which held key economic portfolios and partly represented the interests of aspiring regional capitalists (see Baru 2000). These developments challenged the view that a heterogeneous center-left coalition would stymie the reform process (see Jenkins 1999: 225–8; Nayyar 1999). There were shortcomings and failures. The UF failed to reduce subsidies to relatively privileged constituencies, highlighted by the Fifth Pay Commission, which placed an immense burden on the fisc. The CPM also rightly criticized the government's failure to increase public investment in primary education, basic health and physical infrastructure, and the restructuring of the public distribution system, where half-baked reforms to 'target' the poor created new perversities (see Harriss, Chapter 8 in this volume). On the one hand, these omissions seemed to vindicate the party's decision not to join the government. But its unwillingness to do so undermined its political authority to make such demands or set the policy agenda. The presumed moral hegemony of the Left could not trump the expectations of power-sharing and collective responsibility that multiparty national governments required.

In Centre–state relations, Deve Gowda announced new measures for Jammu and Kashmir and the Northeast, holding state assembly elections after nine years in the former, directing central funds to the latter and making several high-level visits to both regions. The government promised to extend to Kashmir 'maximum autonomy' and resuscitated the Inter State Council. And it accepted the allocation of a greater share of central tax revenues to the states. To be sure, the UF botched several issues. It marred state assembly elections in Kashmir by failing to engage separatist groups and ensure complete fairness (Bose 2003: 138). The government imposed President's rule in Gujarat and Uttar Pradesh under questionable circumstances. And it was unable to resolve longstanding conflicts over inter-state water sharing in the south. Nonetheless, given the vulnerability and composition of the UF, it was surprising that it accomplished anything at all.

Finally, the coalition displayed some flair in foreign affairs. It resisted international pressure to sign the Comprehensive Test Ban Treaty (CTBT) but refused the temptation to test India's nuclear devices. More importantly, its foreign minister, I. K. Gujral, offered non-reciprocal concessions in the subcontinent. The 'Gujral doctrine' facilitated the Ganga Waters Treaty Accord, on terms disproportionately favourable to Bangladesh, finessing a major protracted dispute. The government signed a series of understandings regarding power, water and trade with Nepal. And it resumed high-level dialogue with Pakistan. These were not radical departures. In each instance, however, the UF displayed a more conciliatory approach than previous Congress administrations. Its initiatives belied the view that a federal coalition government of state-based parties would be unable to re-imagine the national interest or how to secure it. In several ways, the UF suggested a possible new vision of federal nationalism.

What undermined these potentialities, however, were its politics. In part, they were internal. The JD broke up again. Personal animosities and political differences led Ramakrishna Hegde, a JD stalwart in Karnataka, to form the Lok Shakti (LS) (see Shashtri 2004). The refusal of Lalu Yadav to resign despite allegations of corruption, and the desire of Sharad Yadav to supplant him, ended with the creation of the Rashtriya Janata Dal (RJD) in Bihar. And the souring of relations between Biju Patnaik and the party, and his later death, led his son to forge the Biju Janata Dal (BJD) in Orissa. The regionalization of the federal party system differentiated the base and orientation of the JD in each of these states: from the prosperous middle-caste agriculturalists in Karnataka, to the Yadav-Muslim combine in the Bihar, to an upper caste-dominated social coalition in Orissa (see Kumar 2004a). But the preceding splits underscored the deeply personalized nature of conflicts in the party.

Nevertheless, the UF government did not collapse due to these fissures, but because of the Congress. In fact, its leading constituents rebuffed the latter on two occasions. In April 1997, the new Congress leader Sitaram Kesri withdrew outside support to the government. Maladroit attempts by Deve Gowda to tarnish Kesri and lure elements of the Congress led to I. K. Gujral becoming prime minister.[8] Yet Kesri's gambit failed to lure a single UF constituent. In November 1997, the Congress ordered the UF to drop the DMK on the basis of the flawed interim Jain Commission Report. But not a single party in the coalition, or faction thereof, broke its ranks. It was the Congress' withdrawal of support, and the failure of either the Congress or the BJP to mount a viable alternative coalition, that compelled the twelfth general election in February–March 1998.

The collapse of the UF government sowed its dissolution as a coalition, however. This was for three reasons. First, many of its parties fought the campaign in their respective states independently or against each another due to the local compulsions of the federal party system. Moreover, the fracturing of the JD cost the party scarce votes. Second, the Congress failed to grasp the exigencies of the third electoral system. Its high command persuaded Sonia Gandhi to lead the party, hoping the Nehru-Gandhi dynasty would restore its fortunes, and decided to contest the polls in most states on its own. But the party failed to improve its tally. Finally, the BJP deftly put together a rival multiparty coalition by projecting the relatively moderate A. B. Vajpayee as its leader and agreeing to shelve its most controversial proposals. These compromises demonstrated astute political judgement. But it equally reflected the growing capacity of various state-based parties to influence the terms of national coalition making.

The BJP emerged at the head of a large multiparty coalition, the National Democratic Alliance (NDA), just shy of a parliamentary majority. To counter it, the CPM announced its support for a Congress-led coalition as part of its 'united front strategy' (Muralidharan 1998), which garnered the support of several weakened constituents of the UF. But the former UF convenor N. Chandrababu Naidu, wary of the rising electoral fortunes of the BJP in Andhra Pradesh, crossed the floor. His decision allowed the BJP-led NDA to capture national power.

The TDP's decision earned the opprobrium of the Left. For many observers, it exposed a naïve faith that India's state-based parties were inherently secular. The Shiv Sena expressed a vernacularized Hindu chauvinism. J. Jayalalitha, the leader of the All India Anna Dravida Munnetra Kazagham (AIADMK) in Tamil Nadu, had been funding temple endowments and 'allying with prominent Hindu priests' in her home state during the polls (Jenkins 1998b: 5–6). And the SAP, BJD and LS were happy to join the BJP in order to weaken their old colleagues in the JD. Hence the belief that '[r]egionalism in India … is not primarily concerned with halting the rise of centralizing orthodoxies or projecting a new vision of the nation, except occasionally by default' (Jenkins 1998b: 4).

Yet this conclusion, while not invalid, is perhaps extreme. First, the official political moderation of the BJP was due to the demands of such parties. Tragically, it was not a fail-safe guarantee, as later events would show. At this stage, however, it worked. Second, by comparison with the pre-1998 allies of the BJP, its new partners from the third force and beyond had defended secularism until now, while other state-based parties remain opposed to Hindutva. Third, the unwillingness of the TDP to support the Congress was understandable. Unlike the Left, SP or RJD, which dominated the Congress on their respective turfs, the TDP was less secure. The exigencies of power, caused by the uneven multiple bipolarities of the federal party system, compelled its decision. Lastly, the TDP was right to suspect the Congress, which had just toppled the UF. Indeed, the Congress would declare at its Pachmarhi session in September 1998 that it opposed federal multiparty coalitions 'unless absolutely necessary'. It was the start of a long political winter.

The dissolution of the third force

The BJP-led National Democratic Alliance (1998-2004)[9]

The first incarnation of the NDA was short-lived. It began with the decision to test India's nuclear devices, a longstanding goal of Hindu nationalists, in May 2008. Rising international pressure on India to sign the CTBT influenced its timing. By equating the tests with 'Hindu pride', however, the BJP sought to claim political credit, outflank its new coalition allies and wrong-foot its rivals. But attempts by the BJP to rewrite school textbooks, introduce new curricula and reconstitute educational bodies sympathetic to Hindu nationalist views encountered stiff opposition from many coalition partners. More ominous was the campaign of violence by the Sangh Parivar against Christians in the tribal belts of Bihar, Madhya Pradesh and Gujarat. In the end, the unwillingness of Prime Minister Vajpayee to obstruct criminal investigations against Jayalalitha or dismiss the DMK state government in Tamil Nadu led her to withdraw support in April 1999. The first BJP-led NDA lasted just 13 months.

It failed to resurrect a third front, however. The continuing political disintegration of the JD was the first reason. Intense sectional rivalries in Karnataka (pitting J. H. Patel against Deve Gowda) and in Bihar (where Sharad Yadav and the influential *Dalit* leader Ram Vilas Paswan sought to weaken Lalu Yadav) stymied a larger OBC front. In fact, these disputes led to the creation of the Janata Dal (United) (JD [U]) in the summer of 1999, which then joined the NDA. Personal rivalries, and the chance to gain spoils at the Centre, caused these splits (see Ramakrishnan and Pande 1999). Whatever their motivations, the JD's implosion was bewildering. It reduced the presence of former socialists in the third force to the SP, RJD and JD (Secular), now led by Deve Gowda.

The second impediment to the revival of a third force was the short-term calculus of its former regional constituents. The DMK exploited the crisis precipitated by the AIADMK by agreeing to join the NDA with its state-level allies. Reportedly, the Left's decision to reach out to Jayalalitha antagonized M. Karuninidhi, the DMK chief, who justified his about-face by saying that 'Jayalalitha's corruption is more dangerous than communalism' (Muralidharan 1999b). This begged credulity. Yet it illuminated how the third electoral system made Centre–state calculations, which hitherto preoccupied national parties, integral to state-based formations too. Like the TDP in 1998, the DMK joined the NDA to accrue national influence whilst protecting its position at home.

Finally, the changed political strategy of the Left vis-à-vis the Congress sealed the fate of a third force after the 1999 general election. The RSP and FB hoped for an alliance with Jyoti Basu as its prime minister-designate (Ramakrishnan 1999). But Sonia Gandhi rejected the idea, leading Basu to vent the view that 'a communist cannot become prime minister of India' (Muralidharan 1999a), three years after the 'historic blunder'. The political times had changed. Consequently the CPM and CPI backed the Congress, arguing that a policy of 'equidistance' between the latter and the BJP was now too dangerous. But its critics were merciless, claiming that a 'domesticated' Left, bereft of powerful mass organizations with a national presence, feared taking responsibility as a 'care-taker administration'. 'The passions of youth', said one, 'have become the lust of old men' (Das 1999). Ultimately, neither interpretation mattered. The SP chief Mulayam Yadav, the key Congress ally in Uttar Pradesh, refused to endorse Sonia Gandhi (Muralidharan 1999b). It was a personal rebuke. But his criticism of her 'foreign' origins, echoing the BJP, suggested that its cultural nationalist arguments had spread. Mulayam also feared losing Muslim support to the Congress and that of OBCs to the BJP, which produced an informal understanding with the BJP OBC leader Kalyan Singh.

An expanded NDA won a comfortable parliamentary majority in the thirteenth general election in September–October 1999. Although buoyed by nationalist fervour after the Kargil war with Pakistan, its tally was largely due to clever state-level alliances and the BJP's prudent decision to contest parliamentary seats in areas of strength, which increased its winning percentage (Yadav 2004). Despite its victory, Yadav and Kumar remained somewhat optimistic about the prospects for the third front:

> The third space, occupied by various non-Congress, non-BJP formations, has not shrunk in any significant way. What has declined, of course, is the vision and organizational capacity of those wanting to create a Third Front in national politics.
>
> (1999)

Yet the distance between its erstwhile protagonists grew. In August 2000, the TDP chief minister challenged the recommendations of the 11th Finance Commission, saying it awarded high-population, low-economic-growth states like Bihar, Uttar Pradesh, Assam and West Bengal, while penalizing the low-population, high-economic-growth performance of Andhra Pradesh, Karnataka and Tamil Nadu (Rudolph and Rudolph 2001a: 1547). The latter were the home states of pro-liberalizers in the UF: the TDP, DMK and TMC, and southern wing of the JD. Naidu's positive self-portrayal belied the facts (see Manor 2004c; Sen and Frankel 2005; Dreze and Sen 1998). Moreover, the new chief ministership of Buddhadeb Bhattacharya saw the West Bengal government woo foreign capital for public–private partnerships in manufacturing, software and urban industrial development, while engaging in 'lockouts, retrenchments and closures' of failing public sector enterprises and allowing social sector spending to stagnate (see Bhattacharyya 1999). Nonetheless, Naidu's protest led to supplementary funds for high growth states, weakening the equalizing basis of previous Finance Commission awards.

The centrifugal tendencies of economic liberalization began to stress inter-state relations (see Corbridge in this volume) and wither the 'third space'. States competed to entice private capital, which now accounted for three-quarters of gross fixed investment (Rudolph and Rudolph 2001a: 1545). Efforts to end beggar-thy-neighbour competition, including a proposal from the CPM patriarch Jyoti Basu, yielded a common sales tax and uniform central value added tax across the states (Rudolph and Rudolph 2001a: 1546). Horizontal inter-state competition became the norm, however, testing the redistributive mechanisms of India's federal political economy. It strained ties between various protagonists of the third force, which had previously begun to challenge the unitary visions of national parties and demand more equitable Centre–state relations.

But most damaging to the credibility of the third force, and opposition politics in general, was the failure of ostensibly secular partners in the NDA to stop the growing communal menace during its second term. Many believed federal coalition politics would punish excessive Hindu militancy. The anti-Muslim pogrom in Gujarat in 2002, which directly involved the BJP state government, exposed this view. The Left denounced the BJP. The TDP, DMK and to a lesser extent the JD (U) distanced themselves. But neither they nor any other member of the NDA demanded political resignations, let alone left the alliance, in response to the violence (see Sridharan 2004a). Their paralysis highlighted the paradoxical effects of the federal party system in an era of diverse coalition governments, which stopped nominally secular parties from joining the Opposition, given their divergent state-level relations vis-à-vis the Congress. Yet it also reflected a brutal political cynicism to weigh the costs of remaining against a possible electoral backlash in the regions. Many parties bore responsibility, including the Congress, for not attacking the BJP. But the collective failure of erstwhile members of the UF belied the promise of the third force.

The Congress-led United Progressive Alliance (2004–2009)

The surprising emergence of the Congress-led United Progressive Alliance (UPA) in the fourteenth general election in May 2004 represented a crucial turning point. Commentators debated its possible causes: a popular rejection of Hindutva, the pro-poor tilt of the Congress, a 'rural revolt' against rising social inequalities (see Mishra 2004; Desai and Manor in this volume). Yet what determined the outcome was the Congress' belated recognition that it had to play the coalition game. The party crafted electoral alliances with key state-based parties in a number of regions – including the RJD, Lok Jan Shakti (LJS) and DMK – as well as indirect agreements with the CPM outside its bastions. The willingness of the Left to support the coalition from outside, while again refusing to join government, enabled the Congress' return to New Delhi.

For Yadav (2004), the emergence of the UPA denoted the 'closure' of the third electoral system. It indicated the 'saturation' of the second democratic upsurge and the 'domestication' of national policy choices. The emergence of a bipolar national contest, in which state-based parties oscillated between the Congress and the BJP, ended the hope of radicalism. It signalled the failure of lower-caste, communist and regional parties to construct a viable third force.

Not everyone agreed. Some highlighted the Congress' difficulty in absorbing its new state-based allies or destabilizing political rivals, and its greater willingness to address the needs of historically subordinate groups (see Rangarajan 2005). Others noted that it was the contest over allies – which together won more than half the national vote in 2004 – that determined the fortunes of the Congress and BJP (see

Sheth 2005). Finally, the UPA government managed to introduce progressive initiatives during its first tenure in office: the Right to Information Act, National Rural Employment Guarantee Scheme and other 'flagship programmes'.[10] According to many, the CPM was a major catalyst of these changes, promoting their adoption while opposing the disinvestment of profitable state enterprises, and greater economic liberalization and foreign direct investment in various sectors (compare Harriss and Manor in this volume). These developments suggested the continuing significance of the idea of the third force.

Its credibility, organization and stability had vanished, however. Subsequent efforts to create a viable third front proved to be incoherent, desultory or futile. The temporary formation of the Jan Morcha,[11] which sought to protect vulnerable peasants from land seizures for special economic zones (SEZs), pitted several erstwhile socialists and the Left against the SP (see Pai 2007). In August 2007, the SP and TDP joined the eight-party United National Progressive Alliance (UNPA), which declared its 'equidistance' from the Congress and the BJP.[12] But it lacked real purpose; there was little to bond its members. Finally, the Left's decision to exit the UPA in August 2008 over the Indo–US civil nuclear agreement (see Vanaik in this volume) suggested a reinvigorated third force. Yet the CPM could not construct a stable alternative formation. The willingness of the SP to rescue the Congress, a party that it had opposed for as long as it had allied with the Left, enabled the UPA to finish its first tenure in office. Indeed, the UPA returned to power in the fourteenth general election in May 2009 with a larger parliamentary tally, vanquishing a much diminished NDA as well as efforts by the Left to project a third front.

Proximate factors had an impact. The shifting declarations and state-level disagreements of the constituents of a putative third force, and their refusal to agree upon a political leader, created a spectre of instability (see Kailash 2009). The JD (S) of former prime minister Deve Gowda aligned with the Left in Karnataka, but competed against it in West Bengal and Kerala, and flirted with the Congress. The newly formed Telengana Rashtra Samiti (TRS) abandoned its alliance with the TDP and the Left in Andhra Pradesh during the campaign. The BJD broke from the NDA before the polls and entered an alliance with the Nationalist Congress Party (NCP) in Orissa, but refused to join the wider alliance. Indeed, the RJD, SP and LJP mounted a 'fourth front'.

But the final outcome also revealed the failure of the third force to deepen popular democratic mobilization and the necessary long-term nexus between economic development and social empowerment (see Yadav and Palshikar 2009). On the one hand, the rise of new regional parties, importance of astute state-level coalitions and the collective weight of state-based parties revealed the continuing impact of the second democratic upsurge and the electoral limits of Hindutva. On the other, though, the verdict exposed the absence of a politics that could bind the increasingly capricious elements and serve the natural social base of a third force. In Bihar, the JD (U)-led NDA capitalized on the protracted governance failures and political exclusion of lower OBCs and Maha Dalits by the RJD and LJP by initiating political reforms and targeting public benefits towards these groups. In Uttar Pradesh, the Congress recovered a foothold by exploiting the failure of the

BSP state government to deliver basic public services and the decision of the SP to associate with the former BJP chief minister Kalyan Singh, alienating his traditional Muslim supporters. In Kerala, despite the achievements of the local development planning (see Heller, Chapter 10 in this volume), the Left suffered a massive defeat caused by high-level rifts over corruption and its alliance with the People's Democratic Party (PDP), which tainted its secular credentials. In West Bengal, the drive towards industrialization through Special Economic Zones (SEZs) had ignited violent conflicts between the Left and its electoral rivals, Naxalites and the inhabitants of rural land designated for expropriation, as witnessed in Singur, Nandigram and elsewhere (see Chatterjee and Jenkins in this volume). The failure of the latest avatar of the third force to overcome its partialities, in other words, allowed the Congress to enter the third space.

Conclusion

It is possible to read the failure to create a durable third force in India after 1989 as the chronicle of a death foretold. Building national power in a country as 'large, diverse and fragmented' as India is inherently difficult (Brass 1990: 19–20). The transformation of India's political economy in the post-1989 era made it even harder. Economic liberalization and popular democratic mobilization have intensified processes of regionalization, creating a federal market polity with proliferating voices, demands and interests. These developments helped to contain, but not eliminate, the threat of militant Hindu nationalism. Collectively, they made it harder for any party, let alone a group of parties, to strike a durable national alliance that cut across multiple boundaries. Constructing a resilient third force in these circumstances was an exceedingly arduous task.

That said, a careful rendering of the third force since 1989 highlights several points that warrant attention. First, its trajectory from the early to the late 1990s suggested a distinct political vision beyond the 'all-pervasive instrumentalism' and 'unending competition for power, status and profit' that allegedly drives Indian politics (Brass 1990: 20). It was neither fully articulated nor consistently realized. Nor did it eliminate the politics of 'ethnic headcounts' (see Chandra 2004) practised by some of its leading parties, which increasingly directed benefits towards particular constituencies and undermined broader political solidarities (see Mehta 2004). Nevertheless, the NF and UF enjoyed some, albeit insufficient, autonomy at the Centre. Indeed, their seemingly myopic character can be attributed partly to the frequency of elections, to their minority parliamentary status and to the rapidly shifting ground of this period, which compressed their time horizons and made it harder to exercise good political judgement.

Second, the two main axes of the third force embraced an understanding of politics that limited their possibilities. Both the JD and Left tended to view power in fixed, indivisible and zero-sum terms. It manifested in different ways. On the one hand, the refusal of the Left to join national coalition governments betrayed a static, moralistic and total conception of power that undermined genuine power sharing amongst the parties. On the other, the unwillingness of many socialists to share power amongst their own reflected a conception of power that prized insubordination, protest and defiance. Following Gramsci, one might say that whereas the Left has been imprisoned in a 'war of position' vis-à-vis the BJP and Congress, too many 'wars of manoeuvre' led to the implosion of the JD. The trajectory of the third force over these years demonstrates the importance of old political virtues: of organization, discipline and self-restraint for the JD, and daring, imagination and the willingness to shoulder the responsibilities of formal political rule for the Left.

Finally, their mutual inability to develop a politics that fused the desire for recognition with the need for redistribution limited their potential. The meagre capacity of the Left to mobilize the lower castes outside its bastions, and unwillingness of the JD and its various splinters to address material deprivation, are well known. The diminishing electoral returns of their respective politics, signalled by the Congress' political revival, underlines these deficits. Whether the Janata parivar or Left Front can develop the political vision, repertoire and skill to transcend their limitations remains a fundamental challenge.

Notes

1 In addition to my co-editors, I would like to thank Partha Chatterjee, Tanni Mukhopadhyay, Philip Oldenburg, Raka Ray, Achin Vanaik and Yogendra Yadav for their criticisms, questions and comments. Any errors that remain are mine.
2 I owe this formulation to Christophe Jaffrelot.
3 Arora uses the concept of 'federal nationalism' to describe the cultural foundations of the Indian democratic regime (2004: 505), in contrast to the outlook, arguments and practices of the third force, as I do in this essay.
4 However, Desai contends the Lok Dal's thwarted desire to use the RSS for itself caused the animosity (2004b: 56).
5 These political leaders were not disempowered individuals – far from it. But their strategies, tactics and manoeuvres of power share a family resemblance with techniques of resistance necessarily practised by micro-level subaltern politics.
6 The government won a majority in July 1993 by bribing the Jharkhand Mukti Morcha (JMM).
7 The CPI had supported Mrs Gandhi and her Emergency in the 1970s before aligning with the Janata.
8 For a remarkably prescient analysis of Deve Gowda, see Manor (1996b).
9 For further analysis, see Ruparelia (2006).
10 More controversially, the UPA also introduced a 27 percent quota for OBCs in central universities.
11 The grouping encompassed the JD(U), Lok Janashakti, CPI, CPM and NCP.
12 The UNPA encompassed the AIADMK, TDP, SP, Indian National Lok Dal (INLD), Marumalarchi Dravida Munnetra Kazagham (MDMK), Kerala Congress (T) and Jharkhand Vikas Morcha.

13 The Congress Party and the 'Great Transformation'

James Manor

Since 1990, the Congress Party has faced challenges posed by three important changes in Indian politics. These are:

- an increased focus on the interests of the 'backward castes' – triggered by the 1990 pledge by V. P. Singh's Janata government to implement the recommendations of the Mandal Commission
- the aggressive pursuit of Hindu nationalism – following a 1990 decision by the Bharatiya Janata Party (BJP) in reaction to Singh's announcement
- the growing importance of regional parties (which had already gathered momentum before 1990).

These changes have evoked mass responses, to varying degrees across India's regions and over time. More recently, we have also seen the emergence of the Bahujan Samaj Party, which draws much of its support from *Dalits* (ex-untouchables). These four trends add up to an overall popular political mobilization – although all four also cut across one another. This chapter assesses the condition of the Congress Party, the impact of these changes upon it, and its responses.

From Indian independence in 1947 until the late 1960s, Congress was the dominant party at the national level and in nearly all states within India's federal system. Opposition parties were disunited and relegated to the margins by Congress, which occupied the centre ground, and much of the Left and Right as well. Congress then practiced intra-party democracy. It had a formidable organization consisting of quite effective state-level political 'machines' that distributed patronage (goods, services and funds) in exchange for electoral support, mainly from prosperous landed groups. Most important debates occurred not between Congress and the opposition, but within Congress. Most key decisions occurred within it.

When other parties mounted serious challenges to Congress in the late 1960s, its leader Indira Gandhi split the party, abandoned democracy within it, and won a huge election victory in 1971 on a promise to reduce poverty – appearing to restore Congress dominance. But her promise went largely unfulfilled, and she set about undermining both the party's organization and formal state institutions, in pursuit of personal rule. This led eventually to the Emergency (1975–7) – after which voters rejected her in 1977.

By 1983, despite an electoral comeback by Mrs Gandhi at the national level three years earlier, every major state had had at least one spell of non-Congress government. Competitive politics had replaced Congress dominance. Indira Gandhi's son Rajiv won a landslide victory in late 1984 amid an emotional upheaval following her assassination, but he governed ineptly, reversing himself on many major policy initiatives. In 1989, he lost a national election – and in the seven general elections beginning in that year, no single party obtained a parliamentary majority. As a result, power has flowed away from the once dominant Prime Minister's Office – to other formal institutions, to a diversity of parties, and to the state level. Congress still contends for power in most states, but it has been reduced to a minor role in several large ones.

This chapter opens with a discussion of the liberalization of the economy by a Congress government after 1991. It went further than the immediate financial crisis required, partly to address the threats implied by the first three changes listed above. Those threats (and their limitations) are then examined in turn. The problems that afflict the Congress organization are then analysed, as is the damage done by – and the party's systemic need for – dynastic dominance. The chapter concludes with a discussion of Congress today, as it heads the ruling coalition of parties in New Delhi – focusing on its troubled organization, its imaginative new strategy, and its ambiguous prospects.

1. Narasimha Rao, economic liberalization and congress

When the Congress Party formed a minority government under P. V. Narasimha Rao in 1991, it faced a financial crisis that might have led to India's first default on its international debts. He and Finance Minister Manmohan Singh responded by beginning to liberalize the economy. Their reforms were cautious and limited by international standards, but by Indian standards quite startling. Their cumulative impact eventually produced a substantial revision of relations between the state and market forces.

A. Narasimha Rao's aims in liberalizing

The political dilemmas faced by Congress played a significant role in persuading Narasimha Rao to go well beyond a minimal response to the financial crisis.[1] Two beliefs about the party loomed large as he devised his new economic strategy. First, he recognized that the Congress organization was plagued by serious factional conflict at all levels and in all regions, and shot through with incapable or destructive people. It was 'like a railway platform ... anyone can come and go as he likes, and can push others aside to place himself in a better position'. He planned to attempt organizational reform, but he knew that this would be difficult and that he might fail. Second, he saw aggressive Hindu nationalism, the 'backward castes' issue, and regional parties as serious threats.

His economic policy was intended to tackle these problems. He liberalized in order to induce economic growth that would yield increased revenue, so that governments would have greater financial resources with which to meet important needs that the private sector would not address. If more adequately resourced official agencies could become more effective, this would reduce the role that his party would need to play. The ghastly condition of Congress influenced his decision to liberalize.

His economic policy was also intended to re-focus political debates and popular preoccupations on economic issues – on growth, but more crucially on development. This posed risks. Higher growth rates and thus greater state revenues might not materialize quickly enough to earn his party electoral benefits, but he saw no promising alternative.

He knew that the issues of growth and development were more mundane and less emotive than caste, religious or regional issues. But he welcomed this because another of his basic aims was to de-dramatize politics, which in his view had become too inflamed for the good of the country and of his party. The more heated politics became, the less able a centrist party like Congress would be to compete with parties to its Left (stressing preferment for disadvantaged castes) and its right (stressing Hindu nationalism). He knew that he was uninspiring on public platforms, but he intentionally cultivated a low-key approach in order to damp down both popular excitement and expectations of the government and the ruling party. He sought to turn his inability to excite into a virtue.

B. *Avoiding confrontation*

To cool politics down, Narasimha Rao sought systematically to avoid confrontation and conflict with other parties and important interests. This was apparent in his approach to every important issue, including liberalization.

After an initial flurry of liberalizing measures to reassure external actors, he carefully proceeded at a deliberate pace, allowing breathing space after each change, to permit tempers to cool before the next step was taken. He picked off diverse interests who were losers in this process, one at a time. After introducing a change that caused pain to one group, he would leave them alone for a while before going further. He then took another modest step that affected another interest group, and then another. And so it went on, incrementally and cautiously – to prevent diverse interests from uniting in opposition to liberalization – but relentlessly.

This frustrated neoliberals. They complained about the excruciatingly slow pace of the process. They wanted dramatic action to achieve macro-systemic change. Narasimha Rao refused to comply – because he sought to avoid confrontation, but also because he was no neoliberal.

As he stated flatly, 'my model is not Margaret Thatcher, but Willy Brandt ... I do not believe in trickle-down economics'.[2] He sought not to give market forces an unfettered role, but to enable them to operate within limits set by the state – so that they would generate wealth that would yield greater government revenues. State agencies would be cautiously withdrawn from areas in which they were unable to perform to society's advantage. But the enhanced revenues which he anticipated would prove *enabling* to the state – as they had done in countries led by social democrats like Brandt. Government would become more capable of playing a redistributive role, and of doing more in areas where the private sector was disinclined to operate – in many development sectors and in poverty reduction. These ideas were anathema to Thatcher. Narasimha Rao was a social democrat – a liberalizer who stood on the centre-left.

There were also things that he did not do. He avoided cuts in the huge government subsidies on many goods. He knew that many subsidies that were said to help the poor disproportionately benefited prosperous groups (something that the Left parties refuse to acknowledge). If they had been cut, funds could have been liberated for genuine poverty programmes. But he took no action – to avoid politically unwise confrontations with prosperous interests. Second, he took little action to promote the closure of loss-making public enterprises, and none to make it easier to dismiss workers – because 'I do not have the right to deprive people of their jobs'. He stated this, unusually, with palpable heat – he firmly believed it. This was the first time in a generation that a national leader of Congress had spoken of moral constraints on his right to take action.[3] Times had changed.

Two quite different ideas inspired inaction on these two fronts. In the first, he held back because it was politically risky, and in the second out of conviction. His management of liberalization was guided by a mixture of Machiavellian calculations and moral judgements.[4]

Neither Narasimha Rao nor Manmohan Singh was/is a neoliberal – contrary to the views of many today. The only genuine neoliberal to hold high office in India since 1991 is P. Chidambaram. But he has been held tightly in check by prime ministers throughout this period – except for a few weeks in early 1997 when he was allowed to introduce numerous market-friendly measures. In that short spell, he arguably liberalized more than BJP-led governments did in six years between 1998 and 2004. But note that he was set loose by a non-Congress prime minister, H. D. Deve Gowda. (That episode, like Narasimha Rao's liberalizing, demonstrates that politicians who make economic policy often operate with greater autonomy from social forces than some analysts believe.)

Narasimha Rao's strong determination to avoid confrontation in this and other spheres, in order to de-dramatize politics, was intended to serve the party's interests. He sought to sustain the capacity of the Congress to cultivate support from a broad array of interests – something that was threatened by strident Hindu nationalism, regional parties and the 'backward castes' issue. But he also sought to revive the social democratic strand of the Congress tradition. The party might cultivate support from prosperous, high-status groups, but it also needed to respond to disadvantaged groups. In his view, it had to do so for both Machiavellian and moralistic reasons – because non-elite groups had more votes, and because this was the just approach.

He largely declined to explain his liberalizing actions, lest that touch off avoidable controversy. He refused to explain himself even to his own party. During visits to Maharashtra and Karnataka in early 1992, this writer found that no state-level cabinet minister in the Congress in either state understood the prime minister's economic liberalization project – except one junior minister in Karnataka who had studied economics at Cambridge. Next to no one outside major corporations and banks, and academic circles in both states, understood the aims or implications of the changes.[5]

So did the Congress Party somehow cause economic liberalization to occur after 1991? The answer is complicated. The party, as a collective entity, did not decide to liberalize. That was done by Narasimha Rao, with crucial advice from Manmohan Singh. But in another sense, Congress can be said to have 'contributed' to the decision. The dire condition of its organization – which undermined its capacity to respond effectively to emergent threats – helped persuade Narasimha Rao to liberalize, in order to shift popular attention to other issues that might prove more advantageous to Congress.

The bewilderment within the Congress Party about liberalization suited Narasimha Rao. He reckoned – shrewdly – that he would get further with it if public debate was limited and confused. He was pursuing what Rob Jenkins later called 'reform by stealth' (1999). He believed that the minimization of confrontation best served the interests not just of liberalization, but also of his government and party.

Let us consider the threats to Congress posed by appeals to the 'backward castes', aggressive Hindu nationalism, and regional parties. On close examination, the first two (but not the third) turn out to be less dangerous to Congress than we might expect.

2. Congress and the 'backward castes' issue

The dangers posed by the 'backward castes' issue have been somewhat exaggerated, for five reasons.

First, the issue lacks evocative power in many states because those groups' interests were addressed before 1990, and/or because other issues have predominated. One or both of these things is/are true in the following states: Andhra Pradesh, Tamil Nadu, Pondicherry, Kerala, Karnataka, Goa, Maharasthra, Gujarat, Madhya Pradesh, Chhattisgarh, Rajasthan, Orissa, West Bengal, Jammu and Kashmir – plus much of Uttaranchal and most of the northeast. Those states contain over 60 per cent of India's population. So in all-India terms, the potency of this issue has been overstated.

Second, before 1990, while in some states opposition parties mobilized the 'backward castes', in others it was Congress itself that did so.[6] So the issue is not an unmitigated threat to Congress, although it has had greater difficulty attracting 'backward caste' support since the issue became salient in 1990.

Third, no long-standing Congress principle restrains it from embracing the 'backward castes'. That issue differs from Hindu chauvinism. To flirt with the latter is to defy party traditions.

Fourth, the issue of reservations for 'backward castes' has, at times, proved to be too narrow and thus politically counter-productive. In 1990, it dramatically signalled the progressive intentions of V. P. Singh's government. But especially when disputes arose among different 'backward' groups over benefits, the issue became a distraction from the more fundamental need for redistribution and poverty reduction. When Congress has taken significant steps to address those broader issues – as it has done since assuming power in New Delhi in 2004 – the evocative power of reservations has diminished.

Finally, the use of the 'backward castes' category has not consistently yielded electoral benefits to parties that champion those groups' interests. The 'backward castes' have often failed to remain a solid vote bank – they have fallen out with one another and with other disadvantaged groups whose votes are also needed to win elections – *Dalits*, *Adivasis* and (to a degree) Muslims.

So the political utility of the 'backward castes' issue is more limited than many believe. So is the threat that it poses to Congress. As we see in section 4 below, regional parties have forced Congress to govern at the national level in a far less domineering manner than before 1990. Among them are parties stressing the 'backward caste' issue – but in only three of India's 28 states.[7]

3. Congress and assertive Hindu nationalism

The threat to Congress from assertive Hindu nationalism is somewhat greater – but only somewhat. Two topics arise here: accusations that Congress leaders have unwisely resorted to 'soft Hindutva', and the problems that beset the Hindu right.

At times, Congress leaders have responded to Hindu nationalism either by giving ground to it[8] or with actions (or inactions) that underplay their opposition to it. In recent times, Congress timidity in opposing Hindu chauvinism was evident in the 2007 Gujarat state election, when its leaders offered few challenges to the anti-Muslim extremism of the BJP government there, and in the decision of the Maharashtra government, which Congress leads, to ignore the findings of the Krishna report into violence against Muslims.

So there is substance in the accusations that Congress has been 'soft' on Hindutva, but they have also been exaggerated. Consider two examples. Some argue that Prime Minister Narasimha Rao played too passive a role in the run-up to the destruction of the Babri Masjid at Ayodhya in 1992 because he secretly sympathized with the vandals who were responsible – in a state ruled by the BJP. In this writer's discussions with Narasimha Rao, before and after Ayodhya, his deep distaste for Hindu chauvinism was vividly apparent. There is a better explanation for his passivity in 1992.

He sought to avoid confrontation not just on economic liberalization, but also in dealing with Hindu nationalists. On three occasions in early 1992, this writer asked him, 'is it not possible that a time will come when actions by Hindu militants will compel you to draw the line and confront them?' Narasimha Rao consistently refused to accept this. 'Confrontation', he said, 'leaves too much bitterness behind'. He was intensely preoccupied with this idea.

His dismay over the confrontational habits of his Congress predecessors was unstated but obvious. Both his temperament and his position atop a minority government inspired an inordinate commitment to accommodation.[9] His tentative approach to the Ayodhya issue was explained by naivety – not covert sympathy with Hindu extremism.

The second exaggeration is the allegation that Digvijay Singh empathized with Hindutva when he was Congress Chief Minister of Madhya Pradesh. But instead of appeasing Hindu nationalists, he was seeking to out-manoeuvre them. He wrote to BJP Prime Minister Vajpayee complaining that the central government was doing too little to address cow protection. This was a ploy. He wanted to be able to refer to this protest on public platforms (as he subsequently did) to prevent the BJP from using Hindu nationalist themes against him. He wanted to force them to attack him on development issues – his ground – and he succeeded.[10]

His firm opposition to Hindu chauvinism became obvious from his response to an attempt by a Hindu bigot who entered Madhya Pradesh to foment anti-Muslim sentiment. Singh promptly had the man jailed in a district town. The extremist professed delight at this, since he expected large crowds to gather to demand his release. None did so. After a few days of waiting, the would-be agitator meekly yielded and left the state. Digvijay Singh's hard line in this instance was not the action of a timid appeaser of extremism.

At times, Congress leaders have actually pursued 'soft' Hindutva, but we must also recognize that some accusations levelled against them are inaccurate. Let us now turn to the problems that beset the Hindu Right, which undermine the threat that it poses to Congress. Two loom large.

First, to capture and retain power in New Delhi after 1998, it had to shelve virtually its entire Hindu nationalist agenda – because all but one of the 23 parties in its coalition opposed it. This exasperated Hindu extremists. One claimed that it was imposing a Muslim theocratic state! The BJP has nudged the political centre slightly towards the religious Right. But thus far, Hindu chauvinism has had little appeal in national – or, except in Gujarat, at state – elections. Indeed, it is disadvantageous. The BJP de-emphasized Hindu extremism during state election campaigns in Madhya Pradesh (2003 and 2008), Uttar Pradesh (2007) and Karnataka (2008) and at the 2009 parliamentary election – to avoid damage.

Second, the BJP has a dismal record at getting re-elected. At the national level, it succeeded once (in 1999) thanks to Pakistani infiltration in Kargil. But in 2004, it lost despite the popular appeal of its prime minister and surging economic growth. At the state level, it has fared worse. Only four BJP Chief Ministers have ever been re-elected: Bhairon Singh Shekhawat in Rajasthan, on solid achievements that no other BJP state leader has matched; Narendra Modi in Gujarat, thanks to crass communal polarization, which doesn't work anywhere else; in 2008, Raman Singh in Chhattisgarh; and Shivraj Singh Chauhan in Madhya Pradesh. But the latter two benefited from a marked surge in government revenues after 2003, which enabled them to spend far more lavishly than their predecessors.

So, except in Gujarat, Congress has not been seriously menaced by aggressive Hindu nationalism. Elsewhere, the BJP has defeated Congress only when it has adopted moderate postures. Hindu extremism is no unstoppable force.

4. Congress and regional parties

Congress has suffered more at the hands of regional parties that have gained ground in many states over the last 20 years than from the 'backward caste' issue or Hindu nationalism. The term 'regional parties' here includes both explicitly and *de facto* regional parties. Until those latter parties – which claim to be national in character – can attract strong support across many states, it is appropriate to treat them as 'regional'.

If we consider regional parties of significance, some – but only six of sixteen – have stressed 'backward caste' issues, and only one (the Shiv Sena in Maharashtra) has pursued Hindu chauvinism. Most have pursued neither.[11] The parties marked with asterisks below have at times developed cooperative relations with Congress.

Most of the parties listed above have weakened Congress as an all-India party. Congress has struggled to regain ground from most. They therefore represent a greater threat to it than the 'backward caste' issue or aggressive Hindu nationalism.

When Congress is confronted by a strong regional party in an individual state, it often begins to resemble its main adversary. There are a few exceptions to this generalization. The most vivid is in West Bengal, where, when it was confronted by the supremely well-organized Communist Party of India-Marxist (CPI-M), it degenerated into an embarrassing rabble.[12] But when it faced the same party in Kerala, Congress developed a solid organization like the CPI-M's, which has kept it competitive in a bi-polar system.

In Andhra Pradesh – where its main opponent has, since 1983, been the Telugu Desam Party, which has always been dominated by a single figure – the Congress Chief Minister since 2004 has assumed similar overweening authority over his party. And so it goes on. This tendency means that 'Congress' assumes very different forms in different states. This has been true since the 1980s (Manor 1982), but it should perhaps trouble national Congress leaders.

Finally, it is worth noting that when Congress loses substantial ground at the state level to regional parties, it eventually becomes weak enough to make it a non-threatening coalition partner for some regional parties. This tends to occur when it becomes the third or fourth strongest party in a fragmented party system – or when (as in Maharashta) a four-party system develops.[13]

Table 13.1 'Backward caste' interests

Stressing 'backward caste' interests	Not stressing them
*Rashtriya Janata Dal (Bihar)	*Nat'list Congress Party (Maharashtra)
*Dravida Munnetra Kazhagam (T.Nadu)	Shiv Sena (Maharashtra)
*AIADMK (Tamil Nadu)	Biju Janata Dal (Orissa)
*Samajwadi Party (Uttar Pradesh)	Telugu Desam Party (Andhra Pradesh)
*Janata Dal-S (Bihar but not Karnataka)	*CPI-M (Kerala)
Janata Dal-U (Bihar but not Karnataka)	*CPI-M (Tripura)
	*CPI-M (West Bengal)
	*Trinamul Congress (West Bengal)
	*Asom Gana Parishad (Assam)
	*Lok Janshakti Party (Bihar)
	Bahujan Samaj Party (Uttar Pradesh)
	*Akali Dal (Punjab)
	Indian National Lok Dal (Haryana)
	*National Conference (J. and Kashmir)
	*J&K People's Democratic Party (J. and Kashmir)

5. Efforts to regenerate the congress organization

By 1990, the Congress organization – which once had both sinew and reach – had degenerated severely. This was mainly the result of Indira Gandhi's abandonment of intra-party democracy, her systematic undermining of the party organization in the interests of personal rule – and then of Rajiv Gandhi's inconsistent management of party affairs. The weakness of the Congress organization invited and facilitated challenges on the 'backward caste' issue, from the Hindu right, and from regional parties.

Once those challenges merged, perceptive Congress leaders – and there have always been some in key posts – saw that the organization required regeneration. Narasimha Rao had known the Congress in better days – before 1970 – when it had been a democratic institution and a formidable political machine capable of cultivating broad popular support. He saw the degeneration as alarming.

He therefore set out to rebuild it. He knew that this would be difficult and would require several years. He knew that serious factional infighting had reached epidemic proportions long before 1990. He specifically recalled one grotesque example in 1985 when Congress members gathered in Mumbai to celebrate the party's centenary. Separate trains from West Bengal arrived simultaneously – each carrying members of a different faction within that state's Congress. As they marched across Mumbai, they spotted one another on opposite sides of a park. The importance of the centenary was forgotten and they threw themselves into a violent, embarrassing melee.[14]

Narasimha Rao saw the root cause of degeneration as the abandonment of intra-party democracy. He sought to re-introduce elections, every two years, to fill all party posts. He knew that the early elections would be untidy, but he believed that eventually, incapable figures would be marginalized and regeneration would occur. He saw this as 'the only realistic way to revive the organization.'[15]

Rajiv Gandhi had announced plans to hold elections on 14 occasions,[16] but none occurred in his time. Narasimha Rao was more determined and in 1993, an election was held. It was a disaster. Factional conflict soared. Massive sums were committed to vote buying, and voters' lists grew bloated with phoney names. Violence between Congress factions was widespread. In some cases, congressmen murdered congressmen, and there was even an instance of congressman *biting* congressman. He eventually concluded that no further elections should take place. This was a deeply difficult moment for him, and it left him rudderless as party leader. He soon reverted to sly machinations, which did him and the party no good.[17]

Readers of euphoric reports in the Indian and international media after the re-election of a Congress-led alliance in the 2009 national election might conclude that this problem has been solved. Commentators claimed that Rahul Gandhi, the son of Rajiv and Sonia, had rejuvenated Congress and Parliament, attracted the youth vote and rebuilt the party organization. All three claims are false. The new parliament was the fifth oldest of the 15 since 1952, younger people voted less often for Congress and its allies than did their elders in 2009,[18] and Congress strategists – including Rahul Gandhi himself – agreed that organizational reconstruction had not yet occurred.[19]

Not *yet*. Rahul Gandhi is determined that it should happen. But the immensity of the challenge becomes clear when we consider what he has achieved so far, and what (in mid-2009) he planned to do next. He has held genuine elections within the Youth Congress. But these only occurred in two small states, Punjab and Uttarakhand, which contain 3.2 per cent of India's population. He attempted an election in Gujarat but was thwarted. He planned to extend this process to all states by 2014. But that means that democracy will have been restored only to a minor front organization – and only after a further five years.

In theory, the Congress Party already holds periodic elections for all offices, but party organizers consistently concede that these are fictitious. Close advisors and observers of Sonia Gandhi indicate that she knows this – since she has expressed scepticism about whether genuine elections, which she favours, are feasible.[20] Redemocratizing Congress will be exceedingly difficult.

Rahul Gandhi also recognizes that the party's habit of choosing election candidates at the last minute has given opponents, who select theirs well in advance, a valuable head start. He has therefore insisted that candidates be named as much as a year in advance – a process which began after the 2009 national election.

He favours a shrewd change in the structure of the Congress. Units of the party at lower levels have always conformed to administrative units (districts and sub-districts) and not to electoral arenas (parliamentary constituencies, state assembly constituencies). This made sense when Congress was dominant, since it enabled the party to exert pressure on bureaucrats at lower levels. But this has prevented it from concentrating its energies on winning electoral contests. The proposed change will facilitate that.

Rahul has also lent support to a strategy that can earn Congress popularity and strengthen its organization in places where rival parties govern – mounting protests against parties in power. Until recently, this approach had rarely been adopted. But it has considerable promise. Consider two examples.

In Andhra Pradesh in the late 1980s, the Telugu Desam Party (TDP) held power. The leader of the state Congress, Chenna Reddy, selected issues on which the TDP had become unpopular and cajoled Congress members from rival factions to launch protests against these injustices. Since the TDP was quick to resort to police action, many Congress protestors were swiftly jailed. This gained Congress public sympathy. It weeded out unreliables from the party organization since they declined to risk incarceration. And when members of warring factions were incarcerated together, many of their suspicions of one another dissolved. Chenna Reddy was adopting a device that produced similar results before independence – *satyagraha*.[21] Congress won the ensuing state election.

More recently, Digvijay Singh, who oversaw the Congress organization in Bihar, asked party activists to divide the state into small segments, to conduct social audits in each to identify popular resentments, and then to mount protests on those issues. He personally led agitations in certain localities to shame others into action. By mounting protests, Congress appeared to be good for something (a departure from before), and party members were drawn together in constructive action (another astonishing change for them).[22]

The use of protests while in opposition can help revive the organization, image and prospects of Congress. Rahul Gandhi proposes to adopt this approach more widely. Indeed, he began during the 2009 national election campaign by joining a *dharna*[23] in Jhansi – a seat which Congress then won. He has more recently backed a search within various states for what one colleague describes as 'street fighters'. This term does not imply that violence will be used, but rather that the party will now support leaders who are prepared to mount challenges to governments headed by rival parties.[24] If this approach is widely adopted, it will begin to regenerate the Congress organization.

That strategy holds far greater promise than a second option, the deployment of the alleged 'charisma' of members of the Gandhi family. Some media reports claimed that Rahul and Sonia Gandhi had excited mass enthusiasm at the 2009 national election, but interviews with reliable observers on the ground in areas where they addressed rallies contradict this.[25] The limited potential of this option was vividly apparent during the Uttar Pradesh state election of 2007, when Rahul Gandhi played the pivotal role in the Congress campaign. The party was embarrassed when its vote share declined from the previous election, from 8.9 per cent to 8.6 per cent. Rahul's own popularity increased during the campaign, but only from 5 per cent to 7 per cent. He was less popular than his party.[26]

One last approach offers greater promise, and has been adopted by Sonia Gandhi in recent years. It entails efforts to negotiate and to enforce from above the uneasy unity among squabbling Congress factions at the state level. Serious factionalism at that level is an enduring legacy of the Indira Gandhi years, when infighting was systematically fomented to undermine regional leaders.

Sonia Gandhi has supported efforts to forge unity within the party, of the kind that occurred before state elections in Madhya Pradesh (1993), Karnataka (1999) and Andhra Pradesh (2004). Two processes must run simultaneously. Serious efforts at sinking factional differences must occur, and faction leaders must be seen to be doing this – as they were, for example, during the 1999 Karnataka election campaign when all major Congress figures boarded the same bus and toured the state – demonstrating unity and propelling the party to victory. When Congress governments are formed in various states, Sonia Gandhi lends solid support to her Chief Ministers. She tells delegations of dissidents to back their Chief Ministers until she acts – which she has never done. This helps to quell squabbling, even though in nearly all states, factional tensions remain. The management of the Congress has changed for the better, but the composition of the Congress has not, and still gives cause for deep concern.

If Rahul Gandhi succeeds in making protests a widespread practice, the composition of the party will begin to change. Unreliables will find the rigours of street demonstrations and possibly jail too much to bear – and they will be marginalized. But at the time of writing, this is only an idea, and it will be difficult to implement.

6. The role of – and the systemic need for – dynastic rule within congress

Members of the Nehru-Gandhi family have loomed large atop the Congress since independence. Narasimha Rao's attempt to reintroduce intra-party elections in 1993 was intended to give party structures more substance as institutions at a time when it appeared that the personal ascendancy of family members might not be restored. But then Sonia Gandhi emerged, the pre-eminence of the family was re-established, and Rahul Gandhi's more recent rise to prominence brings a fourth generation into play.

The family is commonly described as a 'dynasty'. That term is accurate in physiological terms, but it is misleading in terms of politics, party management and policy. There were radical differences between Nehru's approach on all three fronts and that of Indira and Rajiv Gandhi. But astonishingly, it has lately become apparent that the approach of Sonia and Rahul Gandhi differ markedly from that of Indira and Rajiv. They have substantially reverted to something close to Nehruvian ways. Congress activists and leaders find it impossible, even dangerous to acknowledge this, but it is true.

Nehru sought to strengthen democratic institutions within India's new political system after independence, and to sustain democracy within Congress, which had prevailed since 1919 when Mahatma Gandhi introduced it. As a result, he yielded to regional elites within the party on key issues, despite his disagreement. He was also a social democrat who believed that the government should strive to promote social justice. Indira Gandhi differed from her father on both issues. She abandoned intra-party democracy and filled all important posts from above. She also undermined democratic institutions more generally, in the pursuit of personal rule. And while she won her first major election victory in 1971 by promising to 'abolish poverty', she did little to translate the slogan into reality.

Sonia Gandhi emerged as a leader at a time when the inability of any single party to win a parliamentary majority had triggered a massive dispersal of power away from the once-dominant prime minister's office – horizontally to other institutions at the national level, and downward to the state level. She has done little to recentralize power. Even in states that Congress governs, she has left chief ministers largely undisturbed – like Nehru, but unlike Indira Gandhi. And lately, she and especially Rahul have shown an interest in rebuilding and redemocratizing the Congress organization. Finally, since 2004, she has presided over the creation or expansion of an array of programmes that seek to benefit poor people,[27] spending on which exceeded US$57 billion under the Congress-led alliance after 2004. On all of these fronts, Sonia and Rahul Gandhi have operated in the manner of Nehru, and in striking contrast to Indira Gandhi.

On another key issue, however, Sonia Gandhi's view is identical to Indira Gandhi's. The predominance of the 'dynasty' must be sustained. Nehru would have viewed this with the same contempt that he exhibited towards the princely order. For him, the hereditary principle was patently unsuited to a democratic republic.

All systems of dynastic rule are liable to change, since much depends on the capabilities and predilections of successive rulers. This is apparent from the marked differences between the approaches of Nehru and Indira Gandhi, and now in the substantial revival of Nehruvian strategies by Sonia and Rahul Gandhi. Devotees of the 'dynasty' should consider what might have happened had Indira Gandhi been succeeded by her son Sanjay, whose hare-brained schemes during the Emergency earned Congress a humiliating defeat at the 1977 election, and whose unbridled behaviour posed a grave threat to democratic institutions.

The dominance of the 'dynasty' persists because there is a systemic need within Congress for it. Factional conflict was thoroughly institutionalized within the party under Indira and Rajiv Gandhi. The latter sometimes complained about it,[28] but many of his actions encouraged it. Narasimha Rao's abortive attempt to use intra-party elections to overcome it showed how deep the rot had gone. Because factionalism is rife, the party desperately needs an unquestioned, autocratic arbiter atop the organization whose rulings will be meekly accepted by contending forces.

But while Congress needs the 'dynasty', it is also imperilled by it. If hereditary rule is essential to maintaining order with the party, it has proved damaging and it poses serious risks. Consider the damage. Dynamic regional leaders whose ambitions have been blighted by dynastic dominance have left Congress in dismay. Sharad Pawar in Maharashtra and Mamata Banerjee in West Bengal are key examples. Their importance is apparent from Congress' dependence upon them as allies, for its survival in power in New Delhi since 2004 and for its future prospects. The requirement that Rahul Gandhi succeed his mother has also proved damaging. Congress Chief Ministers may have suffered little interference from Sonia Gandhi, but their achievements are seriously under-played, lest they appear to rival Rahul.

And there are future risks. What if a hereditary ruler turns out to be incompetent, destructive or unpopular? What if Sonia and Rahul Gandhi, like Rajiv Gandhi before them, suddenly become unhappy with their strategies, reverse themselves in mid-course, and alienate important interests?

The pathologies that afflict Congress – especially factionalism, partly concealed by the order imposed from on high, but a seething reality everywhere – and the dubious remedy of dynastic rule, may not prove terminal. The party may muddle along for many years yet. But its fortunes depend dangerously – for compelling systemic reasons – upon a single bloodline.

7. Congress today

How might Congress muddle along for some time yet? Rahul Gandhi's proposed changes in the party offer some hope of organizational revival, but the decay runs so deep that he may make only limited headway – and in any case, it will take a long time. Congress will struggle to emerge from obscurity in several hugely important states. In several states where it remains strong, its main rivals are regional parties that it therefore cannot include in alliances needed to win national elections. It may be unable to prevent rival parties at the state level from poaching the credit for constructive programmes it initiates from New Delhi.[29] It relies on the hereditary principle, which is inherently unreliable over the long term.

How can a party that faces such difficulties hope to remain a major force? The answer lies in the difficulties and incapacities of its adversaries, and certain other things. Congress benefits from the tendencies of the 'backward castes' to come into conflict with other disadvantaged groups and to fragment – so that they cannot become a sustainable anti-Congress force.

Its principal adversary, the BJP, faces immense problems. Its Hindu nationalist agenda has generated popular enthusiasm either for very limited periods (as in the six months after the destruction of the Babri Masjid)[30] or in limited areas, notably Gujarat. Its complicity in the anti-Muslim pogrom in that state produced a state election victory in 2002, but deep and lasting suspicion throughout India. Outbursts of bigotry and violence have (thus far) had little staying power as devices for inspiring mass support.

Its party organization lacks the capacity to penetrate below the district level (Manor 2004b). Its national election campaigns in 2004 and 2009 were both inept. The generation that must now lead the party lacks promising figures. One potential future leader, Narendra Modi, would make the BJP's already difficult task of attracting parties to its alliance nearly impossible.

The regional parties that oppose Congress at the state level also face daunting problems. Taken collectively, they pose a greater threat to Congress than does the BJP. But they can seldom be 'taken collectively' – they cannot develop collective coherence, as their disarray at the 2009 election demonstrated. A few leant towards the BJP, others towards an unconvincing 'third front', and still others towards a fourth front. And nearly all regional parties lack the organizational capacity to penetrate effectively to the local level.[31]

With adversaries like that, Congress does not need immense strength. We have here a contest among parties that all suffer serious disabilities. Two other things help Congress. First, if one party is perceived as the main villain in the political drama, others will combine against it – often with devastating results. Congress has been so restrained at the national level since 2004, and so helpful to its allies – one source close to the Prime Minister complained that 'it gives them whatever they want'[32] – that it has avoided this. And as long as Modi looms large, the BJP will appear the more nefarious national party.

Second, not just the 'backward castes' but other social blocs that have sometimes opposed Congress tend to disintegrate over time. That happens because Indian voters tend strongly to shift their preoccupations from one of the huge number of identities available to them to another, and then another – often and with great fluidity.[33] They do not fasten permanently and ferociously on one identity – as in Sri Lanka. This prevents tension and conflict from building up along a single fault line in society. That hurts parties that seek to fix voters' attention on one fault line. The main losers are the Left, which focuses on class divisions and the BJP, which focuses on the division between Hindus and others. This fluidity benefits parties whose lack of ideology enables them to shift their emphases as the popular mood swings – like Congress.

When Congress took power in New Delhi in 2004, its strategists were concerned about disenchantment among disadvantaged groups who had been largely left behind by liberalization and growth. Congress analysts recognized that their victory in the 2004 general election had not – as the media claimed – been the result of a revolt by the rural poor against liberalization and globalization. They saw that Congress had gained more votes in urban than in rural areas. And they saw that in (for example) Haryana and Punjab – two adjacent states with similar numbers of poor people in similar circumstances – the Congress and its allies won impressively in one and were crushed in the other. Such things could not have happened if the rural poor had actually revolted. It was a myth.

But Congress leaders chose not to challenge it. It was a useful misperception, since it made Congress and its allies appear to be more humane than their opponents. Their 2004 government sought to cultivate support from a diverse array of interests. It was able to provide substantial benefits to prosperous groups as a result of a spectacular rise in government revenues after 2003. But it also proceeded as if the myth were true, by committing even more massive resources to new initiatives for small farmers, the rural poor and near-poor, who have great numerical strength. The steep increase in revenues meant that Narasimha Rao's social democratic hope that growth would enhance state resources and capacity had been realized.[34]

The result is an impressive array of initiatives – some of which are making a potent impact. But it is important to stress that the party's (and since 2004, India's) leaders seek to make their main impact through government programmes rather than through the Congress organization. They recognize that, given its weakness, the organization cannot play a constructive role. One senior advisor to Congress recently said that the only thing most of that party's members know how to do is to shout 'Sonia Gandhi Zindabad'. A leading Congress strategist toured India in 2007 and found that the condition of the organization was 'terrible, terrible'. When a political scientist visited various party offices across Uttar Pradesh during the 2007 election campaign there, he found Bahujan Samaj Party activists brimming with ardour. He saw that at least half of the BJP activists were working flat out because 'in their guts' they were burning with spite towards the minorities. But in Congress offices, he found 'only listlessness – cronies and relatives of candidates, and political pimps'. When he told Congress leaders in New Delhi of this, they agreed that this was an accurate description.[35] It is thus logical that India's current leaders should rely not on the party but on government programmes.

Notes

1 This section, and much of what follows on Narasimha Rao's period in power (1991–6), is based on extensive discussions with him during early February 1992.
2 Interview, New Delhi, 11 February 1992.
3 Manmohan Singh then echoed and still echoes that sentiment.
4 It is worth adding that at no time during several long and complex discussions, did the Prime Minister offer a single remark that was inconsistent with a highly sophisticated view of what his approach to the economy (and everything else) should be. This writer has interviewed hundreds of politicians in South Asia, but he has never encountered an intellectual *tour de force* of the kind offered by Narasimha Rao.
5 The main exceptions were a handful of learned journalists whose writings on the subject were largely ignored, and certain figures in the Left parties, which were insignificant in both states.
6 This was true, for example, in Maharashtra and Karnataka. The latter story is told in great detail in Raghavan and Manor 2009.
7 See the list of regional parties in section 4. The three states are Bihar, Tamil Nadu and Uttar Pradesh.

8 See Niraja Jayal's comments on pp. 23–5 of Ayres and Oldenburg 2005.
9 These comments are based on interviews with Narasimha Rao in early February 1992.
10 At the December 2003 state election, that was the ground on which the BJP was forced to campaign. He lost not because he had a poor record on development, and not because of his alleged 'soft Hindutva', but for other reasons (Manor 2004a).
11 Very small states, including all northeastern states – except Assam because of its greater size – have been excluded.
12 Other exceptions include three states where Congress has been marginalized: Bihar, Tamil Nadu and Uttar Pradesh. Still another is Maharashtra, where Congress does not seek to plunder the exchequer and practice systematic extortion as the BJP/Shiv Sena government of the 1990s did. But the predominant pattern is for Congress to come to resemble its adversaries.
13 This argument was first made in Sridharan 2004b. Swaminathan Aiyar made this case in the *Times of India*, 13 July 2008.
14 Interview with P. V. Narasimha Rao, New Delhi, 11 February 1992.
15 His arguments were nearly identical to those made to this writer in the mid-1980s by Myron Weiner. (As far as I know, Weiner never put these ideas into print.) But Narasimha Rao said that he was unaware of Weiner's views in the matter. Interview, 11 February 1992.
16 This figure is based on the monitoring of such announcements by A. G. Noorani and this writer.
17 I am grateful to Sanjay Ruparelia for stressing this last point.
18 This is based on data from the post-poll survey of the Centre for the Study of Developing Societies. I am grateful to K. C. Suri for assistance on this issue.
19 Interviews with Congress strategists from Uttar Pradesh, Madhya Pradesh, Andhra Pradesh and Karnataka in New Delhi, Hyderabad and Bangalore between 19 May and 3 June 2009. Rahul Gandhi was not interviewed, but it was apparent that he decided not to accept a ministerial post and to focus on regenerating the party because he knew that that task had not been completed.
20 These comments are based on interviews with four Congress strategists and two leading journalists, New Delhi, January and June 2009.
21 Interview with Chenna Reddy, Hyderabad, 2 April 1990.
22 Interview with Digvijay Singh, New Delhi, 11 July 2007.
23 A *dharna* is a protest, often involving fasting, which demands action to correct a perceived injustice.
24 This section is based on interviews with Congress strategists in New Delhi in November 2008, and in January and June 2009.
25 This is based on interviews with over 30 perceptive political activists, civil society leaders and analytical journalists from Maharashtra, Madhya Pradesh, Uttar Pradesh, Andhra Pradesh and Karnataka in May and June 2009.
26 Interview with Yogendra Yadav, Delhi, 20 July 2007.
27 They include the National Rural Employment Guarantee Scheme, Bharat Nirman, Sarva Shiksa Abhiyan, the Mid-day Meal Scheme, the National Rural Health Mission, the Total Sanitation Campaign, Integrated Child Development Services, the Jawaharlal Nehru National Urban Renewal Mission and Polio Eradication.
28 For example, he once lamented the infighting in his party by telling the story of '… a merchant who exported crabs packed in uncovered tins without any loss or damage, to the amazement of the importer. The Indian crabs, he explained, pulled one another down and prevented them from moving up!', *The Hindu*, 11 February 1990.
29 Surveys by the Centre for the Study of Developing Societies have found that in some states, Congress at the national level received most of the credit for the massive National Rural Employment Guarantee Scheme, while in others, parties opposed to Congress that headed state governments were given credit.

30 This writer argued – to widespread disbelief – that its effects would be highly temporary just before the destruction occurred, in *The Independent*, 8 December 1992.
31 The great exception to this is the Communist Party of India (Marxist), but it is strong only in three states. The DMK in Tamil Nadu retains some penetrative capacity. The TDP in Andhra Pradesh sought with limited success to acquire this capacity between 1995 and 2004, but its organization has since degenerated somewhat.
32 Interview, New Delhi, 11 July 2007.
33 For more detail, see Manor 1996a. Recent survey data collected by Lokniti in Delhi indicate no diminution in this tendency.
34 The comments above are based on extensive interviews with key strategists – on terms of anonymity – close to Manmohan Singh and Sonia Gandhi in New Delhi in July 2007, November 2008 and May and June 2009.
35 These comments are based on interviews in New Delhi in July 2007.

14 Indian foreign policy since the end of the Cold War
Domestic determinants

Achin Vanaik

Taking 1989 as the cut-off point for investigating the shift in Indian foreign policy would seem to be justified since the subsequent collapse of the Communist bloc and the USSR was a tectonic change of world historic significance. But this reinforces the deeply flawed realist approach of separating the domestic from the international. Contemporary preoccupations with globalization have brought in economics as an 'add on' element to a resolutely realist explanatory framework. Thus neither geoeconomics – the emergence of the neoliberal form of globalization since the late seventies – nor domestic factors are given the weight they deserve in explaining India's shift.

The conventional mainstream explanation goes like this: Nonalignment of whose movement (NAM) India was a leader guided foreign policy behaviour in the bipolar era. India had an economic tilt to the West and a strategic tilt to the USSR. But the collapse of the Second World rendered nugatory the significance of a Third World and its NAM, forcing India to reevaluate its past and to rejig its strategic perspectives. Nonalignment may or may not have served Indian interests, but now it should abandon all illusions in socialism (even in the form of a state-led capitalist developmentalism) and accept history's conclusive verdict by pursuing the contemporary (neoliberal) form of capitalist development, jettison its earlier 'anti-Americanism' since a maturing India always had much closer political, ideological and cultural affinities with the West and US than with Second or Third World countries.

At least this way of justifying an Indian foreign policy shift since 1989 does recognize some sort of historical connection between the domestic economic and the external political even as it remains oblivious of social intermediations in the construction of foreign policy and of the problematicity of the notion of national interest. The authority of this notion as a *routinized* principle of guidance of foreign policy is spurious, resting as it does on a theory of the socially neutral state. National interest is essentially a principle of legitimation not one of either explanation or guidance. Any course of action can be justified in its name.

The key mediation

If national interest does not explain a country's foreign policy then what does? It is the political-moral character of the leadership strata (state managers) that shapes and makes foreign policy decisions consisting of two elements: a 'permanent' bureaucratic elite substantially wedded to its own institutional interests of expanded reproduction and authority and a more transient but also more powerful entity – an elected (in democracies) political elite enjoying formal authority and exercising power over the former. Included also in the 'foreign policy establishment' are those who shape public opinion. The political-moral character of these important sections of society changes over time. Their beliefs and values are shaped by the changes in the power relations between classes and social groups nationally and internationally, as well as by what happens between countries.

Understanding the shift in Indian foreign policy requires understanding the much larger story of why there has been a considerable right-wing shift on all fronts – cultural, political, economic, ideological – over the last 25 to 30 years caused by a complex array of factors; domestic and international, objective and subjective, material and cultural. Unlike realism the approach must be multi-disciplinary but not theoretically eclectic.[1] Foreign policy behaviour is not simply motivated by the seemingly self-evident compulsions to accumulate power resources but is also strongly shaped by the ideas, values and interests held by state managers. Understanding the external means grasping the geoeconomics and geopolitics of uneven and combined global developments expressing themselves through national specificities. Understanding the internal means examining the wider canvas of India over the last 30 years to give a more historically and sociologically informed explanation of how a new kind of foreign policy common sense emerged. The narrative about the main features of Indian foreign policy behaviour since 1991 is then situated within the larger picture.

Some tentative explorations along these lines are all that is attempted here. No political scientist worth her salt would dispute that the Indian landscape has been dramatically transformed by the substantial Hindutva-ization of the Indian polity and society, the 'democratic upsurge' of *Dalits* and lower castes, the burgeoning political-electoral power of regional parties, the greater socio-economic polarization caused by the neoliberal reforms, the insurgency of Indian elites and the 'middle class' faced with burgeoning pressures from below. Yet most 'strategic experts' ignore all this, remaining uncritical of the state's claims to national representation, unsuspicious of its 'official nationalism', insensitive about the fact of competing nationalisms or that official nationalism is itself altered by the changes in the relationship of forces between different social actors that have made it more insensitive to the poor and indigent, more frustrated and communalized, more arrogant and self-aggrandizing and that this has pertinent effects on the Indian state's foreign policy formulations and practices.

Alongside Communism's collapse were socio-economic changes in the advanced countries that greatly strengthened capital vis-à-vis labour as also the dramatic financialization of the world economy. Ascendant economic thought shifted from Keynesianism and developmentalism towards neoliberalism, the most right-wing form of neoclassical economics.[2] But the view that Indian foreign policy changes after 1991 have been determined essentially by changed external circumstances is simply a realist conceit. The meanings and interpretations of even major changes always pass through the filters of the changing beliefs and values that the senior state personnel of India and their acolytes and supporters hold.

Domestic transformations and pressures

Since the beginning of the 1980s the unpredictable interweaving of six basic processes has shaped, and will continue to shape, India. They are: (1) the slow, unsteady but still-forward march of Hindutva; (2) the ongoing forward march of the Other Backward Classes (OBCs); (3) *Dalit* assertion; (4) Muslim ferment; (5) the regionalization of the Indian polity; and (6) the rise of a 'middle class' of mass proportions.

Though the BJP suffered electoral decline in the last two elections, obtaining 138 MPs (2004) and 116 (2009), this does not mean that Hindutva's political-ideological impact is declining. The RSS has an estimated 50,000 *shakas* (branches) all over the country and a million-plus membership entrenching itself in the pores of civil society. Over the last 30 years it has been the force most responsible for the communal and authoritarian drift in Indian society. The centre of gravity of Indian politics moved rightwards with respect to the meaning and practice of secularism and democracy and through the emergence of a more belligerent nationalism.

The upsurge of *Dalits* and OBCs has had considerable domestic but not external impact. Their essentially sectoral preoccupations reflect the socially limited character of their core bases, the restricted scope of a politics immersed in domestic manoeuvrings, the limited visions of their leaderships. The policy perspectives of Mulayam Singh Yadav as defence minister in a coalition government was indistinguishable from his immediate predecessors. Unlike Hindutva ideologues, *Dalit* leaders or intellectuals don't refer to an inspirational past, but nor do they seriously question neoliberal economic perspectives or engage with geopolitics. Since their politics has succeeded in creating a burgeoning 'middle class' among lower castes, their interests have assumed priority and neoliberalism has considerable resonance amongst them.

This undeniable 'democratic upsurge' has not humanized Indian foreign policy behaviour. Also, in determining the formation of national governments regional parties have become crucial. But in regard to national/international policies their political weight has been marginal, with one exception. Virtually all regional parties pay attention to the upper and middle echelons of farmers. There is a divide between export-oriented farmers and those producing primarily for the home market but both converge in supporting India's resistance in the WTO negotiations to the subsidies by the EU and US to its own agricultural producers. The Centre's policy of relaxing capital inflows has been welcomed by some states and regional parties. It allows regional economic-industrial elites and their party defenders to collaborate more freely with foreign capital, reducing dependence on Central funds. That only some states get most such inflows aggravates already serious regional disparities. In the states favoured by FDI flows there emerge powerful social layers in support of such liberalization. In the less-favoured backward states there is the competitive scramble to make themselves more attractive to potential investors, domestic and foreign; so neoliberalism is not seriously challenged.

The regional parties, even those with extra-regional ambitions, have parochial programmes reflecting the geographical/social limitations of their bases. They align with a direction-setting 'national' political formation that does have a national/international agenda. This 'national' hub deals fairly easily through standard bargaining processes with these regional forces, and pushes through its own national/international policies. This was true of the United Front (UF) government of 1996–8, the National Democratic Alliance (NDA) of 1998/9–2004, and the United Progressive Alliance (UPA) of 2004 onwards.

The only regional political formations that do have a genuine nationalist/internationalist orientation are the CPI and CPM. Left political parties, no matter how small, always have an internationalist perspective being classic examples of the principle that it is the programme that makes the party not vice versa. Historically, the party is created as the instrument to bring about fulfillment of programmatically defined tasks and goals. Once such Left parties seek to grow, pressures to dilute the programme so as to widen the party's social and electoral base become enormous. But such Left formations always have a clear internationalist perspective guiding their attitude to foreign policy. However, the impact of the mainstream Indian Left (despite propping up the previous UPA government) have had minimal effect on a Congress party determined to pursue neoliberalism, a soft Hindutva, and a strategic partnership with the US.

It is the 'middle class' and Hindutva that have been the strongest domestic propellers of change in Indian foreign policy behaviour. We have seen the *national* consolidation of the 'politics of Hinduness', but not any national-level expression of the 'politics of Muslimness'. All Muslim communal-political organizations are irredeemably local. The enduring weakness of any 'politics of Muslimness' since Partition means that Central government postures on Kashmir, relations with Pakistan or West Asia (despite the value of remittances by Muslim migrants) or with the US, are singularly unaffected by domestic 'Muslim sentiment'.

However, there is Muslim ferment in India. 'Muslimness' as the dominant collective identity is growing because of Hindutva, communal riots, growing Islamophobia as well as a rising consciousness of their relative disadvantages as a community. But this does not influence Indian foreign policy positively. Instead Islamophobia in foreign policy might lead to domestic policy changes detrimental to the democratic rights and security of India's Muslim population.

The middle class, Hindutva, neoliberalism

The rise of an Indian 'middle class' of mass proportions has created a stable social base for right-wing and reactionary politics, domestically and internationally. Since the Indian Middle Class (IMC) represents the top 15 to 20 per cent of the population they are not a median category acting as a powerful social buffer vis-à-vis the working class, the working poor and the underclass, as in the advanced democracies. Indeed, they are more insecure since social pressure from below is much greater and the governing elite does periodically need to appeal to this multitude. The IMC sees its own sense of status and prestige as intertwined with the global standing of the Indian state. It is the social layer that has most benefited from government economic policies whether in its earlier 'socialistic' phase or in the 1980s 'anti-*dirigiste*' phase or since the NEP of 1991. This combination of IMC values and material interests, this amalgam of a more hedonist and self-centred but also more frustrated and belligerent IMC provides the backbone of mass support to a geoeconomics of neoliberalism and to a geopolitics where India must seek (with US help) to become a great nation.

Since neoliberal economic policies exacerbate inequalities of income, wealth and power, they must be accompanied by a supportive right-wing politics and ideology, which can take variant forms related to nationalist peculiarities. Neoliberalism is not the characterization of a state of affairs but of a general direction of the economy. The existence of the National Rural Employment Guarantee Act (NREGA) – the world's largest employment guarantee scheme, which the Congress credits as greatly helping to improve its electoral performance in 2009 – in no way alters this overall thrust, anymore than the Lula government's *Bolsa Familia* (cash transfers to the poor) has altered Brazil's overall economic direction. Such measures express a 'compensatory neoliberalism' as distinct from a 'disciplinary neoliberalism'. Even the global recession since mid-2008 has led to less reappraisal in mainstream economic thinking in India than in the West. That India has weathered the recession relatively better has been taken by the leaders of the new Congress-led government – now relieved from the pressure of Left parties that fared very badly in the 2009 elections (down from a combined tally of 62 seats in 2004 to 26 this time) – as confirming the wisdom of the neoliberal reform agenda that must now be further pursued. That the publicly owned and therefore much less speculative character of the Indian banking system played a valuable protective role has been cursorily acknowledged but has not changed the dominant mindset.

The 'vacuum' created by the historical political-electoral decline of the Congress was filled up by the dissonant mixture of caste-based politics and ideology, regional assertion, and Hindutva. The great irony of our times is that although socially-electorally, the Congress today is, proportionately speaking, more than ever before in its post-independence history, a party of the lower castes and lower classes, in its policy orientation and behaviour it has never before been so right-wing! Since the 90s, the all-India electoral haemorrhage of the Congress from the top was so much greater than from below. Its upper-caste Hindu vote as a proportion of all upper castes fell from 36 per cent in 1991 to 21 per cent in 2004, while its proportion of *Dalit* (39 per cent and 37 per cent) and *Adivasi* votes (45 per cent and 42 per cent) remained relatively stable between the two election periods. The proportion of Muslims voting Congress actually rose from 38 per cent to 50 per cent. The rise in overall voting percentage of about 2 per cent in the 2009 elections was too small to significantly alter the internal caste composition of Congress support.

Three interconnected factors explain this extraordinary disjunction. First, the emergence of an IMC of mass proportions provided the professional recruiting ground and social base for explicitly self-serving elite-driven policies. Second, a totally new kind of Congress leadership highly compatible with the values and interests of this burgeoning layer and thus very different in its political culture from that of the Congress past emerged. This Congress leadership, starting from Rajiv Gandhi as the 'face of modern India' (and in a context of internal organizational decay), is most responsible for the cumulative programmatic shift of the party to the right that eventually passed beyond the point of no return. This Congress long ago shed the rooted organizational structure, which could have been the source and terrain of a struggle to retain the party's historical character. It has long been 'de-institutionalized' with no check on the leadership apex from within. Finally, there is the enormous pressure exerted by the remarkable rise of the BJP-RSS, in large part also explained by its expanding support amidst this middle class.

The Congress is now a right-wing party but one outflanked to its right (the BJP-RSS) by a formation that is not the Indian equivalent of say, Christian Democracy, but is more dangerously authoritarian, anti-secular/anti-democratic, and communal-racist than either US Republicans or British Conservatives. What is more, the 'Congressization' of the BJP is of less consequence than the 'BJP-ization of the Congress'.[3] For at least the next decade or more, the overall profile is clear – the *normalization* of right-wing politics at the Centre – as two coalition groupings, led by the Congress and BJP, with some degree of interchangeability of junior regional partners, compete with each other.

The bomb

India's nuclear tests in May 1998 marked a definite rupture with India's past, not traceable to any 'logic of neoliberalism' or to the pressures of post-Cold War external developments. All countries that go nuclear do so either because of changed elite self-perceptions or changed threat perceptions, though they all claim that external threats have been the spur. Similarly, Prime Minister Vajpayee officially justified the 11 and 13 May tests by citing the Pakistani and Chinese threats.[4] It was the leaders of the BJP-RSS, not any of its coalition partners (who were kept in the dark), who decided on this course. They were strongly supported by the top leadership of the Department of Atomic Energy (DAE), which organized the tests. Top RSS leaders were pivotal to making this decision, though the RSS is not electorally accountable to the Indian public.

Ever since the 1974 test, the official position of all other parties (including the mainstream Left) was support for keeping the nuclear option open, i.e. ambiguity. But even before the Chinese nuclear test of 1964, the Jan Sangh always demanded that India go nuclear. Clearly this posture owed nothing to fear of Chinese or Pakistani nuclear capabilities (historically predating such developments) but was ideologically driven by Hindutva's vision of how to make a strong India through a militant politicized interpretation of Hinduism's relevance to nation-building.[5] This was Savarkar's classic injunction of 'Uniting Hindus and Militarizing Hinduism'!

But if Hindutva's ascendance to governmental power was decisive in India acquiring the bomb, its widespread acceptance owed everything to the deeper domestic social, political and ideological transformations since the early eighties, most importantly the growth of the IMC and the rise of a more communalized, frustrated and belligerent elite nationalism. Retaining and further developing the nuclear weapons programme is now the shared common goal of all parties, barring the Left, whose opposition is not, however, as consistent as it should be. The completion of the Indo–US nuclear deal is widely seen as the symbolic cornerstone of the Indo-US search for an enduring strategic partnership.

The Narasimha Rao government had in January 1992 established full and normal diplomatic relations between India and Israel. But it was during the NDA period that we had a dramatic acceleration of relations. Prime Minister Ariel Sharon was formally invited to and visited India. The Indian Deputy Prime Minister, L. K. Advani, paid a visit to Israel. Serious military dealings and connections of a kind that had never before existed were institutionalized, with Israeli military help during the 1999 Kargil war being a turning point in this regard. Brajesh Mishra, the national security advisor at the time, consciously laid down the groundwork for closer relations linking support groups amidst the Indian diaspora in the US with the powerful American Israeli Political Action Committee (AIPAC), i.e. also seeing Israel as a vital mediating link in Indo–US relations. Though the Congress-led UPA government does not share the anti-Muslim ideological element of the BJP-RSS, which makes them pro-Israel, it has accepted the strategic 'wisdom' behind the relationship, which again shows how Hindutva has decisively altered key aspects of the foreign policy framework.

India's foreign policy turn since 1991: an overview

For India the two crucial and related events of 1991 were the collapse of the Soviet Union and the inauguration of the NEP by the recently elected Congress government. Though continuous with earlier liberalizing policies, the NEP did represent a decisive *ideological* turn with very significant policy implications. Both New Delhi and Washington then began to talk of forging a new post-Cold War relationship.

India can pursue any of five possible diplomatic strategies in relation to a hegemonizing power like the US. It can (1) bandwagon; (2) balance; (3) hide, i.e. practice neutrality; (4) transcend, i.e. appeal to international law to justify its postures; (5) co-bind, i.e. eliminate a potential threat by tying that country tightly to its own political and economic structures. This fifth option does not really exist for India vis-à-vis the US, though it is what France did to Germany after the Second World War, and what India could do with Pakistan if both countries had a mind to, which they don't. It is what Japan and China could consider doing if they had a mind to (which they don't) and if the US would not strive at all costs to prevent this (which it would).

That India has bandwagoned with the US is obvious. But this denouement was reached in three phases.

Phase I: 1991–8

Soon after the collapse of the Soviet Union, India and the US began talking of a 'strategic friendship', if not a 'strategic partnership'. There were US and Western plaudits for India's NEP. But asymmetry of power meant the terms would be determined by the US, which was not going to shift away from Pakistan. The history of foreign policy reorientation since 1991 is basically the story of India accommodating to US strategic perspectives regardless of the nuclear issue, where it was the US that moved from opposition to acceptance. The India-US diplomatic and military relationship developed slowly, half-heartedly and haltingly.

Phase II: 1998–2004

This phase saw the accession of a BJP-led government and was marked above all by the nuclear issue following the tests of May 1998 and its impact on the triangle of US–India–Pakistan relations. Interrupted by the Kargil War of Spring 1999, when the US backed India and pressed Pakistan to withdraw its troops, this phase saw the most sustained rounds of high-level diplomatic-strategic discussions ever between the two countries. India sought to convince the US that it should accept nuclearization since it was strategically on the same side as the US. The Clinton Administration soon enough accepted this, hence Clinton's Presidential visit to Indian shores. But the Administration also wanted India to clarify what its nuclear ambitions and preparations were and would be, i.e. it wanted it to remain a small nuclear power (SNP).

This was also the period where a strategic triad was being forged between India-Israel-US. After 9/11, India also readjusted to the fact that the US would not sacrifice its alliance with Pakistan to suit it and rationalized this as follows: the Indo–US tie-up is a first-tier relationship compared to the second-tier US–Pakistan relationship. Moreover, this latter relationship is in the long term an aberration, which the US will eventually abandon. It is in India's interest then to put most of its strategic eggs into the American basket.

Phase III: 2004 onwards

The accession of a Congress-led government in 2004 witnessed a further consolidation of the NEP, creating strong economic and media lobbies committed to maintaining a strategic alliance between India and the US. Perceived economic needs are believed to necessitate a close strategic partnership geopolitically. Manmohan Singh has gone on record to declare that his historic contribution was to usher in the NEP in 1991, a globalizing process for which close and enduring Indo–US relations are a must. What was not expected was that the foreign policy trajectory laid out by the previous government would be *accelerated* and naively rationalized as the best way to promote a more 'multipolar' world order, when the US sees such regional alliances as vital to sustaining its global hegemony. While the Clinton Administration favoured gradualism, the Bush Administration decided to dramatically accelerate matters by signalling its willingness to enter an Indo–US nuclear deal that would effectively rewrite both US domestic and international (Nuclear Suppliers Group) rules and norms to reward a rule-breaker (India) on nuclear proliferation matters in return for India's long-term strategic realignment with the US.

The bargain is perfectly understood in both governments.[6] For the US the purpose is fundamentally strategic – paying the price for eliminating intra-elite reservations among Indians. Side benefits include greater sales of civilian nuclear materials and equipment and in due course greater sales of conventional military equipment so that the US and Israel can eventually emerge as the top supplier of military hardware to India, replacing Russia. In India the dominant public response to the Deal, barring the Left, was very supportive. Now concluded, it amounts to de facto recognition and acceptance by the US, NATO, Russia and possibly China of India's nuclear status. It was followed by successful US pressure in the Nuclear Suppliers Group to get that body to grant a waiver enabling India to access civilian nuclear technology and fuel from other countries. This makes India the only country with nuclear weapons and not a signatory to the NPT to get such a privilege. Thus India can now import uranium and expand simultaneously and significantly its military and civilian nuclear programmes. The Obama Administration has endorsed this deal and the secretary of state Hilary Clinton's July 2009 visit to India was mainly meant to follow up on the commercial and strategic implications of this Deal.

The socio-political-ideological foundations for a long-term alliance between India and the US are robust and do not preclude a degree of flexibility in Indian foreign policy behaviour. But India's manoeuvring room would be increased by the wider consequences of what happens to the US geopolitically if its current impasse in West and Central Asia – above all the quagmires of Iraq and Afghanistan – turns into a decisive defeat. The US sees Iran as a key obstacle to its West Asia ambitions and has sought to isolate and squeeze it politically, even holding out a threat of future military assault. The Indian vote in September 2006 in support of transferring the Iran dossier from the IAEA to the Security Council showed that India will not pose serious obstacles to US efforts in this regard, even as it pursues 'friendly' relations with Iran.

Four triangles

A closer look at certain triangles is also imperative. The US aims to be the key balancer in South Asia in the US–India–Pakistan triangle and in East Asia in the US–China–Japan triangle. The US also aims to link the two regions via Southeast Asia by promoting closer dealings between India and Japan. Finally, in the US–China–India triangle, it is the evolution of the US–China relationship (whose future trajectory will essentially be determined by US behaviour) that will determine the India–China relationship. Even a resolution of the longstanding border problem between India and China will not guarantee enduringly friendly relations.

The US wants to promote (within limits) a more right-wing nationalist and ambitious Japan, and also a more geopolitically ambitious India. Official US publications talk of helping to *make* India a major power while calling on Japan to *behave* like the major power it already is. The US needs to both promote a more aggressive Japan to disturb China and also to drive home to China that it would be in its interest to accept the US–Japan Security Pact, which allows the former to control the latter. The US posture towards China currently incorporates two seemingly contradictory postures but is probably the most effective way for it to pursue its longer-term project of nullifying a future Chinese geopolitical challenge, either through its incorporation in a framework of accepted American leadership and hegemony, or by isolating it sufficiently so that the costs of a Chinese challenge are seen in Beijing as too high. Thus the US treats today's China as both a potential opponent and as a potential friend and makes its preparations – military, economic, cultural and political – accordingly. China on its part has every wish to avoid making the US see it as a strategic opponent and therefore to be left to pursue its modernization over the next two decades or more without undue external pressure on it.

In South Asia, the US relationship with India will become increasingly important, worrying many Pakistanis. US (and Western) economic interests in India are general and diverse but only specific and limited for the other South Asian countries. Barring the unforeseen, such as the ascendance of an anti-American regime, Islamist or otherwise in Pakistan, the US will continue to balance between India and Pakistan because each country serves non-substitutable interests. Pakistan serves US geopolitical interests westwards and northwards (West and Central Asia). India serves American geopolitical interests southwards and eastwards, above all as a junior naval partner to control the Indian Ocean. This requires developing India's military relationships not just with Southeast Asian countries like the Philippines, Singapore and Indonesia but all the way to Australia and Japan. The US is quite open about its strategic plans (see US Department of Defense 2002; Blank 2005; and Tellis 2005). It suits US interests to promote Indian ambitions since the American idea is to construct an Asian equivalent of NATO in which India, Japan, Vietnam, South Korea, Philippines, Indonesia, Malaysia and Singapore could be important nodes (linking up with Australia) in the overall project of containing China. To this effect, the US is financially supporting the Indian construction of a Far Eastern Naval Command (FENC) to be based in the Andaman and Nicobar islands close to Indonesia and strategically located between the North Arabian Sea and the Malacca Straits. When completed in 2012 the FENC will be larger and more state-of-the-art than the old Subic Bay base.

An authoritative study spells out US thinking.

> What's in it for the United States? For one, the proposed security system is principally an in-region solution for dealing with two of the biggest international security threats – an over-ambitious China and the spread of Talibanized Islam. Second, this scheme being entirely indigenous, there is none of the odium that attends on US troops deployed locally as in South Korea and Japan ... and finally, it in no way precludes the presence in the extended region of the US armed forces or limits US military initiatives.
>
> (Blank 2005: 79)

The Indian attitude towards an Asian NATO can be gleaned from official statements made by the former Indian Foreign secretary, Shyam Saran, who said, 'In the context of Asia, there is no doubt that a major realignment of forces is taking place'. China was emerging as a 'global economic power'. The US and India could 'contribute to creating a greater balance in Asia'. And to manage the uncertain security situation in this region, it would be necessary to bring in 'more and more countries within the discipline of a security paradigm for this region'.[7]

In this context one notes the growing military relationship between India and Japan. Japan's 'Maritime Self-Defence Force' is now operating in the Indian Ocean region in support of the US occupation of Afghanistan just as Indian armed forces are extending similar auxiliary support to the US in respect of Afghanistan and Iraq. This is Japan's first participation in an overseas military operation since 1945. In October 2008, India and Japan inked a declaration for a 'Strategic and Global Partnership', making the former only the third country after Australia and the US with which Japan has signed such a document.

India has also joined up with the US in regard to its Ballistic Missile Defense – Theater Missile Defense (BMD-TMD) and is not averse to eventually joining the Proliferation Security Initiative (PSI) programme. Both these programmes are guaranteed to perpetuate global nuclear tensions and rivalries, for example, the BMD-TMD project is directed against Russia and China and will push both to enhance quantitatively and qualitatively their nuclear arsenals. China's actions will then have obvious knock-on effects on Indian and then Pakistani nuclear preparations.

By way of conclusion: stable foundations for the present course

So far no mention has been made of the influence of the Indian diaspora, especially in the US. Where do Indian-Americans stand? According to the US Census of 2000, Indian-Americans numbered 1.5 million. Approximately 75 per cent of them have a university education and the average annual income of this community was $60,093, compared to the national annual average then of $38,885. Indian-Americans are an elite and 'model minority', meaning they don't make trouble and are generally quite divorced from the concerns and struggles of the poorest Americans. They enjoy growing public visibility and act as a medium for promoting stronger ties between the Indian and US governments. Their dominant representative bodies seek to connect with and emulate the networking of Jewish-Zionist bodies, such as the American Israel Public Affairs Committee (AIPAC). This diaspora is largely comfortable with the official nationalism espoused by post-Cold War governments in New Delhi and enthusiastic about their neoliberal and pro-American turns.

This Indian diaspora does not lead, make or shape Indian foreign policy but follows and supports. However, its preferences, attitudes and values have a significant impact on Indian political life. The peculiarity of elite nationalism in India today (including Hindutva, which enjoys disproportionately higher support amongst this diaspora) is that so many of its heroic exemplars are Indian-Americans. This reinforces admiration in India for the US as the exceptional land of opportunity and vigour. That professionals in the IMC are sending their children to the US for higher education in ever-greater numbers provides another practical-materialist basis for India's pro-US orientation.

The most important domestic ballasts for pushing foreign policy in this pro-American direction are constituted by the social forces most seriously and strongly represented by the Indian state today. To all those who believe there is an umbilical cord that ties the Indian state to dominant class formations and to the IMC, tracing and explaining the evolution of state behaviour necessarily requires observing and evaluating the evolution of Indian capital. This would mean studying the shifting weights of its fractions, the new balances between the agents of rural and urban forms of accumulation, the rise and decline of industrial-financial sectors, the realignments between domestic and foreign capital and the relationship of state managers and of different governmental departments with domestic and foreign capitals. Empirical studies on this terrain are invariably narrowly focused. It is, after all, only the Left that wants a 'lay of the whole land' as it were, for the purposes of relating this to the study of the evolving character of the state. For others, the Indian state is a fully autonomous political actor that has substantially shed its economic functions over the last 20 years. Questions about its class or social character are the irrelevant 'bees-in-the-bonnet' of the Left.

Neither empirical limitations nor neoliberal disdain, however, should deter us from making some general observations. Contrary to what is widely believed, India did not establish a strong developmental state or a strong 'national bourgeoisie' that would be enduringly hostile to foreign capital and a powerful social anchor for the pursuit of an independent foreign policy.[8] Import-substituting industrialization (ISI) was not intrinsically hostile to export expansion or to eventual integration into the world market but believed this needed to take place when the country was producing higher value-added industrial products. However, the failure to establish a genuine developmental state, the absence of a strong 'national bourgeoisie' and the negative integration of the Indian economy in the world market via expanding imports created a progressively widespread belief (even among the main beneficiaries of the ISI path of industrialization) that the very idea of a developmental state was a huge mistake. The best, perhaps only, way forward was to strongly integrate into the global capitalist economy.

This ultimately meant accepting the neoliberal logic whereby inequalities of all kinds would dramatically increase, foreign capital's presence and weight in the domestic market would substantially increase, industrial restructuring and job loss would take place and rates of employment absorption would decline. But sectors of Indian industry and services would become competitive internationally. There would be expanding markets abroad to compensate for those lost at home. Besides, ever-greater involvement in a burgeoning financial sector at home and possibilities of greater financial activity abroad would maximize chances by the already rich and well-off to accumulate substantial wealth very quickly without going through the time-consuming circuits of investing in the actual production and sale of goods and services.

Urban-based Indian capital and export-oriented sections of the agrarian bourgeoisie now see no alternative to working with and alongside foreign capital by going in for mergers and joint ventures, subcontracting arrangements, or directly competing against foreign capital in the belief that an expanding market will enable it to secure its own market shares. Indian capital will also rely on domestic niche markets and look to export more goods, services and capital. There is thus the emergence of a 'collaborative' or 'internal bourgeoisie', open to a wider range of association with foreign capital, and the nature of these links is not adequately captured by older notions of compradorism or outright dependence.

Indeed, since 1991 there has been a considerable acceleration of the concentration and centralization of both Indian and foreign capital in many important areas. According to the 2007 CMIE database, the Herfindal Index has increased for many industries between 2000/1 and 2005/6.[9] One of the key mechanisms has been the spate of mergers and acquisitions by Indian capital both home and abroad and by foreign capital in India. This process of concentration has also taken place in the services sector.[10] It is the giants of the private corporate sector whether Indian or the major global companies that exercise disproportionate influence on government economic and financial departments and ministries as well as on the top political executives. India's stock market is now strongly connected to global markets and within which Foreign Institutional Investors (FIIs) are a sufficiently strong presence so that their concerns have to feature in government policy behaviour.

The average annual growth rate in the 1980s and 1990s was roughly similar at around 5.7 per cent to 5.8 per cent, even though there were lower rates of employment absorption in the 1990s. However, since 2003 the Indian economy averaged over 8 per cent growth per annum till the recent global recession hit it, lowering this average to a current but still respectable figure of around 6 per cent.[11] The main source of this growth is simply the historically high rates of savings and investments. The former is now around 35 per cent of GDP and investments a couple of percentage points or so higher. Admittedly inequalities have greatly increased; employment absorption remains poor; rates of decline in absolute poverty slow. But so what? The upper and middle echelons of the IMC have been the biggest beneficiaries of the neoliberal turn. Most sections of Indian capital are either supportive of, or reconciled to, such policies. Moreover, as a general rule, it is political arbitrariness and unfairness rather than the mere fact of poverty or socio-economic inequalities that have promoted the kind of political turmoil that sometimes forces the state to change tack. In contrast to the first two-and-a-half decades after independence, in the decades afterwards the strongest socio-political movements have (with a few notable exceptions) had much more to do with identity and culture than with livelihood issues.

Another important change has taken place. In the 1980s it appeared as if the Bharat versus India or rural *kulaks* versus industrial bourgeoisie conflict would escalate or at least carry on. It hasn't. The political importance of the agrarian bourgeoisie remains because of its mass mobilizational capacities. But they have not had anywhere near as much influence as the industrial-financial elites on the Centre's economic policy thrust. Agriculture's overall share in GDP is declining. For 2008–9 it was around 17 per cent. That of the industrial-manufacturing sector is about 18 per cent, while the services sector now accounts for close to 65 per cent. Since growth rates in the services and industrial sectors are much higher than in agricultural, they are considered the spearheads of future growth receiving much greater policy attention. Furthermore, global integration of India's economy has increased differentiation within the agrarian bourgeoisie, making them collectively weaker.

Sociologically speaking then, we might say that there is a recomposition of the ruling class coalition hitherto comprised of the industrial bourgeoisie, the agrarian bourgeoisie with the apex of the bureaucracy playing the coordinating role. The agrarian bourgeoisie is now more differentiated between those increasingly aligned with, and those increasingly disturbed by, neoliberal globalization. Big capital, Indian and foreign, is increasingly powerful. There is a rising financial sector whose weight in the dominant coalition is fast growing, as is that of the representatives of foreign capital. There is the development of a more mobile bloc of transnational capital, inclusive of a sizeable and growing element of Indian-controlled capital, whose influence in the ruling-class coalition and over the Central government is rising. Over the last few years Indian firms have made several hundred acquisitions, big and small, abroad. Maintaining the current direction of Indian foreign policy does not require working to eliminate economic nationalists but to make the other pro-globalization groups relatively stronger.

Where does the US come in? In 2004–5, the US was India's leading trade partner, accounting for 11.1 per cent of total trade. American firms have been the leading investors since 1991, accounting for 17 per cent of the total FDI inflows. But this does not explain the pro-US bias. After all, Indian economic links with others, such as Japan, China and the EU could grow at faster rates in the future. Elites everywhere who benefit from the global neoliberal order must look to the US to play the biggest role in politically sustaining a world order so conducive to capitalist accumulation. It is the US that has to lead in properly organizing the system of multiple states to provide such political guardianship and global policing. States remain the crucial actors and regulators providing the legal, regulatory, institutional and infrastructural framework. They police capital-labour relations to favour the former. They manage the macro-economy. They are the medium (especially if they are electoral democracies) that provide the popular legitimacy for elite rule.

Geopolitics and geoeconomics are thus inescapably intertwined. An ever-expanding and globalizing economy requires a politically stable system of nation-states. It needs 'hegemonic stabilization' or a global coordinator to lay down the rules and norms for behaviour both for states and for the dominant classes that seek to operate through their respective states. This is all the more necessary because capitalism is also always about competition between capitals and between the states that support their 'own' capitals and classes, and this competitive tension must not be allowed to get out of hand. Furthermore, the deepening entry of China and India into this process of global integration will certainly create new stresses and strains. Whether the necessary roles of global coordination, arbitration, management can best be played by a collective hegemon (a concert among the major powers or blocs) or will have to be played by a single hegemon (the US) may be debated. But either way the role of the US is indispensable.

The identification of Indian elites with the US should not, however, be seen as merely a matter of behaving according to the impulses of perceived material and economic interests. A commitment to participating in the US imperial project as a touchstone of one's foreign policy behaviour requires more than a cost-benefit analysis of material gains and losses. Between the hegemon and those who accept subordination to it, albeit masked in the language of 'equal partnership of the two great democracies', there must be a coming together on the level of ideas and values as well. The US leads, or can hope to lead, because its society, polity and economy is admired and in various respects emulated. Indian elites are fixated on the Indo–US partnership not just because it promises to fill Indian pockets or because it massages the 'nationalist' ego. It is also because in some significant measure the US has captured the minds and hearts of Indian elites.

Starting around the late 60s–early 70s a rupture began to form in India at the ideational level even as this had its roots in more material changes. The result was a comparative moral decay. One of the great national movements of the first half of the twentieth century – the Indian struggle for independence – created a political leadership that after independence, for all its faults, had a certain vision of building a new India learning from East and West, but would be a different, better, more just and humane society than the exemplars of either bloc. That distinctive vision is no longer entertained. The collapse of that moral imaginary has been replaced by the determination to emulate a country that in so many respects does not represent the best but the worst of advanced capitalist societies. How on earth can India's elites seriously, consistently and continuously challenge and oppose the country they most want their own to emulate? This is the real tragedy of Indian foreign policy.

Is there any possibility of change from this situation? Yes, if there is a real erosion of the US's global political authority, which could then make it both more desirable and feasible for Russia, China, India, even possibly Iran, to explore greater yet principled collaboration with each other as part of another kind of Asian reorganization very different from the current Indo–US alignment directed against China. In this regard it is what happens in West and Central Asia that probably holds the key. Should the US's political ambitions be decisively frustrated in Iraq and Afghanistan; if its efforts to isolate and weaken Iran come a cropper; if it is unable to move ahead in its efforts to impose a pro-Israeli and therefore utterly unjust 'settlement' on the Palestinian leadership, then new possibilities and new directions for Indian foreign policy do become more possible. This is something to work and hope for.

Notes

1 The most intense debate in IR theory is between neo-Weberians like Michael Mann and his IEMP (ideological-economic-military-political) model of social power and the 'social property relations' approach of the neo-Marxists like Rosenberg (1994), Teschke (2003) and Bromley (2008). My sympathies lie with the latter.
2 Advocates of economic neoliberalism know that the strongest theoretical defence for their position comes from the Chicago School, which argues that 'government failure' is much more dangerous than 'market failure', unlike welfarists (Amartya Sen) in the neo-classical tradition who presumably worry too much about market failures. Government personnel (bureaucrats and politicians) they claim, pursue like everybody else, their self-interest, leading to inefficient rent-seeking activity. But so many of these

very same advocates, including professional economists like Manmohan Singh, Montek Singh Ahluwalia, P. Chidambaram, et al. (respectively Prime Minister, Deputy Chair of the Planning Commission, Home Minister) who are widely seen as the economically-driven architects of the new Indian foreign policy closeness to the US, have no hesitation in talking of that very same government pursuing the national interest. Self-serving politician-bureaucrats, dangerous in deciding on the best economic policies, through the magic wand of realist thinking, become the reliably impartial and genuine pursuers of the 'national interest', when it comes to foreign policies.

3 Most political analysts have argued that given the enormous diversity and cross-cutting cleavages of Indian society, only a 'centrist' force able to appeal to the widest cross-section of the populace could hope to come to power. Thus the BJP/Jan Sangh would have to choose between being a party of the Hindu rassemblement or electorally a mass popular party. To become the latter it would have to become more moderate ideologically. Instead, from the mid 80s, after reaching its lowest electoral level, the BJP-RSS and cohort bodies shifted decisively to the right via the greatest mass mobilization witnessed since the independence struggle – the Ram Janmabhoomi campaign – and in doing so shifted the very fulcrum of Indian politics to the right. But having done so, the BJP is still faced with the problem posed by Indian diversity – the pressure to move towards a more 'moderate' centrism, albeit a newly positioned centre. As for the Congress, it has accommodated to this new respectability of Hindu communalism especially among the IMC, always the key social base for stabilizing elite rule.

4 Within a month this same Vajpayee government declared that the Indian bomb was 'not country-specific' and a year later that the Indian bomb was 'not threat-specific', confirming the basic argument of this writer that it was elite self-perceptions that lay behind the tests.

5 In a book completed in 1994 and published in 1995 I predicted that if the BJP came to power India would probably go openly nuclear. See Achin Vanaik, (1995: 123). As far as I know mine was the only such public prediction made at a time when the CTBT issue was just beginning to grab the headlines in India.

6 This Indo–US nuclear deal must be seen in the context of the earlier path-breaking 'New Framework for the US–India Defence Relationship' that was signed in June 2005. It is this that laid the formal foundation for levels of military-strategic cooperation that was truly historic and which has ever since steadily developed and expanded.

7 'India ready to help US in Asian power rejig' in *The Times of India*, 29 November 2005.

8 See Vivek Chibber's path-breaking work (Chibber 2003, 2005).

9 The Herfindal Index between zero and one measures the concentration by firms in an industry in terms of their collective market share. One means a perfect monopoly and zero means perfect competition.

10 See Barik (2007: 121–2) and Mazumdar (2006: 99–110). The top three manufacturing companies in India are Reliance, Tata and the AV Birla groups. There were 654 software companies listed in 2005 by the Centre for Monitoring the Indian Economy but the top five of Tata, Infosys, Wipro, Satyam and HCL accounted for approximately 57 per cent of total sales.

11 Of course this is only a part of the story. According to the report prepared by the National Commission on Enterprises in the Unorganized Sector (NCEUS) approximately 77 per cent (about 836 million people) fall short of earning Rs. 20 a day. This figure is broadly consistent with the current international standard of poverty of below US $2 a day in purchasing power parity terms. Breaking this down we get 70 million classified as extremely poor, 167 million poor, 207 million marginal, and 392 million vulnerable.

Glossary

adivasi indigenous people; Scheduled Tribes
anganawadis creche
benaami illegal
bhurabal 'brown haired'; used pejoratively to identify upper-caste groups
bustee informal settlement
crore ten million rupees
dalit 'the downtrodden'; untouchable caste groups; Scheduled Castes
dalitbahujan the oppressed majority
dhanda occupational trade
dharna rally
dirigiste strong state direction of economy
gram sabha village council
gram vikas village development
Hindutva Hindu cultural nationalism
izzat 'honour'
kali yuga 'Age of Kali' in Hindu scripture; a 'dark age'
kisan farmer
Lok Sabha 'House of the People'; lower house of parliament
mandir temple
masjid mosque
Naxalites Maoist guerillas; originated in Naxalbari district, West Bengal
panchayat 'five-person' village council
Rajya Sabha 'Council of States'; upper house of parliament
Ramjanmabhoomi movement to build a Ram temple
Rs rupee; note of currency
Salwa Judum 'Purification Hunt'; state-sponsored vigilante groups in Chattisgarh
samman esteem; respect
sangh parivar family of Hindu nationalist organizations
sarpanch head of panchayat
satyagraha non-violent resistance
senas private armies
suvidha comfort; convenience
swadeshi national self-sufficiency

Consolidated bibliography

Adams, J. (1990) 'Breaking Away: India's Economy Vaults into the 1990s', in M. M. Bouton and P. Oldenburg (eds), *India Briefing*, Boulder, San Francisco and Oxford: Westview Press: 77–101.
Agarwala, R. (2006) 'From work to welfare: a new class movement in India', *Critical Asian Studies*, 38(4): 419–44.
Aghion, P., Burgess, R., Redding, S. and Zilibotti, F. (2005) 'The Unequal Effects of Liberalization: Evidence from Dismantling the License Raj in India', mimeo: Department of Economics, Harvard University.
Ahluwalia, M. (2000) 'Economic performance of states in post-reform period', *Economic and Political Weekly*, 6 May: 1637–48.
—— (2002) 'State Level Performance Under Economic Reforms in India', in A. Krueger (ed.), *Economic Policy Reforms and the Indian Economy*, Chicago: University of Chicago Press.
Ahmad, A. (1996) 'In the eye of the storm: the left chooses', *Economic and Political Weekly*, 31(22): 1329–43.
—— (2000) *Lineages of the Present*, London: Verso.
Aiyar, M. S. (2009) *A Time of Transition: Rajiv Gandhi to the 21st Century*, New Delhi: Penguin.
Aiyar, S. A. (2008) 'Swaminomics', *Times of India*, 13 July.
Aiyar, S. S. A. (2007) 'Killing the Best, Aiding the Worst SEZs', *The Economic Times*, available online at http://economictimes.indiatimes.com/opinion/columnists/swaminathan-s-a-aiyar/Killing-the-best-aiding-the-worst-SEZs/articleshow/1888171.cms (accessed 21 March 2010).
Alam, J. (2004) *Who Wants Democracy?* Hyderabad: Orient Longman.
Alsop, R. Anirudh, K. and Sjoblom, D. (2000) 'Are Gram Panchayats Inclusive? Report of a Study Conducted in Rajasthan and Madhya Pradesh', *Background Paper* no. 3, South Asia Social Development Unit, World Bank.
Ambedkar, B. R. (1989) *Writings and Speeches*, volume 1. Ed. Vasant Moon. Government of Maharashtra: Department of Education.
Anderson, K. (2006) 'How can a rights-based approach to development programming help to achieve quality education? Evaluating the education guarantee scheme in Madhya Pradesh', *Asia-Pacific Journal of Human Rights and Law*, 2: 75–109.
Appadurai, A. (2002) 'Deep democracy: urban governmentality and the horizon of politics', *Public Culture*, 14(1): 21–47.
Arora, B. (2004) 'The Political Parties and the Party System', in Zoya Hasan (ed.), *Parties and Party Politics in India*, New Delhi: Oxford University Press: 504–33.

Assadi, M. (1994) '"Khadi curtain", "weak capitalism" and "operation ryot": some ambiguities in farmers' discourse, Karnataka and Maharashtra 1980–93', *The Journal of Peasant Studies*, 21: 212–27.
Athreya, V. (2006) 'Dropping out', *Frontline*, 20 October: 90–2.
Atkinson, R. and Bridge, G. (eds), (2005) *The New Urban Colonialism: Gentrification in a Global Context*, London: Routledge.
Austin, G. (1999) *The Indian Constitution: Cornerstone of a Nation*, Delhi: Oxford University Press.
Ayres, A. and Oldenburg, P. (2005) (eds), *India Briefing: Takeoff at Last?* New York: Asia Society/M.E. Sharpe.
Balagopal, K. (1987) 'An ideology for the provincial propertied class', *Economic and Political Weekly*, 22(36/37): 1544–6.
—— (1988) *Probings in the Political Economy of Agrarian Classes and Conflicts*. Hyderabad: Perspectives Press.
—— (2000) 'A tangled web: subdivision of SC reservations in AP', *Economic and Political Weekly*, 85(13): 1075–81.
—— (2002) 'Reflections on "Gujarat pradesh" of "Hindu rashtra"', *Economic and Political Weekly*, 37(22): 2117–19.
Banaji, J. (1994) 'The farmers' movements: a critique of conservative coalitions', *The Journal of Peasant Studies*, 21(3/4): 228–45.
Banerjee, S. (2003) 'Uneasy convergence of left and right', *Economic and Political Weekly*, 38(32): 3347–8.
—— (2005) 'Hobson's choice for Indian communists', *Economic and Political Weekly*, 40(19): 1935–7.
Banerjee, A. V. and Piketty, T. (2005) 'Top Indian incomes, 1922–2000', *World Bank Economic Review*, 19: 1–20.
Banerjee, A., Bardhan, P., Basu, K., Datta-Chaudhuri, M., Guha, A., Majumdar, M., Mookherjee, D. and Ray, D. (2002) 'Strategy for economic reform in West Bengal', *Economic and Political Weekly*, 41: 4203–18.
Banerjee-Guha, S. (2007) 'Post-Fordist Urban Space of Mumbai: The Saga of Contemporary Restructuration', in A. Shaw (ed.), *Indian Cities in Transition*, Chennai: Orient Longman: 260–82.
—— (2009) 'Neoliberalising the "urban": new geographies of power and injustice in Indian cities', *Economic and Political Weekly*, 44(22): 95–107.
Bardhan, P. (1984) *The Political Economy of Development in India*, Oxford: Oxford University Press.
Bardhan, P. and Udry, C. (1999) *Development Microeconomics*, New York: Oxford University Press.
Bardhan, P. and Mookherjee, D. (2004) 'Decentralization in West Bengal: Origins, Functioning and Impact', paper presented at a conference on Democracy and Human Development: A Global Inquiry, 12 November 2004, Boston University, Boston.
Barik, K. (2007) 'Industry', in *Alternative Economic Survey, India 2006–07: Pampering Corporates, Pauperizing Masses*, Delhi: Daanish Books.
Baru, S. (2000) 'Economic Policy and the Development of Capitalism in India', in F. R. Frankel, Z. Hasan, R. Bhargava and B. Arora (eds), *Transforming India: Social and Political Dynamics of Democracy*, New Delhi: Oxford University Press: 207–31.
Baruah, S. (2005) *Durable Disorder: Understanding the Politics of Northeast India*, New Delhi: Oxford University Press.

240 Consolidated bibliography

Bhattacharyya, D. (1999) 'Election 1999: ominous outcome for Left in West Bengal', *Economic and Political Weekly*, 20 November.

Baviskar, A. (2006) 'The politics of the city', *Seminar*, 516, August: 40–2.

Baviskar, A. and Sundar, N. (2008) 'Democracy versus economic transformation?' *Economic and Political Weekly*, 43(46): 87–9.

BBC On-line News (2006) 'Selling India's Slums', available online at http://news.bbc.co.uk/1/hi/business/5087436.stm (accessed 15 April 2009).

BBC News South Asia (2007) 'Doctor Sought over Illegal Scans', available online at http://news.bbc.co.uk/2/hi/south_asia/7129268.stm (accessed 15 April 2009).

Behar, A. and Kumar, Y. (2001) 'Decentralisation in Madhya Pradesh, India: from *Panchayati Raj* to *Gram Swaraj* (1995–2001)', Working Paper 170, Overseas Development Institute, London.

Beiner, R. (1995) 'Introduction: Why Citizenship Constitutes a Theoretical Problem in the Last Decade of the Twentieth Century', in R. Beiner (ed.), *Theorizing Citizenship*, Albany: State University of New York Press.

Benjamin, S. (2000) 'Governance, economic settings and poverty in Bangalore', *Environment and Urbanization*, 12(1): 35–56.

Benjamin, S. and Bhuvaneswari, R. (2006) 'Urban futures of Poor Groups in Chennai and Bangalore: How these are Shaped by Relationships between Parastatals and Local Bodies', in N. Gopal Jayal, A. Prakash and P. K. Sharma (eds), *Local Governance in India: Decentralization and Beyond*, New Delhi: Oxford University Press: 221–67.

Berman, S. (1997) 'Civil society and the collapse of the Weimar Republic', *World Politics*, 49: 401–29.

Besley, T. and Burgess, R. (2004) 'Can labor regulation hinder economic performance? Evidence from India', *Quarterly Journal of Economics*, 119: 91–134.

Besley, T. Burgess, R. and Esteve-Volart, B. (2005) 'Operationalising Pro-Poor Growth: India Case-Study', mimeo, Working Paper of Department of Economics, LSE.

Besley, T. Pande, R. and Rao, V. (2006) 'Political Selection and the Quality of Government: Evidence from South India', mimeo, Working Paper of Department of Economics, LSE.

—— (2007) 'Political economy of panchayats in south India', *Economic and Political Weekly*, 42(8): 661–7.

Bharadwaj, K. (1995) 'Regional Differentiation in India', in T. V. Satyamurthy (ed.), *Industry and Agriculture in India Since Independence*, New Delhi: Oxford University Press.

Bhatia, B. (2004) 'The Naxalite Movement in Central Bihar', unpublished PhD dissertation, University of Cambridge.

Bhattacharjea, A. (2009) 'The effects of employment protection legislation on Indian manufacturing', *Economic and Political Weekly*, 44(22): 55–62.

Bhattacharyya, D. (1999) 'Election 1999: ominous outcome for Left in West Bengal', *Economic and Political Weekly*, 20 November: 3267–9.

Bidwai, P. (2005) 'For a "New Deal" for labour', *Frontline*, 13–26 August: 109–10.

Blank, S. (2005) *Natural Allies? Regional Security in Asia and Prospects for Indo-American Strategic Cooperation*, Strategic Studies Institute of the US Army War College.

Block, F. (2001) 'Introduction' Karl Polanyi (1944), *The Great Transformation: The Political and Economic Origins of Our Time*, 2nd ed., Boston: Beacon Press.

Bose, S. (2003) *Kashmir: Roots of Conflict, Paths to Peace*, Cambridge, MA: Harvard University Press.

Bourdieu, P. (1984) *Distinction: A Social Critique of the Judgment of Taste*, Cambridge, Massachusetts: Harvard University Press.

Brandolini, A., Cannari, L., Alessio, G.D. and Faiella, I. (2004) 'Household Wealth Distribution in Italy in the 1990s', *Banca D'Italia Temi di Discusione* 530, Banca D'Italia, Rome.
Brass, P. (1982) 'Pluralism, Regionalism and Decentralizing Tendencies in Contemporary Indian Politics', in A. Wilson and D. Dalton (eds), *The States of South Asia: Problems of National Integration*, London: Hurst: 223–64.
—— (1990) *The Politics of India Since Independence*, Cambridge: Cambridge University Press.
Brass, T. (1994) 'Introduction: the new farmers' movements in India', *The Journal of Peasant Studies*, 21: 3–26.
Breman, J. (2001) 'An informalized labour system', *Economic and Political Weekly*, 36(52): 4804–21.
—— (2003) *The Labouring Poor in India: Patterns of Exploitation, Subordination, and Exclusion*, New Delhi: Oxford University Press.
—— (2004) *The Making and Unmaking of an Industrial Working Class: Sliding Down the Labour Hierarchy in Ahmedabad, India*, New Delhi: Oxford University Press.
Brenner, N. and Theodore, N. (2002) 'Cities and the Geographies of "Actually Existing Neoliberalism"', in N. Brenner and N. Theodore (eds), *Spaces of Neoliberalism: Urban Restructuring in North America and Western Europe*, Oxford: Blackwell: 2–32.
Bromley, S. (2008) *American Power and the Prospects for International Order*, Cambridge: Polity Press.
Burman, A. (2007) *Special Economic Zones: Issues in Corporate Governance*, Ottawa.
Business Standard (2007) 'Rehab Policy Good News for SEZs'.
Business World (2006a) 'Sovereign States'.
—— (2006b) 'Zone of Contention'.
Byres, T. J. (1974) 'Land Reform, Industrialization and the Marketed Surplus: An Essay on the Power of Rural Bias', in David Lehmann (ed.), *Agrarian Reform and Agrarian Reformism*, London: Faber and Faber.
Castells, M. (1997), *The Rise of the Network Society*, Oxford: Blackwell.
Chandhoke, N. (2005a) 'Of Broken Social Contracts and Ethnic Violence: The Case of Kashmir', Working Paper No. 75, Crisis States Research Centre, London School of Economics.
—— (2005b) '"Seeing" the state in India', *Economic and Political Weekly*, 60(11): 1033–9.
—— (2005c) *Democracy and Well-Being in India*, Geneva: UNRISD.
—— (2008) 'Globalization and the Indian State: Report on the Findings of a Research Project', unpublished manuscript.
Chandra, K. (2004) *Why Ethnic Parties Succeed: Patronage and Ethnic Headcounts in India*, Cambridge: Cambridge University Press.
Chandran, D. (2006) 'The Richer the District, the Poorer the Sex Ratio', InfoChange News and Features at *Constituent Assembly Debate*, Government of India, available online at http://infochangeindia.org/200601035971/Population/Books-Reports/ The-richer-the-district-the-poorer-the-sex-ratio.html (accessed 19 March 2010).
—— (n.d.) *Constitutent Assembly Debates*, Government of India, available online at http://parliamentofindia.nic.in/ls/debates/debates.htm (accessed 19 March 2010).
Chandrasekhar, C. P. (2007) 'The Progress of Reform and Retrogression in Indian Agriculture', available online at www.macroscan.org/anl/apr07/anl250407Agriculture.htm (accessed 29 March 2010).
Chatterjee, M. (2004) 'The debacle and after', *Seminar*, 539, July.

Chatterjee, P. (1986) *Nationalist Thought and the Colonial World: A Derivative Discourse?* London: Zed Books.

—— (1997) *A Possible India: Essays in Political Criticism*, Delhi: Oxford University Press.

—— (1998) 'Development Planning and the Indian State', in T. J. Byres (ed.), *The State, Development Planning and Liberalisation in India*, Delhi: Oxford University Press: 82–103.

—— (1999) *The Present History of West Bengal: Essays in Political Criticism*, Delhi: Oxford University Press.

—— (2001) 'Democracy and the violence of the state: a political negotiation of death', *Inter-Asian Cultural Studies* 2(1): 7–21.

—— (2004a) 'Singh on a Tightrope: Can the Congress Please its Allies and also Keep India Inc. Happy?' *Telegraph*, 23 May.

—— (2004b) *The Politics of the Governed: Reflections on Political Society in Most of the World*, New York: Columbia University Press.

—— (2008) 'Democracy and economic transformation in India', *Economic and Political Weekly*, 43(16): 53–62.

Chatterjee, P. and Mallik, A. (1975) 'Bharatiya ganatantra o bourgeois pratikriya', *Anya Artha* (May 1975), translated in P. Chatterjee (1997), *A Possible India: Essays in Political Criticism*, Delhi: Oxford University Press, 35–57.

Chattopadhyay, R. and Duflo, E. (2004) 'Women as policy makers: evidence from an India-wide randomized policy experiment', *Econometrica* 72: 1409–43.

Chaudhuri, S. (2006) 'The 1994 Panchayati Raj Act and the Attempt to Revitalize Rural Local Government in India: What Difference does a Constitutional Amendment make?', in P. Bardhan and D. Mookherjee (eds), *Decentralization to Local Governments in Developing Countries: A Comparative Perspective*, Cambridge, Massachusetts: MIT Press.

Chaudhuri, S. and Heller, P. (2003) 'The Plasticity of Participation: Evidence from a Participatory Governance Experiment', University ISERP Working Paper, New York: Columbia.

Chibber, V. (2003) *Locked in Place: State-Building and Late-Industrialisation in India*, Princeton: Princeton University Press.

—— (2005) 'Reviving the developmental state? The myth of the national bourgeoisie', *Socialist Register*, 41: 226–46.

City Mayors (n.d.) 'The World's Fastest Growing Cities and Urban Areas from 2006 to 2020: urban areas ranked 1 to 100', available online at www.citymayors.com/statistics/urban_growth1.html (accessed 20 April 2010).

Coelho, K. (2005) 'Unstating the "Public": an Ethnography of Reform in an Urban Sector Utility in south India', in D. Mosse and D. Lewis (eds), *The Aid Effect: Ethnographies of Development Practice and Neoliberalism*, London: Pluto: 171–95.

Collier, P. (2007) *The Bottom Billion: Why the poorest Countries are Failing and What can be Done About It*, Oxford: Oxford University Press.

Constituent Assembly Debates (CAD) (1949a) Vol. IX, 11 August, available online at http://parliamentofindia.nic.in/ls/debates/vol9p10a.htm (accessed 2 February 2011).

—— (1949b) Vol. IX, 12 August, available online at http://parliamentofindia.nic.in/ls/debates/vol9p11a.htm (accessed 2 February 2011).

Corbridge, S. (2002) 'Cartographies of Loathing and Desire: the BJP, the Bomb and the Political Spaces of Hindu Nationalism', in Y. Ferguson and R. Barry Jones (eds), *Political Space: Frontiers of Change and Governance in a Globalizing World*, Albany: SUNY Press.

Corbridge, S. and Harriss, J. (2000) *Reinventing India: Liberalization, Hindu Nationalism and Popular Democracy*, Cambridge: Polity Press.

Corbridge, S., Williams, G., Srivastava, M. and Véron, R. (2005) *Seeing the State: Governance and Governmentality in India*, Cambridge: Cambridge University Press.

Crane, G. T. (1990) *The Political Economy of China's Special Economic Zones*, Armonk, New York: M. E. Sharpe.

Damodaran, H. (2008) *India's New Capitalists: Caste, Business, and Industry in a Modern Nation*, Ranikhet: Permanent Black.

Das, A. (1999) 'The future postponed', *Economic and Political Weekly*, 34(20): 1666.

Das, S. and Mishra, Y. (2010) 'What does Budget 2010 imply for the social sector?', *Economic and Political Weekly*, 45(13): 64–8.

Dasgupta, J. (2001) 'India's Federal Design and Multicultural National Construction', in A. Kohli (ed.), *The Success of India's Democracy*, Cambridge: Cambridge University Press: 49–77.

Date, V. (2006) 'Travails of an ordinary citizen: a tale from Mumbai', *Economic and Political Weekly*, 41(32): 3473–6.

Datt, G. and Ravallion, M. (2010) 'Shining for the poor too?', *Economic and Political Weekly*, 45(7): 55–60.

Davies, J. B., Sandstrom, S., Shorrocks, A. and Wolff, E. N. (2006) 'The World Distribution of Household Wealth', mimeo, UNU, WIDER.

Davies, J. B, and Shorrocks, A. (2005) 'Wealth Holdings in Developing and Transition Countries', paper presented at the Luxembourg Wealth Study conference, Perugia, Italy, 27–29 January 2005.

de Souza, P. (2003) 'The struggle for local government: Indian democracy's new phase', *Publius: The Journal of Federalism*, 33(4): 99–118.

Deaton, A. (1997) *Analysis of Household Surveys*, Baltimore, Maryland: Johns Hopkins University Press.

Desai, R. (1999a) 'Culturalism and the contemporary right: the Indian bourgeoisie and political Hindutva', *Economic and Political Weekly*, 34(12): 695–712.

—— (1999b) 'The last satrap revolt', *Economic and Political Weekly*, 34(25): 1559–61.

—— (2004a) *Slouching Towards Ayodhya: From Congress to Hindutva in Indian Politics*, 2nd ed., New Delhi: Three Essays Collective.

—— (2004b) 'Forward march of Hindutva halted?', *New Left Review* 30: 49–67, reprinted in A. Sivaramakrishnan (ed.), *Short on Democracy: Issues Facing Indian Political Parties*, New Delhi: Imprint One, 2007.

—— (2004c) 'The Cast(e) of Anti-Secularism', in M. Hasan (ed.), *Will Secular India Survive?* New Delhi: Imprint One: 175–209.

—— (2006a), trans. Jorg Goldberg, 'Indien: Endlich ein Land der Gegenwart?', *Z. Zeitschrift Marxistische Erneuerung*, 67: 60–75.

—— (2006b) 'Neo-liberalism and Cultural Nationalism: A *Danse Macabre*', in D. Plehwe, B. Walpen and G. Nuenhoeffer (eds), *Neo-liberal Hegemony: A Global Critique*, Routledge: New York: 222–35.

—— (2007) 'Dreaming in technicolour: India as a BRIC economy', *International Journal*, Autumn: 779–803.

—— (2008) 'Die Gegenrevolution im Zeitlupentempo: Von Entwicklungsstaat bis Neoliberalen Staat in Indien', in I. Schmidt (ed.), *Die Heimatfronten der Globalisierung: Nationale Klassenkompromisse, Neuzusammensetzung des Proletariats und Transnationale Opposition*, Berlin: VSA Verlag.

Desai, M., Rudolph, S. H. and Rudra, A. (eds), (1984) *Agrarian Power and Agricultural Productivity in South Asia*, Berkeley: University of California Press.
Dev, M. (2004) 'How to make rural India shine', *Economic and Political Weekly*, 39(40): 4415–22.
—— (2008) *Inclusive Growth in India: Agriculture, Poverty and Human Development*, Delhi: Oxford University Press.
Dev, M. and Mooij, J. (2002) 'Social sector expenditures in the 1990s: analysis of central and state budgets', *Economic and Political Weekly*, 37(9): 853–66.
Dhanagare, D. N. (1994) 'The class character and politics of the farmers' movement in Maharashtra during the 1980s', *The Journal of Peasant Studies*, 21: 72–94.
Dogra, C. S. (2008) 'Girl ... Interred', *Outlook*, New Delhi, 28 January.
Dorairaj, S. (2010) 'Verdict for the worker', *Frontline*, 9 April.
Drèze, J. (2004) 'An Unconventional Convention', *Frontline*, 16 July: 124–8.
Drèze, J. (2010) 'Poverty Estimates vs Food Entitlements', *The Hindu*, 24 February.
Drèze, J. and Sen, A. (1995) *India: Development and Participation*, Oxford: Clarendon Press.
—— (1998) *India: Economic Development and Social Opportunity*, Oxford: Clarendon Press.
Economic and Political Weekly (1996a) 'Virtue of Abstinence', editorial, 11 May: 1099.
—— (2006b) Special issue on farmer suicides, 41.
—— (2006c) 'SEZ frenzy': 4095–6.
—— (2007) 'Piecemeal tinkering': 1399–1400.
—— (2009) 'BJP in crisis', 64/35, August 29.
Economic Times (2007) 'Agri Growth Central to Overall Prosperity'.
Exim News (2007) 'Confederation of Indian Industry'.
Fernandes, L. (2006) *India's New Middle Class: Democratic Politics in an Era of Economic Reform*, Minneapolis, Minnesota: University of Minnesota Press.
Fernandes, L. and Heller, P. (2006) 'Hegemonic aspirations: new middle class politics and India's democracy in comparative perspective', *Critical Asian Studies*, 38: 495–522.
Fox, J. (1994) 'The difficult transition from clientelism to citizenship', *World Politics* 46(2): 151–84.
Frankel, F. (2005) *India's Political Economy, 1947–2004: The Gradual Revolution*, 2nd ed., New Delhi: Oxford University Press.
Frankel, F. and Rao, M. S. A. (eds), (1989) *Dominance and State Power in Modern India: Decline of a Social Order*, 2 vols, Delhi: Oxford University Press.
Friedman, T. (2005) *The World is Flat: A Brief History of the Twenty-First Century*, New York: Farrar, Straus and Giroux.
Frontline (2006) 'Starting trouble', 23(25), available online at http://hinduonnet.com/fline/fl2325/stories/20061229002003300.htm (accessed 29 December 2006).
—— (2007) 'Rural resistance'.
Fuller, C. (2003) *The Renewal of the Priesthood*, Princeton: Princeton University Press.
Fuller, C. J. and Bénéï, V. (eds), (2001) *Everyday State and Society in India*, London: Hurst.
Ganguly, S. (1994) 'The Prime Minister and Foreign and Defence Policies', in J. Manor (ed.), *Nehru to the Nineties: the Changing Office of Prime Minister of India*, Vancouver: UBC Press: 138–61.
Ghertner, D. A. (2008) 'Analysis of new legal discourse behind Delhi's slum demolitions', *Economic and Political Weekly*, 43(20): 57–60.
Ghosh, A. and Mitra, M. (2004) 'Decentralisation of urban governance in West Bengal: Role and importance of ward committees', *Urban Management* (journal of the Institute of Local Government and Urban Studies, West Bengal), 11 (September): 29–51.

Ghosh, J. (2007) 'Universalising basic services', *Frontline*, 26 January: 46–8.
Gill, S. S., (1994) 'The farmers' movement and agrarian change in the green revolution belt of north-west India', *The Journal of Peasant Studies*, 21: 195–211.
Gooptu, N. (2007) 'Economic liberalisation, work and democracy: industrial decline and urban politics in Kolkata', *Economic and Political Weekly*, 42(21): 1922–33.
—— (2009) 'Neoliberal subjectivity, enterprise culture and new workplaces: organised retail and shopping malls in India', *Economic and Political Weekly*, 44(22): 45–64.
Government of India (2002) *Foreign Investment: Report of the Steering Group on Foreign Direct Investment*, New Delhi: Planning Commission.
—— (2005) *Jawaharlal Nehru National Urban Renewal Mission (JNNURM): Overview* (Ministry of Urban Development and Ministry of Urban Employment and Poverty Alleviation), available online at http://jnnurm.nic.in/nurmudweb/toolkit/Overview.pdf (accessed 20 April 2010).
—— (2006a) *Economic Survey, 2005–2006*, New Delhi: Government of India, Ministry of Finance.
—— (2006b) Prime Minister's High-Level Committee. *Social, Economic and Educational Status of the Muslim Community of India: A Report*.
—— (2006c) *SEZ Rules, 2006: Incorporating Amendments till May 2009*, Ministry of Commerce and Industry New Delhi, available online at http://sezindia.nic.in/index.asp (accessed 15 April 2009).
—— (2006–7) *Agricultural Statistics at a Glance*, New Delhi: Ministry of Agriculture.
—— (2007) *Economic Survey, 2006–2007*, New Delhi: Ministry of Finance.
—— (2009) *SEZ India*. Ministry of Commerce and Industry, available online at http://sezindia.nic.in/index.asp (accessed 5 July 2009).
—— (2010) *Economic Survey 2009–10*, New Delhi: Ministry of Finance.
Government of Kerala, Planning Board (2001 and 2008) *Economic Review*, Trivandrum.
Government of Orissa, Department of Revenue (2006) *Declaration of Land Classification for Proposed SEZs in Orissa*, Bhubaneshwar.
Government of United Kingdom (2007) *Ending Poverty in India: Consultation on DFID's Plan for Working with Three Indias*, London: Department for International Development.
Govinda Rao, M. (2009) 'The fiscal situation and a reform agenda for the new government', *Economic and Political Weekly*, 44(25): 77–85.
Guha, R. (1983) *Elementary Aspects of Peasant Insurgency in Colonial India*, Delhi: Oxford University Press.
Gulati A. and Narayanan, S. (2003) *The Subsidy Syndrome in Indian Agriculture*, Delhi: Oxford University Press.
Gulati A. and Kelley T. (1999) *Trade Liberalisation and Indian Agriculture*, New Delhi: Oxford University Press.
Gupta, A. (1998) *Postcolonial Developments: Agriculture in the Making of Modern India*, Durham, North Carolina: Duke University Press.
Gupta, D. (1997) *Rivalry and Brotherhood: Politics in the Life of Farmers in Northern India*, New Delhi: Oxford University Press.
—— (2005) 'Whither the Indian village?', *Economic and Political Weekly*, 40(8): 751–58.
Handler, J. F. (2004) *Social Citizenship and Workfare in the United States and Western Europe: The Paradox of Inclusion*, Cambridge: Cambridge University Press.
Harrison, S. (1960) *India: The Most Dangerous Decades*, Princeton: Princeton University Press.
Harriss, J. (1999) 'Comparing political regimes across Indian states: a preliminary essay', *Economic and Political Weekly*, 34(48): 3367–77.

—— (2003a) 'Do Political Regimes Matter? Poverty Reduction and Regime Differences Across India', in P. Houtzager and M. Moore (eds), *Changing Paths: International Development and the New Politics of Inclusion*, Ann Arbor, Michigan: Michigan University Press: 204–32.

—— (2003b) 'The great tradition globalizes: reflections on two studies of "the industrial leaders" of Madras', *Modern Asian Studies* 37: 327–62.

—— (2006) 'Middle class activism and the politics of the informal working class: a perspective on class relations and civil society in Indian cities', *Critical Asian Studies*, 38(4): 445–65.

—— (2007) 'Antinomies of empowerment: observations of civil society, politics and urban governance in India', *Economic and Political Weekly*, 30 June: 2716–24.

Harriss-White, B. and Janakarajan, S. (2004) *Rural India Facing the 21st Century: Essays on Long Term Village Change and Recent Development Policy*, London: Anthem South Asian Studies.

Hart, G. (2002) 'Development/s beyond neoliberalism? Power, culture, political economy', *Progess in Human Geography*, 26(6): 812–22.

Harvey, D. (1982) *The Limits to Capital*, Oxford: Blackwell.

—— (1985) *The Urbanization of Capital*, Baltimore, Maryland: The Johns Hopkins University Press.

—— (2001) *Spaces of Capital*, Edinburgh: Edinburgh University Press.

—— (2005) *A Brief History of Neoliberalism*, Oxford: Oxford University Press.

—— (2006) *Spaces of Global Capitalism: Towards a Theory of Uneven Geographical Development*, London: Verso.

Hasan, Z. (1994) 'Shifting ground: Hindutva politics and the farmers' movement in Uttar Pradesh', *The Journal of Peasant Studies*, 21: 165–94.

Hayek, F. (1944) *The Road to Serfdom*, London: RKP.

Heelas, P. and Morris, P. (eds), (1992) *The Values of the Enterprise Culture: The Moral Debate*, London: Routledge.

Heller, P. (2000) 'Degrees of democracy: some comparative lessons from India', *World Politics*, 52(4): 484–519.

—— (2001) 'Moving the state: the politics of democratic decentralization in Kerala, South Africa, and Porto Alegre', *Politics & Society*, 29(1): 131–63.

—— (2005) 'Reinventing Public Power in the Age of Globalization: The Transformation of Movement Politics in Kerala', in R. Ray, and M. Katzenstein (eds), *Social Movements in India: Poverty, Power and Politics*, New York: Rowman and Littlefield Publishers.

Heller, P. Harilal, K. N. and Chaudhuri, S. (2007) 'Building local democracy: evaluating the impact of decentralization in Kerala, India', *World Development* 35(4): 626–48.

Himanshu, (2007) 'Recent trends in poverty and inequality: some preliminary results', *Economic and Political Weekly*, 42(6): 497–508.

—— (2008) 'Social sector: continuation of past priorities', *Economic and Political Weekly*, 43(15): 29–32.

Indian Express (2007) 'Sizing Up the SEZ Potential'.

India Realty News (2007) 'Farmers Vow Not to Let the State Grab Their Land'.

International Institute of Population Sciences and Macro International (2007) *National Family Health Survey (NFHS-3) 2005–06, Volume I*, Mumbai: IIPS.

India Stat, available online at http://www.indiastat.com/agriculture/2/stats.aspx (accessed 1 February 2011).

Isin, E. (2002) *Being Political: Genealogies of Citizenship*, Minneapolis, Minnesota: University of Minnesota Press.

Jaffrelot, Christophe (1998) 'The Bahujan Samaj Party in north India: no longer just a dalit party?', *Comparative Studies of South Asia, Africa and the Middle East*, 18(1): 35–52.

—— (2000) 'The rise of the other backward classes in the Hindi belt', *The Journal of Asian Studies*, 59(1): 86–108.

—— (2003) *India's Silent Revolution: The Rise of the Lower Castes in North Indian Politics*, New Delhi: Permanent Black.

—— (ed.), (2007) *Hindu Nationalism: A Reader.* Ranikhet: Permanent Black.

Jain, S. and Mukand, S. W. (2003) 'Redistributive promises and the adoption of economic reform', *American Economic Review*, 93(1): 256–64.

Jayadev, A, Motiram, S. and Vakulabharanam, V. (2007a) 'Patterns of wealth disparities in India during the liberalisation era', *Economic and Political* Weekly, September 28: 3853–63.

—— (2007b) 'Imagined problems in computing wealth disparities', *Economic and Political Weekly*, 42: 69–71.

Jayal, N. G. (2006) *Representing India: Ethnic Diversity and the Governance of Public Institution*, London: Palgrave MacMillan.

Jenkins, R. (1998a) 'The Developmental Implications of Federal Political Institutions in India', in M. Robinson and G. White (eds), *The Democratic Developmental State*, Oxford: Oxford University Press.

—— (1998b) 'India's Electoral Result: An Unholy Alliance between Nationalism and Regionalism', mimeo: 1–9.

—— (1999) *Democratic Politics and Economic Reform in India*, Cambridge: Cambridge University Press.

—— (2003) 'How federalism influences India's domestic politics of WTO engagement (and is itself affected in the process)', *Asian Survey*, 43: 598–621.

—— (2004) 'Labor Policy and the Second Generation of Economic Reform in India', in R. Jenkins and S. Khilnani (eds), *The Politics of India's Next Generation of Economic Reforms, Special Issue of India Review* 3(4), October.

—— (2006) 'Democracy, development and India's struggle against corruption', *Public Policy Research*, 13(3): 155–63.

Jenkins, R. and Goetz, A. M. (2003) 'Bias and Capture: Corruption, Poverty and the Limits of Civil Society in India', in M. Blecher and R. Benewick (eds), *Asian Politics in Development*, London: Frank Cass: 109–22.

Jenson, J. (1997) 'Fated to live in interesting times: Canada's changing citizenship regimes', *Canadian Journal of Political Science*, 30(4): 627–44.

Jenson, J. and Phillips, S. D. (1996) 'Regime shift: new citizenship practices in Canada', *International Journal of Canadian Studies*, 14, Fall/Autumn: 111–35.

Jessop, B. (2002) 'Liberalism, Neoliberalism, and Urban Governance: A State-Theoretical Perspective', in N. Brenner and N. Theodore (eds), *Spaces of Neoliberalism: Urban Restructuring in North America and Western Europe*, Oxford: Blackwell: 101–25.

Jha, P. and Parvati, P. (2010), 'Right to Education Act 2009: critical gaps and challenges', *Economic and Political Weekly*, 45(13): 20–4.

Jha, S., Rao, V. and Woolcock, M. (2007) 'Governance in the gullies: democratic responsiveness and leadership in Delhi slums', *World Development*, 35(2): 230–46.

Jodhka, S. (2006) 'Beyond "crises": rethinking contemporary Punjab agriculture', *Economic and Political Weekly*, 41(16): 1530–7.

John, M. and Deshpande, S. (2008) 'Theorising the present: problems and possibilities', *Economic and Political Weekly*, 43(46): 83–6.

Joseph, S. (2007) 'Neoliberal reforms and democracy in India', *Economic and Political Weekly*, 42(31): 3213–18.
Kailash, K. K. (2009) 'Alliances and lessons of election 2009', *Economic and Political Weekly*, 44(39): 52–7.
Kalshian, R. (ed.), (2007) *Caterpillar and the Mahua Flower: Tremors in India's Mining Fields*, Delhi: Panos South Asia.
Kamat, A. R. (1979) 'The emerging situation: a socio-structural analysis', *Economic and Political Weekly*, 14(7/8): 349–54.
Kannan, K. P. and Pillai, V. N. (2004) 'Development as Freedom: An Interpretation of the "Kerala Model"', Working Paper 361, Centre for Development Studies, Trivandrum.
Kapur, D. and Mehta, P. B. (2005) 'Introduction', in D. Kapur and P. B. Mehta (eds), *Public Institutions in India: Performance and Design*, Delhi: Oxford University Press.
Karat, B. (2007) 'Behind the Events at Nandigram', *The Hindu*, 30 March.
Katzenstein, M. Fainsod, Mehta, U. Singh, and Thakkar, U. (2004) 'The Rebirth of the Shiv Sena: The Symbiosis of Discursive and Organizational Power', in Zoya Hasan (ed.), *Parties and Party Politics in India*, New Delhi: Oxford University Press: 257–87.
Kaviraj, S. (1988) 'A critique of the passive revolution', *Economic and Political Weekly*, 23(45–7): 2429–44.
—— (1991) 'On State, Society and Discourse in India', in J. Manor (ed.), *Rethinking Third World Politics*, Harlow: Longman: 72–99.
Khilnani, S. (2004) 'Branding India', *Seminar*, 533.
Klingensmith, D. (2003) 'Building India's "Modern Temples": Indians and Americans in the Damodar Valley Corporation, 1945–60', in K. Sivaramakrishnan and A. Agrawal (eds), *Regional Modernities: The Cultural Politics of Development in India*, Stanford: Stanford University Press: 122–42.
Kochar, K., Kumar, U., Rajan, R., Subramanian, A. and Tokatlidis, I. (2006) 'India's Pattern of Development: What Happened, What Follows', International Monetary Fund Working Paper No. 06/22, available online at www.imf.org/external/pubs/ft/wp/2006/wp0622.pdf (accessed 15 April 2009).
Kochanek, S. (1968) *The Congress Party of India: The Dynamics of a One Party Democracy*, Princeton: Princeton University Press.
Kohli, A. (1990) 'From Majority to Minority Rule: Making Sense of the "New" Indian Politics', in M. M. Bouton and P. Oldenburg (eds), *India Briefing*, Boulder, San Francisco, and Oxford: Westview Press: 1–25.
—— (2001) 'Introduction', in A. Kohli (ed.), *The Success of India's Democracy*, Cambridge: Cambridge University Press: 1–19.
—— (2006) 'Politics of economic growth in India, 1980–2005, parts I and II', *Economic and Political Weekly* 41 (13 and 14).
—— (2007) 'State and Redistributive Development in India', paper prepared for Project on *Poverty Reduction and Policy Regimes* Sponsored by UN Research Institute for Social Development.
Kothari, R. (1967) 'The congress "system" in India', *Asian Survey*, 4(12): 1161–73.
Kremer, M., Chaudhury, N., Rogers, F. H., Muralidharan, K. and Hammer, J. (2005) 'Teacher absence in India', *Journal of the European Economic Association*, 3(2–3): 658–67.
Krishna, A. (2002) *Active Social Capital: Tracing the Roots of Development and Democracy*, New York: Columbia University Press.
Krishna, S. (1997) 'Cartographic Anxiety: Mapping the Body Politic in India', in J. Agnew (ed.), *Political Geography: A Reader*, London: Edward Arnold.

Krishnamurthy, M. (2009) 'Mandi Moods in an Adolescent Town: Early Notes from Harda, Madhya Pradesh', mimeo: paper prepared for workshop on Mofussil India held at LSE, 6–7 July 2009; available from author at UCL.

Krueger, A. (1992) *The Political Economy of Agricultural Pricing Policy, Vol.5*, Baltimore, Maryland and London: The Johns Hopkins University Press for the World Bank.

Kumar, S. (2004a) 'Janata Regionalized: Contrasting Bases of Electoral Support in Bihar and Orissa', in R. Jenkins (ed.), *Regional Reflections: Comparing Politics across India's States*, New Delhi: Oxford University Press: 111–39.

—— (2004b) 'New Phase in Backward Caste Politics in Bihar, 1990–2000', in G. Shah (ed.), *Caste and Democratic Politics in India*, London: Anthem Press: 235–68.

Kunnath, G. (2006) 'Becoming a Naxalite in rural Bihar: class struggle and its contradictions', *Journal of Peasant Studies*, 33: 89–123.

Kymlicka, W. and Norman, N. (1995) 'Return of the Citizen: A Survey of Recent Work on Citizenship Theory', in R. Beiner (ed.), *Theorizing Citizenship*, Albany, New York: State University of New York Press.

—— (2000) 'Citizenship in Culturally Diverse Societies: Issues, Contexts, Concepts', in W. Kymlicka and W. Norman (eds), *Citizenship in Diverse Societies*, Oxford: Oxford University Press.

Lakha, S. (1999) 'The State, Globalisation and Indian Middle-Class Identity', in M. Pinches (ed.), *Culture and Privilege in Capitalist Asia*, London: Routledge.

Lanjouw, P. and Stern, N. (ed.), (1998) *Economic Development in Palanpur over Five Decades*, New Delhi: Oxford University Press.

Lefebvre, H. (1976) *The Survival of Capitalism*, New York: Schocken Books.

—— (1991) *The Production of Space*, Oxford: Blackwell.

Lele, J. (1995) *Hindutva: The Emergence of the Right*, Madras: Earthworm Books.

Lennenberg, C. (1988) 'Sharad Joshi and the farmers: the middle peasant lives!', *Pacific Affairs*, 61: 446–64.

Lewis, W. A. (1954) 'Economic development with unlimited supplies of labour', *The Manchester School*, 22: 139–91.

Lindberg, S. (1994) 'New farmers' movements in India as structural response and collective identity formation: the cases of the Shetkari Sanghatana and BKU', *The Journal of Peasant Studies*, 21: 95–125.

Lloyd, I. and Rudolph, S. H. (1997) *In Pursuit of Lakshmi: The Political Economy of the Indian State*, Chicago: University of Chicago Press.

Lokniti (2009) 'How India Voted', *The Hindu*, May 26.

McCarten, W. and Vyasulu, V. (2004) 'Democratic decentralisation and poverty reduction in Madhya Pradesh: searching for an institutional equilibrium', *Development and Practice*, 14(6): 733–40.

McKean, L. (1996) *Divine Enterprise: Gurus and the Hindu Nationalist Movement*, Chicago: University of Chicago Press.

Maclean, K. (1999) 'Embracing the untouchables: the BJP and scheduled caste votes', *Asian Studies Review*, 23(4): 488–509.

Madheswaran, S. and Attewell, P. (2007) 'Caste discrimination in the Indian urban labour market: evidence from the National Sample Survey', *Economic and Political Weekly*, 42(41): 4146–53.

Mahadevia, D. (2006) 'NURM and the poor in globalising mega cities', *Economic and Political Weekly*, 41(31): 3399–403.

Mahajan, G. (1999) 'Civil society and its Avatars: what happened to freedom and democracy', *Economic and Political Weekly*, 34(20): 1188–96.

Mann, M. (1986) *The Sources of Social Power: Volume 1, A History of Power from the Beginning to AD 1760*, Cambridge: Cambridge University Press.
Manor, J. (1982) 'Where the Gandhi Writ Doesn't Run', *The Economist*, 26 September.
—— (1996a) '"Ethnicity" in Indian politics', *International Affairs*, July: 459–75.
—— (1996b) 'Understanding Deve Gowda', *Economic and Political Weekly*, September 28: 2675–8.
—— (2001) 'Centre-State Relations', in A.Kohli (ed.), *The Success of India's Democracy*, Cambridge: Cambridge University Press: 78–102.
—— (2004a) 'The congress defeat in Madhya Pradesh', *Seminar*, February.
—— (2004b) 'In Part a Myth – the BJP's Organisational Strength', in K. Adeney and L. Saez (eds), *Coalition Politics and Hindu Nationalism*, New Delhi and London: Routledge.
—— (2004c) 'Explaining Political Trajectories in Andhra Pradesh and Karnataka', in R. Jenkins (ed.), *Regional Reflections: comparing politics across India's states*, New Delhi: Oxford University Press: 255–85.
—— (forthcoming) 'Digvijay Singh in Madhya Pradesh: Supplementing Political Institutions to Promote Inclusion', in M. Melo, Ng'ethe N. and J. Manor (eds), *Against the Odds: Politicians and Institutions in the Struggle Against Poverty*.
Marshall, T. H. (1964) *Class, Citizenship, and Social Development: Essays*, Garden City: New York, Doubleday.
Marx, K. (1968) *Capital*, vol. 1, trans. Samuel Moore and Edward Aveling (1887); Moscow: Progress Publishers, chs. xxvi–xxxiii.
—— (1976) *Capital*, vol. 1, ed. D. McClellan. Harmondsworth: Penguin.
Masani, M. (1953) *Our India: 1953*, Bombay: Oxford University Press.
Mauro, P. (1996) *The Effects of Corruption on Growth, Investment, and Government Expenditure*, Washington, DC: IMF.
Mazumdar, S. (2006) 'The Private Corporate Sector', *Alternative Economic Survey, India 2005–06: Disempowering Masses*, Delhi: Daanish Books.
Mehta, P. B. (2004) 'Constraints on electoral mobilization', *Economic and Political Weekly*, 39(51).
—— (2006) 'Being Middle Class is Okay', *The Indian Express*, 7 June.
Mendelsohn, O. and Vicziany, M. (1998) *The Untouchables: Subordination, Poverty, and the State in Modern India*, Cambridge: Cambridge University Press.
Menon, N. and Nigam, A. (2007) *Power and Contestation: India since 1989*, Hyderabad: Orient Longman.
Migdal, J. (2001) *State in Society: Studying How States and Societies Constitute and Transform One Another*, Cambridge: Cambridge University Press.
Mishra, P. (2004) 'India: The Neglected Majority Wins!' *New York Review of Books*, 12 August.
Misra, S. (2007) 'Agrarian Scenario in Post-reform India: A Story of Distress, Despair and Death', Working Paper, Mumbai: Indira Gandhi Institute of Development Research.
Mitra, A. (1977) *Terms of Trade and Class Relations: An Essay in Political Economy*, London: F. Cass.
Mohan, R. (1996) 'Urbanization in India: Patterns and Emerging Policy Issues', in J. Gugler (ed.), *The Urban Transformation of the Developing World*, Oxford: Oxford University Press: 93–132.
—— (2005) 'Indian Economy in the Global Setting', Speech at the 99th Foundation Day Celebration Function of the Indian Merchants' Chamber, Mumbai on 8 September, available online at http://www.rbi.org.in/Scripts/BS_SpeechesView.aspx?Id=211 (accessed 15 April 2009).

Mooij, J. and Dev, M. (2004), 'Social sector priorities: an analysis of budgets and expenditures in India in the 1990s', *Development Policy Review*, 22(1): 97–120.
Motiram, S. and Robinson, J. (2010) 'Interlinking and collusion', *Review of Development Economics* (forthcoming).
Motiram, S. and Vakulabharanam, V. (2007) 'Corporate and cooperative solutions for the agrarian crisis in the developing countries', *Review of Radical Political Economy*, 39: 360–7.
Mukherjee, A. (2006) 'Viewpoint: Trade Zone Hang-ups', *International Herald Tribune*, 28 October.
Mukhopadhyay, S. (2007) 'Giving a Dog a Bad Name', *Business Standard*, 28 October.
Mulay, S. and Nagarajan, R. (2006) 'A Study of Ultrasound Sonography Centres in Maharashtra', Population Research Centre, Pune for the Ministry of Health and Family Welfare, Government of India, available online at http://infochangeindia.org/200601035971/Population/Books-Reports/The-richer-the-district-the-poorer-the-sex-ratio.html (accessed 19 March 2010).
Munck, R. (2002) 'Globalization and democracy: a new "great transformation"?', *The ANNALS of the American Academy of Political and Social Science*, 581: 10–20.
Muralidharan, S. (1998) 'The unravelling of a front', *Frontline*, 24 April.
—— (1999a) 'The end of an ordeal', *Frontline*, 7 May.
—— (1999b) 'An incipient third force', *Frontline*, 16 July.
Nagaraj, K. (2008) 'Farmers' Suicide in India: Magnitudes, Trends and Spatial Patterns', Preliminary Report, Chennai: Madras Institute of Development Studies.
Nagaraj, R. (2004) 'Fall in manufacturing employment', *Economic and Political Weekly*, 39(30): 3387–90.
Nair, J. (2005) *The Promise of the Metropolis: Bangalore's Twentieth Century*, New Delhi: Oxford University Press.
National Commission for Enterprises in the Unorganised Sector (NCEUS) (2007) *Report on Conditions of Work and Promotion of Livelihoods in the Unorganised Sector*, New Delhi: Government of India.
National Sample Survey (NSS) (1998) 'Household Assets and Liabilities in India (as on 30.06.1991)', February 1998.
—— (NSS) (2005a) 'Employment Tables', 61st Round.
—— (NSS) (2005b) 'Situation Assessment Survey: Indebtedness of Farmer Households, NSS 59th Round', New Delhi: Ministry of Statistics and Programme Implementation, Government of India.
—— (NSS) (2005c) *Household Assets and Liabilities in India (as on 30.06.2002)*, New Delhi: National Sample Survey Organization.
—— (NSS) (2006). 'Some Aspects of Operational Holdings in India, 2002–03, NSS 59th Round', New Delhi: Ministry of Statistics and Programme Implementation, Government of India.
Nayyar, B. R. (1999) 'Policy and performance under democratic coalitions', *Journal of Commonwealth and Comparative Politics*, 37(2), July: 22–56.
Nehru, J. (1989) *An Autobiography*, Delhi: Oxford University Press.
Nigam, A. (2000) 'Logic of failed revolution: federalization of CPM', *Economic and Political Weekly*, 35(5).
—— (2008) 'Social Sector Spending Dips in 2007–8', *Financial Express*, 14 January.
Nilekani, N. (2008) *Imagining India: Ideas for the New Century*, New Delhi: Penguin India.
Noorani, A. (2009) 'Decline of the BJP', *Frontline*, 4 July.

252 Consolidated bibliography

O'Donnell, G. (1993) 'On the state, democratization and some conceptual problems: a Latin American view with glances at some postcommunist countries', *World Development* 21(8): 1355–9.

Omvedt, G. (1993) 'Farmers' movement: fighting for liberalization', *Economic and Political Weekly*, 26: 2708–10.

—— (1994) 'We want the return for our sweat: the new peasant movement in India and the formation of a national agricultural policy', *The Journal of Peasant Studies*, 21: 126–64.

Ong, A. (2006) *Neoliberalism as Exception: Mutations in Citizenship and Sovereignty*, Durham, North Carolina: Duke University Press.

Pai, S. (2007) 'The problem', *Seminar*, 571, March.

Pande, R. (2007) 'Rural Banking', in K. Basu (ed.), *The Oxford Companion to Economics in India*, New Delhi: Oxford University Press.

Pani, N. (2006) 'Cart Before the Bullock', *The Economic Times*, available online at http://economictimes.indiatimes.com/Opinion/Columnists/Cart-before-the-bullock/articleshow/814695.cms?curpg=1> (accessed 15 April 2009).

Pant, M. (2005) 'The Quest for Inclusion: Nomadic Communities and Citizenship Questions in Rajasthan', in N. Kabeer (ed.), *Inclusive Citizenship: Meanings and Expressions*, London: Zed Books.

Parry, J. (1994) *Death in Banaras*, Cambridge: Cambridge University Press.

Patel, P. (2005) 'Politics and mobilization of lower classes', *Third Millenium*, 8(4).

Patnaik, P (1995) 'A Perspective on the Recent Phase of India's Economic Development', *Whatever Happened to Imperialism and Other Essays*, Delhi: Tulika.

—— (2009) 'Reflections on the Left', macroscan, available online at http://www.macroscan.org/cur/jul09/print/prnt010709Reflections.htm (accessed 15 April 2009).

Patnaik, U. (1997) 'India's Agricultural Development in the Light of Historical Experience', in T. Byres (ed.), *The State, Development Planning and Liberalisation in India*, New York: Oxford University Press.

—— (2003) 'Global capitalism, deflation and agrarian crisis in developing countries', *Journal of Agrarian Change*, 3(1–2): 33–66.

—— (2007), 'Poverty and Neo-Liberalism in India', manuscript, Centre for Economic Studies and Planning, Jawaharlal Nehru University.

Peck, J. and Tickell, A. (2002) 'Neoliberalizing Space', in N. Brenner and N. Theodore (eds), *Spaces of Neoliberalism: Urban Restructuring in North America and Western Europe*, Oxford: Blackwell: 33–57.

Pew Research Center (2006) 'India: Pro-America, Pro-Bush', *Pew Global Attitudes Project*, available online at http://pewglobal.org/commentary/display.php?AnalysisID=1002 (accessed 15 April 2009).

Polanyi, K. (1944) *The Great Transformation: The Political and Economic Origins Of Our Time* (Second Beacon Press Edition 2001), Boston: Beacon Press.

Portes, A. and Hoffman, K. (2003) 'Latin American class structures: their composition and change during the neoliberal era', *Latin American Research Review*, 38(1): 41–82.

Prasad, C. B. (2001) Interview with S. Anand of the Dalit Media Network, available online at http://www.ambedkar.org/chandrabhan/interview.htm (accessed 15 April 2009).

Purfield, C. (2006) 'Mind the Gap: Is Economic Growth in India Leaving Some States Behind?' International Monetary Fund Working Paper 06/103.

Radhakrishna, R., Shenoi, P. V. and Thorat, Y. S. P. (2007) *Report Of The Expert Group on Agricultural Indebtedness*, Ministry of Finance, Government of India, July.

Radkar, A. and Parasuraman, S. (2007) 'Maternal deaths in India: an exploration', *Economic and Political Weekly*, 42(31): 3259–63.

Raghavan, E. and Manor, J. (2009) *Broadening and Deepening Democracy: Political Innovation in Karnataka*, New Delhi and London: Routledge.

Rai, P. (2009) 'Issues in the general election 2009', *Economic and Political Weekly*, 44(39): 80–82.

Rajalakshmi, T. K. (2002) 'Loaded against labour', *Frontline*, 16 August: 99–101.

Ramachandran, V. K. and Swaminathan, M. (2002) 'Rural banking and landless labour households: institutional reform and rural credit markets in India', *Journal of Agrarian Change*, 2: 502–44.

Ramakrishnan, V. (1999) 'A strategy against communalism', *Frontline*, 24 September.

Ramakrishnan, V. and Pande, S.K. (1999) 'The split and the wait', *Frontline*, 13 August.

Rangarajan, M. (2005) 'Polity in transition: India after the 2004 general elections', *Economic and Political Weekly*, 40(32): 3597–605.

Ranjan, R. (2006) *Special Economic Zones: Are They Good for the Country?* New Delhi: Centre for Civil Society.

Rao, M., Shand, G. R. and Kalirajan, K. P. (1999) 'Convergence of incomes across Indian states: a divergent view', *Economic and Political Weekly*, 34: 769–78.

Rao, M. G. and Singh, N. (2005) *Political Economy of Federalism in India*, New Delhi: Oxford University Press.

Rao, J. M. and Storm, S. (1998) 'Distribution and Growth in Indian Agriculture', in T. Byres (ed.), *The Indian Economy: Major Debates Since Independence*, New Delhi: Oxford University Press.

—— (2003) 'Agricultural Globalization in Developing Countries: Rules, Rationales and Results', in C. P. Chandrasekhar and J. Ghosh (eds), *Work and Well-Being in the Age of Finance*, New Delhi: Tulika Publishers.

Rao, R. K. (2007) 'Special Economic Zones: Gain or Drain', *Business Standard*.

Rao, V. and Paromita, S. (2009) 'Dignity through Discourse: Poverty and Culture of Deliberation in Indian Village Democracies', Policy Research Working Paper 4924, World Bank.

Reddy, D. N. (2006) 'Economic Reforms, Institutional Retrogression and Agrarian Distress', Working Paper, University of Hyderabad.

Riley, D. (2006) 'Civic associations and authoritarian regimes in interwar Europe', *American Sociological Review*, 70(2): 288–310.

Roberts, B. R. (2004) 'From marginality to social exclusion: from *laissez faire* to pervasive engagement', *Latin American Research Review*, 39(1): 183–203.

Roberts, B. R. and Portes, A. (2006) 'Coping with the free market city: collective action in six Latin American cities at the end of the twentieth century', *Latin American Research Review*, 41(1): 57–83.

Rodrik, D., Subramanian, A. and Trebbi, F. (2004) 'Institutions rule: the primacy of institutions over integration and geography in economic development', *Journal of Economic Growth*, 9(2): 131–65.

Rose, L. E. (1990) 'India's Foreign Relations: Reassessing Basic Policies', in M. M. Bouton and P. Oldenburg (eds), *India Briefing: 1990*, Boulder, San Francisco, and Oxford: Westview Press: 51–77.

Rose, N. and Novas, C. (2002) 'Biological Citizenship' (for Aihwa Ong and Stephen Collier [eds], *Global Anthropology*, Blackwell, 2003), available online at www.lse.ac.uk/collections/sociology/pdf/RoseandNovas BiologicalCitizenship2002.pdf (accessed 15 April 2009).

Rosenberg, J. (1994) *The Empire of Civil Society: A Critique of the Realist Theory of International Relations*, London: Verso.

Rudra, A. (1992) *The Political Economy of Indian Agriculture*, New Delhi: K.P. Bagchi.
Rudolph, L. I. and Rudolph, S. H. (1987) *In Pursuit of Lakshmi: The Political Economy of the Indian State*, Bombay: Orient Longman.
—— (2001a) 'The iconization of Chandrababu: sharing sovereignty in India's federal market economy', *Economic and Political Weekly*, 36(18): 1541–52.
—— (2001b) 'Redoing the Constitutional Design: From an Interventionist to a Regulatory State', in A.Kohli (ed.), *The Success of India's Democracy*, Cambridge: Cambridge University Press: 127–62.
Ruparelia, S. (2006) 'Rethinking institutional theories of political moderations: the case of Hindu nationalism in India, 1996–2004', *Comparative Politics*, 38(3), April: 317–37.
Sachs, J., Bajpai, N. and Ramiah, A. (2002) 'Understanding Regional Economic Growth in India', *CID Working Paper No. 88*, Harvard University.
Sachs, J., Mellinger, A. and Gallup, J. (2001) 'The Geography of Poverty and Wealth', *Scientific American*, March: 70–6.
Saez, L. (2002) *Federalism Without a Centre: The Impact of Political and Economic Reforms on India's Federal System*, Thousand Oaks, California: Sage Publishing.
Sainath, M. (2005) 'The Swelling Register of Death', *The Hindu*, 29 December.
Schiff M., and Valdes A. (1992) *The Plundering of Agriculture in Developing Countries*, Washington, DC: World Bank.
Sainath, P. (2005) 'The Unbearable Lightness of Seeing', *The Hindu*, 5 February.
—— (2007) 'The Decade of Our Discontent', *The Hindu*, 9 August.
Sanyal, K. (2007) *Rethinking Capitalist Development: Primitive Accumulation, Governmentality and Post-Colonial Capitalism*, New Delhi: Routledge.
Sanyal, P. (2009) 'From credit to collective action: the role of microfinance in promoting women's social capital and normative influence', *American Sociological Review*, 74(4): 529–50.
Sathyamurthy, T. V. (1997) 'The Impact of Centre-State Relations on Indian Politics: An Interpretive Reckoning 1947–1987', in P. Chatterjee (ed.), *State and Politics in India*, New Delhi: Oxford University Press.
Schiff, M. and Valdes, A. (1992) *The Plundering of Agriculture in Developing Countries*, Washington DC: World Bank.
Schneider, A. (2004) 'Accountability and capacity in developing country federalism: empowered states, competitive federalism', *Forum for Development Studies*, 1(31): 33–58.
Scott, J. C. (1998) *Seeing Like a State: How Certain Schemes to Improve the Human Condition Have Failed*, New Haven, Connecticut: Yale.
Scrase, T. (2006) 'The "New" Middle Class in India: A Reassessment', paper presented at the 16th Biennial Conference of the Asian Studies Association of Australia in Wollongong, June, available online at http://coombs.anu.edu.au/SpecialProj/ASAA/biennial-conference/2006/Scrase-Tim-ASAA2006.pdf (accessed 15 April 2009).
SEBI-NCAER (2000) *Survey of Indian Investors: 2000*, New Delhi: National Council of Applied Economic Research.
—— (2003) '*Survey of Indian Investors: 2003*', New Delhi: National Council of Applied Economic Research.
Sen, A. K. (1999) *Development as Freedom*, New York: Knopf.
—— (2002) 'The Insiders Outside', available online at www.humanscape.org/Humanscape/new/nov02/theinsiders.htm
—— (2003) 'Globalisation, Growth and Inequality in South Asia: Evidence from Rural

India', in C.P. Chandrasekhar and J. Ghosh (eds), *Work and Well-Being in the Age of Finance*, New Delhi: Tulika Publishers.

Sen, S. and Frankel, F. (2005) *Andhra Pradesh's Long March Towards 2020: Electoral Detours in a Developmentalist State*, Center for the Advanced Study of India, University of Pennsylvania.

Sen, A. and Himanshu. (2004) 'Poverty and inequality in India I', *Economic and Political Weekly*, 39(38): 4247–63.

—— (2004) 'Poverty and inequality in India II', *Economic and Political Weekly*, 39(39): 4361–75.

Sethi, A. (2008) 'Some home truths', *Frontline*, 15 August: 38.

Shah, A. (2006) 'Markets of protection: the Maoist Communist Centre and the state in Jharkhand, India', *Critique of Anthropology*, 26: 297–314.

Shah, M. (2008) 'Structures of power in Indian society', *Economic and Political Weekly*, 43(46): 78–83.

Sharma, A. N. (2006) 'Flexibility, employment and labour market reforms in India', *Economic and Political Weekly*, 41(21): 2078–86.

Sharma, R. and Poleman, T. (1993) *The New Economics of India's Green Revolution*, Ithaca, New York: Cornell University Press.

Shashtri, S. (2004) 'Lok Shakti in Karnataka: regional party in bipolar alliance system', *Economic and Political Weekly*, 39(14): 1491–7.

Sheth, D. L. (1999) 'Secularisation of caste and making of new middle class', *Economic and Political Weekly*, 34: 2502–10.

—— (2005) 'The change of 2004', *Seminar*, 545, January.

Sierminska, E. and Smeeding, T. (2005) 'Measurement Issues: Equivalence Scales, Accounting Framework, and Reference Unit', paper presented at the Luxembourg Wealth Study conference, Perugia, Italy, 27–29 January.

Simpson, E. and Corbridge, S. (2006) 'The geography of things that may become memories: the 2001 earthquake in Kachchh-Gujarat and the politics of rehabilitation in the pre-memorial era', *Annals of the Association of American Geographers*, 96: 566–85.

Singh, A. (2006) 'Accountability in Local Governance: Infrastructure Development in the Industrial Townships of Faridabad and Gurgaon', in N. G. Jayal, A. Prakesh and P. K. Sharma (eds), *Local Governance in India: Decentralization and Beyond*, Delhi: Oxford University Press.

Singh, Manmohan, Prime Minister of India (2005) 'PM Launches Jawaharlal Nehru National Urban Renewal Mission', 3 December, available online at http://pmindia.nic.in/speeches.htm (accessed 15 April 2009).

—— (2007) PM's address at the CNBC-TV18 Emerging India Awards, 2007 for Small and Medium Enterprises, 22 June; new PM's speech at the National Awards function for Micro, Small and Medium Enterprises, 30 August, available online at http://pmindia.nic.in/speeches.htm (accessed 15 April 2009).

Singh, N., Bhandari, L., Chen, A. and Khare, A. (2002) 'Regional inequality in India', mimeo. Available online at www.econ.ucsc.edu/faculty/boxjenk/regional_inequality_2002.pdf (accessed 1 February 2011).

Sinha, A. (2004a) 'Ideas, interests and institutions in policy change: a comparison of West Bengal and Gujarat', in R. Jenkins (ed.), *Regional Reflections: Comparing Politics across India's States*, New Delhi: Oxford University Press: 66–108.

—— (2004b) 'The changing political economy of federalism in India: a historical institutionalist approach', *India Review*, 3: 25–63.

—— (2005) *The Regional Roots of Developmental Politics in India: A Divided Leviathan*, Bloomington, Indiana: Indiana University Press.

—— (2007) 'Economic growth and political accommodation', *Journal of Democracy*, 18(2): 41–54.

Sivaramakrishnan, K. C., Kundu, A. and Singh, B. N. (2005) *Handbook of Urbanization in India: An Analysis of Trends and Processes*, New Delhi: Oxford University Press.

Smith, N. (1996) *The New Urban Frontier: Gentrification and the Revanchist City*, London: Routledge.

—— (2002) 'New Globalism, New Urbanism: Gentrification as Global Urban Strategy', in N. Brenner and N. Theodore (eds), *Spaces of Neoliberalism: Urban Restructuring in North America and Western Europe*, Oxford: Blackwell: 80–103.

Solinger, D. J. (1999) *Contesting Citizenship in Urban China: Peasants Migrants, the State and the Logic of the Market*, Berkeley, California: University of California Press.

Somers, M. R. (1994) 'Rights, relationality, and membership: rethinking the making and meaning of citizenship', *Law and Social Inquiry*, 19(1): 63–112.

Sridharan, E. (2004a) 'The growth and sectoral composition of India's middle class: its impact on the politics of economic liberalization', *India Review*, 3: 405–28.

—— (2004b) 'Electoral coalitions in the 2004 general elections: theory and evidence', *Economic and Political Weekly*, 39(51): 5418–25.

—— (2004c) 'The Fragmentation of the Indian Party System, 1952–1999', in Z. Hasan (ed.), *Parties and Party Politics in India*, Delhi: Oxford University Press: 475–504.

—— (2005) 'Coalition strategies and the BJP's expansion: 1989–2004', *Commonwealth and Comparative Politics*, 43(2), July: 194–221.

Srinivasan, K., Shariff, A., Zaman, W. A. and Bierring, C. (1997) *India: Towards Population and Development Goals*, New Delhi: Oxford University Press.

Srivastava, S. (2005) 'Mumbai Struggles to Catch up with Shanghai', *Asia Times Online*, available online at www.atimes.com/atimes/South_Asia/GC16Df02.html (accessed 1 February 2011).

—— (2006) 'India's Rural Poor Climb the Economic Ladder', *Asian Times*, 1 December, available online at www.atimes.com/atimes/South_Asia/HL01Df01.html (accessed 1 February 2011).

Stern, R. W., 2003. *Changing India: Bourgeois Revolution on the Subcontinent*, 2nd ed., Cambridge: Cambridge University Press.

Stiglitz, J. (2008) 'The End of Neoliberalism', *Daily News*, Cairo, 7 July.

Subramanian, S. and Jayaraj, D. (2006a) 'India's Household Wealth Distribution Data: A Critical Assessment', mimeo, Madras Institute of Development Studies.

Subramanian, S. and Jayaraj, D. (2006b) 'The Distribution of Household Wealth in India', paper prepared for UNU-WIDER project meeting, 4–6 May, Helsinki: WIDER.

Sundaram, K. (2007) 'Employment and poverty in India: 2000–2005', *Economic and Political Weekly*, 42(30): 3121–31.

Swaminathan, M. (2000) *Weakening Welfare: The Public Distribution of Food in India*, Delhi: LeftWord.

—— (2008) 'Programmes to Protect the Hungry: Lessons from India', manuscript, to appear in *UN Affairs*.

Tarlo, E. (2003) *Unsettling Memories: Narratives of the Emergency in India*, Berkeley, California: University of California Press.

Teitelbaum, E. (2006) 'Was the Indian labour movement ever co-opted? Evaluating Standard Accounts', *Critical Asian Studies*, 38(4): 389–417.

Consolidated bibliography 257

Tellis, A. (2005) *India as a New Global Power: An Action Agenda for the United States*, Carnegie Endowment for International Peace.

Teltumbde, A. (2005) 'Hindutva, Dalits and the Neoliberal Order', in A. Teltumbde (ed.), *Hindutva and Dalits: Perspectives for Understanding Communal Praxis*, Kolkata: Samya: 46–74.

Tendler, J. (1997) *Good Government in the Tropics*, Baltimore, Maryland: Johns Hopkins University Press.

Teschke, B. (2003) *The Myth of 1648: Class, Geopolitics and the Making of Modern International Relations*, London: Verso.

Thakur, S. (2003) *The Making of Laloo Yadav: The Unmaking of Bihar*, New Delhi: Harper Collins.

Thapa, M. (2005) *Forget Kathmandu: An Elegy for Democracy*, New Delhi: Penguin.

The Economist (2007) 'India's Commercial Capital: Maximum City Blues'.

The Hindu (2000) 'The Budget and Food Security', 9 March.

—— (2006) 'Special Economic Zones Thrown Open to Private Sector in U.P.'

—— (2008) 'Delimitation: Pros and Cons in Karnataka', available at http://www.hindu.com/2008/05/02/stories/2008050253031100.htm

The Times of India (2005) 'India Ready to Help US in Asian Power Rejig', 29 November.

The Tribune (2007) 'Anil Ambani's SEZ in Noida, Not Possible Now', 20 August.

Thomas Isaac, T. M., and Franke, R. W. (2002) *Local Democracy and Development: The Kerala People's Campaign for Decentralized Planning*, Lanham, Maryland: Rowman & Littlefield.

Thorat, S. and Newman, K. (2007) 'Caste and economic discrimination: causes, consequences and remedies', *Economic and Political Weekly*, 42(41): 4121–4.

Tilly, C. (1999) *Durable Inequality*, Berkeley, California: University of California Press.

UNI (2007a) 'Bishnoi Names Sonia in "Deal" with Mukesh Ambani'.

—— (2007b) 'Karnataka Congress to Submit Memorandum Opposing SEZ'.

Unni, J. and Raveendran, G. (2007) 'Growth of employment (1993–94 to 2004–05): illusion of inclusiveness?' *Economic and Political Weekly*, 42(3): 196–9.

Upadhyay, C. (2007) 'Employment, exclusion and "merit" in the Indian IT industry', *Economic and Political Weekly*, 42: 1863–8.

US Department of Defense (2002), *The Indo-US Military Relationship: Expectations and Perceptions*.

Vaidyanathan, A. (1993) 'Asset-Holdings and Consumption of Rural Households in India: A Study of Spatial and Temporal Variations', in *Agricultural Development Policy: Adjustments and Reorientation*, New Delhi and Oxford: Indian Society of Agricultural Economics.

—— (2006) 'Farmers' suicides and the agrarian crisis', *Economic and Political Weekly*, 41(38): 4009–13.

Vajpayee, A. B. (2007 [1969]) 'The Bane of Pseudo-Secularism', in C. Jaffrelot (ed.), *Hindu Nationalism: A Reader*, Princeton, New Jersey: Princeton University Press.

Vakulabharanam, V. (2004) 'Immiserizing Growth: Globalization and Agrarian Change in Telangana Between 1985 and 2000', PhD dissertation, Department of Economics, Amherst, Massachusetts: University of Massachusetts.

—— (2005) 'Growth and distress in a South Indian peasant economy during agricultural liberalisation', *Journal of Development Studies*, 41: 971–97.

Vakulabharnam, V. and Zacharias, A. (2007) 'Caste, Occupational Status and Wealth Inequality in India', mimeo, Levy Institute.

Vanaik, A. (1990) *The Painful Transition: Bourgeois Democracy in India*, London: Verso.

258 Consolidated bibliography

—— (1995) *India in a Changing World* (Tracts for the Times – No. 9), Hyderabad: Orient Longman.

Varma, P. (1998) *The Great Indian Middle Class*, New Delhi: Viking.

Varshney, A. (1995) *Democracy, Development and the Countryside: Urban-Rural Struggles in India*, Cambridge: Cambridge University Press.

—— (1999) 'Mass Politics or Elite Politics? India's Economic Reforms in Comparative Perspective', in J. Sachs, A. Varshney and N. Bajpai (eds), *India in the Era of Economic Reforms*, New Delhi: Oxford University Press: 222–60.

—— (2002) *Ethnic Conflict and Civic Life: Hindus and Muslims in India*, New Haven, Connecticut: Yale University Press.

Vasavi, A. R. (2008) 'Caste, capital and captaincy in the Karnataka elections', *Economic and Political Weekly*, 43(24): 10–12.

Venkatesan, V. (2003) 'The judicial response', *Frontline*, 12 September: 20–2.

Verma, A. (2005) 'The Police in India: Design, Performance and Adaptability', in D. Kapur and P. B. Mehta (eds), *Public Institutions in India: Performance and Design*, Delhi: Oxford University Press.

Veron, R. (2001) 'The "new" Kerala model: lessons for sustainable development', *World Development* 29(4): 601–17.

Vidyasagar, R. (1996) 'New Agrarianism and Challenges for the Left', in T. V. Satyamurthy (ed.), *Class Formation and Political Transformation in Post-Colonial India*, Delhi.

Vyas, N. (2009) 'The Lost Generation of the BJP', *The Hindu*, 13 June.

Walzer, M. (1995 [1989]) 'The Civil Society Argument', in R. Beiner (ed.), *Theorizing Citizenship*, Albany, New York: State University of New York Press.

Whitehead, J. and More, N. (2007) 'Revanchism in Mumbai? Political economy of rent gaps and urban restructuring in a global city', *Economic and Political Weekly*, 42(25): 2428–34.

Weiner, M. (1999) 'The Regionalization of Indian Politics and its Implications for Economic Reform', in J. Sachs, A. Varshney and N. Bajpai (eds), *India in the Era of Economic Reforms*, New Delhi: Oxford University Press: 261–94.

Williamson, J. and Zagha, R. (2002) 'From the Hindu Rate of Growth to the Hindu Rate of Reform', Working Paper 144, Stanford, California: Stanford University Center for Research on Economic Development and Policy Reform.

World Bank (2000) 'Overview of Rural Decentralization in India: Approaches to Rural Decentralization in Seven States; Volume I'.

—— (2006) *India: Inclusive Growth and Service Delivery: Building on India's Success*, Washington DC: World Bank (Development Policy Review, Report No. 34580-IN).

—— (2009) *World Development Report, 2009: Reshaping Economic Geography*, Oxford: Oxford University Press.

Wright, E. O. (1997) *Class Counts: Comparative Studies in Class Analyses*, Cambridge: Cambridge University Press.

Yadav, Y. (1999a) 'Electoral politics in the time of change: India's third electoral system, 1989–99', *Economic and Political Weekly*, 34(34/35): 2393–9.

—— (1999b) 'Politics', in M. Bouton and P. Oldenburg (eds), *India Briefing: A Transformative Fifty Years*, Armonk, New York: M. E. Sharpe: 3–38.

—— (2000) 'Understanding the Second Democratic Upsurge: Trends of Bahujan Participation in Electoral Politics in the 1990s', in F. R. Frankel, Z. Hasan, R. Bhargava and B. Arora (eds), *Transforming India: Social and Political Dynamics of Democracy*, Delhi: Oxford University Press.

—— (2004) 'Open contest, closed options', *Seminar*, 534, February.

Yadav, Y. and Kumar, S. (1999) 'Interpreting the mandate', *Frontline*, 5 November.

Yadav, Y. and Palshikar, S. (2009) 'Between *fortuna* and *virtu*: explaining the congress' ambiguous victory in 2009', *Economic and Political Weekly*, 65(39): 33–46.

Yashar, D. (2005) *Contesting Citizenship in Latin America: The Rise of Indigenous Movements and the Postliberal Challenge*, Cambridge, Massachusetts: Cambridge University Press.

Index

Page numbers in **bold** refer to illustrations.

abortion, sex-selective 149–50
abstract space 7, 68, 73–4, 76, 78
Adivasis 126, 151–3, 166–8, 183, 209, 225
Advani, L. K. 145, 172, 174, 191, 227
affirmative action *see* discrimination, compensatory
Afghanistan 14, 229, 231, 235
agrarian bourgeoisie 22, 173, 178–9, 232–4 *see also* elites, rural
agrarian crisis 80n16
agricultural prices 9, 113
agricultural subsidies 113, **115**, 125n17, 189
agricultural workers 90, 102, 104–5, 108, 116, 118–20, 124n6
agriculture: downturn in 101–5, **103**, 108, 111, 122–3; employment in 29; future of 123–4; investment in 111, **112**; market intermediaries in 115; marketization of 101–2, 113, 116–17, 123; and the peasantry 25, 29–31, 102; shifting out of 63; technology used in 29–30, 82, 84–5, 108–9, 111
Ahmedabad 40, 42, 45, 74, 130
AIADMK (All India Anna Dravida Munnetra Kazagham), xi 197–8
AIPAC (American Israeli Political Action Committee) 227, 231
Akali Dal 100n10
All India Forward Bloc (FB) 194, 198
Ambedkar, B. R. 73, 75, 143
Andhra Pradesh: agricultural collateral in 115; conflict among Dalits in 147; economic reforms in 69; industrialisation in 68; microcredit in 126n39; PPC in 93; regional inequalities in 96, 98; rural elites in 100n11; SEZs in 57–8; state politics in 100n10, 197, 211, 213; wealth distribution in 96

anti-Americanism 184, 221
anti-Brahmin movements 161, 177, 181
Asom Gana Parishad (AGP) 189–90, 194
assets: accumulation of 82, 88, 92, 94, 96, 98; financial 83, 86; growth of in urban areas 89; major categories of **84**; ownership of 84–5, **85**; regional distribution of **98**; valuation of 83
Ayodhya 3, 74, 151, 180, 188, 191, 209

Babri Masjid 119, 151, 182, 188, 209, 217
backward castes: and Congress Party 14, 208–12, 216; identity politics of 154; job quotas for *see* employment quotas; legislative representation of 10; mobilizations of 142, 148; in new economy 94
Backward Classes (BCs): mobilization of 10–12, 72, 147; political citizenship of 2; population growth among 76; reservation of jobs for 13
Bangalore 4, 70, 79n8, 96
Bangladesh 21, 34, 154, 196
bank deposits 83–5
banking, social 115
Basu, Jyoti 189, 194, 198–9
benefit-seekers 30
Bharatiya Kisan Union (BKU) 118, 125n24
Bihar: class politics in 79n10; Congress in 14, 213, 219n12; economic growth in 75, 96; economic reforms in 70; industrialisation in 68; and interstate competition 8; literacy in 76; lower-caste politics in 74, 120; political regime of 72–3, 76–7; population of 71
BIMARU states 163
BJD (Biju Janata Dal) 155n8, 196–7, 201

BJP (Bharatiya Janata Party): appeal to rural elites 119; and citizenship 10; class base of 95; in coalitions 176, 187–8, 197, 210; in coalitions 176, 187–8, 197, 210; complicity in violence of 74; and economic liberalization 12; electoral history of 67, 172–5, 180–2, 193, 210, 223; fear of other parties towards 74; in federal government 177, 183, 198; foreign policy of 228; future of 217; influence of Third Force on 13; and Mandal Commission 191; middle class support for 226–7; and SEZs 58, 63; social policy of 133; in state governments 175; support for NF government 189, 191; and violence 155n8
BJS (Bharatiya Jana Sangh) 172, 181, 191
Block Development Offices 67, 77, 78n4
BoA (Board of Approvals) 51, 57, 59–60
boosterism 38, 160
BPL (Below Poverty Line) 4, 10, 21, 42, 132–3, 152
Brazil 225
BSP (Bahujan Samaj Party) 8, 12, 74, 79n10, 174, 193, 202, 204, 218
bureaucratic-managerial class 24–5, 33
Bush, George W. 228

capital: flows of 95–6; foreign 23, 199, 223, 232–4 (*see also* Foreign Direct Investment); human 5; non-corporate 5, 25–9, 31, 34; social 36, 160, 170n1
capitalist class: power of 4–5, 23–4, 27, 33; structure of 23, 232–4; urban and rural 94, 119
caste: and class composition 119, **120**; and rural class conflict 119–20; schemes of 105
caste/class polarization 177, 182–3
Centre–state relations 66–8, 78n5, 187, 189–91, 195, 200; *see also* India, federalism in
Chennai 70, 79n8
Chhattisgarh: industrialisation in 68; and interstate competition 8; private armies in 77; state politics in 210
Chidambaram, Palaniappan 13, 133–5, 194–5, 207
China: border dispute with 229; Indian competition with 122; nuclear programme of 226; poverty reduction in 9; rural–urban migration in 156n10; SEZs in 50, 52; US policy towards 229–30

Christians, violence against 155n8, 198
churning 11, 161–2
cities: and civil society 161; inclusive 36; official views of 37–8; and the middle class *see* middle classes, and urban space; *see also* urban space
citizenship: aspiration to 151–2; biological 11, 149–50; and consumerism 47, 146; dual 142, 153–4; idea of 141; and influence on the state 157; and local democracy 159; and political society 27; universal 143–5, 148, 152
Citizenship Act 1955 153
citizenship regime (CR) 10–11, 142, 145–6, 148, 150, 154, 155n1
civil rights 64, 158
civil society: applicability of concept to India 160–1; conceptions of 11, 160; and corporate capital 27, 33; exclusion from 27; formation 160–1, 169; interaction of poor with 9, 47; mobilizations of 135–6, 138, 166; and panchayats 164–5; and passive revolution 25; and political society 5–6, 33–4
Clinton, Bill 228
CMP (Common Minimum Programme) 133, 135–6, 194
coalition governments 12
collateral 115
Communist bloc 221–2
compassion 9–10, 127, 138
Comprehensive Test Ban Treaty (CTBT) 196, 198
Congress (Socialist) 189
Congress-O 178, 181
Congress Party: class base of 95, 176–7, 181, 184–5, 225–6; in coalitions 197, 200; and decentralization 165; electoral history of 33, 174–5, 178–9, 204–5; in federal government 191, 217–18; foreign policy of 228; future of 216–17; and Hindutva 182, 209–10, 224; historical progress of 13; implementation of economic liberalization *see* economic liberalization, and Congress; and Indian federalism 66–7; influence of Third Force on 13; left support for 198–9; as model for nation 144; Nehru-Gandhi dynasty in 214–16; organization of 205, 211–15, 218; and protests 213–14; and SEZs 58–9; in state governments 175; support for UF government 195
consent, construction of 36

Constitution of India: 73rd Amendment to 149, 162, 166; 74th Amendment to 56; 93rd Amendment to 136; Article 370 of 193; citizenship in 142–3; and federalism 66
construction workers 43, 138
consumer citizens *see* citizenship, and consumerism
consumerism 63, 72, 146
Contract Farming 123
cooperatives 126n40
corruption: costs of 61–2; perception of 24, 34; and state capacity 49, 62
cotton 31, 111, 117
CPI (Communist Party of India) 194, 198, 203n6, 224
CPI (Communist Party of India) (Maoist) *see* Naxalism
CPM (Communist Party of India (Marxist)): and decentralization 165–6; in federal politics 189, 194–5, 197–8, 200–1, 220n31, 224; in Orissa 58; in West Bengal 5, 47, 57, 163, 211
credit: main sources of **116**; rural dependence on 109, 113, 115
cultural rights 144

Dalits 167; in Bihar 201; and Congress 225; election to panchayats 149; and Hindutva 183; in labour market 95; in local government 169; in Madhya Pradesh 167–8; migration of 151, 153; and OBCs 147; political activism of 193, 204, 209, 223; resistance to 149; and rural mobilizations 19, 118, 123; in Uttar Pradesh politics 79n10
decentralization: and democracy 158; impetus behind 162; industrial 68; and local government 46–7, 163–6; opposition to 168
Delhi: BJP success in 12; gentrification in 6; and interstate competition 8; transport links of 70–1, 73; water supply in 79n8
democracy: capital's indifference to 74; intra-party 204, 212–13, 215–16; local *see* local government, and democracy; middle class attitudes to 6, 34, 40–2, 49, 64, 127, 129, 139; neoliberal suspicion of 127; participatory 157–9, 169–70; patronage 5, 72
democratic deficit 11, 64
democratic mobilizations: elite revolt against 41; identity-based 52; importance of 1–2

democratic upsurge: second 10, 64, 94, 145, 161, 168, 170, 186–7, 193, 201; third 11
demonstrations, restrictions on 42
Department of Atomic Energy (DAE) 226
Desai, Moraji 190–1
Development Commissioner 51, 56
developmental state 18, 21, 24, 162, 232
DFID (Department for International Development) 46, 69, 74–5
dhanda 44
Dharavi 10, 43, 133
dharna 214, 219n23
Directive Principles of State Policy 144
discrimination, compensatory 10, 144, 155n6
DMK (Dravida Munnetra Kazagham) 177, 189–90, 194, 196, 198–200, 220n1
Domestic Tariff Area (DTA) 55, 59
donor funding 146
double movement 2, 4, 36, 128–9, 135

economic growth: and cities 37, 48; in India 4, 8–10, 17, 233; and labour market 9, 129–31; middle class concentration on 34; and political risk 53; and poverty reduction 132; and property market 38, 40; and social instability 42
economic liberalization: and accumulation of wealth 98; and agriculture 56, 101, 111, 113, 116–17, **114**, 173; and Congress 2, 205–9; and consumerism 39; and corruption 7; course of in India 14; and decentralization 13, 78n5, 95, 199; effects on poor of 4; elite embrace of 5; and Hindutva 12, 185; importance of 1–2; and inequalities 94, 146; middle class support for 90, 147; onset of 173–4; opposition to 52, 61, 70, 122; origins of 12; political effects of 192–3; and SEZs 53; and third force 187–8; and urban class relations 35; and urban poverty 6
economic reforms: and asset values 81; and Indian federalism 67–9; limits of state capacity for 61–2; political will for 67; and spread of Naxalism 75; third generation of 50
economic rights 136, 141, 148
education: in Madhya Pradesh 167; peasant expectations of 30; public spending of 10; quotas for 95; taxation for 135; universalization of 134, 136, 165

EGoM (Empowered Group of Ministers) 59–60
EGS (Education Guarantee Scheme) 167, 169
Ekvira Jameen Bachao Andolan 62
electoral mobilizations 24–5, 32, 41, 47
electricity 18, 26–7, 51, 71, 75, 102, 152, 179
elite politics 54
elite revolt 35, 38, 41, 48, 67, 82
elites: landed 15, 23–5, 33; in NCO classification 89; risk aversion of 53; rural 100n11; strengthening of 98; urban 6, 8, 41, 82, 89–92, 94, 178
Emergency 179–80, 182, 190–1, 204, 215
employment: informalization of 129–30; urban 9; white collar **92**
employment protection legislation 43, 130
employment quotas 146–7 *see also* discrimination, compensatory
entrepreneurial cities 35, 37–8, 40, 43, 46, 48
entrepreneurial culture 38, 43, 46
entrepreneurs, the poor as 42–5
entrepreneurship, and nation-building 42–3
EPZs (Export Processing Zones) 50
ethnic conflict 158
Exim Policy 53
expenditure, per capita **104**, **107–8**

Fair Price shops 133
Far Eastern Naval Command (FENC) 230
farmers: large 102–5, 117–19; movements of 118, 120, 122, 179; politicization of 125n25; small 102, 104–5, 115, 117, 122–3, 179, 218; suicides of 9, 29, 122
FDI *see* Foreign Direct Investment
female foeticide *see* abortion, sex-selective
Fernandes, George 188, 192
fertilizers 102, 108–9, **109**, 111, 117, 17
Finance Commissions 67, 163, 199
financial services 39
financialization 222
Food Corporation of India (FCI) 133, 140n11
food prices 116–17, **116**, 131
food subsidies 21, 132–3, 139n6
foodgrains 101, 103–4, 108, 116–17, 119, 131, 133, 138
Foreign Direct Investment (FDI) 70, 81, 96, 201, 223, 234
Foreign Institutional Investors (FIIs) 233
Forward Castes 77, 94
Fourth Front 176–7, 179, 201

Freight Equalization Act 8, 68
Friedman, Thomas 73

Gandhi, Indira 2–4, 67, 178–80, 182, 190, 204–5, 212, 214–15
Gandhi, Mahatma (Mohandas) 15, 118, 215
Gandhi, Rahul 4, 14, 212–16
Gandhi, Rajiv 2, 162, 182, 189, 191–2, 205, 212, 216, 226
Gandhi, Sanjay 215–16
Gandhi, Sonia 14, 58, 192, 197–9, 213–16, 218
Ganga Waters Treaty Accord 196
genetically modified (GM) crops 108–9
gentrification 6, 35, 38–40
Giuliani, Rudy 42
global economic downturn 39
Goa 66, 175, 208
Golden Quadrilateral 70, 73
governance: and democracy 127; urban 38, 43–4, 46, 48, 56
government, minimum functions of 20
governmental technology 18, 20–1
governmentality 31–2
Gowda, H. D. Deve 13, 194–5, 201, 207
Gram Sabhas 164–5, 168–9
Gramsci, Antonio 16n1, 18, 22, 203
Green Revolution: and changes in social structure 117; lagged 102, 108, 111, 117, 123; and marketisation of agriculture 101–2; origins of 3, 12; and PPCs 93; state support for 102
Gujarat: Congress in 213; economic reform in 69; EPZs in 50; genocide of 2002 74, 126n33, 145, 200, 217; and interstate competition 8; literacy in 76; power of capitalist class in 4; President's Rule in 196; state politics in 12, 178, 209–10
Gujjars 147
Gujral, I. K. 13, 189–90, 196

Haryana: BJP success in 12; and interstate competition 8; rural elites in 94; SEZs in 58, 60
hawkers *see* street vendors
health: peasant expectations of 30; public spending on 10
hegemonic stabilization 234
Herfindal Index 233, 236n7
Himachal Pradesh, BJP success in 12
Hindu identity 180–2
Hindu nationalism *see* Hindutva

Index

Hinduism, features attributed to 144
Hindutva: and citizenship 144; Congress's attitude to *see* Congress Party, and Hindutva; crisis of 172–3, 200; and foreign policy 224; importance of 1–2; and Indian diaspora 231; in international context 185; left opposition to 202; middle class support for 90; in Mumbai 6; and NF 191; and nuclear weapons 226; parties supporting 14; in political domain 148, 222–3; rise of 12, 146, 180; and rural elites 102, 119; and SEZs 63; and violence 145, 155n8; and wealth 95
home-based work 44
household assets 81–3, 96
Hyderabad 96
HYV (High yield variety) 108–9

identity politics 47, 154
import substitution industrialization (ISI) 3, 23, 68, 232
inclusion, paradox of 45
India: agrarian bourgeoisie in *see* landed elites; arms sales to 229; autonomy of state in 24, 33, 232; central transformations of 1, 141–2, 148, 150, 154; eastern 7–8, 68, 75–7; economic changes in 3–4 *see also* economic liberalization; federal party system in 146, 175, 179, 186, 193, 196–7, 200, 211; federalism in 7–8, 58, 66–7, 69–70, 74–5, 77–8; fiscal deficit of 71, 132; foreign policy of 221–3, 227, 230–1, 234–5; founding idea of 143; future transformations of 3, 15; Great Transformation of 2, 145; inequalities in 8, 81–2, **107**; land acquisition in 20; military relationships of 230; northern 10, 118, 145, 193; nuclear programme of 226–9; opposition to neoliberalism in *see* neoliberalism, opposition to; overseas citizens of 153–4 *see also* Indian diaspora; population of *see* population of India; protest politics in 31–2; as regional power 14; regionalisation of politics in 70, 180, 223; role of state in 18; social policy in 131–5, 138; state capacity in 49, 62–3, 168–9; structure of state power in 22–3, 128–9; transport infrastructure of 70–1, 77; uneven development of 75–6, 95, 98–9; zones of governance in 55
India Shining campaign 70, 74, 95
Indian Airlines (IA) 71

Indian diaspora 150, 153, 227, 231
Indian National Congress (Tiwari) 194
Indian National Congress *see* Congress Party
individualism 44–6
industrial bourgeoisie 3, 25, 183, 234 *see also* elites, urban
industries, declining 40, 42, 44
inequality, durable 11, 160, 170
infant mortality 76, 150
informal sector 16, 25–8, 31, 36, 108, 162
information technology (IT): exclusion of backward castes 94; growth in 23; lobby for 38; and SEZs 52
infrastructure: costs of 8; role of state in 23; in SEZs 51–2; urban 37–8, 46
Integrated Child Development Scheme (ICDS) 131, 134, 136, 219n27
Inter State Council 189, 195
Internet 71, 79n8
Iran 229, 235
Iraq 229, 231, 235
irrigation 98, 100, 102, 108–11, **110**, 115, 122, 165
Islamophobia 224
Israel 14, 227, 229

Jammu 193, 195, 208
Jan Morcha 188, 201
Janata Dal *see* JD
Janata Party 172, 176, 180–2, 186–7, 189–90, 192, 195
Japan 227, 229–31, 234
Jats 120, 125n25, 190
Jawaharlal Nehru National Urban Renewal Mission (JNNURM) 37, 134, 219n27
Jayalalitha 197–8
JD (Janata Dal) 186, 188–94, 196–9, 202–3; in Bihar *see* RJD (Rashtriya Janata Dal)
JD[S] (Janata Dal (Socialist)) *see* Samajwadi Janata Party (SJP)
JD[U] (Janata Dal (United)) 177, 198, 200–1
Jharkhand: formation of 71; industrialisation in 68; and interstate competition 8; political regime of 76–7
JP *see* Janata Party
jus sanguinis 153, 156n9
justice 9–10, 127, 138–9, 158, 190, 215

Kandla Export Processing Zone 50
Karat, Brinda 57
Kargil war 199, 227–8

Karnataka: EGS in 169; panchayats in 163; regional inequalities in 98; SEZs in 58–9; state politics in 95, 99n2, 210, 214; wealth distribution in 96
Karnataka Rashtra Ryota Sangha (KRRS) 118, 122, 125n24
Kashmir: and Indian federalism 66–7, 193, 195; and Indian foreign policy 224; military adventures in 5; state elections in 196
Kerala: infant mortality in 76; panchayats in 163–6, 169–70; and remittances 93; social mobilisations in 11; state politics in 184, 202, 211; wealth distribution in 96
Kesri, Sitaram 196
Kolkata: actions against street vendors in 73; images of 42; urban spaces in 40
Kolkata Metropolitan Area (KMA) 43, 46, 48
KRRS (Karnataka Rashtra Ryota Sangha) 118, 122, 125
KSSP (Kerala Sastra Sahitya Parishad) 166
Kumar, Nitish 70–1, 96, 192, 199
Kurmis 72, 192–3

LAA *see* Land Acquisition Act 1894
labour rights 54, 129, 137
Lal, Devi 188, 190
land: ownership of 84; prices of 93
land acquisition 7, 56–60, 62–3, 70, 201
Land Acquisition Act 1894 7, 56–8, 65n11
land reforms 56, 101, 117, 124
landed elites *see* elites, landed
Lefebvre, Henri 8, 68, 73–4
Left Front (LF) 47, 73, 186, 189, 194, 203
license Raj 3, 23–4, 192
literacy rates 10, 76
loan waivers 117–18, 125–6n27
local government: and democracy 11, 46, 159; inclusion of poor in 46–7
lockouts 137, 140n20, 199
Lok Dal 180–1, 188, 191–2, 203n3
Lok Jan Shakti (LJS) 200
Lok Sabha 67, 76, 136, 145, 174, 193–4
Lok Shakti (LS) 196–7
LTTE (Liberation Tigers of Tamil Eelam) 192

Madhya Pradesh: Congress in 167; economic growth in 75; infant mortality in 76; and interstate competition 8; literacy in 167; panchayats in 163, 166–70; rural inequalities in 9; social mobilizations in 11; state politics in 183, 210
Madhya Pradesh Vikas Congress (MPVC) 194
Maharashtra: Congress in 219n12; economic growth in 76; economic reform in 69; infant mortality in 76; and interstate competition 8; land acquisitions in 7; literacy in 76; panchayats in 163; patronage democracy in 4; rural elites in 94; sex ratio in 150; SEZs in 58, 60; state politics in 184, 193, 211
Maharashtra Industrial Development Corporation (MIDC) 62
malnutrition 9–10, 131, 150
Mandal Commission 3, 13, 95, 120, 146–7, 180–1, 190–3, 204
Manor, James 13–14, 166–7
Mao Zedong 15, 18
Maran, Murasoli 7, 50
marginality 42, 48
marginalized groups 5, 32–3, 64, 144, 166, 168
market economy, self-regulating 128
Marx, Karl 19, 73, 123
mass politics 49, 52–3, 61
maternal mortality 11, 150
Mayawati 73, 79n10, 193
Mazdur Kisan Shakti Sangathan (MKKS) 136
MBCs (Most Backward Classes) 146–7
Meenas 147
microcredit 21, 43, 126n39, 161
Midday Meal Scheme 131, 133, 219n27
middle castes 94, 174, 177–83, 189
middle classes: attitude to democracy 6, 34, 40–2, 49, 64, 127, 129, 139; civic activism of 40; and civil society 161; and Congress Party 95; consumer identity of 147; and corporate capital 27; enrichment of 98; and foreign policy 224–5; growth of 8, 35, 146, 223; literature on 90; lower 148; overseas education of children 231; social mobilization of 137–9, 146; and social security 132; and urban space 35, 39–40, 146
Millennium Development Goals 36
missiles 231
Modi, Narendra 74, 172, 174, 210, 217
moneylenders 18, 115, 118, 123, 125n19
mono-cropping 111
Most Backward Classes (MBCs) 146–7

multiculturalism 141
Mumbai: gentrification in 6; images of 42; patronage democracy in 5; SEZs in 62; slums in 10, 41–3; urban movements in 161; urban spaces in 8, 40; water supply in 79n8
municipal governance *see* governance, urban
Muslims: in Bihar 8, 72; in BJP discourse 183; political activism of 193, 209, 223–4; and poverty 100n8; and terrorism 74; violence against 155n8, 209

Nagaland 66, 175
Naidu, N. Chandrababu 69, 95, 194, 197, 199
Nandigram 7, 17, 57, 202
national identity 141–4, 155n4
National Rural Health Mission 133, 219n27
nationalism: competing 222; federal 188, 196, 203n2; religious 78, 145
Naxalism 2, 8, 68, 75, 77, 80n18, 98, 154, 202
NCEUS (National Commission for Enterprises in the Unorganized Sector) 25–6, 28, 130, 138
NCO classification 89–90
NCP (Nationalist Congress Party) 201
NDA (National Democratic Alliance) 134, 173–4, 176–8, 181, 187, 197–201, 224, 227
Nehru, Jawaharlal 3, 15, 67, 142–3, 153, 215
neoliberal city 6, 35–6, 39–40, 42, 48
neoliberal subjectivities 37, 46
neoliberalism: definition of 35–6, 127; and citizenship 141; Indian government commitment to 138, 175; middle class support for 225, 233; moderation of 127; opposition to 128, 137–8; politicians associated with 13; and poverty 10; role of state in 234; and social polarization 222
NEP (New Economic Policy) 225, 227–8 *see also* economic reforms
Nepal 68, 77, 80n18, 190, 196
NF (National Front) 13, 180, 186–92, 194–5, 202
NGOs (non-governmental organizations) 6, 30, 42–3, 47, 62, 137–8, 146, 153
Non-Aligned Movement (NAM) 221
NREGA (National Rural Employment Guarantee Act): implementation of 137; and neoliberalism 225; origins of 102, 122, 136, 169; and political society 5; and SEZ Act 50, 54
NREGS (National Rural Employment Guarantee Scheme) 133–4, 139–40, 140n13, 175, 201, 219n27
NRIs (Non-Resident Indians) 69–70, 74, 153–4, 184
NSS (National Sample Survey) 9, 83, 105, 119–20, 129, 133

Obama, Barack 229
OBCs (Other Backward Classes): in Bihar 201; electoral power of 191–3, 223; in NSS 105; political representation of 145–8; reservations for 180, 190; and rural elites 90, 120, 122–3
OCI *see* India, overseas citizens of
Operation Sunshine 73
Orissa: economic growth in 75; Hindutva organisations in 155n8; industrialisation in 68; infant mortality in 76; and interstate competition 8; land acquisitions in 7, 17; party system in 196; SEZs in 58, 60

Pak Visthapit Sangh 153
Pakistan: conflict with 199; conflict with *see also* Kargil war; India's policy towards 14, 190, 224; migration from 11, 143, 151–2, 155n2; US relations with 228, 230
Panchayati Raj 11, 162–3, 168, 170
panchayats 76, 149, 154, 162–8
passive revolution 3, 5, 16n1, 22–3, 25, 33–4
Patna 6, 71–3
patronage 47, 66, 157, 159, 170, 192, 204
patronage politics 10, 168 *see also* democracy, patronage
pavement clearance 41
PDS (Public Distribution System) 10, 102, 116–17, 131–3, 138, 140n11, 152, 195
peasant insurgency 17, 31
peasants: and economic growth 17; eviction of 20–1; indebted 123; and the market economy 22, 25–6; political activity of 30–1, 34; relationship to state 18–19; resistance to land acquisition 17–18; suicide of 122; theorization of 19–20
People's Action for Employment Guarantee (PAEG) 137
People's Democratic Party (PDP) 202

Person of Indian Origin (PIOs) 153 *see also* Indian diaspora
Polanyi, Karl 2, 36, 127–8
Polavaram project 100n11
political economy of India, causal accounts of 1–2
political power 4, 22, 24, 33, 94, 174, 178
political society: definition of 16n2; associations in 28; collective action and 32; criticism of concept 5–6; and non-corporate capital 27; organizations of 27–8; participation of poor in 4–5, 36, 47; and passive revolution 25; subjects of 27
politics: biologization of 149; regionalization of 13, 188
pollution, and SEZs 58
Poorest India 75–6
popular democratic mobilization 1–2, 147, 173–4, 187, 201–2
population of India: growth of 75–6, 105; sex ratios of 11, 149–50; youthening of 5
populism 34, 64, 157, 177–9, 182
Post-Washington Consensus 36
poverty: and asset-poor communities 100n8; conceptualization of 132; and entrepreneurship 43; rural 28–9, 62, 75, 105, 130–1; urban 6, 9, 12, 35–6, 40, 43, 48, 103
poverty reduction: elasticities of 4; trends in 9–10, 103, 105, 130–1
pre-capitalist societies 19
President's Rule 66, 72, 78n5, 196
price scissors effect 113
primitive accumulation: and government intervention 4, 20–2, 30, 33–4, 36; and Indian federalism 69–70; and the peasantry 18–19; and political society 27
private–public partnerships *see* public–private partnerships
private sector: and land acquisition 62–3; provision of social services 134; and SEZs 52; and urban governance 37
privatization 46, 135, 138, 140n14
proletarianization 117
provincial Darwinism 70, 72, 78
provincial propertied classes (PPCs): and BJP 180; and Hindu nationalism 12; power of 122, 173; and regional parties 100n1, 177–9, 181
Public Distribution System *see* PDS
public goods 76, 79n9

public–private partnerships 38–9, 42, 71, 199
public sector 52, 55, 69
public space 40, 73–4, 146, 149, 154
Punjab: Congress in 213; and interstate competition 8; land acquisitions in 7; regional parties in 100n10; rural elites in 94; SEZs in 57–8

Rajasthan: lower-caste agitation in 147; migrant settlements in 151–4; panchayats in 163, 169; state politics in 12, 210
Ramjanmabhoomi 191, 193
Rao, Narasimha 13–14, 192, 194, 205–9, 212, 214, 216, 218, 227
real estate 38–40, 56, 81, 93, 119
Realism 15, 221–2
reform by stealth 49, 208
regional parties: and backwards castes **211**; challenge to Congress 204, 209–11; in coalitions 100, 173, 183, 195; formation of 177–80; opposition to 190; problems of 217; and rural elites 223–4; success in state elections 14
regulations, social 15, 36
relational space 78
religious minorities 144–5
remittances 93, 224
reservations 3, 13, 94–5, 98, 144, 149, 180, 190, 192, 208; *see also* discrimination, compensatory
resource curse 68
retail work 44–5
revanchism 6, 38, 40–2
Revolutionary Socialist Party (RSP) 194, 198
Right to Food Campaign 136–7, 140n16
Right to Information Act 5, 54, 149
rights, bearers of 144
RSS (Rashtriuya Swayamsevak Sangh) 170n1, 172, 174, 180, 182–3, 191, 203n3, 223, 226
rural inequality 103
rural mobilizations 102, 117–18
rural–urban inequality 103, 105, 108
rural–urban migration 19, 93, 108, 120, 122

Samajwadi Janata Party (SJP) 191, 201
Samata Party (SAP) 192, 197
Samyukta Vidhayak Dal (SVD) 190
Sangh Parivar 10, 12, 55, 74, 145, 172, 198
Sarkaria Commission 78n5

Index

Sarva Siksha Abhiyan 134
SCs (Scheduled Castes) 4, 79n10, 91–2, 105, 107, 120–2, 126, 144, 155, 163–4
self-employment 28–9, 43–5, 104, 129
self-exploitation 28, 45
Sen, Amartya 158–9, 235n2
September 11, 2001 228
service sector 93, 122
SEZ Act *see* Special Economic Zone Act 2005
SEZs (special economic zones): definition of 50; and democratic upsurge 64; governance of 55–6, 64; history of 7, 50–1; as hybridized space 63; implementation of 49, 51, 58, 61–3; Indian policy on 51–3, 59–61; opposition to 53–9, 129
SHGs (Self-Help Groups) 43, 167
Shiromani Gurdwara Prabandhak Committee 150
Shiv Sena 5, 119, 193, 197, 21, 219n12
Sikhs 94, 150
Singh, Ajit 188, 191
Singh, Charan 179
Singh, Digvijay 166–8, 170, 209–10, 213, 219n10
Singh, Kalyan 199, 202
Singh, Manmohan 13–14, 37, 75, 192, 205, 207–8, 228
Singh, V. P. 13, 189–90, 192, 204, 208
Singur 5, 202
Sinha, Yashwant 9, 127
slum dwellers 4, 6, 41–3, 45, 108
slums 9–10, 35, 40–3, 46, 133
social citizenship 141–2, 144, 146, 148–9, 151–4
social class: definition of 105; caste composition of **121**
social democracy 149, 207, 215
social exclusion 48, 152
social rights 136, 141, 159, 161
social safety net *see* social security
social sector 131, 135
social security 131–2, 135, 138, 152
social services, expenditure on 134–5
Soviet Union *see* USSR
SP (Samajwadi Party) 60, 74, 79n1, 191, 193–4, 197–9, 201–2
Special Economic Zone Act 2005 7, 49–50, 52–3, 55–6, 59
squatters 27
Sri Lanka 190, 217
Staines, Graham 145

stakeholder citizens 42, 46–7
state governments: autonomy of 95; effectiveness of 76–7; and entrepreneurial cities 38; fiscal dependence on centre 66; influence over 23, 25; and SEZs 51, 54, 56–7, 60; and social services 134
state–society relations 157, 159
states: competition between 8, 24, 199–200; economic growth of 96, **97**; *see also* India, federalism in
status categories **91**–2
street vendors 26–7, 35, 40–1, 43
STs (Scheduled Tribes) 4, 105, 120, 122, 144, 147, 163, 184
subsidies, removal of 113, 207
Supreme Court 78, 127–9, 135–8, 146, 149, 191
suvidha 151–2

Tamil Maanila Congress (TMC) 194, 199
Tamil Nadu: Congress in 14, 219n10; infant mortality in 76; labour rights in 137; Naxalism in 68; party system in 179, 184; power of capitalist class in 4; social security in 133
Tamilaga Vyavasavavigal Sangham (TVS) 125n24
TDP (Telegu Desam Party) 100n10, 126n32, 188, 190, 194, 197–9, 211, 213
Telangana 101
Telegu Desam Party *see* TDP
Telengana Rashtra Samiti (TRS) 201
telephones 79n7
terms of trade (TOT), domestic 113
terrorism 74–5, 172
Thailand 34
third force *see* Third Front
Third Front 13, 176, 179, 187–8, 195, 199, 201–3, 217
Third World 17, 221
Total Sanitation Campaign 134, 219n27
trade unions 66, 70, 127, 137, 149, 162
transition, narratives of 20, 32–3
transport, informal 26–7
Trinamool Congress 177
Tripura 184

UF (United Front) 13, 118, 145, 177, 186–7, 193–200, 202, 224
Unit Approval Committees (UACs) 51
United Nations Security Council 14

United States: Asian policy of 229–30; elite support for 235; Indian trade with 184; India's policy towards 14–15, 224, 227–9, 231–2, 234–5; nuclear deal with 54, 174, 201, 227–8, 236n6
universal franchise 143
unorganized sector workers 25–6, 135, 138
UPA (United Progressive Alliance): Common Minimum Programme of *see* CMP; emergence of 200; foreign policy of 227; influence of Left on 173, 175–7, 201; and regional parties 224; relative performance of parties in 176–7; and SEZs 50, 53–5, 57, 59; and SEZs 50, 53–5, 57, 59; social policy of 133–5, 138, 139n10
urban bias 6, 173, 179
urban class relations 35, 48
urban economy 9, 35, 37, 45, 48, 102, 119, 122–3
urban policy, and neoliberalism *see* neoliberal city
urban regeneration 6, 40
user charges 46, 125n16, 140n14
USSR 221, 227
Uttar Pradesh (UP): Congress in 219n12; economic growth in 75; and interstate competition 8; literacy in 76; lower-caste politics in 74, 79n10, 120; population of 71; President's Rule in 196; rural elites in 94; SEZs in 57, 60; state politics in 73, 76, 179, 184, 193, 201–2, 210, 214
Uttarakhand 71, 75, 208, 213
Uttaranchal *see* Uttarakhand

Vajpayee, A. B. 14, 145, 153, 174, 197–8, 210, 226
Vidarbha 101
Vidhan Sabhas 174
villages, vanishing 9, 30
violence, and political society 31–2

Vishwa Hindu Parishad (VHP) 74, 180
vote-bank politics 6, 41

wages: of agricultural workers 102, 105, **106**; discrimination in 94–5; stagnation of 9, 129
water, exploitation of 111
water provision 11, 72, 75, 79n8
Water User Associations 125n16
wealth: distribution of 8, 81–4, 86–9, **87–8**, 93; Gini coefficients for 85–6, **86**; measuring inequality 99n3; mobility of 86; and new economy 94; and status categories **92**; under-reporting of 83
welfare, Indian government commitment to 4, 9–10, 30
West Bengal: asset holdings in 96; defeat of Congress in 14, 211; distribution of investment in 98; economic reforms in 70, 194, 199; future of peasantry in 29–30; and interstate competition 8; land acquisition in 7, 17, 59; microcredit in 161; panchayats in 163; party system in 184; patronage democracy in 5; SEZs in 57, 60, 202; women politicians in 11
women: and community mobilization 46; employment of 129–30, 148; in informal sector 162; literacy of 167; in local government 11, 149, 163–4, 169; and microcredit 161; and poverty reduction schemes 43–4
women's reservation bill 177
working classes, political mobilization of 42
World Bank 69, 76, 131
WTO (World Trade Organization) 67, 118, 125, 223

Yadav, Lalu Prasad 8, 70, 72, 75, 79n9–10, 80n15, 190–2, 196, 198
Yadav, Mulayam Singh 191, 193, 199, 223

Taylor & Francis
eBooks
FOR LIBRARIES

ORDER YOUR FREE 30 DAY INSTITUTIONAL TRIAL TODAY!

Over 23,000 eBook titles in the Humanities, Social Sciences, STM and Law from some of the world's leading imprints.

Choose from a range of subject packages or create your own!

Benefits for you
- Free MARC records
- COUNTER-compliant usage statistics
- Flexible purchase and pricing options

Benefits for your user
- Off-site, anytime access via Athens or referring URL
- Print or copy pages or chapters
- Full content search
- Bookmark, highlight and annotate text
- Access to thousands of pages of quality research at the click of a button

For more information, pricing enquiries or to order a free trial, contact your local online sales team.

UK and Rest of World: **online.sales@tandf.co.uk**
US, Canada and Latin America:
e-reference@taylorandfrancis.com

www.ebooksubscriptions.com

ALPSP Award for BEST eBOOK PUBLISHER 2009 Finalist

Taylor & Francis eBooks
Taylor & Francis Group

A flexible and dynamic resource for teaching, learning and research.